Anti-militarism

Also by Cynthia Cockburn

FROM WHERE WE STAND: WAR, WOMEN'S ACTIVISM AND
FEMINIST ANALYSIS

THE LINE: WOMEN, PARTITION AND THE GENDER ORDER IN CYPRUS

THE POSTWAR MOMENT: MILITARIES, MASCULINITIES AND INTERNATIONAL
PEACEKEEPING (Co-edited with Dubravka Zarkov)

THE SPACE BETWEEN US: NEGOTIATING GENDER AND NATIONAL
IDENTITIES IN CONFLICT

BRINGING TECHNOLOGY HOME: GENDER AND TECHNOLOGY IN
A CHANGING EUROPE (Co-edited with Ruza Fűrst-Dilić)

GENDER AND TECHNOLOGY IN THE MAKING
(Co-authored with Susan Ormrod)

IN THE WAY OF WOMEN: MEN'S RESISTANCE TO SEX EQUALITY IN
ORGANIZATIONS

TWO-TRACK TRAINING: SEX INEQUALITIES AND THE YOUTH TRAINING
SCHEME

MACHINERY OF DOMINANCE: WOMEN, MEN AND TECHNICAL KNOW-HOW

BROTHERS: MALE DOMINANCE AND TECHNICAL CHANGE

THE LOCAL STATE: MANAGEMENT OF CITIES AND PEOPLE

Anti-militarism

Political and Gender Dynamics of Peace Movements

Cynthia Cockburn
Visiting Professor, Department of Sociology, School of Social Sciences, City University London, UK, and Honorary Professor, Centre for the Study of Women and Gender, University of Warwick, UK

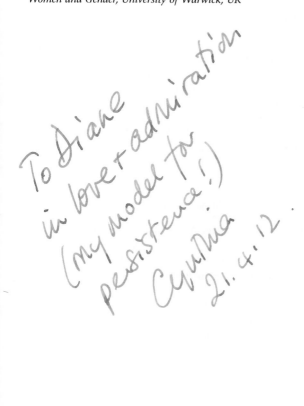

To Diane
in love + admiration
(my model for
persistence!)
Cynthia 21.4.12

palgrave
macmillan

First published 2012 by
PALGRAVE MACMILLAN

Palgrave Macmillan in the UK is an imprint of Macmillan Publishers Limited, registered in England, company number 785998, of Houndmills, Basingstoke, Hampshire RG21 6XS.

Palgrave Macmillan in the US is a division of St Martin's Press LLC, 175 Fifth Avenue, New York, NY 10010.

Palgrave Macmillan is the global academic imprint of the above companies and has companies and representatives throughout the world.

Palgrave® and Macmillan® are registered trademarks in the United States, the United Kingdom, Europe and other countries.

ISBN 978–0–230–35974–1   hardback
ISBN 978–0–230–35975–8   paperback

This book is printed on paper suitable for recycling and made from fully managed and sustained forest sources. Logging, pulping and manufacturing processes are expected to conform to the environmental regulations of the country of origin.

A catalogue record for this book is available from the British Library.

A catalog record for this book is available from the Library of Congress.

10   9   8   7   6   5   4   3   2   1
21 20 19 18 17 16 15 14 13 12

Printed and bound in Great Britain by
CPI Antony Rowe, Chippenham and Eastbourne

To Elsa Maria and Josie Cockburn
born 2 February 2007
For you, for all of us, a peaceful world.

Contents

Acknowledgments

This book is research-based, and my debt of gratitude is first and foremost to those of you, one hundred and thirty in twelve countries, who gave me your time in interview, in group discussions and in conversation, as I undertook these several studies. Thank you not only for the experiences and ideas you shared with me, but also for taking the trouble to review my drafts and steer me through the shoals of fact and opinion. I mention you by name in a footnote to each chapter, but can scarcely do justice to your knowledge, patience and goodwill.

I would also like to thank three co-researchers. Elli Kim, a founder member of Women Making Peace in Seoul, educated me about the South Korean peace and reunification movements. Sarah Masters introduced me to the anti-gun movement, from the vantage point of the International Action Network on Small Arms of which she is acting director and Women's Network co-ordinator. Naoko Ikeda, a PhD candidate in the School of Women's Studies at York University, Toronto, accompanied me to Okinawa and Japan, bringing to view there many realities I would otherwise have missed. The result is Chapter 6, of which Naoko is co-author. Deeply involved as you three are in the situations we studied together, your insight was inestimable, and your good company a gift – thank you for both.

The project would have been I impossible without generous funding support. First, I would like to thank the trustees of the Joseph Rowntree Charitable Trust, who are special in their passion for peace and their enthusiasm for researchers who like to get more involved with their subjects than strict academic detachment permits, to participate and (whenever possible) contribute as well as observe. Thanks too to those thoughtful individuals hidden behind the titles of the Lipman-Miliband Trust, the Maypole Fund and the William A. Cadbury Trust, and to Patrick Lescure in France, who likewise gave me, as well as funding, a sense of political and moral support.

I greatly value the honorary academic belonging and intellectual stimulus provided over many years by the Department of Sociology at City University London, and more recently by the Centre for the Study of Women and Gender at the University of Warwick. Finally, thank you to Amber Stone-Galilee, my editor, and others at Palgrave Macmillan who trusted in the manuscript and have seen the book into print.

Glossary of Acronyms

AA-MOC	Alternativa Anti-militarista – Movimiento de Objección de Conciencia (Anti-militarist Alternative – Movement of Conscientious Objection), Spain
AIDS	Auto-Immune Deficiency Syndrome
AJWRC	Asia-Japan Women's Resource Centre, Japan
ANSWER	Act Now to Stop War and End Racism, USA
ARROW	Active Resistance to the Roots of War, UK
ATT	Arms Trade Treaty
ATTAC	Association pour la Taxation des Transactions Financières et pour l'Action Citoyenne (Association for the Taxation of Financial Transactions and for Citizens' Action), France
BCE	Before the Christian Era
BJP	Bharatiya Janata Party, India and UK
BMS	Biennial Meeting of States (on SALW at the UN under the PoA)
BUKO	Bundeskoordination Internationalismus (Federal Co-ordination for Internationalism), Germany
CCOO	Comisiones de Obreros (Workers' Commissions), Spain
CE	Christian Era
CECORE	Center for Conflict Resolution, Uganda
CGRASS	Centre for Gender Research and Social Science, Hitotsubashi University, Japan
CGT	Confederación General del Trabajo (General Confederation of Labour), Spain
CLAVE	Coalición Latinoamericana para la Prevención de la Violencia Armada (Latin American Coalition for the Prevention of Armed Violence)
CND	Campaign for Nuclear Disarmament, UK
CNOC	Comisión Nacional de Objección de Conciencia, Spain

CNT	Confederación Nacional del Trabajo (National Confederation of Labour)
CO	Conscientious objector
COSTAU	Collectif Strasbourg anti-OTAN (Strasbourg Anti-NATO Collective), France
CPD	Center for Peace and Disarmament, South Korea
CSPR	Centre for the Study of Peace and Reconciliation, Hitotsubashi University, Japan
CStW	Campaign to Stop the War (in Leicester)
CSW	Commission on the Status of Women (at the United Nations)
DDR	Disarmament, demobilization and reintegration
DFAA	Defence Facilities Administration Agency, Japan
DFG-IDK	Deutsche Friedensgesellschaft-Internationale der Kriegsdienstgegner
DFG-VK	Deutsche Friendensgesellschaft – Vereinigte Kriegsdienstverweigerer
	(German Peace Society and United Conscientious Objectors)
DL	Die Linke (The Left Party), Germany
DPRK	Democratic People's Republic of Korea
EASSI	East African Sub-regional Support Initiative for Women's Advancement
EL	Party of the European Left
EL-Fem	Women of the European Left
END	European Nuclear Disarmament
ETA	Euskadi Ta Askatasuna (Basque Homeland and Freedom)
EU	European Union
FECCLAHA	Fellowship of Councils and Churches in the Great Lakes and Horn of Africa
FMO	Federation of Muslim Organizations, UK
FOA	Friends of Al-Aqsa, UK
GDP	Gross Domestic Product
GIIDS	Graduate Institute of International and Development Studies, Geneva

IALANA	International Association of Lawyers against Nuclear Arms
IAMV	International Anti-Militarist Union
IANSA	International Action Network on Small Arms
ICC	International Co-ordinating Committee (of No-to-war: No-to-NATO)
IFOR	International Fellowship of Reconciliation
IL	Interventionistische Linke (Interventionist Left), Germany
ILP	Independent Labour Party, Great Britain
INF	Intermediate Nuclear Forces (Treaty)
IRBM	Intermediate-range Ballistic Missile
ISAF	International Security Assistance Force (NATO-led mission in Afghanistan)
IU	Izquierda Unida (United Left), Spain
IWA	Indian Workers' Association, UK
JCP	Japanese Communist Party (Nihon Kyosan-tô)
JRCT	Joseph Rowntree Charitable Trust, UK
JSP	Japanese Socialist Party (Nihon Shakai-tô)
KAA	Kolectivo Autónoma Anti-militarista, Spain
KAPM	Korean Alliance of Progressive Movements
KARG	Korean Association of Religious Groups
KCRC	Korean Council for Reconciliation and Co-operation
KEM-MOC	Konzientzi Eragozpen Mugimendua – Movimiento de Objección de Conciencia, Euskadi, Spain.
KKG	Kemin Kai Gi (Prefectural People's Conference), Okinawa, Japan
KNCW	Korean National Council of Women
KWA	Korean Women's Alliance
KWAU	Korean Women's Association United
LCR	Ligue Communiste Révolutionnaire (Communist Revolutionary League), France
LCR	Liga Comunista Revolucionaria (Communist Revolutionary League), Spain

LRA	Lord's Resistance Army, Uganda
MC	Movimiento Comunista (Communist Movement), Spain
MdN	Mujeres de Negro (Women in Black), Spain
MDS	Movement for Democratic Socialism (Minshushugi-teki Shakaishugi Undo), Japan
MEP	Member of the European Parliament
MfOK	Movement for One Korea, South Korea
MOC	Movimiento de Objección de Conciencia (Movement of Conscientious Objection), Spain
NAP	National Action Plan (on Small Arms and Light Weapons), Uganda
NATO	North Atlantic Treaty Organization
NATO-ZU	Shut Down NATO
NCNWT	National Campaign against Nuclear Weapons Tests, UK
NFP	National Focal Point (for Small Arms and Light Weapons), Uganda
NGO	Non-governmental organization
NL	National liberation tendency, South Korea
NPA	Le Nouveau Parti Anti-capitaliste (New Anti-Capitalist Party), France
NRA	National Resistance Army, Uganda
NRM	National Resistance Movement, Uganda
NUWSS	National Union of Women's Suffrage Societies, UK
OCPN	Okinawan Citizens Peace Network, Japan
OHUC	Okinawa Heiwa Undo Center (Okinawa Peace Movement Center), Japan
OTAN	Organización del Tratado del Atlántico Norte (North Atlantic Treaty Organization)
OWAAMV	Okinawa Women Act against Military Violence, Japan
PCE	Partido Comunista de España (Communist Party of Spain)
PCF	Parti Communiste Français (French Communist Party)
PD	People's democracy tendency, South Korea
PDS	Partei des Demokratischen Sozialismus (Party of Democratic Socialism), Germany

PG	Parti de Gauche (The Left Party), France
PoA	Programme of Action (United Nations Programme of Action on the Illicit Trade in Small Arms and Light Weapons in All Its Aspects)
PP	Partido Popular (Popular Party), Spain
PRC	Partito della Rifondazione Comunista (Communist Refoundation Party), Italy
PSC	Palestine Solidarity Campaign, UK
PSOE	Partido Socialista de Obreros de España (Spanish Socialist Workers' Party)
PSPD	People's Solidarity for Participatory Democracy, South Korea
PSS	Prestación Social Sustitutoria (Substitute Social Service), Spain
RAF	Royal Air Force, UK
RAGE	Ratepayers against Greenham Encampments, UK
RECSA	Regional Center on Small Arms (East Africa)
REICO	Rape Emergency Intervention and Counselling Centre, Japan
RoK	Republic of Korea
SACO	Special Action Committee on Facilities and Areas Okinawa, Japan
SALW	Small Arms and Light Weapons
SCAP	Supreme Commander of Allied Powers in the Pacific
SDP	Social Democratic Party (Shamin-tō), Japan
SED	Sozialistische Einheitspartei Deutschland (Socialist Unity Party), Germany
SOC	Sindicato de Obreros del Campo (Agricultural Workers' Union), Spain
SOFA	Status of Forces Agreement
SPARK	Solidarity for Peace and Reunification of Korea
StWC	Stop the War Coalition, UK
TAV	Tren de Alta Velocidad (High Speed Train), Spain
UANSA	Uganda Action Network on Small Arms

UDC	Union of Democratic Control, UK
UGT	Unión General del Trabajo (General Labour Union), Spain
UJCC	Uganda Joint Christian Council
UN	United Nations
UNDODA	United Nations Office for Disarmament Affairs
UNDP	United Nations Development Programme
UNIDIR	United Nations Institute for Disarmament Research
UNSC	United Nations Security Council
UPDA	Uganda People's Democratic Army
UPDF	Uganda People's Defence Force
USA	United States of America
USCAR	United States Civil Administration of the Ryukyuan Islands
USSR	Union of Soviet Socialist Republics
VAWW-Net	Violence against Women in War Network
WAM	Women's Active Museum, Japan
WASG	Wahlalternative Arbeit & Soziale Gerechtigkeit (Labour and Social Justice Electoral Alternative), Germany
WiB	Women in Black against War, international network
WIL	Women's International League
WILPF	Women's International League for Peace and Freedom
WLM	Women's Liberation Movement
WLOE	Women and Life on Earth
WMP	Women Making Peace, Japan
WONT	Women Oppose the Nuclear Threat, UK
WPA	Women's Peace Association, UK
WRI	War Resisters' International
WSPU	Women's Social and Political Union, UK
WWG	Women's Working Group (of War Resisters' International)
WWP	Workers' World Party, USA
ŽuC	Žene u Crnom protiv Rata (Women in Black against War), Serbia

Introduction

Women and men, young and old, those of us who join organizations opposing militarism and war bring with us a host of different experiences, hopes and fears, philosophies, objectives and styles. We feel ourselves to be part of something bigger than our local group, part of a movement, even a global movement. But are we a rag-bag of interests or a coherent collective actor? I wanted to know more about the make-up of our movements against militarism and war and for peace, the ways we diverge, how significant our differences are, and how well we hear each other. Over the course of two years I travelled to different countries to find out about groups, organizations and networks, listen to activists and share in some of their activities. I wanted to gain a sense of what we share, how strong and effective we are, or might become. This book is the result.

You might ask why it matters. Isn't it enough that we are all there, one way and another, that we are seen and heard, on the street, on the TV screen and the Web, in the campaign office? In a way, yes, that's already something. But, with every decade that passes, human violence, amplified by developments in media and weaponry, gains a longer reach, has more power to destroy our psyches, our relationships and our world. Our survival may depend on our ability to generate, quite soon, a worldwide epochal movement, one capable of displacing the prevailing idea that violence is normal and inevitable, and substituting a different paradigm: the idea that violence is a matter of choice. It would mean supposing there is almost always a less violent alternative, a less violent thought, word, intention, policy, strategy and action; that we can choose a path that leads, step by step, towards a very much less violent society than the one we live in. For that idea to become hegemonic, to become universal 'common sense', requires a huge and effective social movement. To obtain that sweep and scope, a lot of people must be paying careful attention to each others' thoughts and aspirations, exploring and exchanging methods and negotiating tactical and strategic alliances.

All books about 'peace movements' face a problem of definition. What's included, what's excluded, in the movement being considered here? The movements I examine would for the most part identify with one, or more than one, of three tags: 'anti-war', 'anti-militarism' and 'peace'. Where a war is being fought or about to break out the activists opposing it are likely to call themselves an anti-war movement. Where people are opposing military rule, high military expenditure or the imposition of foreign bases in their country, they may use the word anti-militarism. Where the problem presents itself as a government's propensity to privilege war over diplomacy in its foreign policy, or a long term stand-off between armed powers, the movement is likely to be termed a peace movement. You will notice that sometimes in the following chapters, when it becomes too cumbersome and wordy to list all the components, I abandon logic and take a short cut, referring to 'peace movements' as an envelope for the whole. In the same way I sometimes (optimistically) refer to our 'movement' in the singular, though usually (and more realistically) I write in the plural of our many 'movements'.

Choosing where to look: a panel of cases

This book is the outcome of a two-year funded project of research involving a sequence of studies of disparate elements of the anti-war, anti-militarist and peace movement viewed as a world-wide phenomenon. How did I choose particular instances for study? Why these, why not others? It was hopeless, I knew, to aspire to rigorously 'represent' this movement of movements by a sample of instances. Without a bounded population no representative sampling is possible, and it's in the nature of social movements that their edges are vague, porous and shifting. Rather, I decided to constitute a kind of array or panel of cases to which I might address my questions. As one might assemble for a public enquiry or a television programme a panel of informed people, each capable of contributing some particular experience or expertise to the understanding of a given problem, I chose cases differing by location (Japan, South Korea, Spain, provincial Britain and others), by scale and structure (international network, country-wide movement, local campaign), and by focus (the issue of partition, the arms trade, Israel's Occupation of Palestine, the US system of overseas military bases, and so on). I hoped to see, through these discrete realities, not what *is*, in any definitive sense, but what *can* be, what *occurs*.

While the above may account for the organizations, networks and movements I included in the study, further explanation is needed of the several significant fields of action I left out. One omission is conciliation, the important work of reconciling parties in conflict. A second is humanitarian activity, a huge 'industry' on its own account, responding to the desperate needs of war victims, including refugees. It is often non-governmental organizations (NGOs) that answer to these concerns, though they may have a campaigning wing. In excluding them from my selection of cases I don't mean to suggest they are unconnected with anti-war, anti-militarist and peace activism – there is clearly an overlap. But my particular interest is with the latter. It may be that I allow my perceptual horizon to be defined from where I stand. I mean 'stand', in this case, quite literally. Every Wednesday evening, with few exceptions, for almost twenty years we have stood, a small group of women, in a vigil for one hour at a given site in central London. There we demonstrate opposition to the war policies of our own and other governments. Similar vigils of women who, like us, call themselves Women in Black against War, are a feature of life in other cities and towns around the world. It's from this 'standing' that I began by looking back in time to our antecedents in the British peace movement, a story I tell in the opening chapter, and then looked outwards to locations far removed from London, where I could see people, both men and women, involved in kinds of activism that resonated with our own – oppositional, refusing the logic of war, challenging policy-makers.

There's one important exclusion, however, about which more needs to be said. It derives from the matter of oppression. Poverty and exclusion, as well as bullets and bombs, cause injury and death, so that oppressive conditions are with good cause sometimes termed 'violence' – indirect, impersonal or institutional violence. Some four decades ago, Johann Galtung proposed the term 'structural violence' to describe this pervasive disembodied harm (Galtung 1969). Anti-war, anti-militarist and peace movements, as I see them, are alert to these wrongs, and understand that direct violence is often an enforcement of, or a response to, structural violence. Peace activists know full well that while oppression continues, no peace will be secure. For this reason, they often name their objective as 'peace *with justice*'. Few would believe that a sharp conceptual break can be made between direct and indirect violence, or between the campaigns that address them. However, for the most part the hugely challenging matters of structural inequality, exclusion and oppression are the focus of another set of widespread and growing social movements – those for global economic, land and climate justice. These are not included in my study, but they are part of the world in which my protagonists live, act and make alliances.

The quest for coherence

What my case studies revealed above all was the complexity of anti-war, anti-militarist and peace movements. You will see that, in any given space, I found groups and organizations with similar abstract values – peace, justice, democracy – but rather widely varied practical objectives, such as trying to change voters' minds, influence foreign policy, interrupt a long-running conflict, end the manufacture and export of weapons, discourage recruitment to armed forces, remove guns from the nursery toy-box, or stop military rape. I found various competing political tendencies, some expressed in party membership, others in less formal orientations, and these were often the source of a distinctive analysis of the problem, a 'theory of war'. Repertoires of action I encountered included mass mobilizing, local protest, lobbying, petitioning, information and education, nonviolent direct action and (though rarely, and hotly contested) violently destructive behaviour.

In every case, perverse as it may seem, I positively welcomed the surfacing of tensions, and even antagonisms, within the field of anti-war, anti-militarist and peace activism. Why? Because unavoidably they are present, even if sometimes hidden, and discussing them at once opens to view the efforts being made to clarify them, communicate about them, identify common goals and imagine shared actions. Coherence does not mean, in my understanding, identicality, sameness, but rather the ability to converse and shift, to understand others's meanings, to acknowledge and work with difference, to actively seek bases for agreement.

Since 1995 my research and writing has been about women and women's organizations, and I anticipated mainly women readers. This book is different. I hope many men will read it. My concern this time includes 'mainstream' organizations and activity, by which I mean those of mixed membership, male and female. Although many women are involved in mixed organizations, men are often in leading roles. My focus is on the play of ideas, behaviours and forces within and between such organizations and networks – gender dynamics, yes, but also political dynamics more widely defined. Various versions of socialism, communism and anarchism, for instance, introduce contested analyses of capitalism, class relations and the state. Secularists challenge people of diverse (and competing) religious faiths who nonetheless share their condemnation of war. Pacifists differ as to when, if ever, they might condone the defensive use of physical force. These tendencies struggle for a hearing and for leadership in movements to end war. I pay attention to them all.

Research funding and approach

My research approach over many years has been consistently qualitative. As widely discussed in the methodological literature (for instance Silverman 1985; Strauss and Corbin 1990; Flick 2009; Marshall and Rossman 2011), traditional scientific method, in which the researcher is ideally a detached observer whose presence in no way influences what lies under the microscope, is both impracticable and unproductive in research on organizations, communities and social movements. Getting to grips with such diverse, complex, mobile human collectivities calls for a flexible set of data-gathering techniques including case study, observation, participation, interview, group-work and the assembling of documentation. Qualitative researchers, then, 'study things in their natural settings, attempting to make sense of, or interpret, phenomena in terms of the meanings people bring to them', and they will pick whatever tools promise the best chance of 'getting a fix' on the subject in hand (Denzin and Lincoln 1998: 3).

In the present case I read about the groups, organizations and movements, and their situation in relation to militarization and armed conflict, before engaging with them. I visited them, observed their activities, and sometimes joined them at a meeting, at a rally or on a march. My most important source of information was long, exploratory, open-ended interviews with key actors, framed around six questions. What are your group's *objectives*? What are the main *values* you bring to your activism? What is your *analysis* of the sources of militarism, militarization and war? What *strategies* do you judge most likely to be effective for opposing them, and what particular *activities* do these lead you to engage in? Finally, I asked each one to schematically 'map' for me the other groups, organizations and networks in their particular activist environment, and tell me about the quality and nature of their political *relationships* with them. Of course the interviews often ranged beyond these themes, to deal with group history, current political events and government policies, among other things. I carried out 101 such interviews, and gathered information less formally from a further 29 women and men, in conversation, in group situations, or by phone or e-mail.

And of course I gathered armfuls of documentation. Altogether, in this way, I learned about the work of 76 groups and organizations, some in more detail than others.

In research where no experimental or quantitative data are available to lend conviction, careful observation, accurate reporting and reasoned interpretation are the more important, and the researcher needs to be clear about where she's 'coming from'. Let me say here, then, that I'm a woman and a feminist. I'm not an adherent of any religion and am socialist without being a member of any particular party or tendency. I'm not an absolute pacifist but rather a social reformer, believing that the best we can do is to work a little at a time towards the goals of democracy, equality, inclusion, justice and nonviolence and that it's important to do so prefiguratively, making those ends at the same time our means. These orientations explain my interest in the research topic, my framing of questions, and no doubt also what I accorded more and less significance in my findings. But I hope they do not distort the way I represent other people's differing views. I am active in the London branches of Women in Black against War (WiB) and the Women's International League for Peace and Freedom (WILPF), and in approaching my research informants, I made sure they were aware of our shared, though never identical, engagement in the anti-war, anti-militarist and peace movement.

The principal funders of my research were the Joseph Rowntree Charitable Trust (JRCT), who describe themselves as 'an independent, progressive organisation committed to funding radical change towards a better world'. The Trustees only support projects of research that are likely to contribute to their main aim, the creation of 'a peaceful world, political equality and social justice'.[1] When I visited the Trust office to discuss their support for the project, their research officer Nick Perks asked me what outcomes I foresaw. 'We know you'll *write* something,' he said. 'But what's going to *change* as a result of this research?' So, far from being the 'fly on the wall' of positivist science, who looks but doesn't touch, I did try to contribute, albeit in a modest way, to the work of the groups I visited. I was able to ferry information to and fro, prompt a workshop here or a discussion group there, bring people together who might not otherwise have met to explore their different concerns. I also know, because many tell me, that when activists engage with a researcher, when they are asked to recount, reflect on and analyse their practice, it can helpfully clarify their thinking and renew their sense of direction – even though it is demanding on their time. I see such interventions not as tainting the reality I was studying, but as opening to further useful knowledge about it.

Because of JRCT's commitment, shared by my other funders, to prompt social change, and because the peace movement is itself activist, it might be assumed that the branch of qualitative methodology in play here is what is termed 'action research'. This is not so. There are many definitions of action research, but most suppose the active participation, indeed partnership, of the research subjects in the design and execution of the research (Greenwood and Levin 1998; Reason and Bradbury 2006; Somekh 2006). This was not the case in the project reported here, which was devised by me and *addressed* the organizations studied. On the other hand, my research funding enabled me to pay for short periods of help from, so to speak, 'locals'. In the study of Okinawa and Japan (Chapter 6) Naoko Ikeda, a doctoral student from Japan at York University, Toronto, a colleague in the Women in Conflict Zones Network, not only flew to Japan to join me in the fieldwork but simultaneously acted as my interpreter. She also helped with writing up and is co-author of Chapter 6. In South Korea (see Chapter 7), Elli Kim, who when I met her was Research Director of Women Make Peace, Seoul, helped me establish contacts and accompanied me to interviews, though we employed a professional, and particularly perceptive, interpeter, Lee Se-Hyon. The case of the International Action Network on Small Arms (reported in Chapter 8) is different again. Sarah Masters, co-ordinator of IANSA's Women's Network, travelled with me to Uganda so that we could join in a Week of Action against guns. She greatly facilitated the interviews and meetings we conducted together. Both Elli and Sarah chose to be termed 'co-researcher' rather than 'co-author'.

In terms of 'action', one of the studies differs from the rest. Chapter 5 describes a mobilization against NATO, an activity in which I was personally involved as a member of London Women in Black. Within the context of a transnational network, No-to-NATO, we joined with others in an initiative to engage women from several European countries in protests on the occasion of a meeting in Strasbourg of NATO heads of state. The description of the No-to-NATO campaign included here (Chapter 5) is thus the product of a researcher who is also an activist in the field of her research interest, reflecting on her own experiences and actions. It might perhaps be seen as falling into the category of 'practitioner research' in which 'action researchers enquire into their own lives and speak with other people as colleagues' rather than as 'data' (McNiff with Whitehead 2002: 15).

After each period of fieldwork I (or we) wrote a substantial interim text, which mostly ran to 100 pages, reporting findings and conclusions in the case, and containing many quotations from interviews. I had given each person I interviewed an undertaking that I would not quote them in a publication without first checking back with them, giving them a chance to correct or amplify my rendering of their words. Each interim text, therefore, was returned to the informants involved, with a request for their amendments, particularly concerning any mention of themselves or their organizations. Several months later, when all those who wished to had sent amendments, the text was altered to take account of them. These negotiated interim reports then became the raw material for chapters in the book. Draft chapters were again returned to the people mentioned therein, to be sure they felt no discomfort with the way they are represented in the published version. This elaborate process, for me, is more than an ethical necessity. It gives me greater confidence that my understanding of my informants' reality is not too far removed from theirs.

Starting out: conceptual resources

Qualitative research also calls for a researcher to be clear about the mindset she brings to the subject in hand – the 'interpretive paradigm' that will shape her reading of the world she enters. This is especially important where, as in this instance, that subject is political with a big P. Since the early 1970s I've walked (with many other women) a path we've called socialist feminism. It's a path we've brought into being as we walked it – 'se hace camino al andar' as the Latin American comrades say. There have been many questions along the route, because, as they often add, 'preguntando caminamos': asking, we walk. Socialist feminist? Left feminist? Feminist socialist? With hyphen or without? To those readers (and I hope they will be many) who come to issues of war and peace not by way of feminism, but by way of socialism, anarchism or some other variant of left analysis, it may not be immediately obvious why a feminist approach is relevant to their concerns. I answer them not only by affirming its relevance but by making an even stronger claim. Feminist theory has opened up a pathway *for* the left, a path that leads to a more lifelike model of class power relations and, with it, a more adequate perception of the minimum requirements for successful struggles against both capitalist domination and militarism.

I have brought to this work three concepts, together providing a theoretical orientation. They will be familiar to some readers, new to others: standpoint; intersectionality; and transversal politics. Have patience, those who suspect academic jargon here! Behind the arid terminology is politically useful thinking for socialists, feminists and indeed anyone concerned with war, its causes and its remedies.

Between 2004 and 2006, in a research project that was a forerunner to the one reported here, I visited twelve countries and gathered information on more than sixty women's groups and organizations addressing war. It was published in the book *From Where We Stand: War, Women's Activism and Feminist Analysis* (Cockburn 2007). Women gave me three reasons for their decision to organize separately from men. First, they want to bring to greater prominence the experience of women and girls in militarized societies and armed conflict, which often differs substantially from that of men and boys. Second, they had sometimes left mainstream organizations because they found themselves at odds with their leadership styles and activist methods, and wanted to make their own decisions about these things. But a more challenging reason had to do with the distinctive theory of war women have been evolving. From their standpoint, as women face to face with militarist violence, they perceive a 'sexual division of war' that involves close links between masculinity and militarism. As feminists they understand gender to be a relation of differentiation, inequality and power, founded on violence. Applying this understanding to their life experience, as women in the midst of war, or citizens of countries that source war or profit from others' wars, they perceive gender power relations as an important factor predisposing societies to war, in short as a *cause* of war. This proposition has for the most part gone unheard or been unwelcome in the mainstream movement.

The word 'standpoint' here is not used casually, in the way I spoke earlier of my own 'standing' on a Women in Black vigil in London. I use it in a theorized sense derived from the writings of Marx, most particularly by Georg Lukács (1968). Material life structures but sets limits to the way any one of us understands society. The ruling class and the working class, given the power relation that binds them, must have radically different understandings of the world. The perspective from below, the standpoint of those in struggle against exploitation, is likely to give the more trustworthy view of the realities of capitalist society.

In the second-wave feminism of the 1970s, one current was the selective and critical use of Marx's theory and method to create a feminist historical materialism. Nancy Hartsock in her seminal book *Money, Sex and Power*, adopted the concept of 'standpoint' and argued that, as the proletarian standpoint reveals truths about capitalist society unavailable to the ruling class, so women's lives, differing systematically and structurally from those of men, 'make available a particular and privileged vantage point on male supremacy ... that can ground a powerful critique of the phallocratic institutions and ideology that constitute the capitalist form of patriarchy' (Hartsock 1985: 231). Standpoint, in this sense, it should be noted, does not mean just any individual point of view. It's an account of the world constituted by and in turn constituting a collective subject, a group. It arises from their life activities and is hard won through struggle. It's subversive, contradicting the hegemonic account of how things are. A feminist standpoint, supplementing the account of class power with an account of patriarchal power, the domination of women by men as a sex, the deformations and depradations involved in gender relations, contradicts not only the hegemonic ruling class account of how things are, but also the socialist world view. If a proletarian standpoint is the foundation of a revolutionary movement against the capitalist mode of production, a feminist standpoint could be the footing for a more far-reaching revolution (Hartsock 1985, 1998; Harding 1986, 2004; Haraway 1998; Rose 1994).

Hartsock, like some other socialist feminists, including Hartmann (1979) and Weeks (1998), has maintained Marx's concern with labour, founding her feminist standpoint on women's experience of work, both paid and unpaid. Others, though, have located a standpoint in alternative aspects of women's reality. For example, Sara Ruddick (2004) has argued for 'maternal thinking', Dorothy Smith (2004) for women's bodily engagement in the 'everyday world', and Maria Mies and Vandana Shiva (2004) for women's survival and subsistence in the third world, as generative of feminist standpoints. Basing my case on what I have learned from feminist anti-militarist acivists, I have proposed (Cockburn 2010) that women's experience of violence, militarization and war too may be understood as generating a particular, informative, feminist standpoint. As a feminist standpoint on labour enriches the understanding of capitalist class relations and class struggle, so a feminist 'take' on war potentially enriches the understanding that mobilizes peace movements.

However, adding gender to class is not the end of the story. In bringing to view a sex/gender dimension of power, distinct from but intertwined with an economic/class dimension of power, advocates of feminist 'standpoint' were approaching the theory known as 'intersectionality'. This too has much to say to theorists of capitalism, class and militarism. The concept had its origins in an intervention by women of colour within the US feminist movement around 1990. Kimberlé Crenshaw (1989), Patricia Collins (1990) and others picked up on the critique long made by black women (for example the writings gathered in Moraga and Anzaldúa 1981) that second-wave feminism was marginalizing their experience, building a movement on theories of women's oppression that pretended to universalism while responding only to the realities of white women. As feminists were pointing out to men that the working class was comprised of two sexes, and that women's experience of class relations was not identical to that of men, black women were now pointing out, equally emphatically, that women are not a homogeneous category. Every individual's experience and sense of self differs, they were saying, according to their positionality, not within the power relations of patriarchy alone, but also within those of class rule and white supremacy. These positionalities, they insisted, intersect with each other to shape massively unequal life chances and conflictual subjectivities.

The concept of intersectionality was picked up by social scientists concerned with inequality (for instance, McCall 2005) and lodged in the sociological canon, where it now lives a life independent of feminism and is applied to analysing the nature of disadvantage experienced by different groups, for instance in the labour market and welfare provision. Attention, however, has been directed almost entirely to the intersected positionalities of the individual and group. Neglected has been the meta-level, the intersected power relations inherent in the institutions from which their various forms of disadvantage flow. Patricia Collins (1986) had evoked a 'matrix of domination', but the language of system and structure (mode of production, sex/gender order) fell out of favour in the postmodernist 1990s, so that power itself and the institutions through which domination is effected mostly evaded the intersectional lens.

In delineating a feminist anti-militarist standpoint on war, however, I found it necessary to stress what so many other women had stressed to me: that power, systemically, is *not* singular. Economic class power, the obsession of the left, co-exists and intersects with other dimensions of power, most notably a male-dominant sex/gender order and a system of ethnic or national power embodied in community, religious and state structures. All three systems of domination are founded on violence. Only a combination of structural repression, threat of violence and overt force has sustained class rule, racial supremacy and the subordination of women these many centuries. Intersected as they are, mutually shaping, acting through each other although sometimes in contradiction, they often have expression in the self-same institutions: family, church, corporation, military, state. Women in armed conflict, experiencing rape and abduction as women, genocide for their tribal name and dispossession by corporate plunder, have no doubt that *together* patriarchy, racism and capitalism give rise to and perpetuate militarism and war (Cockburn 2007, 2010). Socialist and anti-racist feminism, then, has reshaped and strengthened the theory of power so that it has become a resource not just for women but for the left, indeed for anyone concerned with the exploitations and oppressions of class, 'race' and gender. Moving beyond the easy notions that 'it's all down to capitalism', and 'all we need is class unity', it has been revealing instead the extent of the mutual oppression, the painfully conflicted subjectivities, that need to be tackled within the 'we' that we hope to mobilize to bring an end to injustice and war.

To this point it might well be felt that what feminist thought has brought to the movement is a poisonous gift. It may offer a more accurate analysis, but by highlighting the mutual oppressions of class, race and sex it stirs up strife and dissension. However, feminists have also begun to evolve and theorize political practices that could help to overcome the mutual oppression and antagonisms generated within the community of individuals by their differing positionalities in relation to power. The term 'transversal politics' was first used by Italian Women in Black activists in Bologna and Torino. 'Politica trasversale' was what they called their approach to working with women who were members of national groups currently at war: Serb, Croat and Bosnian Muslim women; Israeli Jewish and Palestinian women. In describing their attempts to facilitate constructive communication across conflictual differences, they coined the terms 'rooting' and 'shifting', by which they meant a process of 'centring' on another's reality while not abandoning or denying one's own sense of self. Nira Yuval-Davis developed and theorized the idea of transversal politics as a means for escaping the immobilizing dilemma of universalism (there is only one truth) and relativism (there is no truth), and finding a means for dialogue across difference (Yuval-Davis 1994, 1997). A little later, Lynette Hunter and I suggested:

> Transversal politics ... answers to a need to conceptualise a democratic practice of a particular kind, a process that can on the one hand look for commonalities without being arrogantly universalist, and on the other affirm difference without being transfixed by it. Transversal politics is the practice of creatively crossing (and re-drawing) the borders that mark significant politicised differences. It means empathy without sameness, shifting without tearing up your roots. (Cockburn and Hunter 1999: 18)

Transversal politics is not a politics of identity. On the contrary it questions the very notion of identity, marking a clear distinction between the 'tag' or 'name' with which a person is identified by others, and that person's lived sense of self. Progressive dialogue requires recognition of one's own and the other's positionality in relation to different kinds of power, an acknowledgment of the mutual harms done historically and currently in the name of class, gender and ethnonational 'tribe'. In my books about women relating across embittered boundaries in Northern Ireland, Bosnia-Herzegovina, Israel and Cyprus (Cockburn 1998, 2004a) it is possible to see experienced and skilled women hard at work developing the practice of transversal politics.

Sequence of chapters

Having this conceptual orientation in mind will help to make sense of the stories that follow. In Chapter 1 I look at three moments in the life of the British peace movement and ask: what was going on just then in national and international politics, and in relations between women and men, femininity and masculinity? The periods on which I focus are the decades following the Napoleonic wars that ended in 1815; the years that span the Great War of 1914–18; and the early 1980s, when US nuclear missiles were bunkered in British bases. Across this span of time we can see a shift from a profoundly patriarchal peace movement in which women are present but not permitted to speak, to one in which women step forward to act autonomously on the international stage of a world at war, and finally, to a decade when, with good reason in a particular context, women peace activists decide to exclude men.

War Resisters' International, the subject of Chapter 2, is an entire movement within the bounds of one network, a supportive framework for those, worldwide, who refuse obligatory service in the military. More than that, however, it is a movement against armies and war-fighting, and for a just social and economic order. Two major contradictions have been a source of intense debate within WRI over its ninety-year history. The first lies in the difficulty of pursuing a struggle that is both effective and principled – achieving economic and social revolutionary change by means of nonviolent direct action. The second has to do with gender. The majority of conscientious objectors are men, but there has always been a number of women activists in WRI. While the majority of members have recognized that male supremacy is one of the wrongs calling for revolutionary change, only a minority, and mainly women, have integrated this explicitly into their analysis and aspired to change praxis.

I followed war-resistance to Spain, to look in some detail at one of WRI's associate organizations, the Alternativa Anti-militarista: Movimiento de

Objección de Conciencia, and its civil disobedience against the militarism of the Spanish state. Chapter 3 tells the story of how, for twenty-five years, every move the state made to corrall its young men into military service was met by the objectors with a strategy of refusal, dramatizing their pacifism and embarrassing the authorities. AA-MOC shares with other social movements (of greens, squatters, neighbourhoods, women) a prefigurative methodology (nonviolence, horizontal organizing) that differentiates all of them from the traditional left. Women joined the movement first as family and friends supporting male objectors, then as activists making feminist sense of militarism. While some persisted in dual militancy in the male-dominated movement, others left to start Women in Black, a network not only against war but against aggression against women.

Next I decided (see Chapter 4) to take a single city, Leicester in the English Midlands, at a specific moment, the Israeli assault on the Palestinian territory of Gaza between 27 December 2008 and 18 January 2009, and ask who these people were that came out to stand together in the town centre and call for peace and justice. I ask what organizations did they belong to? What were their motivations and their demands? In addition to several secular groups, including the substantial local branch of the Campaign for Nuclear Disarmament which played a central part in the demonstrations, I found a complex array of faith groups drawn into action variously by a profound concern for peace and a passion for justice for Palestinians. The case reveals some of the difficulties and rewards of negotiating a contingent local alliance between profoundly divergent cultures and ideologies.

In 2008 an international mobilization began in France, Germany, the UK and other member states against the North Atlantic Treaty Organization. It was prompted by preparations for NATO's 60th anniversary Summit meeting in Strasbourg, to be attended by the newly elected US President Barack Obama. Chapter 5 describes the mobilization, the political diversity of the participating organizations, and the threatening reaction of the authorities. I reflect on an initiative in which I shared to bring women to Strasbourg to join the demonstration and contribute a 'feminist case against NATO'. A key theme in the chapter is violence – the violence of the state security forces and the violence of some demonstrators – which raised questions concerning the scope and methods of our movement.

In Chapter 6 Naoko Ikeda and I address the Japanese anti-war/anti-militarist/peace movement, which we found to be markedly divided between socialist and communist streams. We devoted particular attention to Okinawa, islands whose people suffer under both Japanese economic and ethnic hegemony and an overbearing US military presence. We found that a tradition of 'co-struggle' here transcends some of the political rifts in the mainland movement. The movement also contains a small number of feminist anti-militarist organizations, differentiated by their analyses and practices. Okinawa Women Act Against Military Violence campaign against both militarism and male violence. With their feminist anti-militarist partners in mainland Japan they differ from the mainstream movement in countering the programme of a resurgent nationalist right across the whole spectrum of reactionary politics, including not only militarism and xenophobia but patriarchalism too.

A mere hundred miles from Japan, across the Straits, is the Korean peninsula. The movement for reunification of North and South Korea, though vulnerable to swings in the policy of both regimes, persists in seeking cross-border contact, campaigning for international understanding of North Korea, and developing practical projects such as the childrens' Bread Factory. As we see in Chapter 7, the tendency in South Korea's reunification movement to an emphasis on nationhood, and its tolerance of the North's nuclear strategy, distance it from an anti-militarist movement that seeks the disarming of the peninsula and the removal of US forces from the region. Some organizations, however, seek to participate constructively in both movements, working towards a peace culture in everyday life, and elaborating the creative project of a democratic 'peace state' encompassing both Koreas.

My final case study, presented in Chapter 8, is not of a country but of another network, the International Action Network on Small Arms. IANSA is a transnational advocacy network that lobbies international agencies and state governments for implementation of a programme of action for the worldwide control of manufacture, export, sale, ownership and use of small arms and light weapons. At the same time, its member organizations are activist groups in many countries campaigning against the proliferation of the guns that stoke war and wreck peace. IANSA's Women's Network supports women's gun-control projects in a wide range of countries and has prompted a Disarm Domestic Violence campaign, stressing the added harm to women resulting from guns in the community and at home. Due to its past and present wars, Uganda is an impoverished country awash with assault rifles and handguns. The gun in a man's hand has become his only guarantee of adult masculine status in a traditional but challenged patriarchy. Women's organizations are calling for the harmonization of gun licensing and domestic violence laws.

In Chapter 9, drawing together the insights I gained from the preceding studies, I pursue some thoughts about anti-war, anti-militarist and peace activism as a social movement, a global movement of many parts. My perception of the groups, organizations and networks I encountered is that they exemplify rather well Alberto Melucci's definition of a social movement as the mobilization of a collective actor, in solidarity around a specific idea, using methods that breach the limits of compatibility with the conventional political system, in a struggle for control of some valued resource (Melucci 1989, 1996). The resource in this case is no more or less than 'common sense'. The peace movement struggles to loosen the grip on our minds of the inevitability of war, the prevailing view of violence as natural and inescapable, and open them to the belief that, for the most part, we can choose to do things differently.

My aim in the research had been to uncover and understand the many elements, differences, divergencies and tensions in this complex movement of movements. Now I can see more clearly that the values of peace, justice and democracy they bring to their activism are shared and a source of coherence. It is in analysis and strategy they diverge. I discuss three divergences in some detail. The first is the tussle in, among and between socialists, communists and anarchists of various hues, concerning the centrality of the capitalist mode of production in fostering militarization and fomenting war. Is it just competition for global markets and the neoliberal interventions of governments that are to blame? And how culpable, in particular, is the USA? Different attitudes towards the Communist alternative (for instance, in the Eastern bloc before the demise of the USSR, and in North Korea today) have been a source of division in some parts of the left, while anarchist groups place more emphasis on the violence inherent in state structures.

The second tension in the movement results from the interjection of a feminist standpoint claiming that power and domination are more complex than they have ever appeared to the imagination of the mainstream left. Recent wars, characterized by rape and ethnic massacre, bear out women's contention that economic interests, while seldom absent from the factors giving rise to war, operate hand in glove with phallocracy and ethnocracy. All three, and more, must be addressed together if militarism and war are to be seriously challenged. The implication stressed by feminists – that transformative change in gender relations, and particularly in forms of masculinity, is necessary work for peace – is not easily accepted in the mainstream, and many women have chosen to organize separately.

The third area of divergence I detect is of activist strategy. Some groups argue for mass mobilization, others for localism; some choose campaigning, others believe in starting with the self, in cultural work against violence. Nonviolent direct action is popular and gaining in inventiveness. But some individuals and groups who embrace violent tactics arouse dissension in the movement. While there is a great deal of mutual toleration and good will at work in the movement, and this should not be underestimated, there is rather little evidence, I find, of a careful and diligent transversalism that could address, clarify and bridge significant differences.

I conclude by turning to some thoughts awoken in me by these many encounters, tropes I detect in current thinking in the movement. They concern violence, as such, not only its extreme expression in militarization and war. One idea that has been prompted both by the nature of post-1990 'new wars' and feminist intersectional thinking is that violence should be seen as a continuum. The conflicts in Bosnia, in Rwanda, in Sri Lanka, the Democratic Republic of Congo and elsewhere have caused many survivors and observers to make connections between war atrocities and the endemic violence in 'peace-time' societies. Gendered and ethnicized violence, latent in pre-war militarization, explodes during war-fighting and persists in post-war criminality. But the continuum of violence is not only one of time. It is also of place (home, street, battlefield), of scale (from fist to bomb) and of type (structural, direct). Instances of violence in the continuum have begun to be seen as causally linked, bringing to mind new strategies of interruption.

A second trope I detect in current thinking in anti-war, anti-militarist and peace movements stresses volition, the idea that we may choose and un-choose violence. It is a minority view. The prevailing understanding is that the violence we observe all around us in human society, deplorable as it may be, is natural, it's 'in our genes', it's our fate. This essentialism is useful to rulers, to those who profit from war, politically or economically, and who have an interest in sustaining militarization. It justifies heavy policing on the home front, too, and an ever-expanding security industry. But some parts of the left also feel an affinity for the assault rifle. Some see revolutionary violence as necessary – and indeed cathartic. Peace movements, by contrast, are defined precisely by rejecting such fatalism, whether biological or historical. While they don't naively proclaim the possibility of a violence-free world, they nonetheless propose a project of violence-reduction. Underlying anti-militarist activism, extended in scope by feminist thinking, is the idea that, at all levels of confrontation from a sexual encounter to global war, alternatives exist. There is more than one way forward. There are less violent and more violent options. The aim is to mobilize a counter-hegemonic idea that replaces the ruling 'common sense', 'Violence is inevitable', with another that says, 'No. More often than not, it's a matter of choice'.

Note

1. See: www.jrct.org.uk (accessed 4 April 2011).

1
Finding a Voice: Women at Three Moments of British Peace Activism

> All the long time the war has lasted, we have endured in modest silence all you men did; you never allowed us to open our lips. We were far from satisfied, for we knew how things were going; often in our homes we would hear you discussing, upside down and inside out, some important turn of affairs. Then with sad hearts, but smiling lips, we would ask you: 'Well, in today's Assembly did they vote peace?' But, 'Mind your own business!' the husband would growl ... Well, for my part, I would say no more. But presently I would come to know you had arrived at some fresh decision more fatally foolish than ever. 'Ah! my dear man,' I would say, 'what madness next!' But he would only look at me askance and say: 'Just weave your web, please; else your cheeks will smart for hours. War is men's business!'.
>
> Lysistrata addresses the magistrate. From the play *Lysistrata*, by Aristophanes, Athens, 411 BCE.[1]

In orienting myself to the gender and political dynamics of today's peace movements I found myself wanting to read into the history of the condemnation of war, looking back to times and places when a spirit of resistance and refusal broke through the common fatalism that for centuries, for millennia, accepted war as natural, inevitable and even necessary. The words of remarkable individuals do reach us from very distant times, voicing anti-war convictions in words similar to ours, even though the political systems, gender orders and practices of war-fighting they experienced were very different from those of today.

19

In the 5th century BCE, the Greek playwright Aristophanes condemned the bloody persistence of both sides in the 28-year Peloponnesian war between Athens and Sparta. In fact, in *Lysistrata* (see the extract that heads this chapter) he directly addressed the gender-and-militarism issue. He pilloried the addiction of men to war, his female protagonists going on sex-strike to coerce their men to forsake their militaristic machismo and put down their weapons. Two millennia later, in 1521, the Dutch theologian Erasmus, in a ferocious polemic, *The Complaint of Peace*, laid the blame for war not on men as men but on the folly of rulers. He railed against pontiffs, princes and kings fighting 'for office, for glory, for riches, for revenge', always 'with unfortunate detriment to the people'. Calling war 'the deadliest bane of piety and religion', he wrote,

> if there is nothing more calamitous to mortals, and more detestable to heaven, I ask, how in the name of God, can I believe those beings to be rational creatures; how can I believe them to be otherwise than stark mad; who ... purchase endless misery and mischief at a price so high? (Erasmus 1521: 2, 23)[2]

Erasmus died in 1536. His century accelerated the process of nation-state formation in Europe. Pavla Miller, in her study of four centuries of change in the gender order, describes a shift from the continually warring 'patrimonial' system of that period to the structure of 'patriarchal' centralized, kingly power that followed. Patriarchy was reshaping the family simultaneously. The Reformation was associated with a gradual intensifying of Church control over marriage and the gender power relation it codified. In both Catholic and Protestant regions the importance of the priest diminished relative to that of the head of household. Man was affirmed as sovereign in the home, and the patriarchal household as the basic unit of order and discipline in society (Miller 1998).

However, these formal structures of society surviving from feudalism, the unquestioned authority of man in his family, king on his throne and God in his heaven, were going to be shaken, as the seventeenth gave way to the eighteenth century, by the radical thinking of the Enlightenment and, in the last quarter of the eighteenth century, by the radical activism of revolutionaries, first in America in rebellion against British colonial rule, then in France in the overthrow of monarchical tyranny. Tom Paine's *The Rights of Man*, published in 1791, summated the novel idea of individual 'rights' in the face of arbitrary power that inspired social movements for the abolition of slavery, civil rights for religious dissenters and parliamentary reform.

That the innovatory philosophers of the late seventeenth and the eighteenth centuries were almost all males should be no surprise. As Carole Pateman tells the story, the Enlightenment did not concern an overthrow of the male-dominant gender order so much as its rearrangement. It was an insurgency against the law of the 'father' by a younger generation of males, in whom male power ruled on. The new 'social contract'[3] establishing equality among the fraternal band of parricides was, Pateman points out, underpinned by an implicit 'sexual contract', that assured the continuation of male supremacy, and extended to all men equally the right to enjoy sexual access to women (Pateman 1988). Nonetheless, the critical questioning of authority spoke volumes to women. Writing simultaneously with Paine, Olympe de Gouges in France published her *Declaration of the Rights of Woman and the Female Citizen*, while a year later, the other side of the English Channel, Mary Wollstonecraft published *A Vindication of the Rights of Woman*, two challenges to male dominance that have never been bettered.

War changed over these centuries too, not only in its technology but in its organization and purpose. The wars of the Reformation, culminating in the extensively destructive Thirty Years' War (1618–1648), affected large swathes of Europe. Motivated by religion and monarchical rivalry, they were fought in many cases by subcontracted mercenary forces. But with the growth of nationhood and national sentiment, armies changed. The American War of Independence and the Napoleonic wars involved the forcible conscription of masses of ordinary citizens. By 1809, in the later phase of the latter, Britain alone had 817,000 men in uniform, one sixth of all males of military age (Ceadel 1996: 167).

It is in the period of these two revolutionary wars, with their new politics, new sense of nationhood and new armies, that the early stirrings of a 'movement' against war is detectable. The loose network of those in England questioning the inevitability of war called themselves 'Friends of Peace'. Many were intellectuals, their views liberal and anti-aristocratic, rooted in non-establishment forms of rational Christianity. They believed in the possibility of progress. Politically they were close to the Whigs in parliament, opposing the heavy-handed Tory government of William Pitt. They sympathized with American aspirations to freedom from British rule, and campaigned bitterly against the war with France, as an attempt to reverse the 1792 Revolution. With Napoleon's coup in 1799 hopes of democracy died, and the war became one against despotism and aggression. Now the petitions and press campaigns for peace expressed a different concern, to stop the bloodshed and prevent the other European powers from imposing their rule over a defeated France.

J. E. Cookson, on whose history of the Friends of Peace I draw in the above account, describes an almost solidly male corps of campaigners among whose names careful scrutiny reveals reference to four women writers: Lucy Aikin, Amelia Alderson, Anna Barbauld and Maria Edgeworth. But Cookson does not comment on the masculine character of the movement he describes (Cookson 1982). We have to look to two other kinds of account to uncover the gender drama going on at this moment. Feminist historians tell us of a set-back to women at the end of the eighteenth century. Male historians of masculinity throw light on what war had to do with it.

The spirit behind the French Revolution was that of the fraternal social contract. It was 'a dethroning of patriarchalist authority and a desacralisation of monarchy', inspired by the ideas of Jean Jacques Rousseau, John Locke and other Enlightenment thinkers (Miller 1998: 77). Women had taken part in this momentous uprising, had invested hope in it. But the directorate and Napoleon step by step reimposed patriarchal controls over women, as they did over workers. As Pavla Miller tells the story, from the second year of the republic, women began to be systematically excluded from formal assemblies and tribunals. Women's political clubs were outlawed. The Napoleonic codes of 1804 confirmed women's dependent status in the family. The new bourgeois public sphere was not the civil society of women and men that some women had imagined it would be. Societies and associations flowered, but 'most of them', as Miller puts it, 'derived their pride and integrity from the categorical exclusion of women and a celebration of what they saw as true manliness' (Miller 1998: 109, see also Pateman 1988).

Meanwhile, out on the battlefield too, something is happening on the gender front. The men who fill the ranks of the new conscript mass armies of the Napoleonic wars are no longer mere hirelings. The state has new specifications for its military and its male population that reshape conceptions of both:

> In order for the state to have secure control of the means of violence, there must be a reliable stream of recruits into the armed forces with the appropriate values and capacities; and there must be a broad popular acceptance of the military as being necessary and even laudable. (Tosh 2004: 49)

Fighting now in fulfilment of a new duty to the nation, those enlisted to fill the ranks are revisualized as soldier-man-citizen. Increasingly male historians have taken an interest in the shaping of men through militarization. Leo Braudy sees the new national armies as bringing 'a shift to a war-based definition of masculinity even more explicit than when war was the business of a particular class in a hierarchic society' (Braudy 2003: 251). By the early nineteenth century, 'the conflation of male citizenship and military service increasingly virilised masculinity, differentiating it ever more emphatically from femininity' (Dudink 2004: 11). In war propaganda the enemy or the traitor are often pictured as female, or as an effeminate or debased travesty of a man. In this evolving gender order the prized qualities of a militarized masculinity rub off on other versions of manhood, in civilian life. 'The nation as a collective form of identity was peopled by a host of figures, positive and negative, supplied by varieties of masculinity' (Horne 2004: 36). The trend was not lost on women. Mary Wollstonecraft stated roundly that militarism threatened women by reinforcing masculine habits of authority and hierarchy. 'Every corps,' she wrote, 'is a chain of despots ... submitting and tyrannizing without exercising their reason' (Wollstonecraft 1792: para 24).[4]

The Peace Society: public men, silenced women

It was in 1815, the year the Duke of Wellington and his 'coalition of the willing' finally put paid to Napoleon on the fields of Waterloo, that peace activism in Britain first gained an institutional form. A Society for the Abolition of War formed, but quickly died. It was followed by the Society for the Promotion of Permanent and Universal Peace, which morphed into the London Peace Society the following year. Inspiring the foundation of auxiliary societies across the country, especially in the north, this was 'the world's first durable peace association with a national reach' (Ceadel 1996: 12). Like their forerunners in the Friends of Peace, the members of the Peace Society were inspired by religion, but it was now less rational Christianity than evangelical. The founders, William Allen and Joseph Tregalles Price, were Quakers of a particular sect that had espoused pacifist 'non-resistance' since the seventeenth century. Nonetheless, though the Religious Society of Friends supplied much of the leadership and the funding, the Society was intentionally non-sectarian and ecumenical, involving Baptists, Congregationalists and other dissenting groups (Phelps 1930).

The Peace Society was a mix of pure pacifists, renouncing all war on principle, and those who retained a belief that, although there are acceptable policy alternatives to most wars, some are just and unavoidable. Beyond the Society's actual membership, a wider movement included an even greater variety of positions on nonviolence, the right to self-defence and the obligation to intervene with arms to protect others. For some, the no-war position was linked to abolishing capital punishment, disciplinary brutality in the army, and the practice of duelling. Motivations for opposing war were also mixed. For some it was a question of religion, for some a philanthropic impulse, for some a matter of social and political justice. For others it was hard-nosed economic realism: wars increase debt, hike prices and disrupt trade. There was considerable overlapping membership with other progressive movements that would surge in the following decades – anti-slavery organizations, temperance and missionary societies, reform movements for the franchise and for the rights of Catholics and Protestant dissenting minorities. Those peace activists who stressed national rivalries as a cause of war found common ground with free trade liberals such as Richard Cobden and John Bright who called for untrammelled international commerce (Ceadel 1996). 'Peace' was a theme also in anti-elite radical politics and eventually in socialism. It is clear that these respectable middle-class peace-minded men believed in the perfectability of humankind and its institutions. Since war had become a matter of custom, it could be eliminated by changing the norm – many peace people pinned their hopes on some system of international arbitration. People were looking on the state in a new way, seeing it, in Christina Phelps's words, as 'a moral person, endowed with a collective will, and therefore capable of being educated to a realization of its international responsibilities and obligations' within the framework of a new international 'community of power' (Phelps 1930: 17).

In the paragraph above I wrote 'peace-minded men'. There were of course also many peace-minded women, but they are less easy to descry. Martin Ceadel is one of the few historians of the nineteenth-century peace movement who is at pains to feature women's role in it. From him I gather the following facts (Ceadel 1996). The founding membership of the Peace Society was overwhelmingly male. Women feature as 10 per cent in early subscription lists. What is more they remained no more than 14 per cent of the membership twenty years after its foundation, and would gain little more ground as the century progressed. This is not, we have to believe, because women knew little about war or lacked enthusiasm for peace. On the contrary, when Elihu Burritt later hit on the handy device of encouraging women to get together to raise funds for mailing his League of Universal Brotherhood 'peace messages' to the press, women responded by forming, by the early 1850s, no fewer than one hundred and fifty Olive Leaf Circles, as they were called, with a busy membership of three thousand women (Laity 2001). No, what accounted for the low female membership of the Peace Society was the transparently conservative gender attitudes of male members. In an article titled 'Appeal to Christian Females on the Subjects of Peace and War', one of them penned this stereotype:

> There is something exceedingly characteristic and beautiful in the idea, of the Female population of the world, with its bewitching smiles and affectionate importunity, removing from the hand of wrathful man the firebrand of war, and gently substituting the olive-branch of peace. (*Herald of Peace*, Oct–Dec 1823, cited in Ceadel 1996: 261)

However, for the time being they should bestow their smiles on each other, in women-only spaces. The Society followed the practice of the British and Foreign Bible Society, of creating separate local auxiliary societies for women, which could accommodate 'the retiring delicacy and modesty of the female character' (*Herald of Peace*, April–June 1824, ibid: 260). The first ladies' auxiliary was set up in Tavistock in 1821, others followed in Gisborough, Leeds and Lymington in 1823. In 1824 the Peace Society took the bold step of opening its annual meeting to 'Females', though they were not permitted to speak. That they eventually (silently) availed themselves of the open door is suggested by an article in *The Times* that reported of the 1840 Peace Society annual meeting: 'the assemblage was very numerous … the greater portion being ladies' (ibid: 302).

We know that by then many women, deeply troubled by the problem of war, were speaking in other venues and expressing themselves in print. Leonora Knapp, Mary Roberts, Elizabeth Pease, Mary Howitt, Maria Hack, Mary Hughes – these and several others surface as writers and activists in the histories of the early and mid-nineteenth-century peace movement. Many were inspired by the example of American women who came to Britain in 1840 to attend an anti-slavery convention. Having crossed the Atlantic, these women delegates, such were the sensibilities of British men, were banned from the main hall of the convention. Their American colleague William Lloyd Garrison, a radical campaigner for abolition, chose to sit with them in the gallery to which they were relegated, as a statement of his belief that women should be regarded as persons (ibid.).

Some light is thrown on the gender relations of this period by Leonore Davidoff and Catherine Hall in their study of the English middle class in the early nineteenth century. The war with France, they point out, had been a significant cultural watershed. The redefinition of men and masculinity described by Leo Braudy, John Horne and Stefan Dudink, mentioned above, had involved a changed perception of femininity too, an intensified idealization of women in terms of the industrializing nation-state. But while middle-class men found a new arena for self-expression and social power in a burgeoning civil society, the scope of their wives and daughters contracted. There had been a long tradition of women preachers and ministers in some of the dissenting congregations from which the Peace Society drew many of its members. But Methodism banned women preachers in 1803. Even among the Quakers, where the ministry of women was widespread and well-regarded, 'canons of gentility' began to cost them their predominance in Quaker meetings. Some women may have continued to speak in places of worship, but in the myriad voluntary associations and societies that played such an important role for men in this period, where males found new scope for self-expression and leadership, women were not to be heard (Davidoff and Hall 1987: 139).

It is perhaps not so surprising, then, that women had their work cut out to find a space to activate their peace politics within the nineteenth-century movement. They were there. In the second half of the century, women such as Josephine Butler, E. M. Southey, Ursula Bright, Priscilla Peckover, Ellen Robinson, Frances Thompson and Mary Lamley Cook – these and others somehow found ways to organize, publish and speak. But for the most part it was in spite of men, rather than with their support. Leaders of the Peace Society continued to reiterate that they would not endorse women speaking in public on its behalf. A Workmen's Peace Association was founded (in 1870) that lived up to its name by excluding working women. Eventually, in 1874, four decades after it was first mooted, a Ladies Auxiliary of the Peace Society was established at national level. It would not, however, be until 1889 (all but a century after Mary Wollstonecraft wrote her *Vindication of the Rights of Woman*) that the Society would invite a woman to join its National Committee (Laity 2001; Ceadel 2000).

Meantime, peace had not prevailed very long in Europe after the defeat of Napoleon. Militant nationalism and economic imperialism gave rise to renewed hostility among the European states. Within states and empires there were wars of national self-determination. The mid-century Crimean war was followed by civil war in America. There were British imperial forays in the Near and Far East, the Franco-Prussian war, the Russo-Turkish war and, as the century came to a close, the Boer war.

Clearly the peace movement had no purchase on government policy, and even among the public the advocates of peace, whether within the Peace Society or without, remained a small minority often drowned out by popular enthusiasm for war.

In 1869, two years after a Parliamentary Reform Act failed for the second time to give the franchise to women, John Stuart Mill published his startling treatise *On the Subjection of Women*. He was one of very few men who would speak for women when women themselves were silenced. He did not mince words. He wrote of the condition of women as 'the primitive state of slavery lasting on ... [a] social relation grounded on force' (Mill 1869[1991]: 477). He wrote of men's worship of their own will, of their sense of entitlement to command:

> The principle which regulates the existing social relations between the two sexes, the legal subordination of one sex to the other is wrong in itself, and now one of the chief hindrances to human improvement ... it ought to be replaced by a principle of perfect equality, admitting no power or privilege on the one side, nor disability on the other. (ibid.: 471)

In the latter part of the century many women withdrew from other movements, including peace activism, to put their energies into the struggle for the female franchise. Peace, like war, went on being waged predominantly by men. But their numbers too were by now depleted.

The Great War: the masculine birth of nations

Otto von Bismarck, the statesman with the erect bearing, feathered helmet and big moustache who united Germany and created an empire, loved war. He said, in 1862: 'The great questions of the time will not be resolved by speeches and majority decisions ... but by iron and blood.' His academic admirer, the historian Heinrich von Treitschke, liked to lecture on *virtus*, virility, the restorative manliness of war (Oldfield 2000). These men were dead by the turn of the century, but their passion lived on in the breasts of a number of the German and English élite, in the politicians and generals competitively amassing the means and forces of coercion that sustained their rival empires. Another man, of contrary opinion, wrote an instant bestseller warning that in a territorial war between these empires, such was the integration of modern European economies, neither would gain. Norman Angell's *The Great Illusion*, published in 1909, immediately sold by the thousand, which suggests that, although the organized peace movement in Britain was in eclipse, many ordinary people were anxious to avert the impending war (Robbins 1976). They included internationalist liberals, speaking Angell's language of the futility of war, and people of the old pacifist Christian denominations, speaking their customary language of war's immorality. But the rejection of war was more emphatically articulated now by the growing socialist and Marxist current in British politics, including the Labour Party, the Independent Labour Party (ILP), the Communist Party and the British Socialist Party, that saw capitalism as the root of the problem, and international working class solidarity as the only answer. There was however a divergence between those who justified revolutionary violence and those for whom opposition to the imperialists' war meant opposition to class war too (Shaw 1987).

The war came, of course. Ironically, the men that took Britain into the most murderous conflict of all time were of the Liberal Party, before long in coalition with the Conservatives. Even a majority of the Labour Party, which by now had forty Members of Parliament, supported the war effort and Labour eventually had a representative in the Cabinet. Outside Parliament, however, many socialists remained opposed to the war. Several of the leaders of the ILP joined Norman Angell and E. D. Morel, famous for his campaign against slave labour in the Belgian Congo, in forming the Union of Democratic Control (UDC) (ibid.). Even this body, however, did not actually call for British withdrawal from the hostilities but, like the League of Nations Society formed some months later, argued for an early negotiated peace instead of the pursuit of 'victory'. Other survivors of the old peace movement, pacifists of the Quaker and other Christian minorities, were more wholehearted in opposing the war. Some came together to form the non-denominational Fellowship of Reconciliation. When compulsory service for men of military age became a certainty, a No-Conscription Fellowship was set up, a mix of socialist anti-militarists and religious pacifists who welcomed the opportunity of practical work supporting conscientious objectors in their ordeal of court-martial and imprisonment (Hinton 1989; Ceadel 2000; Robbins 1976; Young 1997).

The significance of masculinity for nationhood became dramatically visible in the moment of entry into the war. In the early months of the fighting, many men, swept up in the surge of patriotism, volunteered to serve 'for king and country'. By early 1916 a million of them would have crossed the Channel. Manliness was overtly invoked by the recruiters. As Leo Braudy puts it, the gender norm in the nationalist propaganda touched each person, seeming to be 'a necessary building block of their sense of self' (Braudy 2003: 78). After a while, men of fighting age seen in the street in civilian clothes were liable to be given a token of cowardice by women of Admiral Charles Fitzgerald's Order of the White Feather. A recruitment poster read:

> To the Young Women of London : Is your 'Best Boy' wearing Khaki? If not don't <u>YOU THINK</u> he should be? If he does not think that you and your country are worth fighting for – do you think he is <u>WORTHY</u> of you? [5]

Most young males did not need this bullying. They queued up to enlist for the sake of masculine honour and national glory. But the positive gloss put on war-fighting would not survive the mud of the trenches. On the first day alone of the battle of the Somme, 1 July 1916, 20,000 men died and another 35,000 were wounded to gain a strip of territory one mile wide and three and a half miles long. The Somme would eventually account for 1.5 million casualties, 400,000 of them British (Hinton 1989: 63). In the war as a whole between 8 and 9 million combatants would be killed.[6] The Great War more than any other fits am Jones's concept of male 'gendercide', the selective mass killing of ung men on the basis of age and nationality (Jones 2000).

The Great War caused crisis and division among the women of the suffrage movement, as it did among socialists and Marxists. Activist women had been at pains for some time to locate themselves in and between two causes – the long hard struggle for the vote, and the campaign to keep the country out of war. In 1914 there were two strong suffrage organizations, the National Union of Women's Suffrage Societies (NUWSS) with 50,000 members, and the smaller Women's Social and Political Union, more extreme in campaigning method. The war would split both organizations. In each case the majority declared support for the government, but some members of the NUWSS executive resigned, and a splinter group departed from the WSPU (Berkman 1990).

On the other side of the Atlantic, in January 1915, three thousand women assembled at a conference for peace in Washington DC. Some of them conceived the idea of making contact with women in allied and enemy countries in order to bring them together in a neutral space to discuss how to stop the slaughter. They announced an International Congress of Women to be held at The Hague in neutral Netherlands. Four months later, no fewer than 1136 delegates from twelve countries, including 'enemy' states, attended this extraordinary, indeed treasonable, event, held over four days in April 1915, only a hundred miles north of the battle of Ypres. One hundred and eighty British women applied for permission to attend. Only twenty-four were granted pass-ports, and they were stranded at the docks by a last-minute Admiralty ban on Channel crossings. Three British women who happened to be abroad at the time were however able to take part. The Congress adopted twenty resolutions, including a call for ceasefire, for an initia-tive of mediation between the belligerents by neutral countries, and for women to be formally represented in the process of devising a peace settlement. To carry this message to the war-makers, the Congress appointed two groups of travelling envoys who managed to gain audi-ences with national leaders in the USA and thirteen other countries. Some received the women respectfully. None acted on their demands (Bussey and Tims 1980; Liddington 1989).

It was the issue of whether or not to support the Hague Congress that precipitated the split in the British suffrage movement. Those who supported the initiative, and left the NUWSS and WSPU, transferred their suffragist loyalties to the firmly anti-war International Women's Suffrage Alliance, while as pacifists they took up the role of British wing of the International Committee of Women for Permanent Peace, born of the Congress. Calling themselves the Women's International League (WIL), the British women promoted its feminist anti-militarist demands, despite castigation as traitors. But for some WIL women there was now a dilemma. Given the urgency of the situation, should they, also or instead, be putting their energy into the mainstream organizations – the Union for Democratic Control and No-Conscription Fellowship, founded and led by high-profile men such as E. D. Morel, Fenner Brockway and Bertrand Russell?

An account by Keith Robbins suggests that this choice was a hard one for at least two women. Helena Swanwick, a leading suffragist and outspoken critic of the war, did not hide her belief in the affinity of masculinity and militarism. The war, she wrote, was men's 'silly, bloody game of massacring the sons of women'. Nonetheless it was now being put about that the UDC would welcome an input from women. She somehow felt 'sick of segregation' and decided to join the Union's executive (Robbins 1976: 46). She nonetheless remained active in WIL, writing, 'I think women have got to organise women and to make them think as women. Men generally won't trouble to organise women at all, but if they do, it is always to think as men and work, in a one-sided way, for men'. Other women expressed a similar view: no way did the male leaders intend suffrage-seeking women to have a clear and visible presence in the mixed movement. So, effective and necessary though the mainstream organizations were, Swanwick did not feel that 'all the anti-militarist women should just throw themselves in with [them]' (ibid: 99). A second woman activist, Catherine Marshall, widely described as having been an exceptionally able, energetic and skilled campaigner, had resigned as parliamentary secretary of the NUWSS on the war issue. Although she became a member of the Women's International League, for much of the war she would give all her strength to administering the No-Conscription Fellowship. At one point Helena Swanwick tried to persuade her to reduce her role in the mixed movement and devote herself more to WIL. Instead, it was from WIL that she resigned (ibid.).

With the armistice of 11 November 1918 the bloodshed finally ended. In the early summer of 1919 the leaders of the victorious powers assembled in Paris to decide the terms of the peace. The leaders that would produce the Treaty of Versailles were male to a man – President Wilson had not acceded to the American women's request for the inclusion of women delegates. However, the women activists took their own initiative. Two hundred women from seventeen nations gathered in Zurich for a second International Congress of Women, while the official negotiators were meeting in Paris. The assembled heads of state were spared the sight, not only of women, but of representatives of the defeated powers. By contrast, the women's Congress, in neutral Switzerland, was attended by German, Austrian and Hungarian women. The war-time blockade of the defeated countries was still in place despite the ceasefire, and some of the women delegates were clearly starving. The text of the Treaty of Versailles was issued during the days of the Zurich meeting. Its terms were roundly condemned by the women, as by peace movements everywhere, as savagely punitive, a continuation of the war by other means. They called the famine, pestilence and unemployment inflicted on the defeated countries a disgrace to civilization, and passed resolutions which were taken to the negotiators in person by a small group of women. Among the envoys were Charlotte Despard and Chrystal Macmillan from Britain (Kuhlman 2008). These women boldly speaking truth to power could have been the granddaughters of women in the mid-nineteenth-century Peace Society, the generation who were not permitted to open their mouths in the presence of men.

There had always been at least two reasons for organizing women for peace. One was merely instrumental – to swell the ranks of the mainstream movement. The other was politically innovatory – to articulate a women's take on war. The document resulting from the Zurich Congress shows how far the movement had progressed with the latter. Women had by now devoted many years of political thought and theoretical argument to discerning the link between two power relations, that between the dominant and subordinate sex and that between powerful and weak nations. Now this understanding was encapsulated in a Women's Charter. It stated, among other things, that the social, political and economic status of women must be recognized as being of supreme international importance. Women should be eligible for every position in the anticipated League of Nations. It demanded the full franchise for women immediately, in all member states of the League. Women must be freed from dependence and assured equality in all fields including pay, property rights, and access to education and employment, on the grounds that recognition of women's services to the world as wage earners and homemakers is essential to peace. In other resolutions the Congress-women showed concern for minority rights and racial equality; progress to self-government for colonized peoples; fair distribution, and certain controls on capitalists and war-profiteers; public economic support for the work of motherhood; an end to the traffic in women; rights of asylum-seekers and protection from deportation. Above all the women called for an end to the 'right' of any government to make war, and expressed sympathy for workers' uprising, combined with an appeal to nonviolence.[7]

After Zurich, the women's international peace network took the name the Women's International League for Peace and Freedom (WILPF). An office was opened in Geneva, and by the mid-1920s there would be a membership of 50,000 across forty countries (Liddington 1989). The Women's International League became the British branch, and would later adopt the full name. It is still active today.

The settlement imposed on the vanquished nations by the men of Versailles did not, of course, as the women foresaw, achieve lasting peace. It led to a second World War within a generation. What is more, it squandered the opportunity for a new deal for the working class, a new deal for disadvantaged nations, and a new deal for women. As to the latter, Erika Kuhlman concludes, the policy-makers had a gender agenda. Their reason for keeping women far from the peace table, refusing to make the vote for women in all the belligerent countries a condition of peace, and returning women wage-workers to the home, was a determination to reimpose gender normalcy. Only re-domesticated women would re-populate the societies depleted by the killing (Kuhlman 2008).

It was a moment of nation-making for a new world order. And nothing is more symptomatic of the inherent masculinity of nation and citizenship in 1919, as in 1815, than the fact that the settlement failed to give women an important right they had demanded in the Women's Charter: the right to their own national identity, regardless of the nationality of their husband. On the contrary, there seemed to be a conspiracy to reinforce the patrilineality of nationhood: fifteen European nations introduced *new* legislation annulling a woman's nationality on marriage to a foreigner. It was clear that, in a kind of reversal of the immaculate conception, it is men alone, men without women, who have the capacity to give birth to a legitimate nation (Kuhlman 2008; Sluga 2004).

Nuclear weapons: internationalism, direct action and women-alone

In the aftermath of the Great War, the peace movement flourished. It was clear to everyone that nothing had been gained by that terrible episode of industrialized conflict, and the losses were immeasurable. Hopes were pinned to a new international order: the League of Nations Union had a quarter of a million members in Britain by 1925 (Ceadel 2000: 273). But the League was powerless against Imperial Japan's military aggression in the Pacific, the rise of fascism in Spain and Italy, and Nazism in Germany in the 1930s. The left had been inspired by revolution in Russia, disappointed by the reversal of revolutionary movements elsewhere. Now it was crucially alert to the menace from the extreme right. But even among pacifists who were not socialists, fewer and fewer, as a second world war approached, felt able to deny the necessity of armed resistance to Hitler. The causes of peace and justice had never been further apart. During the war years only the most absolute of pacifists would adhere to WILPF, the Women's Co-operative Guild, the Peace Pledge Union and War Resisters' International.

The final act of the war, however, the Allies' instantaneous and gratuitous massacre of more than 100,000 Japanese civilians by two atomic bombs (the eventual death toll from radiation would be far higher), reunited peace movements everywhere around one shared and urgent cause. Overnight, achieving world disarmament became an issue not merely of peace but of human survival. The Soviet Union had a functional nuclear weapon by 1949. Britain exploded its first atomic bomb in 1952 and tested a hydrogen bomb four years later. The development of a British nuclear weapon was the secret decision of a caucus of ministers, debated neither by Parliament nor Cabinet (Liddington 1989). The apocalyptic beauty of the mushroom clouds rising over the Pacific islands flickered on the black-and-white television screens in the corner of millions of living rooms. Many people were appalled. It prompted the creation in February 1957 of a National Campaign against Nuclear Weapons Tests (NCNWT). A year later it would become the Campaign for Nuclear Disarmament (CND).

Most of the self-appointed Executive Committee of CND, as Christopher Hinton remarks, were 'middle-aged men with established public reputations'. Bertrand Russell was President, with Canon Collins in the Chair (Hinton 1989: 161). But women were actively involved in the anti-nuclear movement from the start. The NCNWT had been the initiative of the two North London branches of the Women's Co-operative Guild. Women made up around two-thirds of the membership of NCNWT and early CND (Liddington 1989: 193). Peggy Duff, Pat Arrowsmith, April Carter and others who would become significant anti-nuclear campaigners were among an estimated 2000 women, wearing black sashes, who marched from Hyde Park to Trafalgar Square in protest against nuclear weapons in May 1957 (Carter 1992). A female majority in CND however did not mean feminism, either in terms of activist method or anti-militarist analysis.

Undifferentiated by gender politics, the strategy of the men and women of CND focused crucially on persuading the Labour Party to a policy of unilateral disarmament and voting it into power (Taylor 1987a, 1988). Over the coming decades there would be moments of success in the former, but during periods of Labour government, when it could have stopped the nuclear programme, the party clung to the 'deterrent', Britain's stake in the international power game. Some criticized the Campaign for its single-minded pursuit of Labour Party policy-makers, its failure to galvanize the working class itself. Some put this down to its middle-class character – membership drew heavily on public and welfare sector professionals and employees, and included many teachers and doctors (Mattausch 1989). Some were dissatisfied with CND's deference to the law, and supported the Direct Action Committee and the Committee of One Hundred whose activists courted arrest and imprisonment through nonviolent civil disobedience.

As CND struggled for the soul of Labour, so over the years (and indeed to the present day) people of various left tendencies would join CND in the hope of steering its policy towards their political interests. Despite this it managed to remain a relatively inclusive and undogmatic organization, thanks to the great diversity in its many active local groups, and perhaps also to the counterweight of Christian pacifism. Though the Communist Party itself was in gradual decline, members were to be found in both the leadership and rank and file of CND, where they were a mainly constructive presence – though at times during the Cold War there were tensions around differences of attitude towards the Soviet Union and its nuclear arsenal. The political ferment of the late 1960s enlivened and reshaped the left, but around a new set of concerns. By the early 1970s the intellectual New Left, and a revived Trotskyism in the International Socialists and International Marxist Group, as hostile to the Communist Party as they were to Labour, were animated less by nuclear weapons than by US imperialism and the Vietnam war, the Northern Ireland 'troubles' and the effects of economic crisis on domestic realities. Insofar as the Bomb featured for them it was less as cause than as symptom of a greater evil, capitalism, and if they involved themselves in anti-nuclear campaigning at all in the 1960s and 1970s it was in the hope of converting CND to revolutionary anti-capitalism (Taylor 1987b).

Meanwhile, feminism, to most perceptions dead and buried since the Second World War, sprang back to life along with '1968' student rebellion. During the 1970s a new consciousness awoke in women of every age-group and inspired struggles for across-the-board equality and respect, recognition of domestic labour, reproductive rights, sexual autonomy and, by the late seventies, an end to male violence against women. Anti-militarism however was not in the minds, even as a memory, of most second-wave feminists – so far. But things were about to change dramatically.

The Conservative Party, led by Margaret Thatcher, won the general election of May 1979. On 12 December that year it was announced that US intermediate range nuclear missiles (IRBMs) were to be deployed in European NATO member states, targeted on westward-pointing Soviet SS-20s. Like the North Atlantic Treaty Organization itself, this was clearly a US ploy to ensure that a third world war, like the first two, would be fought on European, not American, soil. It was soon learned that Britain would receive 140 cruise and Pershing II missiles, by an executive decision that had once again by-passed Parliament. Lulled by a period of détente in Western–Soviet relations and the achievement of a ban on atmospheric nuclear tests (1963) and a non-proliferation treaty (1968), anti-Bomb activism was at a low ebb, and a diminished CND was reduced to sharing a small office with WILPF. Now, galvanized by the imminent location of American IRBMs in British bases, the Campaign revived. National membership shot upward from 4287 to 110,000 between 1979 and 1985 (Taylor 1987a: 121). Ironically, CND achieved its ultimate goal of winning over the Labour leadership to unilateralism when it no longer counted for much – Labour would not win another general election for eighteen years.

Meanwhile the peace movement's political and gender dynamics received a jolt from two sources. In the past CND had been criticized by some for clinging to a self-satisfied conception of Britain as a continuing power in the world, capable of leading others by good unilateralist example (Hinton 1989; Taylor 1987a). In this new phase of the anti-nuclear movement, when the missiles were being introduced not only into UK military bases but Europe-wide, a genuine transnational partnership became not an option but a necessity. European Nuclear Disarmament (END) was established by E. P. Thompson and others in 1980, on CND's left flank. It looked outward to links not only with other European NATO states but with progressives and dissenters in the Soviet Union and East-Central Europe. END-ism appealed to the Labour left in CND, but never became the 'governing outlook' (Hinton 1989: 188).

The second new dynamic, introduced by women, kicked in the following year. Many women in Britain had been inspired by a dramatic act of colourful, creative, nonviolent civil disobedience in the USA, the Women's Pentagon Action of 16 November 1980. Some, in Leeds and elsewhere, came onto the streets calling themselves WONT, Women Oppose the Nuclear Threat. In June 1981 the UK Secretary of State for Defence announced that 96 cruise IRBMs and their warheads were to be located at the Royal Air Force Base on Greenham Common in Berkshire. Helena Swanwick had once complained, back in the Great War, that 'men had dropped their end of the burden of living' (Oldfield 2000: 13).[8] Now a group of women in Cardiff, Wales, carefully put down their own end of this same burden, and left home for peace. They walked a hundred and twenty miles, arriving ten days later at the gate of RAF Greenham Common. They requested a televised encounter with government representatives. Ann Pettit, an initiator of the walk from Cardiff, later wrote that their objective had been 'to gatecrash the closed world of the media debate on defence issues' (Pettit 2006: 42). Dissatisfied with the response they received from Ministry of Defence personnel on arrival, four women chained themselves to the fence. When released, they declined to leave, spontaneously setting up an encampment, first in front of the main gate, later pitching tents and constructing plastic shelters at other entrances around the nine-mile perimeter of the base.

The campers grew in numbers and notoriety, developing ever more imaginative ways of getting over, under and through the fence to gently disrupt the life of the occupying US military. They would be there on the wet and windy day the missiles were flown in. I was there too. The roar and down-draught from the massive transport planes seemed to crush us to the grass. On 12 December 1982 an estimated 30,000 women would 'embrace the base'. We linked arms, ankle deep in the mud, and sang. We decorated the fence with thousands of little symbols of everyday life, while also clipping useful holes through the wire mesh, which came to have a disheveled look, like incompetent knitting. There were increasingly serious attempts to evict the camp from March 1984 when cruise missile convoys started to leave the base on exercises. Numbers dwindled after the Intermediate Nuclear Forces (INF) Treaty was signed in late 1987, agreeing the withdrawal of cruise, Pershing II and SS-20 missiles from their stand-off. But there were still women around to see off the last missiles as they left Greenham Common for Arizona in 1992.[9]

Three things about the Greenham Common Women's Peace Camp contributed to changing the political profile of the peace movement. First was its internationalism. The women were much closer to END than to CND in this, quickly reaching out (long before laptops and cellphones would simplify such connections) to women's antimissile and antinuclear groups at bases in Australia (Pine Gap), the USA (Seneca Falls), in Italy (Comiso), in Japan (Hiroshima and Nagasaki survivors) and elsewhere, including Women for a Nuclear Free and Independent Pacific. Visits were exchanged. In this they followed the transnational tradition we have seen in the Women's International League for Peace and Freedom, many of whose contemporary members supported and contributed to the camp. Second was its methodology. CND had distanced itself from the Direct Action Committee of the 1950s and later the high-profile nonviolent civil disobedience of the Committee of One Hundred. The Campaign's own response to the announcement about the IRBMs was its customary move, a mass demonstration. The women on Greenham Common by contrast, like the nonviolent direct activists of twenty years earlier, and indeed like the suffragettes sixty years before that, put their bodies into play every day, a stubborn but nonviolent affront to orderly military policing. They did their best to let the fresh air of publicity enter the base with them, to show the public precisely where the weapons were bunkered, to sleep, dance, cook and take photographs on the forbidden land, to take and drive military vehicles, paint defiant messages on buildings and runways, and then use the courts of justice to articulate a feminist opposition to Cold War bloc-politics and militarism. They also aimed for a prefigurative methodology in day-to-day administration of the camp, trying to ensure that the means always reflected the desired end of a nonviolent, equal, respectful kind of community. In contrast to CND, there was no constitution, no structure, no executive committee, only individual women learning and contributing as they came and went.

Third, and above all else, they did gender. While the women who walked from Cardiff had called themselves Women and Life on Earth: Women's March for Disarmament, they had welcomed a handful of men among them in a support role. A few men were associated with the camp in its early days. Some women welcomed this, while others emphatically did not. Various experiences eventually led in February 1982 to a women-only meeting at which a majority decision was taken that

> all future actions should be women-only, that only women should live at Greenham, and that the camp should always attempt to deal with women representatives of the authorities and women journalists. The men living there at the time were asked to leave, and it was suggested that they might camp on another part of the Common. (Roseneil 1995: 39)

Despite the uproar this provoked, there were a number of sound reasons for the woman-only decision. Some men had shown themselves to be out of tune with the nonviolent spirit of the camp, and more likely to be aggressive in the course of direct action. It was observed that the police responded with their own violence more to men than to women protesters. The men were felt to be a drain on women's energies, failing to contribute their share to domestic provisioning and camp maintenance. It was symbolically important to show the public the strength of women's feeling against the missiles, and to express a feminist antimilitarist case, which included a critique of patriarchal gender relations, in particular of masculinity. Above all, it reflected the lesson learned in feminist consciousness-raising groups throughout the 1970s: organizing as women alone undermines dominant gender relations. It is empowering to women.

The moment of the decision to exclude men was traumatic and formative for the camp, and reactions differed widely. Certainly some men responded with anger and incomprehension, but others accepted the ruling graciously. Over the coming years supportive men would visit the camp in daylight hours and help in practical ways. Among the women, responses to the women-only decision also differed. Ann Pettit was distressed by it. She had never intended it to be this way (Pettit 2006). Sybil Oldfield, who was later a visitor to the camp, vehemently condemned the exclusion of men as fascistic (Oldfield 2000). Caroline Blackwood was sorry for those men who would certainly have fitted in very well at Greenham, but agreed the decision could hardly be selective – it had to be any man or no man (Blackwood 1984). However, those women who lived longest at the camp were inevitably the most positive. Barbara Harford and Sarah Hopkins wrote that, when the dust had settled,

> the rightness and necessity of that decision has been borne out time and time again ever since. Thousands of women identify with Greenham because they see women taking initiative that builds on, rather than denies, women's strength. For many women it has been the first time in their lives that they have become politically involved ... When men look at the world, everywhere they see other men in positions of power, leadership, men being assertive – images that reinforce male self-esteem ... If you ask where in the world women can see other women doing something which they admire and respect and which gives them a sense of their own power and their own value, there are precious few places. We need to build a positive image of ourselves in a way that isn't so much anti-men as pro-women. And we need the space to do that. (Harford and Hopkins 1984: 4)

The separatist case was legitimated by the profoundly gendered nature of the politics surrounding the camp. It was, after all, mainly men the camp was confronting. Their principal protagonist may have been a female Prime Minister, but her lieutenant was Michael Heseltine, Secretary of State for Defence. When the campers experienced obscenities and harassment from US soldiers, bullying by civilian and military police and bailiffs, invasions at night by local youths and strictures from self-important barristers and magistrates, it was in the main from men. Even when some women were involved, for instance in harassment of the campers by residents' groups, the sense of it was misogynistic. The treatment of the Greenham Common Women's Peace Camp was a response, Sasha Roseneil later concluded, that 'operated with patriarchal purpose, to crush women's most visible collective involvement in public politics since the suffrage movement' (Roseneil 1995: 135). It was therefore logical, sensible and reassuring to be able to organize resistance to the onslaught of mainly masculine reaction as women among women.

How did CND respond to this turn of events? When the Cardiff women announced their plan to walk to Greenham, CND, after several requests, lent them £250 to print leaflets (Pettit 2006). Big deal, the women felt. When they chained themselves to the fence, on

4 September 1981, and subsequently settled in for a long stay, the CND leadership responded with similar caution. They did agree, however, to Ann Pettit addressing their Hyde Park rally a month later. There was anxiety about the confrontational aspect of what was going on at the base and, as it developed into a women-only affair, some annoyance. What right did this bunch of women have to keep the larger, more experienced, mixed organizations from mounting a major resistance to the government's sell-out of this patch of British land to Ronald Reagan? The merits and demerits of the women's camp were debated in the letters pages of *Sanity* and *Peace News*. Some said it was divisive. It was preventing the full weight of the people's opposition to cruise missiles being felt at this key site. Others recognized, as James Hinton puts it, that 'the women of Greenham Common affected parts of the public psyche that more conventional campaigning could not reach' (Hinton 1989: 183). The fact that the media responded to the campers with a mixture of patronage, scorn and hostility did not help CND to love them. A piece of research commissioned by CND, but never published, stated: 'The Greenham women are burying a potentially popular cause in a tide of criticism levelled against them on personal grounds. They are discrediting a cause to which they profess allegiance' (*Report of Research*, 1983, cited by Roseneil 1995: 149).

Though national CND came near to splitting on the Greenham issue, there was strong support for the peace camp in many local CND branches, with their predominantly female membership. CND members were among the women who came to live there. One of them, Sarah Hopkins, later wrote that, seen from within her CND local, the Greenham activists 'made me feel awe, guilt, excitement, pride and envy sometimes all at once' (Harford and Hopkins 1984: 21). Many women of CND local and regional branches became regular visitors to the camp, bringing food and firewood, sometimes staying over. Meanwhile, in the CND apparatus, where feelings for Greenham were extremely mixed, one voice spoke consistently for the women. Bruce Kent, Catholic priest, at that time CND's General Secretary, published a letter in *Newbury Weekly News*. He praised the women's courage for continuing to remind the country, often in the face of mindless hatred, that nuclear weapons are both illegal and immoral. The 'mindless hatred' was an allusion to the furious Berkshire locals of RAGE (Ratepayers against Greenham Encampments). 'Thank God,' wrote Kent, 'for the many others who offer the hand of friendship, concern, and love' (Blackwood 1984: 49).

The Greenham camp was not the only group rocking CND's boat. Soon there were mixed camps at Molesworth and Faslane. Local groups were inspired to do nonviolent direct action at nearby military and industrial sites. Looking back, Kate Hudson (currently CND's General Secretary) sees it as symptomatic of CND's maturity and its skilled leadership at this time that it was able to 'embrace this spontaneous upsurge of groups and activities, to share its knowledge and experience, its ability to articulate public concerns, and to give direction to the mass mobilisations that followed' (Hudson 2005: 135). The Greenham Common Peace Camp pushed the Campaign itself to imagine new forms of protest. For example, they wished to hold a major demonstration at Greenham Common RAF Base over Easter 1983. Unwilling to impose the unwelcome participation of men, they removed the pressure from the women by organizing instead a 70,000-person, fourteen-mile human chain linking Greenham to the atomic weapons establishments at Aldermaston and Burghfield.

The women, for their part, were sceptical about CND. To many of them that 'human chain' exercise seemed less like compromise by CND than obduracy. Why couldn't they take their demo to Molesworth? So they had done their own thing that weekend, and organized a fancy-dress Teddy Bears' Picnic inside the base. It was not that the women refused all contact with men or mixed organizations. They felt fine, for example, playing their part in Cruisewatch. They monitored missile convoy departures from the base, blockaded the exits, and alerted the mixed teams of men and women that took delight in tracking the massive transporters round the countryside, teasing the military, publicising their every move. What it was in CND that turned off both the original Cardiff walkers and the eventual campers was what they saw as its establishment culture, its self-importance and earnest propriety, its lack of imagination and daring, its endless meetings and petitions. In Ann Pettit's opinion, 'a little screaming, a little shouting' didn't go amiss (Pettit 2006: 42). More damning, Beth Junor felt, was the fact that CND would use the camp, but contribute very little practical help or funding. 'We were regarded within the hierarchy of the "peace movement" as tokens to be cashed in when needed, but more symbolic than real' (Junor 1995: 86).

In 2008 I interviewed Nicola Butler, who became involved with national CND some years after the heyday of the Greenham Women's Peace Camp.[10] She believes the camp was, in the end, influential on how CND worked. Of course, despite its large female membership, CND has never spoken with a feminist voice. But by the mid-nineties, when Nicola was CND National Campaigns Coordinator, 'It was unquestionable that women could and did and should organise autonomously – that women could have meetings, even in CND, without men'. It was a far cry, she said, from the days when Joan Ruddock could cause perplexity by asking to be addressed by the gender-neutral term 'chairperson'. 'The Greenham years were a good learning time,' Nicola said, 'and CND was genuine in its response.' Whether the feminist intervention influenced government policy is of course unknowable. The 1987 INF Treaty bears Mikhail Gorbachev's imprimatur, not that of women peace campers. But David Fairhall, for instance, concludes that while the Greenham Common Women's Peace Camp was only part of a much wider movement, the women

> dragged the fundamental issues out into plain daylight. Above all they changed public expectations, so that when a rare chance came to cut the knots into which the deterrence strategists had tied themselves, even the Iron Lady felt obliged to take it. (Fairhall 2008: 189)

Towards a holistic analysis of war

In this chapter we have seen a sequence of moments when various philosophical, religious and political beliefs and mobilizations have given a particular character to the British peace movement, steering it this way and that. Whether the dominant tendency in the peace movement was rational, evangelical, liberal, reformist, radical, socialist or revolutionary, it was masculine voices, manners and values that prevailed. Nonetheless, since the early nineteenth century women have persistently done their own thinking and worked with each other for peace. At first, they had no choice but to talk among themselves, since men of the London Peace Society and its auxiliaries around the country would not tolerate women raising their voices in public. As the Society gradually opened up to women activists, women had to make a difficult decision, to continue to organize as women alone, or co-operate with men, lending their energies to the mainstream movement.

The hard choice we saw Helena Swanwick and Catherine Marshall debating at the start of the Great War is still faced by women today. In later chapters we shall come across many examples of feminists who feel it important to maintain solidarity and unity with men, adding to the strength of mixed organizations in the struggle for peace and social justice. Yet few men of those 'mainstream' organizations acknowledge male oppression of women, reform their own practices, make room for feminist women in the leadership, support women's liberation and adopt this objective alongside other aims of the organization. Their failure to do so entails women in a 'double militancy', with men and against men, that drains their strength and eventually drives some to depart. Yet (the 'yet and yet' that is symptomatic of contradiction) the creation of separate women's organizations, while necessary and productive, ruptures the solidarity of women. While both those who stick with the mainstream and those who make the woman-only choice may genuinely be committed to twin objectives of 'peace' and 'gender change', women sometimes blame each other for prioritizing one over the other.

Despite being separatists, the Greenham Common women had to justify themselves to some feminists who believed that by putting their energies into the nuclear disarmament campaign they were allowing themselves to be co-opted into a men's movement, betraying their hard-won women's liberation consciousness and selling out their feminist principles and radical analysis. A workshop was held in London on 'The Women's Liberation Movement versus the Women's Peace Movement or How Dare You Presume I Went to Greenham'. In a pamphlet resulting from the workshop, Frankie Green and the other authors expressed the view that women working to end war were yet again doing the world's housework, cleaning up the mess men make. As to being 'women-only' that meant nothing – you get women-only in the Women's Institute and the local launderette, they said. The Greenham Women responded vigorously. The essence of their reply was: feminism is feminism, and we do it where we find ourselves.[11]

The case that 'the pursuit of peace is no part of feminism' was also made academically. Janet Radcliffe Richards, for example, wrote, 'although there may be excellent reasons for an all-female protest camp at Greenham, the idea that peace is a feminist issue is not one of them' (Richards 1990: 213). She was able to maintain this position by failing to remark on connections between the masculine authoritarianism of civilian and military systems, and between male violence against women in peace and in war, connections feminist anti-militarists (as we shall see in later chapters) continually assert and on which they challenge men.

Doing things separately as women has no doubt always had more than one potential reason. Who knows whether the women of the Olive Leaf Circles in the 1840s resented being the excluded sisters on the fringe of Elihu Burritt's League of Universal Brotherhood, or were pleased to be able to do something practical, sewing, knitting and weaving together to raise money for peace propaganda. Maybe they even valued the space the Circles allowed them as women to develop autonomous ideas about war, peace, women and men. It is possible all these feelings were present as the tea was poured. Later in the century women in

Manchester set up an autonomous Women's Peace Association (WPA). Martin Ceadel suggests that it saw its role as the limited one of mobilizing women as 'a distinctive constituency' for peace, getting more hands on deck, rather than claiming a feminist insight into the causes of war (Ceadel 2000: 100). However the very fact that the Manchester women decided to establish their WPA outside the Peace Society framework, at a moment when the latter had just reiterated its ban on women speaking for the Society in public, suggests that they were intent on expressing some ideas of their own. When, later, in the Great War, women in Glasgow set up the Women's Peace Crusade (it spread rapidly across the country) it was not to bring women on board the mainstream peace movement but to express working-class women's outrage at government's wanton wastage of working-class men's lives in the trenches, and at the food shortages and misery the war was inflicting on families (Liddington 1989). Some of the same women would have been involved in the rent strikes of this period and a leading activist, Ethel Snowden, was a socialist and ILP member.

We have seen that by the 1980s it was not exclusion from the nuclear disarmament mainstream that led women to organize as women-only, but their alienation from it, and anger with men's everlasting failure to respond to feminist demands. This meant that, unlike the ladies' auxiliaries to the nineteenth-century Peace Society, they could not be taken for 'the women's section', there to augment numbers by adding female adherents to a masculine project. There are, however, other misapprehensions that can and did occur concerning the reason for being women-only. Sasha Roseneil has analysed the thinking among women at the Greenham Common Women's Peace Camp as having three strands: maternalism, feminism and materialism (Roseneil 1995). Women anti-war activists in the past and even today sometimes speak as mothers. For those who are indeed mothers this may be a realistic and cogent 'achieved' standpoint, a collective politics based on experience. It can at times come perilously close to playing into an ideology of 'separate spheres', the domestic for women, the rest of the world for men. But often it is a theme exaggerated and manipulated by the media, always ready to photograph baby bootees pinned to the military fence. As to the second theme, feminism – yes, women organizing in women-only anti-war groups are certainly bringing into play insights into a socially constructed affinity between masculinity and militarism that derive from a feminist theory of patriarchal power.

The third strand of thinking, materialism, Sasha Roseneil explains as women's response to their experience or perception of the concrete effects of militarization and war on women (ibid.). And it is indeed the case that women often feel they have more scope to stress these in women-only groups. Materialist in the Marxist sense, however, is something the left suppose women-only peace activists are *not*. There is a widespread assumption that they are, necessarily, not 'of the left', that they have chosen a course of action that in identifying gender oppression must be blind to class exploitation. This historical sketch has shown, however, that many women peace activists have been socialists, anti-nationalists and anti-imperialists. In the ensuing chapters we shall see many more women. The women I met in Spain (Chapter 3) gave me a T-shirt. The words across the chest read *Quien es socialista y no es feminista carece de amplitud; quien es feminista y no es socialista carece de estrategia.* Whoever is a socialist and not a feminist lacks fullness; whoever is a feminist and not a socialist lacks strategy.

Notes

1. Online at: http://drama.eserver.org/plays/classical/aristophanes/lysistrata.txt (accessed 20 September 2010).
2. Online at: www.archive.org/stream/complaintofpeace00eras#page/2/mode/ 2up (accessed 20 September 2010).
3. The term entered philosophical discourse with the publication in 1762 of Jean-Jacques Rousseau's treatise *The Social Contract*.
4. Online at: www.bartleby.com/144/1.html (accessed 20 September 2010).
5. Online at: www.spartacus.schoolnet.co.uk/FWWfeather.htm (accessed 20 September 2010).
6. Estimates from 'Source List and Detailed Death Tolls for the Twentieth Century Hemoclysm', at: http://users.erols.com/mwhite28/warstat1. htm#WW1 (accessed 24 September 2010).
7. Online at: www.wilpfinternational.org/DOC/resolutions/1919word.doc (accessed 24 September 2010).
8. Oldfield here is citing Helena Swanwick (1935) *I Have Been Young*, published by Gollancz.
9. See the many detailed accounts of the Greenham Common Women's Peace Camp written from various points of view, some at the time, some in retrospect, for example Blackwood 1984, Cook and Kirk 1983, Fairhall 2008, Harford and Hopkins 1984, Junor 1995, Pettit 2006, Roseneil 1995 and 2000.
10. I would like to express my appreciation to Nicola Butler for her insights.
11. The first document cited here is an anonymously authored collection of radical feminist writing, dated 1983, titled *Breaching the Peace*. It was published by Only Women Press, London. The second, a response to the former, is an anonymously authored pamphlet published in 1984 and titled *Raging Womyn*. No publisher is cited.

2
War Resisters and Pacifist Revolution[*]

The movements to end war that have surged and faded around the world over the course of more than two centuries have had many and varied component organizations. One among them stands out as peculiarly focused in its resistance to war *as such* and its determination to find, to invent, nonviolent means of eradicating it. At the same time it has had a longevity and international scope that make it less of an organization than an entire movement in itself. It is War Resisters' International (WRI), the subject of this chapter.

WRI arose out of the Great War of 1914–1918. As we saw in Chapter 1, a Military Service Act was passed in 1916, introducing compulsory military service for all unmarried men between the ages of 18 and 40 resident in Britain. The Act contained a conscience clause, tribunals offering objectors either non-combatant military roles or substitute service. Those conscientious objectors (COs) who not only refused soldiering but rejected any kind of service to the war-making state were court-martialled and normally sentenced to two years' imprisonment.

The war had placed comparable constraints on the freedom and rights of young men in all the belligerent states, and the experience awakened

[*] For help with this chapter I am greatly indebted to the following who not only afforded me interviews, often more than once, but also responded with care to my request that they read and comment on this chapter and an earlier research report. Andreas Speck, Ippy D, Hilal Demir, Howard Clark, Joanne Sheehan, Jungmin Choi, Patrick Sheehan-Gaumer, Roel Steynen, Sergeiy Sandler-Yogev, Sian Jones, Tali Lerner, Xavier Leon, and Yeidy Rosa-Ortiz. Andreas Speck, a fulltimer in the WRI office, and Howard Clark, international Chair at the time of my study, were particularly generous with their time, and I owe a great deal to their insights. I was also greatly helped by e-mail correspondence with Dorie Wilsnack, Ellen Elster and Majken Sørensen. My warmest thanks to all of you.

a postwar awareness among pacifists in many of these countries of a three-fold need: for a system of moral and practical support for individual conscientious objectors, a campaign for their rights, and a movement to prevent such a war recurring. In 1921 at a conference in the Dutch town of Bilthoven, an international organization was formed with the name 'Paco' (*esperanto* for peace). Two years later, the office of Paco was moved to London, the name was changed to War Resisters' International, and H. Runham Brown, a British war-time conscientious objector and member of No More War, became secretary. He would remain a key actor in the movement for twenty-five years.[1]

By 1925 WRI had no fewer than forty-two member organizations in twenty countries. Their representatives came together at an international conference at Hoddesden in Hertfordshire in July that year. They adopted a Constitution and Statement of Principles, and affirmed a Declaration which, with small modifications, would remain the basis of WRI belonging:

> War is a crime against humanity. We therefore are determined not to support any kind of war and to strive for the removal of all causes of war.

Individuals affirming this credo might be members. Organizations signing up to it became 'sections'. Other organizations, whose constitution or structure rendered them unable to formally adopt the Declaration, could become 'affiliates' of WRI.[2] A small central apparatus was established to serve, as it still does today, as a clearing house for ideas, a centre for news and a medium of contact for member groups.

For nonviolent revolution

The early ideologues of the movement gave War Resisters' International a bold and far-reaching aim. It was not to be a mere support group for conscientious objectors to military service, nor even simply an anti-militarist movement. It would aspire to bring about *nonviolent revolution in society*. The ills this revolutionary impulse addressed were seen as, first, 'the state' from whose absolute authority it was WRI's task to liberate the individual and humankind; and, second, 'capitalism'. A resolution passed at the 1927 Council meeting committed WRI to work 'for the supercession of Capitalism and Imperialism by the establishment of a new social and international order based on the principle of co-operation for the common good' (Prasad 2005: 110). The method was to be 'nonviolence'. To some this term might suggest passivity, but this was far from WRI's meaning. From the start they interpreted non-violence as an energetic, risk-taking and creative process: *direct action for change*.

It is the goal of nonviolent revolution that, as I see it, generated the first of two major contradictions that would be a source of internal struggle in WRI in the course of its 90-year history. I should add straight away that by 'contradiction' I do not mean merely a 'problem', something ill-thought through, avoidable or mischievously divisive. On the contrary, the contradictions that have so challenged WRI, and continue to preoccupy it today in thought and praxis, are *necessary* difficulties arising from the diversity of human beings and the intractability of the real world. The contradiction that arises from the near-impossibility of revolution and the non-negotiability of nonviolence is closely related to that addressed to some degree in most if not all anti-war, anti-militarist and peace movements: the desire for justice and the simultaneous desire for peace. While injustice rules there can be no peace. Injustice presents itself to us as intractable to all but violence. Yet violence cannot be a source of peace. Yet ... peace with justice remains imperative. These are the successive negations that characterize contradiction. In WRI every-one has believed the first and last proposition. It is debating the second and third in order to agree a practice that has challenged coherence and achievement.

In uneasy alliance within War Resisters' International in its early decades were several political tendencies. Some groups and individuals were motivated by spirituality or religious belief. Many COs in the Great War had been Quakers or Tolstoyans.[3] The impulse of other mem-bers was secular, humanist and humanitarian. There were also socialists and anarchists of different hues. Among the former were members of the Labour and Socialist International.[4] Some defined themselves as Marxists. However, many other WRI members and member organiza-tions were anticapitalist and anti-imperialist on moral and ethical rather than analytical and political grounds. Wolfram Beyer notes that while the religious, moral and spiritual element in WRI tended to use a language of 'war' and 'peace', the politicals more readily invoked 'militarism' and 'anti-militarism' (Beyer 1980).

Revolutionary change by active nonviolence (or peace with justice) is an extraordinarily ambitious goal. The questions 'is it possible?' and 'how can it be done?' were a source of much heated debate and sometimes of division in WRI. The anarchists and anarcho-syndicalist members and member organizations were more consistently anti-militarist than the socialist ones. In 1904 an International Anti-militarist Union (IAMV) had been founded in the Netherlands by the anarchist Ferdinand Domela Nieuwenhuis. Its contemporary members, still active in war resistance, were critical of Marxists and socialists on the grounds that not all of them, indeed few of them, opposed *all* militaries – they made an exception for the notion of a 'people's army'. It was a position that followed logically from the socialist ambition to take power from the ruling class, whether by parliamentary or revolutionary means, and to control the state and its means of coercion. The anarchists, however, brooked no exceptions.

The tension between anti-capitalist socialists and anti-state anarchists in WRI became evident in divergent attitudes to disarmament among the member organizations in different countries. Some favoured calling on states to abolish their arsenals: disarmament by policy. Others looked instead to mass refusal of military service: disarmament by example. An informative case is the range of positions apparent within and outside Russia in the early 1920s. Those WRI members and member organizations inclined to socialism trusted Lenin's promise that the Bolshevik revolution would be capable of delivering peace as well as a new economic and class order. Others, inclined to anarchism, rejected Leninism's centralizing statism and the transitional aim of a 'dictatorship of the proletariat'. In their analysis, the individual, not the working class, is the maker of history. Those for whom pacifism itself was the key ideology, including conscientious objectors in the post-revolutionary USSR (for there were WRI members there), despaired of the Soviet experiment from day one. As Stalinism took hold, their pessimism was confirmed.

The 1930s and 1940s were difficult decades for WRI. No sooner had it come into its strength and begun an international campaign for disarmament and an end to military conscription than fascism emerged in Germany, Spain and Italy, producing a crisis of conscience for pacifists. Now the violence/nonviolence choice was not about how to promote life-full revolution but to how stop life-threatening reaction. In 1934 the Canon of St Paul's Cathedral, Dick Sheppard, issued a pledge that soon generated 100,000 postcards committing their signatories to refuse participation in a war. His initiative led to the Peace Pledge Union, which would become, as it remains today, one of the British member organizations of WRI. But as the viciousness and ambition of the fascist regimes became more and more apparent, many signatories revoked their pledge. Some WRI members likewise revoked their refuser's Declaration. Several leading personalities, including Albert Einstein, Bertrand Russell and Fenner Brockway, reneged on war resistance during the 1930s, believing there was no alternative but to stop Hitler and Mussolini by military means. During the Second World War WRI turned its attention to setting up relief committees, helping conscientious objectors and war refugees, and condemning practices such as night-bombing.

Cold War and hot liberation movements

At an informal conference in June 1945, War Resisters' International debated the postwar prospects for their two key aspirations: radical change to end oppression, exploitation and militarism, and peaceful method. The two big shifts occurring around them in the immediate postwar world were the consolidation of a two-bloc power system and the gradual dismantling of the colonial empires. The North Atlantic Treaty Organization (NATO) was founded in 1949, the Warsaw Pact in 1955. The Cold War set in. WRI members distanced themselves from both the Western bloc and the state apparatus of the Soviet Union. They refused official co-operation with the World Council of Peace, sponsored by the USSR and its satellite nations. They looked favourably on the emergence of a nonaligned group of countries. A. J. Muste's proposal for a 'Third Camp' was the theme of the WRI international Council meeting in 1954. The word 'camp' was preferred to 'bloc' because it suggested an assembly of co-operating movements and individuals, in contrast to alliances of governments and political parties in whom WRI placed no trust.[5]

This formulation would not long avoid dissension within WRI however, for the diversity of political orientation among members and member organizations that had marked the inter-war period lived on in the postwar decades. There was a liberal traditional pacifism, its proponents happiest when campaigning on the limited front of legal rights for conscientious objectors.[6] To the left of them, however, the anarchist-inclined pacifists of WRI continued to sustain an uneasy relationship with some Marxist-inclined, Soviet-leaning elements. As late as 1972, at the Triennial conference in Sheffield, a clash occurred between one of the weightiest member organizations of the International, the German DFG-IDK,[7] and the majority of the international Council. Though its membership was politically diverse, DFG-IDK at that time was led by communists. They had produced a paper that made clear their belief in 'only one revolution – socialist revolution – which had both a violent and nonviolent wing' (Prasad 2005: 439). It led to differences, for instance, concerning the relative legitimacy of Czechoslovak resistance and Soviet intervention during the 'Prague spring' events of 1968. Howard Clark, who would later be international chair of WRI, was present at that Triennial meeting. Reflecting now on DFG-IDK's ideology he told me in interview, 'They were communists who used to say: there are three allies that will transform the world – the socialist bloc, the third world liberation movements and the Western peace movements'. After serious debate the Council decided not to expel DFG-IDK, for all its divergence from WRI's established principle of detachment from both powers in the Cold War. The tension characterized by DFG-IDK's 'difference' remained unresolved within the network.

Another surfacing of the contradiction inherent in WRI's goal of 'revolution by nonviolent means' or 'peace with justice', was in disagreement about the conduct of independence and liberation struggles. Mahatma Gandhi's nonviolent campaign to free India from British rule was profoundly inspirational to WRI, and his death by assassination in 1948 was felt as a terrible loss (Clark 2007). But despite the coherence and dignity of Gandhian passive resistance, *satyagraha*, many progressive people (DFG-IDK among them) doubted that colonized or oppressed populations could be freed from domination, always and everywhere, by nonviolent means alone. The resistance of the Vietnamese people to the massive onslaught of the USA, and *'la lucha armada'* against dictatorships in Cuba, Nicaragua and other Latin American countries, inspired a whole generation of young Westerners in the sixties and seventies. WRI therefore trod a careful path through the thicket of its besetting contradiction. The Council issued a working document on *Liberation Movements and War Resisters' International*. It affirmed the identity of WRI as 'first of all a freedom movement', and stated that its unwavering commitment to nonviolence should not be read as hostility to liberation struggles. But it posed an explicit question to 'brothers and sisters in the movements of violent liberation'. It was 'whether they are really certain that out of the bloodshed of the revolution a just society can be created' (Prasad 2005: 385).

Emerging from the brotherhood of man

The second major contradiction inherent in WRI's determination to analyse and understand oppression and war, and invent effective practices of resistance to both, had to do with sex/gender. While the majority of WRI members were males, there was a female minority. And, given the power dynamic in sex/gender relations, this was bound to entail a political diversity. While the majority recognized, or were prepared to concede, that male supremacy is one of the ills calling for revolution, it was a minority (and mainly women) who integrated this explicitly into analysis and aspired to change praxis. The majority of men, and some women, ignored or evaded the issue.

While this second contradiction was latent from the beginning, it only erupted into antagonism in the second half of WRI's history, from the early 1970s. Antagonism or agonism? It was not hatred nor destructiveness, in the main, that characterized this struggle but creative engagement and argument between actors of differing standpoint. Those who have so energetically 'agonized' over the gender contradiction in war resistance (and we shall see more of this in the Spanish context in Chapter 3) have done peace and anti-war movements an important service. This second contradiction lies in the fact that in the two world wars it was men, overwhelmingly, who were the war-makers and the conscripts. WRI had been active during a period in which masculinity was demonstrably serving militarism, and militarism shaping masculinity. Its resistance to war therefore logically called for an analysis of patriarchal power and presaged gender revolution among the other dimensions of revolutionary change. Yet rather few male war resisters grasped this. Yet women were a minority, and often a marginalized minority, in WRI and its member organizations. Yet ...

In 1928, when WRI gathered a number of like-minded organizations into a Joint Advisory Council (later termed the Joint Peace Council), two of them were women's organizations: the Women's International League for Peace and Freedom and the International Co-operative Women's Guild (both mentioned in Chapter 1). WRI had to this point shown no awareness of women's critique of sex inequalities, nor did it include in its concept of social revolution the gender dimension of change posited by feminist and proto-feminist organizations of the period. The language and policy formulations of WRI in this period are unselfconsciously masculine. The Statement of Principles of 1925 makes no mention of sex equality. There is continual reference in WRI rhetoric to 'a worldwide *brotherhood*' and 'our fellow *men*' of all classes, colours and creeds. Sisters do not feature. At WRI's fourth international conference, held at Digswell Park in the UK in 1934, the leading activist of the IAMV, Bart de Ligt, produced a compendious plan of action. His plan was about 'man' and 'men'. But a mention is made here for the first time of women's organizations. Women should be enlisted by men for the peace effort, much as they have been enlisted by governments for the war effort. The patronage is overt. Women's organizations are needed, in de Ligt's view,

> where women do not yet or have only for a short time taken any interest in social questions and where in connection with their

maternal and social functions they require special education ... it is of the greatest importance that women should become conscious of the fact that in modern war the industrial, intellectual and social work of women behind the front is as necessary as the men's work at the front ... (Prasad 2005: 155)

Throughout its first half-century the WRI was an organization that provided a platform for self-confident – and sometimes self-important – male leaders like de Ligt and Herbert Runham-Brown, of strong opinions and unhesitatingly rhetorical. Notwithstanding, there were some significant women actors in WRI. Grace Beaton was General Secretary for no fewer than twenty-three years (1933–56). Dr Helene Stöcker played an important role in the German war resisters' movement. And we catch a rare glimpse of females here and there in accounts of specific actions. For example, there were three women (April Carter, Vicki Rovere and Jette Mikkelsen) involved in WRI's mission to Moscow, Warsaw, Budapest and Sofia to protest against the Soviet invasion of Czechoslovakia in 1968 (Prasad 2005: 391). Three years later a report on the march from Geneva to Madrid in support of Spanish CO Pepe Beunza mentions seven Spanish marchers imprisoned for doing *auto-inculpación*,[8] including 'two girls' (Prasad 2005: 423). More characteristic of the histories, however, is an absence of female actors, and a lack of comment by the authors on that absence. Indeed, the female pronoun is so rare in the narrative that when it does occur, usually in reference to a nation-state ('her government', 'her people'), it is quite jarring, and confirms the impression of an unselfconsciously patriarchal organization.

Things were about to change, however. The writing of postwar feminist pioneers such as Simone de Beauvoir and Betty Friedan, and the experience of women in the political renewal of 1968, led to a women's movement in the 1970s that shook up WRI as it did the wider world. WRI's 13th Triennial in 1969 was held in the USA at the height of flower power, yet it had still been possible to have fourteen commissions ('theme groups' they were called), including one on student and youth movements, *without* including one on women. However, the subsequent Triennial, held in Sheffield in 1972, adopted a resolution on 'sex roles'. The term is quaint, given the moment. The (sociological and psychological) concept of sex role had already given way to a very different (feminist and activist) perception of women's sex and gender oppression. The resolution stated, 'The WRI supports liberation from sex roles as an integral part of the nonviolent revolution, and opposes all forms of discrimination based on sex or sexual preferences'.

It was backed by certain concrete proposals: WRI should eschew sexist language and illustrations. Fuller participation of women should be encouraged, and childcare facilities to enable this should be contributed equally by women and men (Prasad 2005: 439).

Further evidence of a shift in WRI towards a new awareness of women and gender oppression is the contrast between two important documents produced three years apart. *Manifesto for a Nonviolent Revolution*, authored by George Lakey, was submitted to discussion at the 14th Triennial in Sheffield in 1972. The only glimmer of awareness of feminist thought in this paper is the use (for the first time in a WRI document)[9] of the neutral pronoun 's/he'. The redrafted manifesto that succeeded it in 1975, authored by Michael Randle (international Chair of WRI,1966–76), was titled *Towards Liberation*. It seems to have been written in a different world altogether, stresses cultures and cultural change, and even cites Juliet Mitchell's *Woman's Estate*. It includes the standard Marxist perception that 'the kernel of [women's] repression under capitalism has been the subjection of women to the double task of market wage labour and non-market house labour', but it does go on to observe:

> Women's sexuality too has been alternatively denied and exploited. She is the goddess or the whore. In neither instance is she accorded a human status and it is the demand for a human status that is at the core of the women's liberation movement. Yet this demand – apparently so simple – has profound implications for the economic and social order and for the way in which both men and women see themselves and their relationships.[10]

Feminism now began to introduce a greater consciousness of good 'process', and WRI began to feel its way towards 'gender balance'.[11]

Feminist anti-militarism and the 'continuum of violence'

The 15th Triennial conference, that of 1975, was the first to have a women's theme group.[12] It coincided with the first United Nations Women's Year and the start of the UN Decade for Women. In WRI it was the beginning of a flurry of feminist activity which would last till the early 1980s. The women's initiatives were 'a reaction to male dominance' in the organization, and the women involved 'experienced various negative responses against having created a woman-only space'.[13] In 2008 I interviewed Joanne Sheehan, who had been at that 1975 Triennial as a delegate from the War Resisters League of the USA. She remembers it being said: 'This is separatism! It's not anti-militarism, it has nothing to do with supporting conscientious objectors.' But the women now had a sense of direction. The next step was an international women's conference, held in 1976 in Les Circauds, southern France. Ellen Elster was there. She wrote to me recently:

> It was the time when the 'new' women's movement was growing, and women were discussing their own situation, as the 'coffee-servers' in the organization, but also looking at the connection between anti-militarism, nonviolence and feminism ... This gathering was my first meeting with WRI women. It was a very decisive moment for me. I came there with a very low self-esteem, and was frightened to death, but met women who were curious about who I was, found what I had to say was interesting. I also found out that the other women had had the same fright as I had. I came out from the gathering with new friends and contacts, inspired to go deeper into the themes [of] anti-militarism, nonviolence and feminism and connecting with women in different parts of the world through the years.[14]

Four years later, in 1980, a second international women's gathering was held, on the theme 'Women and Militarism', at Laurieston Hall in Scotland. The aim, as Ellen recalls it now, was to recover that space they had found at Les Circauds in which to discuss and develop the growing consciousness that women have a distinctive understanding, play distinctive roles and therefore have some different needs from men in the peace movement. Ellen proposed the plan to the WRI Executive of which she was now a member. Some of them just didn't get it. She found herself 'arguing for money, space and program with a group of older patriarchs who couldn't understand the point of having a women-only gathering'. Yet the Laurieston agenda could have been seen as a substantial contribution to WRI's mission. The discussions there resulted in a clear statement opposing women's incorporation into the military, declaring the need for women also to resist alternative service for the state, and refusing the 'emancipation' of women through adopting men's militarized roles.[15]

Through the persistence and clarity of a small group of women, WRI was the context from which emerged an innovatory feminist anti-militarist analysis. At Les Circauds, a 'Feminism and Nonviolence' study group had been set up. It met regularly for six years and, after publishing several contributions to the feminist journal *Shrew*,[16] eventually produced, in 1983, a substantial and innovatory 60-page pamphlet, *Piecing It Together: Feminism and Nonviolence*.[17] It was a remarkable document for its time. Its authors, when they started work, had found little literature to build on. They felt they had to do their own spade-work. They started by making a conceptual link, that would be foundational in anti-militarist feminist thinking, between sexual violence and the violence of armed conflict. 'There is a profound relationship,' they wrote, 'between the fact that individual women are commonly attacked and beaten up and that a nuclear war threatens the entire world' (Feminism and Nonviolence Study Group 1983: 5). They introduced the notion of 'a continuum of violence':[18]

> As nonviolent feminists we have watched a growing acceptance within the WLM [Women's Liberation Movement] that individual men attacking individual women is one end of the continuum of violence which leads inexorably to the international military abuse of power ... what we are aiming for is an integration of the two critiques of violence ... (ibid.: 39). We cannot fight for peace and ignore the violence on the streets and in our homes; we cannot successfully confront the violence of our everyday lives without struggling for total change (ibid.: 24) ... The continuum of violence emanating from patriarchal power pervades all our lives, from the nuclear family to the nuclear state. (ibid.: 18)

The group authors of *Piecing It Together* invoked the concept of 'structural violence'[19] ('for us violence includes conditions which themselves kill' [ibid.: 6]) and used it to legitimate a concern of anti-militarist feminists with the struggle of black women, lesbians, prostitutes and homeworkers against 'being tortured and brutalised with male tools of control, whether drugs or electric shocks, pins or pricks, operating knives or flick knives or just plain dirty money ... this is structural violence at its most profound and it is time for men to realise that they are responsible for it ...' (ibid.: 43). They were explicitly positing gender relations as causal in war: '... sexual divisions in society operate to support and perpetuate wars' (ibid.: 9). They singled out two principal ways in which people are led to support and participate in wars: coercion and persuasion. Persuasion includes gender expectations, thus, 'people gradually become unfeeling, a false notion of honour is developed and men especially learn to relate to the world from a distance' (ibid.: 10). In a way that ten years later the post-structuralist/postmodernist turn had rendered all but impossible, the authors of *Piecing It Together* looked for the roots of war in *systems*. The 'structural underpinnings' as they put it, not only of sexism, racism and poverty but also of nuclear weapons, are 'the system of patriarchy, with capitalism and the State as basic and linked aspects of that system'. Anticipating today's concept of 'intersectionality' (see my Introduction), they stressed the importance of understanding their 'interconnectedness' (ibid.: 15).

Piecing It Together was politically important for several reasons. For one thing, the timing was right. It came out at just the moment to enrich and inform the thinking of women active in the campaign against nuclear missiles, which, as we saw in Chapter 1, had begun in the USA with the celebrated Women's Pentagon Actions of 1980 and 1981, and was continuing at this time with the Greenham Women's Peace Camp in the UK. In terms of content, its importance lay, first, in its explicit feminism. Reiterating and expanding on the demands of the Women's Liberation Movement, it outflanked the contemporaneous feminist critics of women's peace activism, viz. that women had again turned their attention from their own needs, rights and liberation to taking care of the world (see Chapter 1, p. 43). Second, its adamant refusal of any conception of women's engagement with war as being to do with biology, nurturing or motherhood prevented it being hostage to those who claimed the women's peace movement was 'essentialist'. Third, it sustained a critique of masculinity in WRI, the peace movement and the left, and called for change in men:

> ... [D]espite the difficulties, men have to be part of the solution if they are not to continue to be part of the problem. In the meantime we try not to let men drain the energy we have for other women and we work with men on our terms. Women have been men's source of inspiration, consolation and energy for thousands of years; we are due centuries of 'energy credit'. (ibid.: 34)

As regards WRI, the women addressed its central value, principle and strategy, that is to say nonviolence, and reshaped it for feminism. They refused any sense of passiveness or proneness in civil disobedience that could reproduce and amplify women's victimhood. At the same time they opposed, as 'alternative machismo', making heroes of those activists who most often contrive to get arrested or sent to jail.[20] They were looking for a liberatory practice that was not deformed by gender stereotyping.

In 1979–80 a financial crisis hit WRI. Myrtle Solomon took over the day-to-day management of the International and, many would say, saved it from collapse. Solomon was very influential in the organization, and unusual in being a woman figurehead. She was not, however, a feminist and she did not further the feminist agenda. In interview, Howard Clark recollected, 'Myrtle took us right back to the basic agenda of WRI: conscientious objection. The basic problem is the nature of CO. However hard you try to dress that up, it's blokes!'.[21] Howard had first got involved with WRI in the early 1970s, when as a young man, he worked for some years on the editorial and production team of *Peace News*, at that time a WRI member organization. When, after an absence, he reconnected with WRI in the early 1980s he felt the new feminist assumptions in the International had faded in that interval. He was shocked to hear how once more, at the 1982 Triennial, the women had to fight to obtain a women's space. Things seemed to have slipped backwards in WRI. Ellen Elster, who remained on the Executive till 1982, and was a Council member after that, recalls a continued struggle against a resistant organization. She wrote to me, 'We had to fight during those years, continually reminding people about the need for a women's space, taking account of women's views'. Indeed, the women had found it hard work in 1982–3 to obtain acceptance for the publishing of *Piecing It Together*. 'I would say that it was not published *because* of WRI but rather *in spite of* WRI,' Ellen wrote.[22]

The struggle for the feminist agenda

For its first half century, not only was WRI very masculine in style – its leadership comes across as disquietingly élitist. They often refer to their organization as comprised of 'intellectuals', with responsibilities towards the less enlightened masses. Thus Herbert Runham-Brown wrote, 'Only a few think – the great mass feel and learn only by object lesson' (Prasad 2005: 121). Hans Kohn, of the pre-Israeli Jewish settlers in Palestine, speaking at the Triennial conference of 1928, is recorded as saying, 'We and the War Resisters are merely an outpost of all other men who do not possess the power of theoretic exposition, and the sacrificial courage of the martyr; of the humble and the dumb, who cannot speak for themselves' (Prasad 2005: 125).

Some of the humble and dumb were clearly understood as residing in what used to be called the 'underdeveloped' world, for until the 1990s the great majority of WRI's member organizations were in Europe and the USA. Few of its gatherings had been held outside Western Europe. In the 1990s, however, WRI began to fulfil its potential for being a worldwide organization. The Berlin wall was chipped to pieces by the people it had divided, a supremely symbolic act of nonviolence. The Soviet Union disintegrated and the USA stepped forward to proclaim the New American Century and full-spectrum world dominance, their Project for the New American Century.[23] The globe spun into view.

Women's activity in WRI both fostered and responded to its new internationalism. In the summer of 1987 a women's international gathering at Glencree, in Ireland, drew women from member organizations far beyond Western Europe. Ulla Nowakowska, the only one of several Polish women to get an exit permit, brought news of women in the nonviolent struggle, then at its height, between the trade union Solidarity and the communist government. Four women drove to Ireland from Yugoslavia and reported on their government's attempt to introduce obligatory military training for women. Two South African women spoke about their dual campaign against apartheid and military conscription. Women from Thailand and Hong Kong spoke, and three participants from Women for an Independent and Nuclear-Free Pacific described the effects of nuclear testing on Pacific islanders. There were workshops on feminism; on boys and war toys; Greenham Common Women's Peace Camp; and on the very difficult matter of the relationship with women engaged in armed liberation struggles (for no more did women than men, feminists than non-feminists, escape the No. 1 contradiction). The gathering ended by agreeing a set of demands on WRI and its member organizations including equal representation for women on decision-making bodies and adoption of a feminist analysis of violence.[24]

By now WRI women had established a Women's Working Group (WWG) which would give the active women, and especially newcomers to WRI, a valuable space of belonging. Majken Sørensen remembers joining the WWG ten years later. 'It was a great inspiration to me, and I felt it as a safe space for me. I was very young ... everything was rather overpowering ... it was a very good feeling to know that I could count on these women'. The initiative brought, Majken recalls, a 'freshness' to WRI.[25] In 1987 the WWG began to publish a twice-yearly newsletter, *WRI Women*, from which it is possible to trace the themes that mattered most to them. Although they never recovered the creativity of the moment that produced *Piecing It Together*, they continually drew on the insights of that earlier period. Thus, the central element of the feminist agenda they were now trying to lodge on the WRI mainstream agenda was a recognition of the continuum of violence. The sporadic violence of war is one with the perennial violence against women, they were saying. You cannot address one without addressing the other.

At successive Triennials between 1988 and 1994 there were women's 'commissions' or theme groups – one was on women and militarism, another on military prostitution, sex tourism and related topics. Then, in 1992, the WWG organized a women's gathering, at Bangkok in Thailand, on the theme 'Women Overcoming Violence'. Howard Clark remembers, 'Bangkok was a huge event for WRI ... No WRI conference in my experience was discussed as much or prepared as thoroughly'. This big undertaking was extensively discussed at Council meetings for two or three years previously, and also at the Triennial of 1991.[26] The gathering covered important ground. Shelley Anderson[27] wrote afterwards, the conference 'made clear that women are indeed at the centre of any effort to create peace and prevent war. The question however remains: how many policymakers realize this? And what are women going to do?'.[28] Note that this was five years before the UN Security Council would address this very question and eventually, pressed by women's NGOs, pass its Resolution 1325 on *Women, Peace and Security*.

Was all this changing WRI? Was the feminist agenda shaping the main agenda of the organization? It seems not. In *WRI Women*[29] Ulla Eberhard wrote of the Women's Working Group that its issues

> never touch the lives of WRI men, nor the WRI in general. We are off on the side, meeting and planning. We are not stirring up change in the full organization ... We need to begin strategizing how we are going to integrate feminist thinking into the mixed organization.

To Dorie Wilsnack, an indication of the gender gap in WRI in the mid-nineties was that its male members leapt to attention in support of men refusing to fight in the various nationalist armies of the Yugoslav wars, yet appeared unable to respond to the mass rapes there,[30] immobilized perhaps by fear of fostering nationalist exploitation of the issue. Of the Triennial in São Leopoldo in 1994, Maggie Helwig wrote, 'Women were very visible at the Triennial – though few of the many other theme groups dealt with the issue of gender as it related to their topic in any serious way'.[31] What she is saying, I think, is that there was little evidence of any transformation, due to feminist insights, of the perception of what was the 'real business' of WRI.

There seem to have been two difficulties (men apart) in the feminizing of WRI. As Joanne Sheehan remembers it, first there was the problem that the very struggle by women to be included, to make a space for themselves and to shape WRI's agenda, drained energy from the task of feminist questioning and analysis. The creative moment of

Piecing It Together was never recovered. Second, the key activists wanted to continually reach out to a fresh intake of women from a wider range of countries. Ironically, the internationalizing of WRI came at a cost, bringing discontinuity and loss of focus for the WWG. 'We didn't want to work just "with our own". We wanted to make progress as an international group. But once a project becomes larger, broader, more international, the politics and process change. They always do, and that is a challenge.' The women's movement in society at large was fading by the mid-eighties and in eclipse throughout the nineties, so that the project of achieving the feminist agenda for WRI 'was never embraced as strongly by new members as it was by those of us who were not only part of it from early days, but ... came of age at a particular time in the feminist movement'.[32]

If WRI women were finding it hard to shape, deepen and sustain an articulation of feminist anti-militarism, the men for their part do not appear to have been attempting during these years to create an anti-militarism that was feminist. WRI's theorists of militarism were not following the nudge in that direction given by Michael Randle back in the seventies. Yet, as Ulla Eberhard had warned in 1988, there is a 'Gordian knot' connecting patriarchy and the military. 'To try to untie this knot from one end only won't work'.[33]

The feminists in WRI were however about to make another substantial effort to shift the mainstream agenda. Between 1994 and 1998 the organization set about rewriting its Statement of Principles as part of the process to renew its Strategic Plan. Ellen Elster and Joanne Sheehan, activists in the Women's Working Group, volunteered to co-ordinate this demanding process.[34] There are several places in the Principles and Plan, documents that still govern the work of WRI today, where the feminists' input is evident. One of the 'overarching objectives' defined for WRI is that 'gender perspectives [be] integrated into WRI's anti-militarism work, drawn from different cultures and traditions', with concrete measures for implementation.[35] The Strategic Plan included a list titled 'What is WRI doing well?'. Among these positive points, WRI was felt to have 'a willingness to see its program in perspective of gender, ahead of many other organizations organising both men and women'. Listed among 'WRI's weaknesses', rather candidly, was that 'some affiliates have difficulties accepting a feminist perspective'.

Joanne Sheehan became WRI's first feminist international Chair in 1998, the year of a Triennial in Poreć, Croatia, to which the Principles and Plan were presented. This meeting was more shaped by feminism than anything that had gone before.[36] Instead of having women/gender as one theme group among others, this time there was a 'gender day' in which *all* the theme groups were required to focus on the gender aspects of their topic. Ellen Elster wrote a paper for the occasion titled 'Masculinity as a Cause of War: Victimization of Women as a Result of War'. In it she wrote:

> WRI has an analysis of the world as looking through a man's glasses ... In a gender perspective masculinity will be [seen as] one of the causes of war. It is men who are in a position to start war, to produce the weapons for war, they are still the soldiers [who] fight war.[37]

After the high point of the 1998 Poreč Triennial feminist activism in WRI would be sporadic.[38] Yet a base line had been established. There was henceforth an understanding, as Ellen put it recently 'that women are affected differently by militarism and war, that women's work may be different in the work for peace and a nonviolent society ... [and] that women may voice different views which may add a more feminist contribution to the discussion'.[39] It was by now taken for granted that there should be a substantial women's/gender input to Triennial conferences and Council meetings.

War resistance today

Looking back over the history of War Resisters' International from the vantage point of 2008, I have pointed up what seem to me to be two major contradictions that have challenged the organization, causing internal struggles, deep thinking and sometimes inventive solutions. No.1 is that while all the progressive forces around and inside WRI passionately wanted social revolution, the default route to such change is a violent route.

WRI rejected that as a matter of principle. But the problem remained: to find a strategy that could 'do' social change nonviolently, that could visibly contribute to the achievement of justice without war and liberation without guns.

The No. 2 contradiction running through WRI's story also stems from intractable realities. War is a highly gendered affair, and soldiering, conscription and refusal to serve have for the most part been the experience of men. Yet only a very few men in WRI allowed this gendered reality to shape their understanding of war or strategies of resistance. Yet there were women in the war resistance movement, and we have seen how, during the 1970s, they began to evolve an understanding that patriarchy, particularly its tendency to shape masculinity as violent, is one of the interlocked systems of power at the root of war. Yet patriarchal power relations were inherent in the organization. So, despite the presence of some anti-patriarchal men, the adoption of the feminist agenda onto the main agenda was patchy. More so, the adopting of feminist process and practice.

To step into the present (2009), two examples of WRI member organizations, Vredesactie in Belgium and New Profile in Israel, illustrate serious work addressing these two contradictions respectively.

Active nonviolence: Vredesactie

Currently, WRI has two major programmes of work. One is its Nonviolence Programme. This includes transnational work around the issues of the arms trade, military contracting and financial services to 'the war machine'. It also involves development of resources, including a recently published *Handbook for Nonviolent Action*, and making those resources available by networking in the international anti-militarist and anti-globalization movements. The aim is to help people find 'the power to shape their own lives and to influence the course of events around them' and specifically to exert this power 'against oppression and exclusion, for participation, peace and human rights'. The intention is to 'prepare for nonviolent confrontation' and develop 'alternatives to economic globalisation and corporate rule'.[40] The Nonviolence Programme, in other words, addresses, head on, WRI's No. 1 contradiction.

Perhaps more than any other member organization of WRI, it is Vredesactie that exemplifies the international's Nonviolence Programme. Vredesactie is a group of nonviolent anti-militarist activists, the only organization in the Flemish part of Belgium that defines itself specifically as pacifist. These thoughtful activists shift the focus of their campaigns not in response to transitory events, but according to their analysis of needs. Roel Stynen is a member. He told me in interview: 'Vredesactie is oriented to campaigning. We think strategically, with defined goals.' In addition to direct action they do journalism and educational work around perceived needs. 'We are rather consistent. We look for relevance,' Roel says.

NATO, with its nuclear arsenal in Europe, has been an important focus for Vredesactie, evoking a series of campaigns. One they called 'Bombspotting' involved a series of acts of civil disobedience, including the incursion of thousands of people into an air force base hosting US nuclear weapons. Subsequently, in 'NATO Game Over', with partners from other countries, they carried out civil disobedience against NATO's headquarters in Brussels. 'War starts from Europe' involved nonviolent direct action against the military 'intervention' infrastructure in several European states, to get across the message that, though NATOs bombs drop far away, they are despatched from near where we live.

The organization has a number of paid staff members, working from an office in Berchem, and a self-defining core group of activists who do most of the analysis and planning. A network of local groups enables them to spread the campaigns locally and draw more people into participation. 'It's a chance to build people's capacities, so they take it on as their own thing.' Decisions in Vredesactie are made by consensus. There is no co-ordinator, director or chair. 'Co-ordination meetings' are frequent, and involve the staff together with any others who wish to take part. 'General meetings', at which policy is discussed, take place four times a year and, again, anyone who wishes to be involved may attend. They have 'working groups' (for example, one supporting local groups, another for press work), and staffers are supportively involved in each of these. Everyone participating in Vredesactie is encouraged to take a share of responsibility, and there is no tolerance of an individual dominating. 'There's an allergic reaction to that,' Roel says. 'We have tried to introduce this way of working to the local groups too. We don't train in it or make it a necessary condition. It's more a common sense.' The organization's democratic and horizontal approach is, in fact, 'not very explicit as process, more a kind of general habit, a way of doing things that's become normalized'.

In Vredesactie's immediate environment are three opposed tendencies. They are the ones we have noted in WRI as a whole. There are members of parliamentary parties such as Social Democrats and Greens that are critical of the USA, even maybe of NATO, but support the idea of a European alternative, which means the militarization of the European Union. Vredesactie are very explicit in opposing that. Secondly, there are those – often Trotskyists or former communists – who are oriented towards the traditional peace movement, with a liking that Vredesactie does not share for large demonstrations, marches and rallies. Besides, there is an analytical difference. For instance, 'Some of the socialists will criticize NATO as a front for the USA. We criticize it as an instrument of military intervention. We do make it clear in our analyses that NATO is dominated by the USA, but that's not our main point. After all, the right agree with the left on that!'. Thirdly there are those, on the anti-authoritarian or anarchist left, who are anti-war and favour direct action, but are not necessarily for 'peace' and not committed to nonviolence. Vredesactie try to maintain a working relationship with each of these three tendencies, while being clear about differences. They avoid explicitly associating the organization with a particular ideology because, they feel, to do so would result in being less inclusive. They even avoid using the word 'capitalism' on their website, referring instead to 'economic motives' in war. Roel Stynen told me:

> Many of us who are involved would probably say, if asked, that we are anti-capitalist or anti-state. But we want to avoid making people who can't agree with 'anti-capitalism' or with being 'against the state' feel that they can't join in what we do. Those who are more familiar with ideology would pick it up anyway: states visibly protect the economic interests of 'their' capitalist corporations by military means.

One source of coherence and co-operation is that Vredesactie stress *militarism itself* as a cause of war. 'People in power see militarism as a means of solving political problems ... For instance the intervention over Kosovo. Some people saw it as a way of solving that political problem, which we would absolutely reject.' Pointing to militarism and militarization itself as a problem, rather than 'capitalism' or 'the state' (and this is my interpretation), enables Vredesactie to mount actions, such as those against NATO or nuclear weapons, in which social democrats, socialists and anarchists can work side by side. The actions must be nonviolent – that is axiomatic. But Vredesactie are prepared to include people in their actions for whom nonviolence is merely instrumental – so long as they observe Vredesactie's guidelines for a nonviolent practice and are willing to take part in trainings to build this capacity.

Vredesactie, then, is one of the best examples of a WRI member organization that is inventing and fine-tuning forms of nonviolent direct action for profound change in society. However, it is not a major contributor to resolving WRI's No. 2 contradiction, that of gender in war resistance. Rather than transcending this, it evades it. While these activists have an instinctive dislike of sexism and homophobia, and observe a rough gender balance among the part-time staff, men predominate numerically in the membership and the NVDA. There have never been women's meetings or women's initiatives in Vredesactie, and there is no connection with the Belgian women's movement, Roel says. The very considerable analytical skills in Vredesactie are not applied to exploring the relation between gender and militarism. Very different in this respect is another of WRI's member organizations, New Profile.

New Profile, Israel

New Profile fits most clearly within WRI's second major programme, which they call 'The Right to Refuse to Kill'. This embodies the international's active support not only of conscientious objectors in those countries where military conscription still prevails, but also of deserters from professional armies. Israel requires military service at eighteen years of age for all its citizens, male and female, with certain exceptions and variations. For instance, Christians and Circassians have the option of serving; Druze women are not called on to serve; and Israeli Palestinians are precluded from enlisting. Men must serve for 36 months and may be called to the 'reserve' until they are 41 years of age (51 years in some cases). Women serve in the first place for 24 months and have an obligation to the reserve until they are 40 unless they become pregnant or have children. Much of the Israeli Defence Force is deployed in maintaining the Occupation of the Palestinian territories of the West Bank and Gaza, and many of its conscripts are called on to serve in the 'territories' or on their borders. For Israelis who believe it is wrong, the thought that they may be asked to play a part in perpetuating the Occupation is often a cause of refusal.

New Profile was established in 1998, by Israeli Jewish women who had for some time previously been members of a study group on 'women in militarized society'. A key activist was Ruth Hiller, whose son was a conscientious objector. Male COs, whom the law was treating more harshly than females, were particularly attracted to New Profile, but have rarely been more than a quarter, at most a third, of its members. New Profile calls itself 'a feminist organization of women and men'.[41] They have three main projects. The first is a counselling network, helping those who do not want to accept the draft, offering legal aid, supporting those in prison. Second, they organize youth groups in different cities of Israel. They work with teenagers who are still at school, encouraging them to think about militarization, feminism, the purpose and activity of the Israeli Defence Forces. Third, with partner organizations they run summer camps for young people, with activities and workshops designed to put across a radical critique of society and militarization, economy and ecology.

Two New Profile members told me their experience of the organization. Tali Lerner was drafted into the military in 2002 at the age of nineteen. She deserted the following year, acting alone and unsupported. Some time later she joined New Profile and has worked mainly as a counsellor and in the summer camp programme. I asked Tali about gender identities in New Profile. She describes herself, 24 years old now, as 'gay, loud and strong' and says she's happy New Profile includes male members because she's more comfortable in a mixed group than an all-women group. She feels her lesbianism has given her a head start as a woman. 'My ability to be the kind of woman I want to be comes from being a lesbian – because being a lesbian broke with such a basic aspect of being a woman in society. The rest was easy. Other people don't have expectations of me to be a certain way as a woman.' From Tali's perspective the core activists of New Profile tend to be 'older, white, educated and middle-class women'. She comments, wryly, 'Most of the New Profile men are more self-effacing, actually, than the women. And they seem more aware of what it means being white and male.' Younger women are getting involved however, because there are now more young women than young men refusing military service.

Sergeiy Sandler-Yogev refused military service and was imprisoned for two terms during 1994 and 1995. He was in touch with an experienced Israeli war resister, J. Toma Šik, who was then counselling a small group of contemporary COs. When he left Israel in 1995, the group formed an Association of Conscientious Objectors to carry on the activities. When Sergeiy got involved with New Profile, a year or two after it was formed, he immediately liked it for the strong presence of women, the casual and inclusive nature of the discussions and the organization's horizontality – the absence of an office and permanent staff, of office holders or 'spokes-persons'. He quickly became active, counselling and organizing trainings.

New Profile became a member organization of WRI in 2005. While it is similar to other WRI member organizations in addressing conscientious objection and militarization, and in its horizontal and inclusive processes, it differs from the international in several ways. First is the fact that, as well as being, like most Israeli oppositional groups, 'on the left', it has been, from the start, explicitly *feminist*. Feminism in this case is not the product of a long struggle within a male-dominated organization. On the contrary, women have always been in the majority, and the link between feminist and anti-militarist theory and politics was there from the first moment. Besides, because of female conscription, some high-profile COs in Israel are women.

Secondly, New Profile has quite a few academic members and is more analytical about what it does than some CO organizations. Cynthia Enloe's groundbreaking analyses of women and militarization are central to their thinking (for example, Enloe 2000). They are unhesitatingly vocal about the causality of patriarchy in militarism and war. They believe that just as society cannot be rid of militarism unless gender relations change, likewise equality for women and a more human shaping of masculinity cannot be achieved without the demilitarization of Israeli society. While even some feminist organizations hesitate to express a public critique of militarized masculinity, for fear of alienating potential allies, in New Profile they don't shy away from the 'M-word'. Sergeiy says, 'We're so far out anyway that we don't care. Even masculinity is sayable. There's no problem'. Third, their processes and methods are not dissimilar in intention from those of other WRI affiliates, but the latter usually see the horizontalism and inclusiveness as anarchist in spirit (if not in name), while within New Profile these qualities are understood as feminist. As Tali puts it, they are about 'creating a feminist facilitation of the self and others'. New Profile is an associate, rather than a section, of WRI because not all of them would call themselves pacifists. Although they would never use violent methods (violence is generally repugnant to the Israeli left, Sergeiy insists) they have never actually signed up to principled nonviolence, assuming it to be implicit in their feminism: 'Challenging patriarchy, we never had to specify nonviolence as a concept. It was natural.'

An important moment for feminist life in WRI was a seminar the International organized in partnership with New Profile in 2007. This picked up some of the main themes of the feminist anti-militarist analysis that had been evolving in WRI over many years. Presentations included one by Olga Miryasova on the gender aspects of abuse of soldiers in the Russian military. She stressed how obligatory military service and brutal 'hazing' (*dedovschina*) reproduce patriarchal forms of masculinity, and indeed, cultivate what she called 'emotional insanity' and evasion of responsibility in men. Isabelle Geuskens, manager of the Women Peacemakers' Programme of the International Fellowship of Reconciliation, a long-time partner network of WRI, reported that 'men not seeing gender as an issue that concerns them is one of the biggest obstacles women peacemakers face'. Boro Kitanoski of Peace Action, Macedonia, a member of the WRI Executive at the time, gave a cogent analysis of the toxic alliance between militarism, nationalism and patriarchy in the Balkans. 'Gender roles,' he said, 'are the foundation of the big war system.'

Transcending and surviving

A reading of WRI's Statement of Principles suggests the organization is tackling its No. 1 contradiction by several helpful manoeuvres. The first has been to seek a language that avoids rhetoric or dogma, whether socialist or anarchist, that might provoke alienation and schism. For example, in the Statement of Principles one finds little reference to the capitalist mode of production as such. A more characteristic formulation is 'the pattern of economic exploitation', or 'corporations in the industrialised and materially rich world'. References to 'injustice' substitute for explicit anti-state rhetoric. Secondly, the need to define WRI as specifically anti-capitalist or anti-state, which would leave it hostage to sectarian tendencies, is sometimes avoided by identifying militarism itself as a prime cause of war and prime object of protest and refusal. This is visible in the Statement of Principles, but more clearly in the fact that most member organizations, like Vredesactie, put their creative nonviolent activism into action specifically against militaries, weapons systems and wars, although the methods they are inventing are important resources for the anti-capitalist and *altermondialist* global social movements. Thirdly, care is taken to avoid arrogant dogmatism concerning the principle of nonviolence. Thus the Statement recognizes that fascism or episodes of genocide, for instance, 'may pose a problem of conscience'. 'Each conflict merits analysis,' it continues, and 'we are aware of the limits to what our approach offers in the short term. Therefore, we take the long-term view'.[42]

Similarly the Statement of Principles shows that an opening to the feminist agenda has been achieved without alienating (most) non-feminist men partly by dint of avoiding specificity and emphasizing inclusiveness. High value is placed on human 'diversity'. A relationship of regard between different kinds of people, and between humans and the natural world, is stressed:

> WRI seeks to join with others in building a world ... based on rela-tionships of equality, where basic human needs are fulfilled, where women and men have an equal voice, different cultures and ethnic groups are accepted by one another, borders do not divide, and the natural environment is respected.

All forms of 'domination' are condemned. A key cause of violence and war is identified as structures of domination, in the plural, where male supremacy can unobtrusively find a place:

> Domination is found in the oppression of the less powerful and in the subjugation of nature itself; relationships of domination can be based on factors such as gender, class, cultural and ethnic differences, and exist between and within nation states.

War Resisters' International is not an explicitly feminist organization in the manner of New Profile. New Profile has a majority of women mem-bers, and was founded by feminist women, while WRI has a majority of male members, and in its early years was unselfconsciously patriarchal. That need not be the end of the story however, provided two developments occur. They are still possible, and some would say are happening. One is that men as a whole 'come out' as men, making a gender case against militarism and war. And, since the turn of the millennium, a few men have indeed stepped forward with a conceptual critique of patriarchy and an anti-sexist/anti-homophobic practice. We have noted Sergeiy Sandler in New Profile. Others, in Turkey, have taken the experience conscientious objectors have always had of being slandered as 'not real men', and stood the implied shame on its head, lampooning military masculinity and asserting their own subversive alternative. Andreas Speck, when he took up a staff position in WRI's office in 2001, brought an experience of years of legal struggle and civil disobedience as a refuser of conscription to the German military. A gay man with firsthand knowledge of the malign effects on men of the patriarchal gender system, he has written and spoken a good deal about masculinity in relation to militarism (Speck 1998, 2007). At the New Profile 'Gender and Militarism' seminar he told of both political reasons for his own act of refusal, and, more personally, a profound discomfort with the militarized masculine environment that awaited him and other conscripts in the army. One explicitly anti-patriarchal man in WRI has been, as international Chair of WRI from 2006 to the present moment (2009), well-placed to support these others, and feminist women, in attempting a gender transformation of the war resistance movement. Howard Clark, as early as 1978, in a pamphlet published by *Peace News*, expressed an emphatically pro-feminist spirit (Clark 1981) and continued to speak in support of feminist initiatives in WRI. Despite these heartening examples, however, the feminist women I interviewed or with whom I exchanged correspondence in 2008 and 2009 were cautious-going-on-sceptical about the extent and pace of change in WRI. Words are not the same as deeds, they felt. And even theoretically anti-patriarchal men may, in practice, sustain an environment in which women feel unsupported, in which it is difficult for them to assert leadership.

The second transformative development that slowly continues in WRI is the leap from male refusal of military service, via female refusal of conscription (where that occurs) to a refusal of militarization in everyday life and culture. The analysis with which women presented WRI in *Piecing It Together* has helped actions like the withholding of military taxes to be valued as acts of refusal. In 2004 twelve Turkish women in a WRI member organization, who themselves were neither involved in the armed forces nor threatened with military service, declared themselves to be conscientious objectors. They did so not in support of male COs but on their own account. Ferda Ülker said in her declaration:

> Militarism is always like an unannounced and shameless guest in every aspect of life, especially for women in this geography; in the streets, at home, at work, in our relationships, at our fields of struggle, and everywhere. I declare that, today, as much as before, I shall defy every secret and obvious form of militarism and show solidarity with anyone who defies militarism. As much as militarism is determined to affect my life, I am determined to continue my struggle. (Ülker 2010: 110)

WRI could have died, could yet die, with the professionalizing of armies and the decline of obligatory military service. If it survives it will be due to this perception that militarization penetrates all our lives, whether we are men or women, gay or straight, in the military or outside it.

Notes

1. My documentary sources for this chapter are as follows. As concerns the history of War Resisters' International up to 1975 I draw almost exclusively on two secondary sources. The first is a compendious history of WRI by Devi Prasad, who was its General Secretary from 1962 to 1972 and international Chair from 1972 to 1975 (Prasad 2005). The second is the slighter and more politically oriented unpublished thesis on WRI by Wolfram Beyer (Beyer 1980) made available to me in WRI's London office. These two historians for their part delved deeply into the primary sources in WRI's archive (now housed in the International Institute for Social History in the Netherlands) which includes minutes of meetings, reports of conferences, a multitude of documents produced over the years by members, officers, WRI sections and affiliated organizations, and issues of *The War Resister* and *Peace News*. As concerns the period from the early 1970s until the period of my research in late 2008, I draw on documentation to which I had access in the London office of WRI and on its website.
2. Since their status changes from time to time I refer to them all here by the generic term 'member organizations'. In 2008 WRI had 83 member organizations in 43 countries.
3. Jehovah's Witnesses refuse military service, but are not part of the movement for conscientious objection.
4. Inheritors of the Second International founded in 1889.
5. *The War Resister*, published by WRI, Autumn 1954.
6. Wolfram Beyer is critical of this tendency, which he termed 'bourgeois democracy', and believed to be dominant in WRI in the postwar decades (Beyer 1980).
7. Deutsche Friedensgesellschaft-Internationale der Kriegsdienstgegner.

8. For an explanation of this term, see Chapter 3, pp. 78–9.
9. Howard Clark, e-mail communication, 14 April 2009.
10. From the website, www.wri-irg.org (accessed 22 January 2009).
11. Howard Clark. e-mail communication, 14 April 2009.
12. There were also gender-aware men's meetings at the 1975 Triennial. George Lakey, who had come out as bi-sexual, facilitated one of these (Howard Clark, e-mail, 14 April 2009).
13. Quoted from the project proposal to funders for the women's history project, online at www.wri-irg.org (accessed November 2008).
14. I am drawing here and in the following paragraph on Ellen Elster's e-mail communication of January 2009.
15. 'Total resistance to military service', signed by women attending the International Conference on Women and Militarism, August 1980, Laurieston, Scotland. Online at www.wri-irg.org (accessed 10 January 2009).
16. For example, 'Neither Victim nor Assassin', *Shrew*, Summer 1978.
17. The members of the working group were Gail Chester, Diana Shelley, Lesley Merryfinch, Jo Somerset, Jill Sutcliffe, Sheryl Crown, Jenny Jacobs and Gay Jones. Not all of these authors were members of WRI. There was an overlapping membership with the Campaign for Nuclear Disarmament (CND), the Campaign Against the Arms Trade (CAAT), Women Oppose the Nuclear Threat (WONT) and labour movement organizations.
18. The notion of a continuum of violence would emerge again in the 1990s. An article I wrote with this title in 1998 was often cited thereafter (Cockburn 2004). I am sorry now that I did not know of the groundbreaking work on this concept by the Feminism and Nonviolence Study Group, twenty years before.
19. See Chapter 9, p. 257, for clarification of the meaning and use of the term 'structural violence' in relation to peace movements.
20. See further discussion of pacifist 'heroism' in Chapter 3, p. 92.
21. Howard Clark, e-mail communication, 14 April 2009.
22. Ellen Elster, e-mail communication, March 2009.
23. Online at: www.newamericancentury.org (accessed 9 May 2011).
24. *WRI Women*, published by War Resisters' International, No. 2/1,1988.
25. Majken Sørensen, e-mail communication, January 2009.
26. Howard Clark, e-mail communication, 14 April 2009.
27. Shelley Anderson was a significant actor in feminist developments in WRI, from her base in the Netherlands headquarters of the International Fellowship of Reconciliation (IFOR), a network separate from but always close to WRI. She founded IFOR's Women Peacemakers Programme, which was closely linked to the WRI Women's Working Group.
28. *WRI Women*, published by War Resisters' International, 1996/01.
29. *WRI Women*, No. 12. Undated, but probably 1992, the year of the Bangkok gathering.
30. Dorie Wilsnack, e-mail communication, January 2009.
31. *WRI Women*, 1995/01.
32. Joanne Sheehan, e-mail communication, 29 June 2009.
33. *WRI Women*, No. 2/2, 1988.
34. Other women too, particularly members of the Women's Working Group, played a significant role in developing the Plan between 1994 and 1998.

They included Dorie Wilsnack, Maggie Helwig, Vanja Nikolić, Carmen Magallon and Christine Schweitzer.

35. Online at: www.wri-irg.org (accessed January 2009).
36. Joanne Sheehan, e-mail communication, 29 June 2009.
37. I have slightly amended the English in this quotation, with the author's permission.
38. A highpoint was an international workshop in Chiang Mai, northern Thailand, 'Asking the Right Questions: Nonviolence Training and Gender Consultation'. The five-day event was attended by women from Sierra Leone, Kenya, Australia, Zimbabwe, Burundi, Aceh, Thailand, Nigeria, Uganda, Madagascar and Georgia among other countries. And in 2010 an anthology of writings by and about women conscientious objectors was published (Elster and Sørensen 2010).
39. Ellen Elster, e-mail communication, January 2009.
40. Online at: www.wri-irg.org/programmes/nvp (accessed January 2009).
41. There are some things that males may not do in New Profile. For instance the organization is affiliated to the Coalition of Women for Peace, and that is a women-only organization, so NP do not send male representatives to those meetings. Although men do travel abroad for New Profile, there is a preference for sending women representatives.
42. This and the following quotations are from 'WRI Statement of Principles', online at: www.wri-irg.org/statemnt/stprinc-en/htm (accessed 20 December 2010).

3
Legitimate Disobedience: An Anti-militarist Movement in Spain*

Anti-war, anti-militarist and peace activism encompasses a great variety of forms of engagement. None is so personal, so costly to the individual, as the refusal of obligatory military service. Many conscientious objectors have made their decision, and paid the price for it, alone. Often the objector is treated with ignominy and scorn by those around him and the state finds ways of intimidating and humiliating him before imposing a jail sentence. Organized support for resistance to conscription therefore has a unique place in the spectrum of activism to end war, because it both collectivizes the individual's experience, making the punishment more bearable, and harnesses personal rage against the war-prone state into an effective social movement. In Spain the twenty-five-year campaign against forced soldiering was inventive, often humorous and always nimble-footed, never allowing the state's manoeuvres to bring it to a halt. When conscription ended at the turn of the millennium, it was in part because the authorities were

---

*My principal sources for this chapter are the publications and website of the Movimiento de Objección de Conciencia (MOC), later renamed Alternativa Antimilitarista (AA-MOC), and interviews with a number of members and former members during some weeks in Spain in late 2008. I would like to thank the following for interviews they afforded me:
Alberto Estefanía Hurtado, Almudena Izquierdo Olmo, Ander Eiguren Gandarías, Concha Martín Sánchez, Enrique Luna Mellado, Guillem Menxeta Peris, Idoia Aldazábal Lotina, José Manuel López Blanco, Juanma Ruiz Sánchez, Manuel Soriano, Miguel Arce, Mireya Forel, Pau Serrano Magdaleno, Pedro Carmona, Pura Peris Senent, Santiago Almiñana, Sofía Segura Herrera and Yolanda Juarros Barcenilla. Thanks also to Carlos Pérez and Noemí Canelles for communicating with me by e-mail, and to Antón Apaolaza and Victoria Frensel for helpful conversations and interpretation of some interviews.

bone weary of the struggle to corral unwilling men into the barracks. They saw, too, that the resistance was a crucible for anti-militarist and anti-state thought and action.

In the amnesty that followed the death of Franco in 1975, 285 conscientious objectors were among those released from the dictator's prisons. Many of them had refused military service on religious grounds – they were Jehovah's Witnesses. There had however been a few bold pioneers of political military refusal, and the numbers would surge with the return to democracy. The Constitution of 1976 provided for the continuation of obligatory military service but also recognized conscientious objection, and introduced the option of 'substitute social service' (*prestación social sustitutoria*, hereinafter PSS). As they came of age in the following years many thousands of young men now declared themselves CO. At first, however, the state lacked the will to confront them. A legal reform was contrived to enable 'deferred conscription' (*incorporación aplazada*), under which young men refusing the call-up were put indefinitely on hold.

Collectivizing many individual acts of refusal

When the Movement of Conscientious Objectors (*Movimiento de Objetores de Conciencia*, MOC) was formally constituted in January 1977 there was already an issue around whether refusal of military service should also involve a refusal of PSS: 'total objection'. In their first Ideological Declaration in 1979, MOC acknowledged the provision of PSS as 'progress'. Nonetheless, as an organization they firmly denied the right of the state to impose *any* kind of service on the citizen. Like War Resisters' International, to which it would affiliate, in this founding document MOC described its path as nonviolent revolutionary struggle (*lucha revolucionaria*), opposing not only the army but the state's entire military structure and the repressive, violent and authoritarian values militarization confers on society and fosters in human behaviour. They promised to develop an alternative notion of defence – global, popular and nonviolent (MOC 2002: 304).

When the Spanish Socialist Workers' Party (*Partido Socialista de Obreros de España*, PSOE) came to power in the elections of 1982 it set about drafting a new law to bring order to the embarrassing chaos of conscription. Passed in 1984, it took five years to come into effect, due to a challenge to its constitutionality. Meanwhile, however, a National Commission on Conscientious Objection (*Comisión Nacional de Objección de Conciencia*, CNOC) was set up to hear cases. Already by 1985 it had dealt with no fewer than 15,000 collective declarations of refusal to serve and many more remained outstanding (MOC 2002: 324). In 1986 Spain held a referendum on whether to remain in the North Atlantic Treaty Organization (NATO), which it had joined four years earlier. The majority of the country voted 'Yes', but the process was turbulent and the energetic campaigning for a 'No' vote increased popular distaste for state militarism, especially in the more assertive of the regions (*comunidades autónomas*), always alert to Spanish power play.[1]

MOC was growing in confidence and effectiveness. Their 'total' objectors, refusing not only conscription into the armed forces but also the state's concession, substitute social service, termed themselves '*insumiso*' and their rebellious actions '*insumisión*' – refusal to submit. They worked with the trade unions, and progressive employers such as certain local authorities and universities, to encourage non-compliance with the state in the matter of providing jobs for conscientious objectors under PSS. They boycotted the employing institutions that signed up to the plan. By 1990 there would be six times as many men in full *insumisión* as performing PSS. Of these 2450 *insumisos*, 130 were in prison (MOC 2002: 325).

I heard the stories of several individual conscientious objectors who had made their refusal at different moments of the active decades of the 1980s and 1990s. Manuel Soriano, member of the MOC group in Sevilla, told me that even as a teenager he had felt a clear aversion to hierarchy and authority. He knew refusal of military service was possible, but had no idea how to proceed with it. As he approached military age, he heard of MOC and before long was going along to meetings, learning about organized objection. 'Gradually a perspective of anti-militarism matured in me,' he said. When he declared himself CO he was called to substitute social service. At first he accepted, and was drafted to a children's project. But he just sat there and refused to work. He then politicized this refusal of PSS, and got involved in a MOC campaign against the contract the local authority of Sevilla had made with the Spanish government to employ the conscientious objectors.

It was a decade later, at the end of the eighties, that Alberto Estefanía Hurtado, now in KEM-MOC, as MOC is known in Euskadi (the Basque Country), declared himself a conscientious objector. He had deferred his service for study, and subsequently got involved in co-operation projects for development in the Philippines, Peru and Mexico. He was in Croatia during the war there, and witnessed the starvation and suffering it caused. Then he came back to Spain and saw 'all this money being spent on the military'. In preference to serving in the Spanish army, he told me, 'I joined the *insumisión* campaign, which led to a year and a half in prison, because it denounces militarism and works for a world without armies'. Guillem Menxeta Peris, in Valencia, was called up in 1992 when he was nineteen. He came from a combative family of Catalan nationalists who had little love for the Spanish state. It came naturally to him to refuse both the military and substitute service. 'It was all part of the system,' he says. He served fifteen months in a civilian jail. The worst thing about prison, he said, was being rendered submissive, so that you became somehow flat and still – 'like water'. It was the movement that transformed the experience of imprisonment for him, as for others. 'We were prepared. We kept in touch with the world outside. We would help other prisoners, for instance with legal matters. We resisted being broken by the system.'

Many conscientious objectors were imprisoned over and again for successive instances of disobedience. Ander Eiguren Gandarías, like Alberto a member of KEM-MOC in Bilbao, was condemned four times, the last two for entering military installations. Depending on the crime and the period, a term of imprisonment might be in a military or a civilian gaol. While the military prison was formidable for its high degree of security and discipline, once you were inside the imposing walls it was in many ways a more tolerable regime than that of a civilian prison, where there was drug addiction and AIDS infection, and a great deal of violence among the inmates, and between prisoners and warders.

The first line of support for the *insumiso*, the first step in collectivizing his experience, midway between the individual and MOC, was his own 'support group' of family and friends. Sofía Segura Herrera lives in Sevilla. She was in the support group of her son Javier, an *insumiso* in the 1990s, during the last period of *insumisión*. Even when her children were little she had proposed to them that they would be conscientious objectors 'when they grew up'. So Javi knew he could count on her for support. But, she says, 'I didn't imagine he would take me seriously!' For almost two years the support group had weekly meetings. Among Javi's young friends neither the boys nor the girls, at the start, could be said to have had an anti-militarist consciousness. But Javi himself was very aware of the political implications of *insumisión*, and theorized his actions thoroughly. Sofía said she had found it hard to accept that 'young men like my son would have to be incarcerated. Prison was no place for anyone. It cost me dear'. But Javi saw it differently. A long prison term has its own value, he told her, 'because this is not only about not going into the military. What we're doing is about spreading information and awareness of the militarism of the state and society'.

Pura Peris Senent, who lives in Valencia, is the mother of conscientious objector Guillem Menxeta Peris. She was active in his support group, along with her husband, daughters and a number of Guillem's friends. She had already seen her older son Lluís through the process, but with Guillem it felt different, because he was refusing a legal route through which he could have avoided prison. He served the mandatory sentence of 'two years, four months and a day' in a civilian prison. Although he naturally felt a bit apprehensive about imprisonment, he knew pretty well what to expect. He had prepared for the moment by listening to the accounts of those who had been in prison before him. While he was shut away his support group worked hard. Apart from regular meetings, Pura and friends made a weekly programme on a local 'free radio' station, Radio Klara, calling it 'Leave me in peace' (*Deixeu-nos en Pau*). They wrote letters to Guillem and visited him regularly. 'The prison officers hated the *insumisos*,' Pura said. 'They had so many visitors and there was all this press coverage. The guards and prison functionaries didn't like it at all and made life impossible for the prisoners, and for the visitors.'

The *insumiso* support groups varied in how political, how militant and how anti-militarist they were. They were not part of MOC, but their members learned a way of relating and behaving that was in tune with MOC's principles, and some individuals joined the local group. Almudena Izquierdo Olmo, whom I met in Madrid, sees the support groups as having been an valuable interface between the activism of MOC and the less aware populace, because their members worked in every kind of job, they were school teachers, nurses, office workers, and as such were embedded in the non-militant world.

Denying legitimacy to the militarist state

One effect of PSOE's law had been to exempt from service 15,000 of the old 'deferred' (*aplazada*) CO cases, for whom the state was simply unable to find the needed prison places or PSS jobs. Once again, however, MOC refused to accept the militarist state's 'generosity'. They responded by inventing the notion of the 're-objector' (*re-objetor*), the one who declined his exemption only in order to re-declare as a refuser. From now, and throughout the 1990s, MOC would escalate its provocations of power in this way, keeping pace with each new attempt of the state to impose its will. Court cases were used creatively to delay judgments and keep cases in play. Particularly annoying to the authorities was the activists' practice of *autoinculpación*, or 'self-blaming'. Pedro Carmona, now living in Sevilla, described to me how, when the state failed to call him for service, he had taken this step of incriminating himself. They were telling the state, 'I wouldn't serve if you wanted me to. Therefore I too am guilty for my friends' refusal to serve. Put me in prison'. With more than sixty thousand young men awaiting trial at the time, the state had little choice but to ignore Pedro. In a similar spirit to *autoinculpación*, COs who received short sentences sometimes refused them in solidarity with those who received longer terms. In 1993 a concession was made that some prisoners would be freed from prison in the daytime, required only to return each night. Some of those granted this 'sleep over' favour refused it, seeing it as the government's ploy to undermine popular solidarity with *insumisos*. Looking back on this period Carlos Pérez, in Valencia, wrote to me: 'MOC's strategy was to reject these privileges. The *insumisos* once again acted in a public and concerted manner, refusing to go obediently back to prison to sleep. They were then relegated back to ordinary terms of imprisonment.'[2]

In 1997, in a further rebellious step, MOC began a campaign they termed `*insumisión* in the barracks' (*en los cuarteles*). A man called to service would accept conscription, don the uniform and have the haircut, but would fail to report back for duty after his first day of leave from the barracks. In this way he became, legally speaking, a 'deserter' from the armed forces and incurred a longer prison sentence than a mere *insumiso*. However, by now it was dawning on policy-makers that prison was no deterrent to military refusal, and they decided to play a different card, inflicting another form of punishment on *insumisos* called *inhabilitación* (disqualification). This measure limited their freedoms in regard to employment, banning them from public sector jobs (such as teacher) up to the age of 38, when their liability for military service expired. It was a clever move by the state. Long drawn-out and less visible than imprisonment, *inhabilitación* could undermine solidarity and weaken the impact of the civil disobedience campaign. It was a specially hard punishment for these idealistic young men who would naturally have gravitated to jobs with social purpose. MOC termed it 'civil death'.

Given the disorder attending obligatory military service, it was no surprise that, when the rightwing Popular Party (*Partido Popular*) won the elections in 1996 the new president, José Maria Aznar, announced that the armed forces would be totally professionalized by 2003. The move also responded to changed circumstances in the international field. Spain was now a member of NATO. In NATO operations as well as in United Nations peace-keeping missions, the armed forces would have to stand up to international scrutiny. Besides, war-fighting was involving ever more advanced technology. The Spanish government understood it needed a modern military – no more press-ganged and recalcitrant school leavers but a force of well-trained, experienced and enthusiastic career soldiers (Gordillo 2002). However, the young men of the last generation to be subject to compulsory militarization naturally felt even more aggrieved by the idea than those that had gone before. By the end of the 1990s refusal to serve had become the norm rather than the exception. The CNOC had a staggering 130,000 applications in 1997 alone (MOC 2002: 326). The *Partido Popular* kept its promise. In the year 2000 the last batch of conscripts was submitted to service and in 2001 the last reserve soldiers went home from the barracks.

Conversion of the armed forces into a twenty-first-century-style military was no triumph for MOC, whose revolutionary aim was to close down the army, demilitarize the state and end war. But it was perceived as a victory of a kind for all those whose disobedience had made the system unmanageable. And one lasting effect of three decades of anti-militarist activism was that the new model army, when it came into being early in the millennium, was hardly perceived as a good job option. Xabier Agirre Arunburu, one of the Movement's members, invited to address the Commission responsible for the transition to the new model army, warned the senators and congressmen that the military was deeply unpopular and the country's youth were little disposed to be soldiers (Arunburu 2002). And indeed it turned out that, for lack of volunteers, the armed forces had to make do with only 75 per cent of the personnel they needed (Zamarra 2009).

Post-professionalization: a state-wide anti-militarist movement

In 2001, soon after conscription ended, MOC held a congress of its branches throughout Spain in order to map out its future. The plan involved working for the abolition of the military in Spain, the withdrawal of Spanish troops from Afghanistan, the removal of the US-Spanish base at Rota, near Cadiz, and a stop to NATO developments in Spain. They would also revive 'tax resistance'. From the early 1980s MOC had encouraged people and enterprises, as a gesture of disapproval of the state's militarism, to withhold from their annual income tax payments a sum representing the proportion of the state's total tax revenue destined for the national defence budget, usually about 5 per cent. The individual or organization not only deprived the fiscal authorities of this sum but diverted it to some social, nonviolent or anti-military project of their choosing. However, the campaign had never been accorded as much importance as refusing military service, and the revenue diverted had been meagre. Now it would be given a new emphasis.

Soon after this, it was decided to preface MOC's name with the words *Alternativa Anti-militarista*. AA-MOC today is a network of local activist groups, with a degree of informal co-ordination between them at the level of the Spanish state.[3] What has kept them going, with conscription now a thing of the past? Listening to members' accounts and reading back into the documentation suggests to me that the movement is inspired, now as always, by four values. The first is justice, which leads them to oppose exploitation, exclusion and inequality of all kinds. The second is respect for the individual. The contemporary Ideological Declaration gives as a goal 'to instil respect for each and every person, never confounding the living individual with the socially defined role of which she or he is the bearer'.[4] This meant resistance against any form of domination, whether of class, gender, race, ethnicity or religion. The same document continues, 'MOC's means of struggle will always tend to destroy concentrations of power and foster the exercise of power from the base'.[5] Third is opposition to militarism as mindset and militarization as practice, linking it specifically with the state as the key instance of 'domination'. Thus, the second Declaration (1986) reads, 'We understand militarism as the conjuncture of interrelations and functions that prevail in all authoritarian societies in which the state, the fundamental apparatus of political, social, economic and cultural domination, uses armies as an instrument for maintenance and expansion of the ideology of domination'.[6]

AA-MOC's fourth and supremely important value is nonviolence, a word it deploys with a long reach. It is not only a practical commitment to nonviolent actions but also a badge of identity (*sena de identidad fundamental*) for the individual member and the organization, and an ethic guiding the transformation of both. The movement opposes, by nonviolent means, a wide spectrum of violence, psychological, cultural and military.[7] A world rid of all these kinds of violence is AA-MOC's ultimate goal. 'Our aim would be a just and nonviolent society, with no place for armies or wars,' Alberto Estefanía Hurtado told me. Nonviolence is also a way of doing things. Expressed in direct action (NVDA) it becomes a road for getting to goal. The website describes NVDA as a revolutionary process, disobeying in an active manner for the purpose of changing the structures, values and attitudes that sustain injustice.

AA-MOC's values spring from several belief systems. One is Christianity, or at least spirituality. During the period in which conscientious objection became a social movement, there was a significant subcurrent of 'liberation theology' in Spain, in which Catholic priests with a critique of the ecclesiastical hierarchy worked at grassroots level, especially in poor urban communities, on projects of social justice. Concha Martín Sánchez (formerly of MOC Madrid) told me, 'They might look like hippies but quite a few conscientious objectors, especially the early ones, came from a Christian background'. And indeed several did say in interview that it was their faith that had led them to refusal. Another well-spring of values in AA-MOC is Marxism, particularly a belief in the historical significance of capitalist economic exploitation, and of the proletarian experience and potential. However, Spain has a long tradition of anarchism, and the Marxism of AA-MOC is mediated through one of its best known and long-lived expressions – the anarcho-syndicalism of some trade unions allied to the International Workers Association. Leadership roles and hierarchy are rigorously avoided, autonomy from prevailing structures is stressed, as well as 'developing in workers the spirit of association, practising mutual aid and solidarity ...'[8] Miguel Arce, whom I met in Cantabria, is one of those who identifies himself as an anarchist, 'although very far from groups that call themselves anarchist, but are actually very dogmatic'. He, like some others I spoke to, used the term 'libertarian', not as a political tag so much as to suggest a way of functioning. Alberto for instance had said 'I don't think MOC as such is, properly speaking, an anarchist movement. It's libertarian'.

Interestingly, Manuel Soriano told me that, the way he sees it, 'The most important value in MOC is actually a constant *questioning* of values and their effects. Bringing injustice and lies to the light of day. Countering them with an educational approach'. This very scepticism about the supremacy of any given value may suggest another kind of inspiration in MOC, less easily labelled than Christianity, Marxism or anarchism but recognizable in firsthand accounts I heard from members. It is a spontaneous humanism, unmediated by ideological doctrines, generous, rebellious and stubbornly optimistic.

Doing something to end the evils of militarization and war, however, seems much more attractive to AA-MOC than analysing their causes. Alberto said, 'To try to analyse, philosophically or metaphysically, why war exists isn't very important for us. It's a fact. We simply have to try to abolish its causes and its consequences. In the here and now'. And I did indeed find much more written and said in MOC on strategies and actions than on values and analyses. Its website makes it clear that the ultimate objective is the demilitarization of society (*la desmilitarización social*).[9] Starting with the Spanish armed forces, they wish to see armies abolished, an end to war and to preparation for war. They see this as an everyday revolution (*una revolución cotidiana*) that affects every facet of our lives, making changes that start from and add impulse to the 'little daily, collective, grassroots revolutions that are going on in present time'. When they write and speak of their 'anti-militarism' they mean on the one hand critique and confrontation, but always, on the other, proposing and building alternatives, a transformation of economy, work, culture, education, politics and personal relations that would obviate the *raisons d'être* of armies and other instruments of social control that facilitate the taking and maintenance of power. Thus they term themselves 'radical' in a literal sense, because they question the very roots of 'the system', aiming to 'eradicate' causes rather than simply denounce scandalous effects.

Doing disobedience

A collection of writings from three decades of the movement for conscientious objection, published by MOC in 2002, was titled 'In Legitimate Disobedience' (*En Legítima Desobediencia*) (MOC 2002). The phrase sums up the movement's stance: when the militarist state makes illegitimate demands on the citizen, disobedience is justified and indeed necessary. So their main strategy is civil disobedience, which involves non-collaboration with the structures, offices and functions of the state, both civilian and military. They denounce the state's intentions and practices, and confront government ministries, military commands and bases, and enterprises producing military equipment or weaponry. They protest against the engagement of Spain's armed forces overseas, against military exercises and events celebrating the military. They put out counter-information that challenges the official acount of events.

AA-MOC actions are both long-term and 'of the moment' (*puntual*), Miguel told me. Long-term programmes include their campaign for conversion of military industries to civilian production, their educational work in schools and against children's 'war toys'. Actions on the spur of the moment give scope for more drama. A NATO ship arrives in port – and a group of MOC activists will attempt to board it. The state signs up to an international war – and MOC goes to a government building and attempts to enter and occupy it. Such actions are symbolic. They cannot possibly achieve what they appear to intend. Miguel explained, 'You don't actually take over the ship, or stop the country going to war. But you do have an impact on people's awareness'. With that eye to public opinion, many of AA-MOC's actions are designed to make the state and its military appear ridiculous. On one occasion, for example, a group of men and women, in wild fancy dress, went out to a military training ground where stood a large old tank used for target practice. They painted this symbolic object pink, from the tip of its gun to its hatches and its treads, leaving not an inch of khaki uncovered (see cover photo). A similar approach, one of gentle ridicule, is found in MOC's logo, which is a soldier's helmet set upside down, converted into a flower pot for a childlike daisy.

In the past, when *insumisos* were being hunted by the law, they would make no effort to evade arrest and punishment. On the contrary, they would proudly state their reasons for disobedience. If they hid from the authorities it was only so as to choose for themselves where and when they would be arrested. A member of MOC Sevilla described an occasion when an *insumiso*, Jacobo, was on the 'wanted' list, due to serve a prison term. How could they inveigle the police into arresting him with maximum publicity? His supporters decided to climb into a US-Spanish military base, demanding its conversion to agricultural use. Four of them, including Jacobo, found a way into the base, taking symbolic olive trees to plant. Others stayed outside, facilitating the action, filming it and contacting the media for publicity. The intention was to achieve a high-profile arrest for Jacobo. They were immensely frustrated when the police failed to recognize him and he was doomed to remain a free man a little longer.

In 2003, when it was announced that Spain would join Bush's 'coalition of the willing' to bombard Iraq, a group in Cantabria, depressed by the way mass demonstrations had failed to change the government's trajectory to war, decided to take direct action. Miguel Arce told the story. The *Partido Popular* was in power. Their HQ was in an apartment block. A group went into the building, each to a different floor. Some rang the bell of the PP office. When it was opened to them they calmly but firmly walked in. They explained, Miguel said, 'We've come to occupy this place, but there is no need to worry about a thing'. They went to the windows and hung banners down the outside of the building saying 'No to PP's war for oil' (*No a la Guerra del Petrolio*). Outside, two activists with a ladder climbed up and sat on the window ledges. They were eventually removed from the building. There was a trial, which they milked for humour and publicity. They were sentenced to a short spell in prison. When released the activists invited the press to meet them at the prison gate, and emerged wearing smart business suits. 'Look,' they told the journalists, 'the prison service aims to reinsert offenders into society as respectable citizens. So here we are, this is the result. We are quite reformed, and won't be repeating the offence – until we change our minds'. Which of course they very soon did.

In the long term all of AA-MOC's work is directed towards imagining and developing an alternative society, one that is not militarized, not dependent on a military conception of defence. They ask themselves 'what is *social* defence, what could it be?'. This means questioning the idea of 'enemies'. Pura Peris Senent showed me a photo of her son Guillem and his friend Santiago Almiñana when they were *insumisos* in MOC Valencia, holding a banner asking, 'Who is the real enemy?' and answering their own question – it's poverty, it's failure to supply adequate public services, starved as they are by defence spending. Social defence means applying 'a transformative and emancipatory ethic' in such a way as to be not just 'an anti movement but one that builds an alternative' (MOC 2002: 246).[10] They want, as they put it, to create collective and co-operative spaces, 'alternative realities' that have value in the here and now, but also prefigure on a small scale what they wish to bring into being on a global scale.

Anti-militarism, prefigurative movements and the left

The anti-militarist movement in Spain is not a stand-alone phenomenon, but one of several contemporary social movements among which there is a deep affinity of values and style. Sporadically, here and there, a *'plataforma'* is created, bringing them together for a common purpose. They also encounter one another in local and regional Social Forum events.[11] One such movement is the *'ecologistas'*, the greens. A host of small green groups have sprung up in recent years, many of them addressing a particular local project or scandal, eventually united in a state-wide network *Ecologistas en Acción*. AA-MOC and the *ecologistas* are often to be found demonstrating side by side on, say, an action against a military site. *Okupa*, too, the squatting movement, has always had a warm affinity with *insumisión*. *Okupa* was stronger in the 1990s than today, but still there are some high-profile squats, such as the Patio Maravillas in Madrid that Yolanda Juarros Barcenilla took me to visit. When it comes to evictions, these days, the movement chooses to respond nonviolently – something that may have 'rubbed off' on *Okupa* from the movement for conscientious objection. Certainly, I learned, activists against the construction of a high-speed train, the *'anti-TAV'* campaign, have sought advice from AA-MOC on nonviolent method.

During the dictatorship, when political parties were banned, neighbourhood (*barrio*) organizing was one of the few means of popular self-expression. The tradition lives on in some *autonomías* today, and I met several people who had transferred their energies from AA-MOC to community action. Pura, Santiago and their friend Pau Serrano Magdaleno come to mind, tussling with the a rightwing (PP) local authority of Valencia over unpopular urban development plans for their residential areas. Santi was making the link between anti-militarist and neighbourhood activism by organizing military tax resistance with the aim of redirecting the money held back from the state's defence budget to these *barrio* projects. The most integrated situation I found was in Sevilla. Here AA-MOC, Women in Black (*Mujeres de Negro*, of which more below) and *RedPaz* (Peace Network) have together to set up a centre they call the Peace House (*Casa de la Paz*). It is adjacent to a squatted community centre on the lively Plaza del Pumarejo, a tiny square in the heart of an old residential quarter. The groups in the *Casa de la Paz* try to 'live out of doors' in the square as much as they can, joining in the strong neighbourhood movement against redevelopment.

What the anti-militarist, *ecologista*, *Okupa* and *barrio* activists have in common is process, the way they do things, the quality of relationship they aspire to, within and beyond the group. For example, they would be very careful indeed as to funding, never accepting money from sources that might constrain the uses to which it is put. They would not only be autonomous, free from political party control or influence, but also non-hierarchical, inclusive and sharing. They often use the word '*asamblearismo*' to describe their preference for an organization in which the decision-making lies ultimately in the general meeting of members, at whatever level this occurs, from local to national. The style is sometimes called libertarian. More precisely it is prefigurative. Two widely used catchphrases are 'coherence of means and ends' (*coherencia entre medios y fines*), and 'we make the road as we walk it' (*se hace el camino al andar*). If there are differences and tensions among and between these various parts of the new social movements they tend to have to do with divergent versions of anarchism. This was illustrated for me by Santiago, who described the divergence of MOC from a former Valencian anti-militarist collective (*Kolectivo Autónoma Anti-militarista*) that was successful for a while in the 1990s, drawing its young members mainly from *Okupa*. While the militants of KAA would go into hiding to defy and evade the state, MOC's *insumisos* chose to use their arrest, trial and imprisonment creatively as a public act to spread the attitude of anti-militarist disobedience.

The allied prefigurative social movements as a whole contrast themselves rather sharply with the various political parties of the 'official' or parliamentary left and the tendencies of the extra-parliamentary or 'extreme' left, with whom alliances, when they occur at all, tend to be cautious, tactical and short-lived. The parliamentary left is United Left (*La Izquierda Unida*, IU), an alliance of leftwing socialist, republican and green groups, led by the Communist Party of Spain (*Partido Comunista de España*, PCE). It is a minority participant in national and local elections, and occasionally joins forces with PSOE. The party opposes Spain's co-operation in US war ventures and campaigned against Spain's membership of NATO, but it does not question the militarism and wars unleashed by Communist-identified leaders, such as Milosević in the case of Yugoslavia. On occasion IU have favoured conscientious objection, but given their aspiration to participate in government, they have been an unreliable ally for the anti-militarist movement. The trade union movement in Spain is markedly divided between communists, socialists and anarchists. Enrique Luna Mellado of MOC in Sevilla, described AA-MOC as closest to the anarchist unions, the National Confederation of Labour (*Confederación Nacional del Trabajo*, CNT) and the General Confederation of Labour (*Confederación General del Trabajo*, CGT). They also feel respect for the Agricultural Workers' Union (*Sindicato de Obreros del Campo*, SOC) that has practised exemplary nonviolence in occupations of farmland. It is distant from the bigger Workers' Commissions (*Comisiones de Obreros*, CCOO) and the General Labour Union (*Unión General del Trabajo*, UGT). The latter have withheld support from the anti-militarists' protests against weapons manufacturers, due to their antagonism to any threat to jobs in the industry.

AA-MOC and other prefigurative social movement groups have an uneasy relationship with the extra-parliamentary left, a shifting array of Marxist, Trotskyist and Maoist groupings. For a period in the seventies and eighties the two strongest (and the most problematic for MOC at that time) were the Revolutionary Communist League (*Liga Comunista Revolucionaria*, LCR, 1971–1991) and the Communist Movement (*Movimiento Comunista*, MC, 1976–1992). The former were Trotskyists, in the 4th International tradition, vanguardist and rigorously class-based. The latter, with a larger membership, began as Maoist but evolved over time a more eclectic communist ideology. They came together from the early nineties in a confederation variously called the Alternative Left (*Izquierda Alternativa*) or *Liberación*. There have been, however, a multitude of other small parties in similar traditions at different moments and in the different *autónomas*. The high point of the anti-militarist activity of LCR and MC was in the 1980s during the period of the anti-NATO referendum campaign.

AA-MOC differs from the left first and foremost in its political analysis. While the Trotskyist, Maoist and Communist tendencies point the finger at 'global capitalism' and 'imperialism', AA-MOC tend to identify configurations of power in general, not economic power specifically, as the cause of war. In process, too, these small groups and parties of the extra-parliamentary left, with their adherence to a dogmatic 'line', autocratic practices and a strategy of entrism, are at the other end of the spectrum to AA-MOC and other prefigurative movements. They assume themselves to be destined leaders of an anti-war movement yet have an ambivalent relationship to militarism. Their style is itself somewhat militaristic, being one of attack, rather than a modelling of alternatives. As Almudena described them, 'They are not like MOC, who live their disobedience, who are happy to be arrested and explain their refusal to people, to be educative. They just want to attack the government'. During the conscription era they did not consistently oppose it. In fact, for a while they maintained a position dating from the dictatorship, that it was useful for adherents to enter the army and learn fighting skills that could eventually be used against the state. They scorned MOC's nonviolence, which they deemed counter-revolutionary.

Nonetheless, during the eighties, as MOC proved its effectiveness by mobilizing tens of thousands of *insumisos*, the left parties, both parliamentary and extra-parliamentary, jumped on the bandwagon of conscientious objection. Concha Martín Sánchez remembered: 'They noticed that a lot of youngsters were attracted to CO ... The left thought that engaging them in a campaign of conscientious objection was a useful way of increasing pressure on the government of the time, it was a tool against Felipe Gonzalez.' She went on to surmise, 'I think also that they wanted to control everything on the left, including pacifism. MOC was a stumbling block to that'. At first they tried to control MOC by entrism, but that strategy failed, thanks to MOC's *asemblearismo* and structurelessness. They then set up a movement of their own called *Mili-KK* (pronounced '*kaka*', slang for shit). Mili-KK had a character very different from MOC however, attracting (Miguel said) 'stone-throwing youths who relished confrontation'. Santiago said, 'Mili-KK used *insumisión* instrumentally, just for the objectives of the political movement they belonged to. They did not aim to end militarism'. And Enrique recalled, 'With the Trotskyists the relationship was tense. Where Mili-KK was weak they continued to work with MOC, but we made it clear that joint actions would be nonviolent, and that was respected. But it was a struggle'. Mireya Forel, whom I met in Sevilla, spoke from personal experience in the Liga Comunista Revolucionaria (see p. 97 below). She says now of the Trotskyist tendency, 'They are very sincere but they want to control everything that moves. They have a definitive theory on every last thing. They don't listen, they can't learn. They are afraid of plurality'.

In the context of Basque politics, the extra-parliamentary left co-exists with a nationalist left that seeks independence from the Spanish state. An armed struggle to this end has been waged since 1959 by ETA (*Euskadi Ta Askatasuna* – it translates as Basque Homeland and Freedom). The party closest to ETA and part of the wider Basque National Liberation Movement is *Batasuna*, formerly known as *Euskal Herritarrok* and *Herri Batasuna*. Naturally, *Batasuna* are problematic as allies of MOC, since, though they are bitterly opposed to the Spanish armed forces, they are by no means anti-militarist or nonviolent. Alberto of KEM-MOC said of *Batasuna*,

> they won't participate in an anti-militarist action or campaign for its anti-militarism, but they might do so if some aspect of the action seems likely to harm the Spanish state. That is, they won't struggle against the Spanish army because it's an *army*, but because it's *Spanish*. Our position is really different: we are against all armies, whatever flag they march under.

Santiago likewise spoke of differences between MOC and the Catalan and Valencian nationalist parties that called for *insumisión* against the Spanish army but were far from being pacifists, since they wished to leave open the possibility of a future Catalan armed force.

The relationship between MOC and the extra-parliamentary left seems however to have improved over time. Thus Ander Eiguren Gandarías said: 'Things are pretty relaxed now. In the eighties it was more antagonistic, to the power of a thousand. It has changed a lot.' This is presumably due to the weakening of the extreme left groups, who cannot realistically aspire today to control the social movements of anti-militarism, *ecologismo*, *Okupa* and the *barrio*, that are given immunity against its methods by their horizontality, the absence of a leadership. Instead they are concentrating their efforts on the more fertile recruiting ground of students in the universities.

Unlike the left groups, AA-MOC has never attempted to colonize other organizations, networks and movements, nor does it fiercely promote its name and identity. Miguel Arce illustrated this very clearly. When I asked him to name the organizations and movements in his political environment in Cantabria, he deflected the question, saying 'MOC's idea is not to relate to *groups* but to expand the proportion of ordinary *people* that are active. Here a lot of people think that initials such as MOC don't actually unite people, they divide them from each other. So we decided to draw more people in with MOC-type processes, rather than with a name'. To this end they decided to call themselves, more loosely, the Nonviolent Direct Action Group (*Grupo de Acción Directo Noviolencia*). This spirit is reflected in an article by Rafael Ajangiz, written in 1996. He describes MOC as '… a network of networks in which physical distances don't signify political distances and where to speak of centre and periphery makes no sense'[12] (Ajangiz 2002: 271).

Antipatriarchalism: the principle and the practice

Obligatory military service in Spain applied only to men, so naturally it was men that founded the movement for conscientious objection and formed its main membership. Women, however, were never excluded from the movement and from the early days MOC had women activists, some of whom first got involved as members of *insumiso* support groups. We have heard the voices of quite a few of them earlier in this chapter. Besides, MOC from the start had identified patriarchy as one of the structures of power they aimed to dismantle. In their first Ideological Declaration (1979), they describe themselves as confronting not only the military structure, the armed forces, but also the militarist values and the human behaviour they encourage, 'machismo, authoritarian, repressive and violent interpersonal relations'.[13] In the second Ideological Declaration, seven years later, the reference to patriarchy was even more explicit. The first paragraph included the words:

> MOC is committed to the struggle to overcome the present oppression exercised over women, empowering feminist work which develops in the organisation as a renovating and non-*machista* spirit in personal relations. Equally, MOC is engaged in the critique and denunciation of the function of the army and militarism as transmitters and glorifiers of *machista* and patriarchal values.[14]

The Declaration also lists transformed sex roles as one aspect of the organizational model for which MOC's anti-militarism strives. 'We give special attention to doing away with the sexist roles and stereotypes imposed by patriarchy, because this is the most widespread discrimination shaping and limiting women and men in every sphere of life'.[15]

In this spirit, quite early on they changed MOC's name from Movement of Conscientious Objectors (*objetores*, a male noun) to Movement of

Conscientious Objection (*objeción*). Nonetheless, a reading of MOC's online archives and printed publications reveals a significant predominance of male authors. As Yolanda Juarros Barcenilla told me, in reality, 'there was always a hierarchy in MOC. Certain of the *insumisos* and their lawyers were the ones who thought through the strategies and brought them to the network'. Several of the women and men I interviewed told me how local groups had continually tried to overcome the problem that, as Juanma Ruiz Sánchez, a member of Sevilla MOC, put it, 'men were the ones who went to prison, and this involved a dynamic in which women felt themselves to be not heard'. Their ideal had been for women to join equally with men in the daring parts of MOC's actions – confronting police and army, chaining themselves up, climbing cranes, breaching fences and entering bases. In the best circumstances, as Alberto described it,

Women and men were equal. We shared roles. When planning actions we would usually have no regard to gender. If we needed an agile person, agility was what we needed and gender didn't come into it. We didn't even make any distinction between women and men when it came to safety and risk. What we paid attention to was the risk for any person, regardless of sex. On one occasion we did an action in which five women broke into a military site. We wanted to 'visibilize' women's participation, which was rather eclipsed by masculine protagonism in *insumisión*.

Sometimes, however, this principle of equality gave way, despite much discussion and many regrets, to a practice in which women and men did play different roles. Miguel had found it was men more than women who were keen to take risks. 'If someone has to hang from a rope a man is more likely to volunteer,' he said. If it turned out that there was only one woman in a group committing itself to an action, they might, albeit reluctantly, exclude her. It was inadvisable to expose a lone woman to risk of arrest, Miguel explained, because the police and prison service always separated the sexes, and she would be isolated. An equal role for women was fostered by MOC's general principle that everyone in the group should be seen as identically responsible for an action. The routine response to the police question 'Who's in charge here?' was always 'All of us'. But the law courts annoyingly discriminated in favour of women. For fear of a public reaction they seldom gave prison sentences to those women who broke the law through acts of civil disobedience, or were *autoinculpados* in support of men's 'crimes'. This impunity defeated MOC's object.

Masculine heroism is generated by militarism, and the war hero is, trans-historically, a key character in the patriarchal drama. It was therefore part of MOC's refusal of militarism to avoid reproducing the heroic male role in the person of the conscientious objector, the brave man willing to face imprisonment, engaging single-handed with those other 'enemies' – the judges, the commanders, the prison governors. They made serious attempts to avoid certain male activists becoming 'rock-and-roll stars', as they put it. I heard from one group, KEM-MOC in Euskadi, that relished mounting what they called 'blood actions'. Ander Eiguren Gandarías and Idoia Aldazábal Lotina told me when I interviewed them in Bilbao of a moment when the political conjuncture had been particularly adverse, and their group were determined to draw the attention of media and public to the state's brutality by provoking a strong reaction from the military and police. They entered and occupied a building. The police forcibly ejected them, beat people up and threw some into a police van, which set off fast down a narrow street. One of the MOC men, in an unpremeditated action, threw himself in its path. The van swerved to miss him. Ander spontaneously followed suit. Both activists narrowly avoided being hurt. Ander explained, 'The state tries to invisibilize us. We started to do "blood actions" like this so that the media could not ignore us'. But other MOC groups, perhaps the majority, disagreed with this type of action because it promoted personal acts of heroism and sacrifice, abandoning the principles of collectivity and care. All the same, they too sometimes found the anti-heroic ideal difficult to maintain. Miguel said, 'We are always discussing it. But it's one thing to have the idea and another to actually do it'. The contingencies of campaigning left little space for finding 'another way' of living gender. Looking back, Juanma said 'MOC's strategies inevitably involved conflict, going to the limit. It was always emergencies, fire-fighting. Those were times of strong and direct feelings. People were really young, and they had a lot on their minds like holding down their jobs, emotional problems too'.

So I heard widely differing evaluations of the practical outcome of MOC's principle of anti-patriarchalism. Santiago felt positive about it. He said: 'In MOC we saw the army as an expression of masculinism in society. We saw that the feminist struggle was ours too. We opposed a masculinist way of thinking and living in society.' Pedro Carmona, gay, an *insumiso*, but not a member of MOC, saw it otherwise:

> In MOC publications and statements in some cases you would find a couple of sentences about gender, but never a constructive discourse

that made that an important issue. The intention was good. They were sincere, but superficial. Gender is fashionable after all. 'Women', 'ecology', 'nature', 'patriarchy', 'machismo' – it's relatively easy to put these words into play, and it gives you credibility. But in some cases they were just reproducing heterosexual stereotypes.

Inventing feminist anti-militarism

If, as Concha said, 'getting patriarchy out of our lives, out of our behaviour, was not straightforward', neither was getting patriarchy *into* the theory of anti-militarism. In 2007, women in Sevilla, looking back on the 1980s, remembered how they had experienced

> an absence of feminist reflection on the patriarchal structures and values that generate the monopoly of violence, of territorial conquest and occupation. Even in the face of violence we couldn't manage to get beyond a narrow denunciation of sexism, leaving undone any deeper analysis of the meaning of militarism in the structures of patriarchal power.[16]

As Concha went on to explain to me, not all MOC women made the development of feminist anti-militarism a priority. After all, they had widely differing backgrounds. Some came from feminism, some from anti-militarism, and others were entirely new to political work. They were always rather few in number, and had to work hard to explain, both inside and outside MOC, why they were in the movement at all. They had to make it clear over and again that they were not there as girlfriends, sisters or mothers of *insumisos*. They were in the anti-militarist movement by their own political choice, for their own reasons. Some women felt a growing need to meet, talk and organise a 'dual militancy', be active not only as *people* in MOC but as *women* in MOC with a feminist agenda. So in some local groups they set up what came to be called women's '*comisiones*', in which they could sometimes get together as women apart from men. From these separate spaces they made contact with other feminist groups in their localities or regions. They reached out internationally too. The Women's Working Group of War Resisters' International, described in Chapter 2, was a point of connection. All the time they were not only talking but writing, evolving a specifically feminist analysis of militarism. As we have seen, the Ideological Declarations mentioned patriarchy among the systems of power fostering militarism, but women felt the perception had more profound implications than MOC as a movement had yet uncovered. They began to theorize the intimate connection between gender power relations and war, and thence to visualize the relation 'feminism–anti-militarism'. This was their conceptual task. They wanted 'a full debate within the peace movement on the theme of sexism, and a debate on militarism within the women's movement'.[17]

When, in 1988, the Spanish state passed a law to enable incorporation of women in the armed forces in roles more substantial than the auxiliary positions they had heretofore held, women found themselves with a unique (feminist) critique of the military to add to MOC's anti-militarism. The 'official' feminist movement, including the state-funded *Instituto de la Mujer*, like the parliamentary left, favoured women's incorporation into the military. They had struggled for equality of opportunity in all fields of employment. How could they make an exception for the armed forces? MOC women argued fiercely that anti-militarism should prevail over the arid principle of sex equality. There was nothing to be gained in their view by women acceding to the masculinist cultural model the army represented, voluntarily signing up to 'a school of blind obedience, submission, exploitation and machismo'.[18] Like other MOC members they wanted the army abolished, not reformed (MOC Madrid 1998).

In the course of several years of discussion, reading and reflecting on their own activism, feminists in MOC produced many papers and two significant booklets, one in 1991 titled *Woman and Militarism* (MOC, *Grupo de Mujeres Anti-militaristas*, 1991), a second seven years later, called *Anti-militarism and Feminism* (MOC Madrid 1998). They drew on feminist theory from many countries. No direct reference is made to the WRI Feminism and Nonviolence Study Group, and its product, *Piecing It Together*, described in Chapter 2. Perhaps language was a barrier. However the analysis is very similar. Like the UK group, the Spanish authors stressed the significance of the economic, of poverty and exploitation, among the causes of war. They expressed a wish to 'deepen' feminism beyond a singular focus on sexuality, violence and prostitution to take in a concern with the Third World, ecological issues, and work for peace through change in education (MOC 1991: 27). The 1998 booklet evoked Celia Amorós on patriarchy as a '*sistema metaestable*', a system clearly surviving through successive modes of production and forms of political structure. In a system sustaining masculine subordination of both women and certain male '*degenerados*', violence, they argued, is bound to be ubiquitous and continual. The powerful, those who gain by the system, find ways of legitimating it, making it seem natural, the only thinkable condition (MOC Madrid 1998: 1). Drawing on Amparo Morena, the authors noted 'the very close complicity (*complicidad estrechísima de contenidos*) between violence and virility'. Patriarchy and militarism are intertwined so tightly you can hardly tell them apart, while anti-militarism and feminism become two sides of a single coin (ibid.). There was no question of substituting women's for men's values, rather the point was to end gender dichotomy itself (MOC 1991: 37, 47). They were clear that they had no wish to force some kind of union of feminism and anti-militarism, or to subject (*supeditir*) one to the other. Neither social movement should lose its autonomy. It was simply a matter of starting to build a theory and practice from the observation that Western societies are both patriarchal and militarist (MOC Madrid 1998: 8).[19] Feminist anti-militarism, or anti-militarist feminism, however one wished to name it, was a necessary response to lived realities. How could the movement reach its goal of demilitarization without women's involvement? And how could a nonviolent, non-hierarchical society fail to entail the liberation of women?

The majority of men in MOC gave these ideas a nod of endorsement. They did not disagree with the idea that gender was implicated in militarism and war. On the other hand they did not give it any expression in their anti-militarist practice. And a minority dismissed the feminists' analysis. Ander of KEM-MOC, Bilbao, told me their branch believed that 'gender is not the principal issue here. To promote it as such is weak, poor (*debil, pobre*)'. I think he meant 'an impoverished analysis'. And he added, 'Behind it there is an attitude'. He went on to explain to me the reasoning for the scepticism in the branch about gender politics. 'All decisions in MOC are group decisions. On that terrain, gender disappears. Everybody, male or female, has an equal voice'. So they, in KEM-MOC, tend to satirize the gender issue. We make fun of 'women-and-militarization', he said, this hyphenated thing that the feminists are always attempting to theorize. 'It's all women-and-this, women-and-that. Sometimes we say women-and-apples (*mujeres y manzanas*)!' They are exasperated by the way feminists single out women's suffering, women's needs, the effects of war on women. 'This isn't the point,' Ander said. 'It's no good building an analysis and action on the basis of gender. Power has no gender. The problem is not gendered, nor is the solution.'

As some men may perhaps have feared, the women's *comisiones* led gradually to some women leaving MOC with its specific focus on anti-militarism to get more involved in other, different, women's movement activities. But some looked for anti-militarist feminist allies in other countries. By 1990 the Berlin wall had fallen, the Soviet Union was imploding and the growth of nationalism was threatening to bring down federal Yugoslavia in ethnic war. Yugoslav feminists, particularly those in Belgrade, the Serbian capital, saw they had to fight for their survival against the misogyny of resurgent nationalism, militarism, clericalism and patriarchy. Their writings on the relationship between these malign phenomena over the coming years would be widely influential on women in many countries, not least Spain. On Wednesday 9 October 1991 women in Belgrade held their first street demonstration against war, in Republic Square in the centre of the city. They called themselves Women in Black against War (*Žene u Crnom protiv Rata, ŽuC*) and stood silently, for one hour, dressed in black, the target of nationalist abuse. The name and the style were borrowed from a well-known anti-Occupation movement in Israel, transmitted via Italian anti-war and anti-Occupation feminists calling themselves *Donne in Nero* (Cockburn 2007). When, early in the war, a group of MOC men visited Belgrade, with the intention of giving support to conscientious objectors, *ŽuC* were the most active and progressive movement they encountered – and indeed they found the women to be sheltering some Serbian male COs. A fertile connection between Belgrade and Spain ensued, assisted by the fact that Staša Žajović, a key activist in *ŽuC*, spoke excellent Spanish. On return the MOC travellers organized the first of what would become numerous speaking tours by Staša in Spain. Staša expressed the wish that her tour be hosted jointly by MOC with feminist groups in the towns she visited. Many women from Spain then visited Belgrade and other parts of ex-Yugoslavia, and were among the feminists from all over the world who gathered in Novi Sad, despite the armed conflict, for *ŽuC*'s annual gatherings (*encuentros*). This led to strong alliances between women in the two countries.

Double militancy: careful choices

After the millennium, when conscription ended, the membership of MOC changed. No more *insumisos*. After 9/11, those who were drawn to the movement came to oppose the 'war on terror', the attack on Afghanistan, the invasion of Iraq. In MOC there had always been, Yolanda Juarros Barcenilla told me, two kinds of business. There was the 'khaki' activism, opposing uniforms, barracks and armies. And there were non-khaki activities such as peace education and tax resistance. Women, and Yolanda herself, who is a teacher, had on balance been involved more in these and hoped that in the new times they would be given more priority. Indeed the network decided it should be so. But it was not so easy to dislodge the khaki element from dominance. It was the 'hard' projects, direct action against NATO, bases, arms manufacturers, that inherited the protagonism of the *insumisión* campaign. The younger people who joined MOC Madrid, Yolanda said, not only brought changes in objective and focus, they also brought a change of attitude, particularly towards the handling of differences. When there was disagreement, some voices were now allowed to prevail over others. Where a careful and conscious handling of 'certain mismatches', as she put it, would have been helpful, 'there was a silence'. Some of the Madrid women, including Concha, had belonged to *Mujeres de Negro* as well as MOC. 'Until then our dual militancy had been perfectly acceptable,' she said. 'I never heard any negative remarks about it. It was after 2000, when new people joined MOC, that it ceased to be positively accepted.'

In Sevilla, two women told me about the careful choices they had made about where to put their energies, both during and after the age of *insumisión*. Mireya Forel and Sofía Segura Herrera described their different trajectories. Mireya's early years were spent in Switzerland and France. Her first political move as a young woman was away from her family's allegiance to the Communist Party towards Trotskyism, which seemed to her a healthy response to Stalinist authoritarianism. In 1976, while still young and new to Spain, she joined the *Liga Comunista Revolucionaria* (LCR) in Andalucía, in which she eventually held a post of some responsibility. However, she was very touched by the women's movement that was having such an impact all over Europe at that time. The group of the LCR she belonged to was open to both *ecologismo* and feminist issues, but always and only within the frame of their particular Marxist orthodoxy. Mireya felt more and more the need for an autonomous feminist space, something that was anathema to the *Liga*. She finally left LCR in 1985 – although she found the separation very hard. During the anti-NATO campaign she got to know some of the MOC activists in Sevilla, and liked their style of nonviolent resistance. But it was not until 1991 when, as a reporter, she covered a story about *insumisión*, that she joined MOC.

Mireya was drawn to MOC by their analysis of the state and militarism, but she was perplexed by their lack of analytical depth when it came to patriarchy. When a little later she met *ŽuC*, the Women in Black group in Belgrade, they had a huge impact on her precisely because, right in the middle of an armed conflict, they were systematically evolving a theory of the intersection of patriarchy, nationalism and militarism

(Cockburn 2007). She found answers to a lot of questions that had been worrying her and, enriched by her own Marxist heritage, she was able to progress towards a critique not only of capitalism but of 'modernity'. She told me that she began to see that 'in modern civilization a new kind of patriarchy had evolved, expressed in exclusion, conquest, the will to domination, white male supremacy, the legitimation of violence as a means of resolving problems'. Certainly there were differences between socialism and capitalism, but both applied violent processes to global questions, not dissimilar from the violent masculinist processes through which women were reduced to, and shaped as, dependent – or were murdered (literally and figuratively). As a result of the encounter with *ŽuC*, Mireya and other MOC women set up a Women in Black (*Mujeres de Negro, MdN*) group in Sevilla. It was not merely a secession from MOC. Eighty percent of the membership was young women from the local *Okupa*, the *ecologista* and *barrio* movements with their newly minted feminism.

Sofía, as we saw, had been active during the 1990s in her son Javi's support group. She tells how sometimes when they were on an anti-militarist demonstration, Javi would say to her, 'why don't you go and walk with the *Mujeres de Negro?*' But at that time these women seemed rather weird to her, with their black clothes and their banners. What are they about? she wondered. One day, in 1997, Mireya approached and invited her over. Sofía joined *MdN* soon after this, scarcely knowing why, but somehow wanting to delve deeper into feminist and anti-militarist ideas:

> *Mujeres de Negro* in Sevilla was a small group, and still is. There were some young women, very vibrant. It was very different from other groups I'd known, the way they reflected on their actions, and on their interactions with the people in the street. It was a comfortable space where you could express yourself as a woman. In mixed groups men have more space, more security, more power. In a woman-only group everything seemed easier.

In a typescript paper titled *Memoria*, some of the women recently recalled the history of *Mujeres de Negro* in Sevilla (*Mujeres de Negro Sevilla* 2007). On return from visiting *Žene u Crnom* in Belgrade, some women had wanted to form a network in Spain – but should it be specifically a support group for *ŽuC* or a country-wide network with its own identity? An *encuentro* was called, attracted more than a hundred women, and resulted in the founding of a state-wide Network against Aggression against Women: Women in Black (*La Red contra las Agresiones contra las Mujeres: Mujeres de Negro*). Each local group would have its own character, no formula was imposed. As in the case of MOC, the greens and other grassroots movements, this diversity and fluidity proved an asset in resisting the inevitable incursions by women cadres of the left parties and tendencies. In Sevilla the *Mujeres de Negro* group decided on weekly meetings with occasional 'days of reflection' for deeper discussions. They developed links with other *MdN* groups in the province, the state and other countries, attending annual meetings in Spain and what would become a series of biennial international Women in Black gatherings. In this way, the Sevilla women felt part of 'a big international family'.

Sofía told me how *MdN* in Sevilla had evolved certain working principles. They seldom act alone, preferring to look outward for connections, for partners. It was in this spirit that, as mentioned above, *Mujeres de Negro* stayed close to MOC in Sevilla and in 2002 joined the Peace Network (*RedPaz*) to set up the Peace House, *La Casa de la Paz*, with office and meeting space. When I met them they were there still, almost a single entity. Much of their work is educational and cultural, organizing workshops and giving talks on many subjects to women's groups, in schools, and in the community. But they also deem 'street work' important. The are often '*en la calle*', holding silent vigils, in classic *MdN* style, but also performing 'die-ins' and other acts of street drama. There have been times they have stripped and painted their bodies with 'blood'. They have climbed ladders, changing the street names that honour military men so that instead they commemorate women. They have wrapped military statues in vast cloth banners. They have inscribed long wordy messages across the Plaza. *Mujeres de Negro* in Sevilla characteristically focus on sexual violence, asserting the integrity of women's bodies – a theme that women always found it difficult to address within the context of MOC. Sofía is a photographer and artist and she uses these skills to good effect in *Mujeres de Negro*. *MdN* Sevilla's calendar for 2008 contains her photographs of their own womanly body parts bearing written messages. She says: 'It is a cry, our bodies being used to shout antimilitary messages. For once this is not the victimized female body. It's our bodies used on our own terms.'

The hard choice Yolanda and Concha in Madrid, and Mireya and Sofía in Sevilla, have had to make, whether to persist in double militancy as feminists in a mixed organization, or to abandon it to give a hundred per cent of their energies to a women-only project, is the same choice I have shown British women were obliged to make in several historical periods (Chapter 1). In Spain, some have chosen to leave and put their energies into *Mujeres de Negro*. However, many others, in Bilbao, Madrid, Sevilla, Valencia and other places have elected, as many did in Britain, to stay and work with men in the mixed environment. Some feel feminist criticisms of their male comrades are unfair. One said of the partnership between men and women in MOC:

> It's very nice, it's wonderful, it's liberatory and influences the work. Men are also victims of the gender role system. Like I as a woman experience oppression, so do men. For men or women it's the same thing. Women addressing the same questions in a women-only group are missing out on that.

I was referred to Carlos Pérez in Valencia as one of the most consistent actors in AA-MOC country-wide. I asked him to summarize the present position on women and gender in MOC. He responded in an e-mail in December 2008. In numbers, women and men in MOC are more equal today than in the days of *insumisión*, he said. But addressing the problem of patriarchy in relation to militarism, that is another matter. 'It's not currently a theme addressed in the network's discussions, nor is it a specific area of work ... This isn't to say that it doesn't exist, but rather it's a 'tonality' of MOC's anti-militarism that's been handed down over the years in the debates and reflections that took place particularly in the period of *insumisión* ...'[20] A suble word, 'tonality'. It affirms AA-MOC, I think, as an organization sufficiently sophisticated to hold gender politics relevant, as one that does not ignore or deny such a politics. In that respect, the ridicule we heard expressed in KEM-MOC is by no means representative of AA-MOC. On the other hand it suggests that, as we shall see to be the case in other contexts, foregrounding patriarchy as profoundly implicated in militarism and war, and as an impediment to the attainment of peace, remains 'women's work'. Meanwhile, the following chapter takes us back to Britain, to a local movement where the gender dynamic is secondary to another: that of ethnicity and religion.

Notes

1. Under the 1978 Constitution all regions of Spain were afforded the option of proclaiming themselves 'autonomous communities' (*comunidades autónomas*). Spain today has seventeen such *autonomías*. Euskadi (the Basque Country) and Catalunya are particularly committed to affirmation of linguistic and cultural identity.

2. E-mail communication, December 2008.
3. The movement has found expression in the periodical *Mambrú*, and in various other magazines and journals issuing from AA-MOC's branches in different periods. In recent years co-ordination has been facilitated by the Internet. There is an e-mail listserve, 'listamoc', and several websites. The site titled 'Insumissia' (www.antimilitaristas.org) although designed with a wider remit, has become over time 'the' AA-MOC site. In a personal communication Carlos Pérez (AA-MOC, Valencia) wrote of it: 'Although we allow ourselves occasional 'heterodoxies', the tone in general is within the frame of the work and ideology of AA-MOC as a state-level network.'
4. Translations from Spanish texts and e-mails are my own. Here the original reads: '... el respeto a toda persona, distinguiendo siempre entre la personal y el personaje o papel social que representa ...' (online at: www.antimilitaristas. org, accessed 14 December 2008).
5. 'Los medios de lucha del MOC tenderán siempre a destruir la concentración de poder y a potenciar su ejercicio desde la base' (MOC 2002: 307).
6. 'Entendemos el militarismo como el conjunto de interrelaciones y funciones que se dan en toda sociedad autoritaria cuyos Estados, aparatos fundamentales de dominación política, social, económica y cultural, se sirven de los ejércitos como instrumento de mantenimiento y expansión de la ideología de la dominación' (MOC 2002: 306).
7. From *Declaración Ideológica, Texto Integral* (from the website *Insumissia* at: www.antimilitaristas.org, accessed 14 December 2008).
8. '... desarrollar en los trabajadores el espíritu de asociación, practicar el apoyo mutuo y la solidaridad ...' (online at: www.cnt.es, accessed 14 December 2008).
9. See the website *Insumissia* at www.antimilitaristas.org (accessed 14 December 2008).
10. '... una ética transformadora y emancipatoria' ... 'no como un movimiento "anti", sino constructor de algo alternativo.' *Declaración Ideológica, Texto Integral* (online at: www.antimilitaristas.org, accessed 14 December 2008).
11. Since the first World Social Forum in 2001 in Porto Alegre, Brazil, local, national and regional social forum events have been occurring, including in some parts of Spain. While an expression of the alter-globalization movement, forums also address local issues, in the spirit of 'think globally, act locally'.
12. '... una red de redes donde la distancias físicas no se traducían en distancias politicas y donde hablar de centro y periferia no tenía sentido' (Ajangiz in MOC 2002: 272).
13. '... machismo, relaciones interpersonales autoritarias, represivas y violentas ...' (MOC 2002: 303).
14. '... el MOC se compromete en la lucha por superar la actual situación de opresión que se ejerce sobre la mujer, potenciando tanto el trabajo feminista que en él se desarrolla como un espíritu renovador y no machista en las relaciones personales. Asimismo, el MOC se empeñará en la crítica y denuncia de la función del ejercito y del militarismo como transmisor y exaltador de valores machistas y patriarcales' (MOC 2002: 305).
15. 'Especial atención dedicaremos a la superación de los roles y estereotipos sexistas que impone el patriarcado, por ser la discriminación más generalizada al

condicionar y limitar a todas las mujeres y hombres en todos los ambitos de la vida' (online at: www.antimilitaristas.org, accessed 14 December 2008).

16. This was their reflection, after forming a separate *Mujeres de Negro* group, on earlier times in MOC. 'Recordaba la ausencia de reflexiones desde el feminismo sobre las estructuras y los valores patriarcales que generan el monopolio de la violencia, de las conquistas y ocupaciones territoriales. Ante la violencia no llegábamos aún a superar la estricta denuncia del sexismo, dejando de lado un análisis más profundo de lo que significaba el militarismo dentro de las estructuras del poder patriarcal' (*Mujeres de Negro*, Sevilla 2007).

17. '... falta un debate amplio sobre el tema del sexismo dentro del movimiento por la paz, y un debate sobre el militarismo dentro del movimiento feminista' (MOC 202: 132).

18. '... obediencia ciega, machismo, autoritarismo ...' (Braunw et al., 1984: 14).

19. '... no se trata de unir antimilitarismo y feminismo indefectiblemente, ni de establecer unas prioridades estratégicas o ideológicas que supediten uno al otro. No se pretende que uno de los dos movimientos sociales pierda su autonomía en beneficio al otro. Simplemente, comenzaríamos por reconocer en el modelo occidental de organización político-social una manifestación bifronte patriarcal y militarista' (*Mujeres de Negro*, Sevilla 2007).

20. '... respecto al tema del antimilitarismo antipatriarcal en AAMOC ... Actualmente no es un tema que se plantee en las discusiones de la red ni es un área de trabajo específica ... Esto no quiere decir que no exista, sino que más bien es una "tonalidad" del antimilitarismo del AAMOC que ha ido heredándose a lo largo de los años partiendo de debates y reflexiones que se dieron sobre todo en el ciclo de la insumisión ...' (Carlos Pérez, e-mail communication, December 2008).

4
Midlands City: Faiths and Philosophies Together for Palestine*

I was born in Leicester, seventy-six years ago. In those days, when my parents were young, the city was a centre of manufacturing, famous for its production of hosiery – knitted fabric and garments such as vests and socks in cotton and wool. Its factories had tall smoking chimneys. Their workers lived in surrounding narrow streets of terraced housing, built in the red brick that is characteristic of this region. The social class structure was strongly marked here. The company owners, directors and senior managers lived in more spacious detached houses in the wider streets of suburban areas and in nearby villages, encroaching on the estates of the landed gentry.

---

*This chapter is based on information received from the following people, to whom I would like to express my warm thanks for conversations that in many cases went far beyond what might be termed an 'interview'. Alan Hayes and Michael Gerard of the Secular Society; Canon Dr Andrew Wingate and the Rev David Clark of the Christian faith communities; Annette Wallis of Leicester Quaker Peace Group; Anna Cheetham and Richard Johnson, at that time co-chairs of Leicester Campaign for Nuclear Disarmament; Asaf Hussain, lecturer in Islamic civiliza- tion at the University of Leicester and director of the Public Diplomacy Research Organization; Avtar Sadiq, Vice-President of the Indian Workers' Association; Chris Goodwin of Leicester Campaign to Stop the War; Claire Wintram of Just Peace; Ismail Patel, director of Friends of Al-Aqsa; Jane Foxworthy of Leicester Palestine Solidarity Campaign; Jenny Pickerill of the Department of Sociology, City University, London; Liz Brandow and Lorraine Mirham, of a quiescent Leicester branch of the Women's International League for Peace and Freedom; Manzoor Moghal of the Muslim Forum; Minou Cortazzi Rowshan, Jan Macdonald and Avramesh Mahboubi of the Bahá'í community; Suleman Nagdi, MBE, DL, Public Relations Officer of the Federation of Muslim Organizations Leicestershire; Parvin Ali, director of Fatima, the Forum for Advocacy, Training and Information in a Multi-cultural Arena; Peter Flack of the National Union of Teachers and Leicester Social Forum; Zina Zelter of ARROW and Women in Black in Leicester.

The most marked cultural variance in Leicester in my childhood was brands of Christianity. Places of worship included Catholic churches, Methodist and other nonconformist chapels, in the shadow of the many spires and towers of the hegemonic Anglican 'Church of England'. There was a synagogue in Highfield Street, but the Jewish community, a mere couple of hundred in the year of my birth, was beleaguered by anti-semitism. Simon de Montfort, whose charter of 1231 CE banished Jews from living in Leicester 'in my time or in the time of any of my heirs to the end of the world' was still honoured in the city.[1] Leicester's population in the 1930s was almost entirely 'white'. It would be many decades before Afro-Caribbean migrants, and then, in much greater numbers, Asians would arrive, get employment and set up businesses. Today the city's employees for the most part work in modern buildings of concrete and glass, manufacturing has been displaced by new technology and service industries, wholesale and retail businesses, and the 2001 census showed fully 38 per cent of Leicester's inhabitants to be something other than 'white British' (or Irish). A provisional estimate for 2009 suggests an increase in this figure to 60 per cent.[2]

I happened to be visiting my family in Leicestershire over the Christmas period of 2008, when news broke of a sudden heavy air attack by the Israeli military on Gaza, the coastal enclave that is part of the Occupied Palestinian Territories. A fragile truce between the Israeli state and Hamas, the ruling party in Gaza, had expired some days earlier. Israel's stated reason for Operation Cast Lead, as they called it, was to put an end to Hamas's harassment of nearby Israeli communities with short-range rockets. But as well as targeting Palestinian rocket installations, administrative buildings and police stations, the Israeli Defence Forces destroyed many civilian homes, schools and hospitals in the air attack and the land invasion that began on 3 January 2009. By the time a ceasefire was called two weeks later, not only several hundred Hamas fighters, but an estimated 1400 Palestinian civilians, including many women and children, had died in this one-sided war (Amnesty International 2009).

I later read in the local newspaper that on Saturday 3 January there had been a small but impassioned demonstration of protest by Leicester people against the Israeli aggression. Around two hundred people had gathered around the Clock Tower, the iconic structure at the heart of Leicester's city centre. The event coincided with a national demonstration in London, which rallied thousands in Hyde Park and marched on the Israeli embassy in Kensington. By Leicester Clock Tower, the municipal Christmas tree was still standing. Protestors tied small flags in Palestine's national colours on the surrounding fence. Certain groups were identifiable by banners and placards. Someone had brought a loud-hailer and people from various groups borrowed it to make short speeches. There was a deal of shouting and chanting of slogans.

So I wondered to myself: who were they, these people who felt compelled to join others at the Clock Tower to express their anger? I saw the gathering as manifesting a local 'anti-war' sentiment and action from which I could learn something about the grassroots realities of peace movements. The Israeli assault of 27 December 2008, however, was not just 'any war'. As well as angering people opposed in principle to the pursuit of politics by violent means, it outraged particular groups already distressed by the long history of Zionist appropriation of Palestinian land by settlement and force of arms, displacement of Palestinian people and, dating from the 1967 war, the Occupation by Israel of the West Bank, Golan Heights and Gaza. What were the organizations involved, how did their co-operation on this occasion come about, what linked them before and afterwards, and what were the satisfactions and difficulties inherent in these activist relationships? I quickly learned that the 3 January demo at the Clock Tower was only the first event in a short burst of activity. The subsequent Wednesday, 7 January, at 5 pm there had been a second gathering, smaller and less noisy than the demonstration of the previous Saturday. It was already dark, and people brought candles. The same day there had been a gathering for multi-faith prayers for those affected by the conflict, in front of the Town Hall, not too far from the Clock Tower, and a third rally at the Clock Tower took place in daylight on Saturday 17 January, as Israel was about to declare a successful end to Operation Cast Lead. I decided to include these events within my study.[3]

Spontaneous response to an act of violence

It turned out that three organizations had been primarily involved in mounting the Saturday 3 January demo. This is how it came about. On 27, 28 and 29 December television news carried distressing coverage of Israel's onslaught on Gaza. But it was just after Christmas and before New Year. Many were still on holiday, so reactions were slow. On the afternoon of 30 December, a Tuesday, Anna Cheetham, at the time co-chair of Leicester Campaign for Nuclear Disarmament (CND), went to help at her friend's allotment, where she bumped into Mick Jarmaine, chair of the Leicester Campaign to Stop the War (CStW). After their spell of gardening, they shared a cup of tea. The conversation naturally turned to the attack on Gaza. They agreed their two organizations should organize a demonstration on the coming Saturday. Their natural partner in such an action would be the Leicester Palestine Solidarity Campaign (PSC). But Jane Foxworthy, their usual contact, they knew to be away. However, they must do something! What? A demonstration at the Clock Tower? This could be spontaneous since, as a matter of custom and practice, it requires no police permission. As Anna remembers it, 'I said to Mick, "Let's just call it. I'll bring the CND flag and the megaphone".' This, I'm told, is the way actions often come together in Leicester.

After this chance meeting and impromptu start, the communication system that links groups and organizations in Leicester concerned with war, militarism and peace was set in motion. It involved e-mail, phone and use of public media. Leicester CND is a branch of the national Campaign for Nuclear Disarmament, founded in 1958.[4] The Campaign is unique in its sustained focus on the threat of nuclear war and its unequivocal aim of unilateral and global nuclear disarmament. However, many members, including the leadership of the Leicester branch, embrace the Campaign's other activities (opposition to the 'war on terror', for instance, and to NATO expansion) and wish to see it therefore as a more generally anti-militarist organization. Anna's co-chair Richard Johnson describes the 183 members of the Leicester branch as 'mainly white British, middle class, characteristically over 60 years of age, and with a clear majority of women'. The branch has multiple and productive connections with many local groups, organizations and networks, so that it plays an important linking role in the Leicester anti-war, anti-militarist and peace movement. When Anna came back from the allotment she sat down at her computer and sent a message round the Leicester CND e-list and another list of addresses she calls her 'like minds'.

Mick Jarmaine, for his part, went home and phoned Chris Goodwin, the second key activist in Leicester Campaign to Stop the War. Leicester CStW is independent from, though affiliated to, the national Stop the War Coalition. With no more than five or six active adherents, it is tiny in comparison with Leicester CND and differs in having no organizational structure or formal membership. They are simply a small band of reliable women and men, co-ordinated by Chris Goodwin (my principal informant), who meet once a week at the Secular Hall on a Thursday evening. The group has a more working-class identity and a more explicitly anti-capitalist and anti-imperialist stance than Leicester CND. Their forte is achieving public demonstrations by partnering or co-ordinating other groups, and in this way play a key role in the local movement. Though their members are few, their contact e-list is very extensive. Chris now mailed out to call people to the Clock Tower.

Chris Goodwin is a good example of the tendency of active individuals in Leicester to be members not just of one but several anti-war or related organizations. The overlapping memberships are important to how mobilizations work. As it happens, Chris, besides her main commitment to CStW, is also an active member of the Leicester Palestine Solidarity Campaign, so she was the one to call its secretary with news of the plan hatched by Stop the War and CND. Leicester PSC is one of 40 branches of the national Palestine Solidarity Campaign, which has its head office in London.[5] PSC campaigns for the right of self-determination for the Palestinian people, their right of return to the place from which they were displaced, and the withdrawal of the Israeli state from the Occupied Territories. Its Leicester group is small, with five or six activists, but draws on greater numbers of supporters for events. Chris also mailed the very inclusive list of the Leicester Social Forum and that of the Leicester Civil Rights Movement, of both of which she is a member. Someone contacted Zina Zelter, a motivator in both a local group of Women in Black against War (WiB),[6] and ARROW (Active Resistance to the Roots of War), a handful of men and women who take nonviolent direct action against local weapons manufacturers. On the morning of the demonstration, Chris spoke on Radio Leicester.

However in addition to these principal actors there were members of several other groups and organizations present at the Clock Tower demo. It was not a matter of group 'representation'. As Michael Gerard of the Secular Society (who was there) put it, 'It's more people than organizations'. Rather, the individuals present belonged to a range of organizations that would be concerned about such an occurrence as the Israeli attack on Gaza, and any one of them, like Chris Goodwin, might be a member of two or even three. Importantly, Just Peace was present in the shape of Claire Wintram and Michele Benn. This group aim 'to be a different, alternative Jewish voice in Leicester, amid a big Muslim community, opposing Israeli government dogma'.[7] These women, who would have been expelled from this city 800 years ago, are now seeking justice for a people driven from their homes by Jews. Michele told me that it felt 'important to stand up as a Jew ... We thought about making a placard saying "Jews against the war in Gaza" but we didn't get it together in time'. So they went 'as individuals'. The Religious Society of Friends has many adherents in Leicester, so Annette Wallis and several other members of the local Quaker meeting and its

Peace Group were present with their simple blue and white 'peace' placards. A small cluster stood as Women in Black, some activists of the Leicester Social Forum and some members of Amnesty International's local branch were there, and certainly also members of various Christian denominations, some of them in a progressive network called Christians Aware. As usual at any such event, various political parties were in evidence. Though absent on this occasion, Peter Soulsby, Labour MP for the Leicester South constituency, is a member of CND and is always willing to turn out speak at rallies and demonstrations such as this. Members of the Green Party were noticed. And the 'extraparliamentary left' were in evidence in the shape of the Communist Party of Britain, the Socialist Workers Party, the Socialist Party and the Alliance for Workers' Liberty. Though few in numbers, members of these parties will often attend such events, bringing a stall and selling their papers.

What about the city's ethnic minority communities? Avtar Sadiq and perhaps other members of the mainly Hindu and Sikh Indian Workers' Association were at the Clock Tower that first day. As to the Muslims, no organizational banners were evident, but there were quite a number of individuals from among the South Asian, Somali and other Leicester Muslim communities. The Leicester Palestine Solidarity Campaign, who are mainly white British, would have been certain to put out a call to Friends of Al-Aqsa (FOA), an organization predominantly of Indian Muslims, with whom they share a concern with Palestine.[8] But, being a national organization, FOA were at this very moment focused on London. When the news broke about Gaza they had immediately issued a press release for national as well as local attention. They sent five coaches down for the national demonstration in Hyde Park, organized by the national Stop the War Coalition, that same Saturday. FOA took the lead however in organizing the subsequent Clock Tower gatherings on Wednesday 3 January and Saturday 17 January. Ismail Patel, its director, later told me that on these occasions perhaps 50 per cent of those present were Muslim, 40 per cent white British (the same cast of organizations as the previous Saturday) and 10 per cent 'others', including supporters of the Indian Workers' Association. Certainly the lively majority this time were Muslims, possibly 40 per cent of them women, with their children. Some Muslim youth in hoodies with *Free Palestine* printed on the back were in evidence. The FOA distributed five thousand leaflets. The demonstration experienced no heckling or aggression from the public, and, as anticipated, the police did not intervene.

What were the messages around which these people of varied affiliation adhered? The placards of Leicester Campaign to Stop the War read

'End the Israeli Occupation', 'Free Palestine', 'Israeli ceasefire now', and 'Stop the Israeli carnage'. Those of CND read 'Stop the massacre of the Palestinian people', 'Stop Israeli war in Gaza', and 'Join us here today and do whatever you can to help us end arms sales to Israel'. Leaflets developed these themes, including the perennial calls to boycott Israeli goods, end the Occupation, dismantle the settlements and allow self-determination for the Palestinian people. At the 3 January demonstration there were two loud-hailers, one brought along by CND, the other by the Palestine Solidarity Campaign. It is customary to have a kind of 'open mike' arrangement at these events, where anybody may request to use the hailer. So CND's Anna Cheetham, PSC's Jane Foxworthy and Claire Wintram of Just Peace all spoke, as did Avtar Sadiq. Several others stepped forward to make short speeches, including a man identifying himself as Afghan. Friends of Al-Aqsa got some rhythmic chants going: 'End the bombing, end the siege', and 'Free, free Palestine – Occupation is a crime'. There were many cries of 'Allah-u-Akhbar!' (God is great), and other slogans and calls in Arabic.

These demonstrations (rallies or vigils, however one might term them), although no more than a gesture, were somehow cathartic to those who attended. Everyone told me how deeply they had felt the attack on Gaza. 'It was the unbelievable inhumanity of it. Everyone everywhere felt it. Protests were bound to happen. Demonstrations served a good purpose and were the visible expression of public opinion,' said Manzoor Moghal of the Muslim Forum, a think tank on Muslim matters. Annette Wallis of the Quaker Peace Group said, 'It was unbearable, the ferocity of it. It was wonderful to be able to do something, however small'. Claire Wintram of Just Peace felt, 'There's so much anger, distress and commitment. People feel powerless but they want to effect change. It's important to take action'. Quite a lot of the demonstrators, certainly at the 3 January event, were not associated with any peace-oriented organization at all. Peter Flack, of the National Union of Teachers and Leicester Social Forum, said, 'People who would never normally go to demos were outraged at the level of carnage and felt duty bound to protest. A lot of people were drawn in just by the issue.'

Interfaith relations put to the test

Likewise, it is certain that the multi-faith prayers held at 1.30 pm on Wednesday 7 January in the Town Hall square attracted not a few bystanders who never normally pray. This public pray-in was the initiative of the Faith Leaders' Forum, a handy mechanism for a concerted response whenever there is a crisis affecting faith groups in the city. The Forum's press release with the call to prayer, above the name of the Bishop, did not place blame uniquely on Israel. It mentioned the violence in various parts of the world and then referred to 'the escalation of violence in Gaza and Israel. The suffering is clearly immense, whatever the past long term or immediate causes … We call now for an immediate end to the fighting, with Hamas agreeing to halt the rocket attacks, and Israel withdrawing from Gaza …'.

The event was opened by the then Mayor of Leicester, Manjula Sood, a woman and member of the Hindu community and of the Leicester Council of Faiths. The Bishop presided over the prayers. Several Christian denominations were represented, including the Catholic Church, the Methodists, Seventh Day Adventists and United Reformed Church. Ibrahim Mogra, an imam well respected locally and nationally, officiated for Leicester's Muslims, and Ramanbhai Barber, President of the Shree Sanatan Mandir temple, for the Hindus. It appears that the city's Sikhs, Jains and Buddhists, though invited, were not represented on this occasion, their absence perhaps due to the short notice and the fact that the event was in the middle of a working day. The Jewish community of Leicester[9] was represented by Tony Nelson, a former President of the Leicester Synagogue and vice-chair of the Leicester Council of Faiths, who read the 130th Psalm. The Orthodox Synagogue on the other hand is known to be strongly supportive of the Israeli state. In response to the call to prayer the Rabbi had made it known that he felt his attendance would be inappropriate, on the grounds that the violence in Gaza was an 'internal Israeli affair'. Minou Cortazzi Rowshan, at that time Chair of the Forum and the only other woman to speak, offered the Bahá'í prayer. The Anglican Christian Canon, Andrew Wingate, read a poem for Gaza. The Chief of Police was present – not for security purposes but in the interests of community solidarity.[10]

In contrast to the demonstrations at the Clock Tower, at the prayers there were no placards or banners, nor was there any shouting or chanting. There could hardly be communal singing, of course – these many faiths have no common hymnal. Politically, the prayer event differed from the Clock Tower demonstrations. At the latter, despite their diverse composition, the gathering clearly condemned the military and political actions of Israel and called forcefully for an end to the Occupation and for the self-determination of Palestinians. Many of those present would explicitly or implicitly have condemned the UK government's policy of support for Israel, its participation in the 'war on terror' and its perennial militarism. At the prayers, by contrast, though no doubt a trained ear would have detected subtly different political loadings, the agenda was one of 'just peace', carefully avoiding any apportioning of responsibility and guilt. Canon Wingate remembers the content as having been confined to prayers for: an end to violence; the alleviation of suffering; and wise leadership by the politicians concerned. David Clark, former Church of England rector of a Leicester parish and long active in inter-faith work, observed that the prayers were cautiously worded: 'Everyone was very careful. They were evenhanded.'

It was the prayer event that alerted me to the significance of religion, non-religion and anti-religion in this small 'moment' of a peace movement. As I listened to peoples' accounts I began to feel their satisfaction in having brought together, even for a couple of weeks around a specific act of war, organizations and individuals of so many and widely differing beliefs and philosophies. Leicester is one of the most ethnically complex cities in Britain, and its largest cultural components are distinctive religious groups. The city has two hundred and twenty-eight places of worship.[11] The national census of 2001 showed Christians, of many denominations, to be 45 per cent of a total of 280,000 inhabitants. The next largest religious group is Hindus, both Sanatan and Vaishnava, with 15 per cent. There are slightly fewer Muslims, who total around 11 per cent, mainly Sunni, but including some Shia, Ahmadiyya and others. The 2011 census is expected to show a shift in these proportions, in favour of Muslims. The survey of places of worship showed there to be, in addition, communities of (in alphabetical order) Bahá'í; Buddhist (Therevada); Jain; Jehovah's Witness; Jewish (Orthodox and Progressive); Mormon; Sikh and Spiritualist.

Despite this religious diversity, apart from the abstention of the synagogue from the Town Hall prayers, no inter-faith tension was apparent at the Gaza events. The Anglican Church in Leicester is very practised at inter-faith work, of which the Bishop, Tim Stevens, is a strong advocate. The city's Council of Faiths, founded in 1986, is recognized as a prominent member of the country-wide Inter Faith Network.[12] The Leicester Faith Leaders' Forum that initiated the Town Hall prayers was formed in response to the terror attacks of 11 September 2001, and is intended to bring together key figures in the religious communities. Another asset in the diocese is the St Philip's Centre for Study and Engagement in a Multi-Faith Society, which provides training for multi-faith awareness and hosts Muslim-Christian Dialogue groups and a Hindu-Christian Forum. Such structures have also proved effective in sustaining Hindu-Muslim and Hindu-Sikh dialogue in Leicester when it has failed in some other cities during times of communal conflict in India.

Leicester's Muslim organizations: for 'peace' or 'Palestine'?

The inter-faith structures are related directly to the anti-war, anti-militarist and peace movements, but in an ambiguous way. They can be seen on the one hand as contributing to peace and nonviolence, on the other as a state-sanctioned strategy to handle and defuse the anger in Arab, Muslim and other ethnic minority communities evoked by UK foreign policy – such as military interventions in Afghanistan and Iraq, and support of the Israeli government.

I was given a helpful introduction to Muslim realities in Leicester by Asaf Hussain, who teaches Islamic civilization at the University of Leicester. He told me there is a great deal of Muslim diversity in the city and a degree of tension between the various communities. First there is a range of ethno-national groups. There are sizeable communities originating in Pakistan, Bangladesh and Somalia, but Muslims of Indian origin, mainly Gujarati-speakers, are the most significant political presence. Some Leicester Muslims are Shia, but a bigger proportion are Sunni Muslims. Of the latter, some are of the Sufi tradition. However there is a local predominance of Deobandis, an Islamic sect dating back to 1867, when certain Muslims of the Sufi tradition that prevailed from the Middle Ages came under the influence of Saudi Arabian Wahhabis encountered on the Hadj. Where Wahhabis and Deobandis stress dogma, Sufis ascribe more importance to the depth of one's love of God. Being more cultural than political, Sufism is regarded by Wahhabis as 'weak', and, in the Indian context, too co-operative with Hinduism. In Leicester, Deobandis of Indian origin together with other Wahhabi Muslims, including approximately 15,000 recent Somali immigrants, greatly outnumber Sufi Sunni Muslims, who are mainly, in terms of national origin, Pakistanis and Bangladeshis. There is a marked difference in the character of the mosques of the two Sunni traditions. The 'flagship' mosque of the Deobandis in Leicester is the Masid Umma Mosque, while the heart of the Sufi Sunni community is the Leicester Central Mosque. There is also a small presence in Leicester of members of the Ahmaddiya sect who are severely ostracized by other Muslims.

The Deobandi Muslims of Leicester, Asaf Hussain told me, though conservative, are moderate relative to some other Wahhabi groups. They have gained significant leadership positions within several institutions in the Leicester Muslim community in recent years, on which their presence confers (in the eyes of some others) a cultural conservatism, particularly evident in matters of gender. They have a wary relationship with the local Hindu population, which harbours a strong element of Hindu nationalism. Hindutva violence is always a latent threat to local Indian Muslims and their families living in India. The Deobandis must work hard for recognition and engagement in Leicester City's municipal structures, where their influence is outweighed by that of the Hindu élite.

Deobandis constitute the leadership of Friends of Al-Aqsa, the pro-Palestine group mentioned above as active in the Gaza events. FOA, a nation-wide organization with its head office in Leicester, takes its name from the 8th-century Al-Aqsa mosque in Jerusalem threatened by Israeli Jewish ambitions for exclusive possession of the Temple Mount site, sacred to both religions. The Association publishes a weekly news bulletin on their website, a quarterly paper, *Al-Aqsa News*, and an analytical journal. Its members and volunteers collect material and financial aid for Palestinians and organize campaigns and demonstrations for their rights. I interviewed FOA director Ismail Patel. Their 1000-plus activist members are almost all practising Muslims, but the organization's aims and objectives are political rather than religious. 'Our overall aim is justice and peace in Palestine,' Ismail Patel told me in interview. 'Justice is not a theological concept for us – in that we are different from the mosques'. Despite FOA's national identity, Leicester city is a particular focus of action. 'Local relationships are important for us to maintain. There is a great deal of co-operation between us and local groups,' Ismail said.

Friends of Al-Aqsa are affiliated to another significant Muslim body, the Federation of Muslim Organisations Leicestershire, which was also visibly involved in the Clock Tower Gaza protests. Established 26 years ago, it is an umbrella body, elected and non-sectarian, made up of both Sunni and Shia. Its 187 affiliates include mosques and other Muslim organizations, charities and schools. Suleman Nagdi MBE, DL, a leading figure in the organization and currently its Public Relations Officer, told me in interview that the Federation does 'a balancing act' that combines co-operative relations with the authorities and protest against the 'war on terror', which of course many in Leicester interpret as a 'war on Muslims'. 'There is a loyalty issue. Your loyalty to the country is questioned very, very quickly as a Muslim. Contest the government you offend one side, don't contest it and you offend the other,' he said.

Weighing in on one side of the balancing act, Suleman Nagdi is (as we see) the recipient of the Medal of the British Empire. He has been a Justice of the Peace, and represents the Queen as Deputy Lord Lieutenant of Leicester. As well as being a member of the Leicester Council of Faiths and the Faith Leaders' Forum, and Chair of the Muslim Burial Council of Leicestershire, he received a National Police Association award, and sits on the Police Advisory Board. Civic engagement of this kind is characteristic of leading Muslim personalities in Leicester. The Federation plays an active part in interfaith activity in the city, and Leicester is known for football matches in which mosques compete with the police force, and an annual cricket match between Christian clergy and the imams (with a Jewish umpire).

Weighing in as counter-balance, the Federation of Muslim Organizations in Leicester regularly issues statements against the harassment of Muslims under the Terrorism Act, organizes coaches to participate in national demonstrations against government policy (protesting against the attack on Iraq, for instance), and on such occasions it unhesitatingly co-operates with the Stop the War Coalition, CND, the Socialist Party and the Socialist Workers Party. During the attack on Gaza they issued press statements, participated in protests in London and mailed their affiliates to draw them to the Clock Tower demonstrations. Former FMO president, Abdulkarim Gheewala, protested keenly against the press statement issued by the Bishop and the Faith Leaders' Forum for relativizing the onslaught on Gaza by situating the events of December/ January in the context of other current conflicts such as Sri Lanka and Darfur.

The considerable and continuous effort of co-operation made by the Christian and Muslim 'sides' in Leicester pays off at times such as the Israeli attack on Gaza. When there is a strong shared motive for action like this, the communities stand together – quite literally, for a short while, in a public space. What is more, as we have seen, key organizations of these and other faiths at such a time are capable of standing shoulder to shoulder with actively non- and even anti-religious organizations. There remains, however, a doubt in some minds about how deeply, if one were to delve beneath 'peace' and 'justice', the motivation would be found to be shared. I heard these doubts most clearly expressed by non-religious, 'host community', anti-war activists. For example, when FOA, the Federation of Muslim Organizations and other Muslim bodies join in protesting against the Israeli Occupation of Palestine and the Western military campaigns in Iraq and Afghanistan, are they motivated by a disapproval of war itself, of militarization, of violence in general? Do they dream of 'peace'? Or are they only concerned with the interests of Islam and the Muslim communities? The spokespeople for Muslim and Christian beliefs I interviewed were mostly too tactful and well-mannered to voice their own doubts. The kind of reassurance they might reasonably seek is that the concern shown by the British peace movement for war victims in Gaza, Iraq and Afghanistan extends to the defence of Muslims' civil rights in the UK.

All the non-Muslim partners in the movement that I spoke with expressed warm appreciation of the co-operation they get from FOA and the Federation. They are pleased by the alliance, and proud of it. The Leicester Palestinian Solidarity Campaign, for example, which shares FOA's focus on Palestine, finds this common ground sufficient to the moment. Jane Foxworthy pointed out that in Palestine there are many villages where Christians and Muslims live side by side peacefully and respectfully. This could be a good basis for confidence in Muslim-Christian dialogue in Britain. Of Leicester PSC's relations with FOA, she says, 'We collaborate on the main focus of both our organizations, which is to support the Palestinian struggle for freedom. The discussion would never get to the stage of us falling out. I don't think we would get into situations where these political differences would appear on a deep level'.

Others, however, expressed caution, aware that they do not engage sufficiently in discussion with their Muslim partners to know how deep and secure the alliance is. Leicester CND for example, is a broad-spectrum anti-war and anti-militarist organization. Richard Johnson of Leicester CND said:

> We don't really know where the points of convergence and divergence are. We inform each other. For instance, we may ask them, 'What are you doing?'. They may tell us, 'The mosques are sending coaches to the demo'. How is it seen? There could be a slight doubt there. Do they have their own agenda? Is it an anti-Israeli one more than an anti-war one? We don't exchange ideas about it. You could argue there is no need for discussion. But I'm sure there are more things we could say to each other.

With this in mind, Richard had recently started inviting people of different origins and identities, standpoints and philosophies to occasional informal evenings of 'dialogue' in his home.

Belief in God, faith in humanity

The church-goers and mosque-goers in Leicester's anti-war movement are at least united in their monotheistic belief. Other actors in the movement are critical of both (and indeed all) religions. Some are in organizations that are atheistic by principle. The Leicester Secular Society, founded in 1851, is older than the national body and in fact the oldest in the world.[13] Rejected from others' meeting halls due to their philosophy, they early on built their own place, the Secular Hall in the city centre. Scientific rationalists, adherents of the secular movement, aim to establish a civil society without reference to the supernatural. Alan Hayes, president of the Leicester Secular Society, finds religions divisive. 'People will use their religion to justify themselves, to separate people from each other.' Michael Gerard, another active member of the Society, points out that a great many of Leicester's inhabitants are in fact secularists. In the 2001 census almost 49,000 individuals stated that they had 'no religion', while a further 20,000 did not give a religion. Together these constitute nearly a quarter of the population. Yet in terms of structures the non-believers are overwhelmed by the religious. 'There is such an imbalance. The churches are huge. The Secular Society has a tiny handful of members – even if we represent a large silent population of non-believers.' David Clark, a former Church of England Rector, acknowledges that, in the Christian churches, 'There is an ancient, almost subconscious, hostility to active atheists'. And Michael admits, 'In any case there is resistance from some on our side too'.

Another atheist organization involved in the Gaza activities is the Indian Workers' Association. The IWA was founded in 1938 and became a national organization in 1958, with branches in many British cities. Leicester, with its huge Hindu population, is an important branch. It welcomes all Hindus, Jains and Sikhs who espouse an Indian rather than a religious identity. It would indeed not exclude secular Indian Muslims. The IWA is close to the Communist Party of India (Marxist), and in the UK context is in tune with the Communist Party of Britain (publishers of the *Morning Star*). Avtar Sadiq is the national Vice President. He told me their political ideology is anti-capitalist and anti-imperialist, and their aims are: keeping people informed on social, political and economic developments in India; fighting discrimination and racism; and linking Indian workers to the trade union and labour movements in the UK. Here Avtar added, 'Please note: *not* the Labour Party!'. They fight for liberation of countries under oppression, including Palestine. But as well as being active over the Gaza crisis, they aim to link Indian workers to the wider anti-war and peace movement, and Avtar is a member of Leicester CND. The Association must keep a wary eye on the extreme Right, in the shape both of the British National Party (East Midlands branch) and the local Bharatiya Janata Party (BJP, Hindu nationalists).

It occurred to me for the first time in Leicester that prayer must be acknowledged as fully part of the repertoire of action of the anti-war, anti-militarist and peace movements. While some lobby, inform, campaign, agitate and demonstrate for peace, others pray for it. The faith groups that assembled in Leicester's Town Hall Square to pray for peace between Israel and Palestine had similarly prayed to avert the 'war on terror' and the attack on Iraq. But for at least two of the groups present the link between worship and peace is more profound. The primary practice of the Religious Society of Friends is meeting for silent worship, in most cases with no human leader and no fixed programme.[14] Leicester has a Friends' Meeting which draws up to eighty people each Sunday. It has a number of groups and committees, one of which is the Quaker Peace Group. Annette Wallis is its convenor. They hold a quiet weekly vigil in the town, with a simple peace message for passers-by. Work for peace, she explained to me, is not an optional extra for Quakers. Rather, 'peace is fundamental. If you live faithfully as a Quaker you will be working for peace'. A famous phrase from the Quaker Peace Testimony reads: 'All bloody principles and practices we do utterly deny, with all outward wars and strife, and fightings with outward weapons, for any end, or under any pretence whatsoever, and this is our testimony to the whole world.' It is a vow that has historically set a wide distance between the Quakers and the Christian churches that in antiquity gave their blessing to military crusades and today seldom condemn Western war policies if they can be given a 'humanitarian' or 'just war' spin.

The Bahá'í community too has a natural interest in the problem of injustice and war, believing it is prejudice and inequality (on all dimensions including wealth, race and gender) that cause disunity and sometimes war. Work for peace and human rights is therefore central to their faith and, as with the Quakers, Bahá'ís are of necessity part of the anti-war and peace movement.[15] I had a chance to interview Minou Cortazzi Rowshan, Jan Macdonald and Aramesh Mahboubi of the Leicester Bahá'í community. They told me that the Bahá'í religion originated in Persia, now Iran, in the mid-nineteenth century, where from the start it was treated as heretical, so that many Bahá'í have lived in a worldwide diaspora. Possibly six thousand Bahá'ís live in the UK, around thirty of them in Leicester. Believing in one God, and seeing a fundamental harmony in the world's theist faiths, the Bahá'í are in their element in the Leicester Council of Faiths, and it is characteristic that they were represented at the interfaith prayers for Palestine. 'Bahá'ís associated with people of all faiths in a spirit of fellowship,' Minou Cortazzi said. 'And that is a law, not just something that's thought to be a good idea. The greatest harm in the Bahá'í vision is disunity.' As to strategies for peace, the Bahá'í are not averse to lobbying politicians, writing articles and using the Internet – they frequently do so to alert the world to the injustices against the Bahá'í in Iran. However, as an actor in the peace movement the distinctive strategy of this faith group is not argumentation, petitioning, marching and protesting. It is prayer, which they believe is effective in itself. 'Prayer alone can achieve peace.' Minou added, however, that while they use prayer in all their affairs, Bahá'ís also constantly put their prayers into action in day-to-day work for peace. 'We do not pray with no action to follow. One of the Bahá'í writings states "Let your prayers be beautiful actions".'

Like most other options in the anti-war, anti-militarist and peace movements' repertoire, praying as a strategy evokes differing opinions. For the Bahá'í prayer, simply, *is* anti-war strategy. There are those, including Muslims, Christians and those of several other faiths, who find it necessary if not obligatory to pray – for peace, among other things. A wider group still, while not engaging in prayer, have no objection to others doing so. However, for convinced secularists, praying for peace can be obscurantist, misleading and deflect from useful activism. Avtar Sadiq of the Marxist IWA is clear that religion has no relevance in the modern world and no place in political life. He says: 'I don't oppose people who have an individual relation with "god", but I believe it should be a private matter. It is not something in which governments should be involved.' However, apart from the membership of the IWA and the Leicester Secular Society, both 'politically' secular as organizations, many individual members of other organizations are personally agnostic or atheist and feel varying degrees of antipathy for organized religion. Chris Goodwin of Leicester Campaign to Stop the War says:

> I'm a secularist myself. I think people are entitled to their religion and we welcome people from all groups. On the other hand, I don't think [religion] is particularly helpful to the cause of peace. I don't think, myself, that praying for peace makes a difference.

Claire Wintram of Just Peace feels 'Religion has been hijacked by politicians. Personally I would rather write angry letters to the Prime Minister than pray to god. But that's their choice'. Anna Cheetham of Leicester CND, who doesn't believe in a deity, nonetheless (surprisingly perhaps) attended the prayers at the Town Hall. She told me later, 'I didn't pray or lower my head but stood in support of their wish to be together'.

Her comment on the event was, 'They made statements, but not about what was happening. Just "thinking about those who are dying" and "praying for an end to it"'. That, for her, was not enough. She recalled another occasion when praying had felt positively inappropriate. In 2003 she had attended a meeting organized for George Galloway, the socialist activist and MP, by Friends of Al-Aqsa. In the middle of the meeting it had been announced, 'We must hurry the agenda because it's time for prayers'. Anna says, 'I thought they meant to end the meeting, but no. [The Muslims] just prayed then and there, and we had to wait. This is not suitable for a public meeting'. Michael Gerard, also present at this event, had similarly objected to the interruption. He'd felt, 'You are shoving your religion down our throats'.

It is certain that many religious adherents are equally repelled by atheist discourse and lifestyles, but the spokespeople for Muslim and Christian beliefs I interviewed were too well-mannered to voice it. Only the Bahá'í, in their gentle way, told me of the limitations of the political road to peace, in contrast to the road of prayer. 'Bahá'í works towards the Great Peace and the Kingdom of God on Earth. [Secularist] anti-war activists are working towards what we Bahá'í call a "lesser peace". But the work they do is admirable, and who are we to judge them?'

Feminism, faiths and peace activism

Feminist anti-militarist organizations were not much in evidence in Leicester at the time of this study. The local branch of the Women's International League for Peace and Freedom had fallen into abeyance. Women in Black against War had declined in number and become too few to sustain weekly vigils, until propelled back onto the street by the assault on Gaza. However, as elsewhere in the UK, in Leicester many women as individuals are active for peace and in some cases are a majority of the membership in many of the mixed organizations. I met several women who identified as feminists, and some who were actively pursuing feminist issues. Their situation differs, however, from that of the feminist anti-militarists that feature in other chapters of this book. To do effective work for peace in Leicester, with its large ethnic minority population, the feminists are obliged to develop a working relation-ship with faith-based organizations, the most influential of which are emphatically patriarchal.

Imagine the challenge this poses to someone like Claire Wintram of Just Peace, who, like many other anti-militarist feminists, sees patri-archy, along with capitalism and nationalism, as among the causes of war. Claire describes herself as 'an unreconstructed feminist'. She has co-authored a book on feminist consciousness-raising (Butler and Wintram 1991). She said of herself, 'I've lived my whole conscious life as a feminist. But for me it has to be *feminist* – not just "women". Not women and nail varnish. Feminism for me is anti-patriarchy, anti-militarist. Our entire lives are marginalized by both these things'. This analysis means Claire has to negotiate carefully her relationship to the Muslim, Christian and also (because of Just Peace's concern with Israel) the Jewish religious structures around her. 'Religion is all part of patriarchy. I'm sceptical. So I skirt around the edges, I distance myself from it,' she says. Zina Zelter sees Women in Black's way of organizing, its silent vigils, as 'feminist traditions'. And like Claire she feels, 'Yes, patriarchal values are definitely one of the roots of war'. But she differentiates patriarchy from men 'as such'. 'It's that patriarchy polarizes things. The patriarchal structure encourages us all, men and women, to be the way we are'. Anna Cheetham of Leicester CND is another who emphatically describes herself as feminist, and Richard Johnson, co-chair, is supportive of feminism and looks to achieve gender balance in the branch. Anna says she has come to believe there is 'a difference between male and female minds'. The way men are brought up to behave and think is functional for militarism. 'It's how the military wants them.' Unlike Zina, who sees value in a women-only group, Anna chooses to be involved in a mixed organization: 'Men are part of society. I'm not anti-men.'

Women with a strong grounding in socialist thought often temper the feminist analysis of patriarchy as contributing to militarism and war. Chris Goodwin of the Campaign to Stop the War said, 'I wouldn't say it was *not* part of the picture'. But she went on, 'It's not a *major* part. Yes, rape is used in war. But after all, men are raped too.' Her commitment to CStW rather than, say, Women in Black, is a conscious political choice:

> Women's vigils are not my thing. I was active on women's issues in the 1970s. But I don't feel I want to go down that road again. It tends to give the impression that war is a women's issue rather than a general issue. Women in my experience are not passive – they can be violent too. It's capitalism and imperialism that are the main cause of war.

Nor is it only secular women who bring a gender critique into their work for peace and justice. Annette Wallis, convenor of the

Quaker Peace Group, in response to my question about women and feminism, said:

> I've been learning things through my life. For example, that we really do need to use gender-inclusive language. And my God is *not* a man! So I've come to understand that feminism is necessary. It's important to understanding war. So often the ones considered 'great men' are actually war heroes. We are learning what testosterone does! And that's without devaluing what men can do. It makes you feel some sympathy for men, actually, rather than antagonism.

Towards a realistic and sustainable alliance

Zina, and other women anti-war activists of the organizations that draw their membership mainly from the white 'host' community in Leicester, would dearly love to have a strong and meaningful partnership with women of the Muslim communities in opposing Israel's oppression of Palestinians and, more generally, the West's 'war on terror' in Afghanistan and elsewhere. But they have so far found no way of achieving it. One difficulty is a lack of visible political engagement on the part of women in the Muslim communities. Thinking of the Gaza moment, Asaf Hussain told me,

> So many women died in that attack! You would think there should be a powerful women's response. But Leicester Muslims keep their wives inside. There's no sign of women's groups in this city. And if there were they wouldn't be strong enough to reach out to white British women. Their husbands would suspect them.

Manzoor Moghal's assessment was: 'It's not surprising if white British feminists find it difficult to get a large measure of support among Muslim women. While a few, the more educated, may join the men on a demonstration, most would be unwilling or would not be supported by their menfolk.' He put this down to the dominance of Deobandi Muslims in Leicester among whom, he said, segregation of the sexes in public is the norm. Unlike Sunni mosques of the Sufi tradition, Deobandi mosques provide no place for women, who are expected to pray at home.

It is not feminists alone, but also many other 'white' British women, and indeed some Muslim women and men, who deplore the practice of sex-segregation and are, besides, critical of the *hijab* head cover as an obligatory dress code. The full-cover *niqab*, increasingly seen in Leicester, disturbs them even more. But while some allow these cultural differences to impede their attempts to reach out to Muslim women, others do not. Anna Cheetham says, 'In this country women struggled for freedom. I wish women who came here could learn that. They say women choose to wear the *hijab*. But it's not true. They would only know if they were freely choosing if they had not been brought up in a patriarchy'. In 2003 she had attended that meeting for George Galloway organized by Friends of Al-Aqsa. She had been shocked to find women and men being directed towards opposite sides of the hall. 'This was a *public meeting*! They said non-Muslim women might sit on the men's side as 'honorary men' – but I don't want to be an honorary man!' Since then she has chosen not to attend events organized by Muslim groups that are likely to involve segregation.

Suleman Nagdi is at pains to point out here that one should distinguish the mosques from those organizations of the Muslim community that are political rather than religious actors. The Federation of Muslim Organizations Leicestershire do not themselves organize segregation, he says. 'No! We accommodate segregation but do not promote it. Often it's family units that travel together. If there is a women's bus or section, it is because women ask for it, they feel threatened in mixed situations.' He points out that the Federation fosters women's activity. For some years they had a 'ladies' subcommittee' that organized monthly meetings with speakers on themes such as social welfare, childcare, needs of the elderly, and today women are directly elected to the Federation's Executive Committee. Likewise the FOA, a political rather than religious organization, do not follow the segregating practice of the mosques. They number many women among their activists and volunteers and ensure that women comprise 50 per cent of the executive committee.

Besides, some women peace activists of the 'host' community feel they should not set terms and conditions on contact with the Muslim community with which Muslim women cannot comply. Zina Zelter is impatient with the inability of some 'white' British women to compromise on these cultural differences. She says:

> It matters to me that here I am living in Leicester, in this very, very mixed city, and I'm stuck in a white middle-class peace community. People get hung up on questions like 'Will women have to sit at the back of the coach?'. They won't look at the Muslim community and understand how *they* feel.

She believes the distance could be closed. 'It's due to something we're not yet doing. And not enough of us are worried about it.' And she added, 'I don't mind excluding people who don't believe in dialogue. But I don't want to exclude people just because our comfort zone is different from theirs'. Claire Wintram of Just Peace had even found segregation of the sexes could offer a welcome opportunity for contact with Muslim women. She and Helen, a Just Peace friend, had been to London on a coach trip organized by Friends of Al-Aqsa to protest about the Israeli invasion of Lebanon:

> There were no other non-Muslim, white, women. And we women had to sit at the back of the coach. I don't feel happy about their practice of separating men and women, but we had an amazing engagement with some of the women, precisely due to that. They were astonished that we were Jews. Later some came to Just Peace events.

So I found many divergences and tensions in the *ad hoc* alliance of organizations that gathered in Leicester in the first two weeks of 2009 to protest against the Israeli assault on Gaza. The difficulties encountered in forging realistic and deep relationships between those of different faiths and philosophies are not the subject of as much discussion, exposure and exploration as some would like to see. A research project on the anti-war movement by sociologists at City University, London, carried out a few years before my own, came to a similar conclusion. The researchers interviewed a wide variety of Leicester anti-war activists, at a time when the mobilization against the attack on Iraq was still clear in people's memories. They found considerable willingness among Muslims and non-Muslims to demonstrate side by side, yet noted a 'paucity of dialogue' between the allies. In part, they believed, 'this was for the sake of maintaining a fragile unity and to avoid the risk of giving offence, yet the failure to engage also functioned to perpetuate a distorted notion of what it means to be Muslim' (Gillan et al. 2008: 190). The particular focus of the research was on the anti-war movement's use of communication technologies. They found that the Internet had been 'a poor facilitator for communication beyond those already closely connected with other activists and it [had] not been used as a forum through which to make links across difference'. E-mail discussions, they observed, were revolving 'between familiar voices and opinions, not as a space for difficult dialogue' (ibid.: 99).

Of course there is a danger that if you talk about differences you may deepen them, so that they come to seem irreconcilable. A tension may turn into an antagonism. On the other hand, a deeper understanding and empathy might be achieved that would permit a more sustainable alliance over a broader range of issues. The present reality is that the movement, if indeed we can call it this, is a matter of contingency, groups of people rubbing along together in reaction to the moves of history. An event happens, you see who else feels roughly the same about it as you do, you get together to 'do something'. 'If they support the working class I'll support them.' 'They may be non-believers but they'll swell the ranks.' In contingent mode, the discussion of tensions is absent. Several people insisted to me, 'We just don't talk enough'. 'We are walking side by side and no discussion.' 'This is not an alliance, if alliance means dialogue.'

On the other hand, as many people affirmed, there was cause for rejoicing that the tensions were not proving so severe as to undermine all possibilities of co-operation. Basic values of peace, justice and democracy are understood as shared, even if detailed analyses and demands are not the subject of explicit negotiation. People do respond to each others' calls to meetings, to demonstrations. They use each other's meeting places: Muslims will go to the Quaker Friends Meeting House; believers may use the Secular Hall. They do forward each other's e-mails, join the bus, or drop in on the vigil. They do come and hold one end of someone else's banner or lend their loud-hailer. 'We all pull together,' someone said. And another, 'It doesn't matter who puts out the call, we'll turn up'. 'It's hopeful that so many in Leicester are seeking peace.' 'It's typical Leicester, everyone will be there!'

Notes

1. Online at: www.jewishgen.org/JCR-UK/community/Leicester.htm (accessed 2 April 2011).
2. Office of National Statistics data, online at: www.guardian.co.uk/news/ datablog/interactive/2011/may/19/ethnic-breakdown-england-wales (accessed 19 May 2011).
3. There were certainly other happenings concerned with Gaza at this time in Leicester that I heard mentioned, but decided not to pursue. For instance, while I include events in which Muslim organizations participated in a wider movement, I do not include events organized mainly within the Muslim communities, by student groups and others.
4. See their website: www.cnduk.org.
5. See their website: www.palestinecampaign.org.
6. See their website: www.womeninblack.org.
7. The title 'Just Peace' is in use by several organizations, especially in connection with Palestine. A short description of Leicester Just Peace can be seen

online at: http://beehive.thisisleicestershire.co.uk/default.asp?WCI=Site Home&ID=11983 (accessed 2 April 2011).

8. See their website: www.foa.org.uk.

9. I was given an estimate of 500 individuals, with perhaps another 1000 unassociated with synagogues.

10. In this account of the prayer event I draw on the recollections of Canon Andrew Wingate and the Reverend David Clark.

11. List prepared by the Leicester Council of Faiths in 2004.

12. See their website: www.interfaith.org.uk.

13. See the websites: www.secularism.org.uk and www.leicestersecularsociety. org.uk.

14. See their website: www.quaker.org.uk.

15. See their website: www.bahai.org.uk.

5

Saying No to NATO: Divergent Strategies*

'N – A – T – O. What's that stand for, then?' This was the question a lot of Londoners asked us when we handed them our leaflets. We uncovered a surprising ignorance about the world's most powerful military alliance, the massive war machinery within which British armed forces are shaped to fit and function. In the foregoing chapter we saw that Spain's anti-militarists have been acutely conscious of the North Atlantic Treaty Organization and organized energetic resistance to Spain's membership of the alliance. In France too there has been a lively awareness of NATO's significance, since President de Gaulle defied US dominance by pulling France out of its military command – a policy recently reversed by President Sarkozy.[1] The same cannot be said of Britain, where protest has been mounted against particular NATO engagements, such as the bombing of Belgrade in 1999 and the current mission in Afghanistan, but little attention has been paid to the Alliance, its growing reach and ambition, and the implications of membership. NATO is not an issue for the average Brit. Leafletting around central London, we were a group of women who decided to draw attention to NATO on the occasion of the North Atlantic Treaty Organization's November 2010 summit

*This chapter differs from others in the source of the material here presented, in that I write not as an academic researcher but as an activist in Women in Black against War and the Women's International League for Peace and Freedom, reflecting on some anti-militarist actions in which I have played a part alongside others. Please see the Introduction (p. 7). I would like to thank Kate Hudson, then national chair of the Campaign for Nuclear Disarmament, John Rees, of Stop the War Coalition's steering committee, and Andreas Speck, staff member of War Resisters' International, who were all three involved in No-to-NATO, for affording me interviews which greatly enriched my understanding of the events described in this chapter.

meeting. Our T-shirts spelled out SAY-NO-TO-NATO, and our leaflet spelled out why.

I had become aware, a couple of years before this, of an activist network in member states organizing opposition to NATO. In November 2008, when I was in Geneva for the annual general meeting of the Women's International League for Peace and Freedom, I learned that WILPF had signed up to an appeal being circulated by an initiative calling itself 'No to War: No to NATO', and had sent a representative to an early meeting of the committee mobilizing protest at NATO's 60th-anniversary meeting of Heads of State, due to take place in Strasbourg on 3–5 April 2009. Soon after this I got together with three other women to plan a feminist input to this event. Together we could call on the resources of three networks. Irmgard Heilberger was a member of the German section of WILPF. Marlène Tuininga was active in Women in Black (WiB) and president of WILPF in France. I also have dual membership of WiB and WILPF, while Anna Gyorgy, based in Bonn, was just then re-activating Women and Life on Earth (WLOE), a network dating back to the 1970s. We decided to put out a call on our respective international e-mail lists encouraging women to come and be a visible presence on the streets of Strasbourg during the Summit. The Women and Life on Earth website (www.wloe.org) and an e-list set up for the purpose would be our main organizing mechanisms. Anticipating between thirty and fifty participants, we prudently made a block booking of inexpensive hotel accommodation in Strasbourg for the relevant dates in April. We knew very well the city was going to be packed with media, protestors and official delegations, their advisers, security guards and drivers during the three days and nights of the Summit.

Together the four of us went to a No-to-NATO preparatory 'activists' conference' in Strasbourg in February, attended by five hundred people from nineteen countries, and here we learned more about the plan for opposing the Summit. It would have four components: a mass demonstration, a week-long peace camp, nonviolent civil disobedience in the form of blockades of major roads, and a two-day counter-conference. Finding no reference to women or gender in the proposed conference programme, we got agreement to inclusion of a workshop, to be offered jointly by our three organizations, developing a feminist critique of NATO's version of 'security'. We also proposed an identifiable place for women's organizations in the rally and march. Both ideas were supported by other women we met at the activists' conference, including some from the international *Marche Mondiale des Femmes*, and the French *Organisation de Femmes Egalité*.

The elements of a campaign

The organizations and networks engaged in the No-to-NATO mobilization were and are politically, organizationally and geographically a mixed bag. The widest version of 'membership' would be the list of signatories of the No-to-NATO Appeal launched in 2008 – several hundred organizations from twenty-seven countries, including United for Peace and Justice in the USA, and some women's networks including WILPF and the London branch of WiB.[2] The composition of the International Co-ordinating Committee (ICC) was necessarily much narrower. Partly due to the location of the forthcoming Summit, in Strasbourg/Kehl, on the very border between France and Germany, the principal actors were from those two countries, though there was an input too from the anti-war, anti-militarist and peace movements of Greece, Spain, the Czech Republic, Turkey and other member states. The UK was represented by the Stop the War Coalition (StWC) and the Campaign for Nuclear Disarmament (CND). Taking a positive view, the organizing group could be said to be a richly diverse array of locations and standpoints. More realistically, perhaps, it could be seen as a contingent grouping with alarming political divergences. The participating organizations can be clustered, with a little pushing and pulling, into three categories: first, peace, anti-war and other 'movement' organizations and networks; second, parliamentary political parties; and third, groupings of radical left anti-capitalist and anarchist tendencies.

Peace and anti-war movements

The weightiest and most consistent members of the ICC were the peace and anti-war movements, among them the venerable French *Mouvement de la Paix* (Peace Movement), whose co-president, Arielle Denis, was its co-chair.[3] Founded in 1948, the *Mouvement de la Paix* opposes war, nuclear weapons and the arms trade, and works towards international relations based on justice, democracy and co-operation between peoples. It has a structure of local committees in numerous towns and cities in France, and its peace work includes petitions, debates, exhibitions, conferences and demonstrations. It has historic links with the *Parti Communiste Français* (French Communist Party, PCF) with whose fortunes it has been somewhat tied. However, the membership of the *Mouvement de la Paix* is broad, including many Christians and progressives of various kinds, and the PCF line has never been stressed. In recent years it has consciously distanced itself from the Party. The *Mouvement de la Paix* gives an impression of solidity and (in the No-to-NATO context) of conservatism.

Also large and respected, the UK's Campaign for Nuclear Disarmament (CND) was another peace movement represented on the International Coordinating Committee of No-to-NATO. Committed to nonviolent campaigning against nuclear weapons, it tracks and opposes their development, manufacture, testing, deployment and use by any country (Hudson 2005).[4] Clearly CND's main take on NATO is that it is a belligerent alliance in which nuclear weapons are 'shared' and deployed in the UK and other European countries. However many people join CND's local and regional branches as a 'peace movement' in a more general sense, opposed to wars and militarization. The Campaign has a working partnership with the Stop the War Coalition and the Muslim Alliance of Britain, and this threesome is capable of pulling out large crowds in London and other cities in opposition to war and threats of war.

Less a peace movement than an anti-war network, StWC was also represented on the No-to-NATO International Coordinating Committee. The Coalition came together in 2001 in the wake of the attacks of 11 September on US targets, with the aim of stopping the war against 'terrorism' declared by George Bush and his allies (Murray and German 2005).[5] It has individual members and local groups, but more importantly a large array of organizational affiliates. StWC's efficient campaigns and demonstrations show the hallmarks of the left tendencies that initiated it, among which a major actor was the Socialist Workers Party. SWP is a development from the International Socialists (IS) and was for some time Britain's most substantial Marxist, Trotskyist and revolutionary socialist party. It does not contest elections, but did for a while lend its support to the Respect Party that put forward parliamentary candidates. Furnishing organizational resources for global justice and other campaigns, as well as StWC, they write of themselves: 'We strive to be the anti-capitalist, anti-imperialist voice of the movements we build.'[6]

The German peace movement does not feature large national organizations such as the French *Mouvement de la Paix* and the UK's Campaign for Nuclear Disarmament. Its numerous smaller organizations, many of which date back to the 1980s, are clustered in networks, notably Co-operation for Peace (*Kooperation für den Frieden*),[7] and the Federal Council Peace Forum (*Bundesausschuss Friedensratschlag*).[8] The *Kooperation* and one of its affiliates, the Network Peace Cooperative (*Netzwerk Friedenskooperative*)[9] were involved in the No-to-NATO co-ordinating committee. Also prominent in the preparatory work for the events in Strasbourg were the German and French branches of ATTAC, an international association formed in 1998. The French branch is known for its campaign for a 'Tobin tax' on international financial transactions, while the German ATTAC is rooted in a nonviolent direct action tradition, and more oriented to environmental issues, and challenging public spending cuts and privatization.[10]

The parliamentary parties

The collapse of the Soviet system in 1989 severely challenged the West European communist parties, but some parties, or fragments thereof, survived to reform and create new anti-capitalist alliances to the left of social democracy, often modernizing their left politics in an opening to green, feminist, anti-racist and anti-war concerns (Hudson 2002). During the 1990s, Members of the European Parliament (MEPs) of this political orientation began to work more closely together and by 1999 thirteen parties were able to launch a common platform at the European elections. They included *Rifondazione Comunista* (Communist Refoundation Party, PRC) in Italy and *Izquierda Unida* (United Left, IU) in Spain, which emerged from the struggle against Spain's accession to NATO in the late eighties. There was, and still is, no British party adhering to this union. Their theme included 'anti-neoliberalism, job creation, a tax on international capital flows, an end to privatization of the public sector, measures to combat racism, the cancelling of third world debt and the dissolution of NATO'. They subsequently took the name the European Left Party (EL).[11] Some members of the EL, and of EL-Fem, its women's organization, were active in the No-to-NATO mobilization.

Germany has its own rather successful Left Party, *Die Linke (DL)*, founded in 2007.[12] Also operating in this space to the left of social democracy, it plays a significant role in the European Left (EL). After German re-unification, the Socialist Unity Party (*Sozialistische Einheitspartei Deutschland*, SED) East Germany's ruling party, became the Party of Democratic Socialism (*Partei des Demokratischen Sozialismus*, PDS) 'embracing the democratic red, green, feminist and pacifist politics typical of the new European left' (Hudson 2009). The PDS subsequently formed an electoral alliance with the Labour and Social Justice Electoral Alternative (*Wahlalternative Arbeit & Soziale Gerechtigkeit*, WASG), won 54 seats in the Bundestag, and in 2007 merged to create the Left Party, *Die Linke*, subsequently absorbing several smaller entities on their left wing. *Die Linke* maintains a strong anti-war stance, and Tobias Pflüger, at that time a *Die Linke* MEP, played a leading role in the preparations for No-to-NATO's Strasbourg protests.

The French Communist Party (*Parti Communiste Français*, PCF) was among the French political parties supporting the No-to-NATO initiative. A survivor from the early years of the twentieth century, its membership declined during the nineties, and it gained a reputation as tending towards social democracy, due to its participation in the Mitterand government. In practice the PCF is allied in parliament with Greens and other left groups, and at Strasbourg its MEPs are part of the European Left (Hudson 2002).[13] To the left of the PCF in the French political scene, two brand new small parties were both in evidence at the No-to-NATO mobilization. The New Anti-Capitalist Party (*Le Nouveau Parti Anti-capitaliste*, NPA) has absorbed the membership of the former Communist Revolutionary League (*Ligue Communiste Révolutionnaire*, LCR) and drawn in new members from trade unions, the student movement and individuals of the non-party anti-capitalist left. It is attempting to be broader and less dogmatic than the Trotskyist LCR and, under the energetic leadership of Olivier Besancenot, had established 400 local branches and gained an estimated 10,000 members within a few weeks of its foundation in February 2009.[14] It profited from the widespread dissatisfaction with the Socialist Party, seen as incapable of challenging the unpopular presidency of Nicolas Sarkozy (Mullen 2009). The Left Party (*Parti de Gauche*, PG) was created almost simultaneously with NPA early in 2009.[15] It is led by former senator Jean Luc Mélenchon, accompanied by other defectors from the Socialist Party. Although, like the NPA, the PG claims a space to the left of the Socialist and Communist parties, it defines itself not as a revolutionary but a 'radical reformist' party. For electoral purposes it allies with the Communist Party against the NPA. The *Parti de Gauche* is inspired by its namesake, *Die Linke*, but is smaller, and lacks *Die Linke's* minority radical left elements (ibid.).

Radical left and anarchist tendencies

Besides the parliamentary parties mentioned above, the assembly of organizations mobilizing against the NATO Summit included an array of tendencies that keep a distance from the formal political sphere, significant among them the German Interventionist Left (*Interventionistische Linke*, IL).[16] The IL is a network providing a federal structure for relatively small anti-capitalist, anti-state and anti-fascist groups. It describes itself as of the 'undogmatic radical left', thereby marking a rejection of Communist, Marxist and Trotskyist rigidities and vanguardism. After experience of the divisive anti-neoliberal and *altermondialist* activism against a sequence of world economic summits, the intention of those who formed IL was, as a sympathetic article in *Red Pepper* put it, to help the radical left groups to emerge from 'their largely self-imposed isolation' and 'show a willingness to work together with those who have different goals'. While still being ready to 'push (even break) the boundaries of legality' the radicals should be prepared in some contexts to adapt to the wishes of the less militant (Trott 2007). *Interventionistische Linke* activists came to No-to-NATO fresh from a G8 Summit at Heiligendamm at which they had featured prominently in a high-profile civil disobedience action.[17]

The IL arises from and is related to the anarchist/libertarian *autonomen* (autonomist) groups of Germany, some of whom are its affiliates. Their history goes back to the late 1970s and 1980s, when they were active, on a larger scale than today, in the squatting movement and in demonstrations against nuclear energy and airport expansions. Some of these groups adhere to a principle of nonviolence, while others call for what is euphemistically termed 'tactical diversity', that is, not excluding attacks on state targets and property. Engaging in direct confrontation with the police and other authorities, it is they who furnish to various protest movements some of the element popularly known as 'the black bloc'. The *autonomen* are difficult to identify and locate, but their activities can be traced through a host of websites and blogs. Some have come together since as long ago as 1977 in an annual Federal Co-ordination for Internationalism (*Bundeskoordination Internationalismus*, BUKO). Their interest in No-to-NATO naturally inclined towards the proposed peace camp and direct action, variously interpreted.

Preparing a weekend of action: hopes and fears

One of the earliest moves for a mobilization in opposition to NATO's 60th-anniversary Summit was at a meeting in May 2008 of the above-named BUKO. From this had emerged an alliance of the Interventionist Left and other *autonomen* calling itself 'Bye-bye NATO' (Schmidt n.d.).[18] Around the same time, the more middle-of-the-road peace, anti-militarist and anti-war movements were holding meetings in Germany and France. On the French side, the *Mouvement de la Paix* and the *Ligue Communiste Revolutionnaire* participated, and on the German side, along with IL were the Federal Council Peace Forum of Kassel (*Bundesausschuss Friedensratschlag Kassel*), DFG-VK[19] and Representatives of the Left (*VertreterInnen der Linken*). Also involved was the international organization IALANA, the International Association of Lawyers against Nuclear Arms, whose director, Reiner Braun, would eventually become co-chair with Arielle Denis of the No-to-NATO International Co-ordinating Committee (ICC), and its effective convenor and facilitator. The two countries' movements came together at a meeting in

Stuttgart in October 2008 from which was issued the 'official' Appeal that organizations everywhere were invited to sign.[20] Some considered its authors had watered down the robust radicalism of the original 'Bye-Bye NATO' document earlier issued from BUKO. It now called for protest 'against NATO's aggressive military and nuclear policies' and observed that 'NATO is an increasing obstacle to achieving world peace', but omitted to identify NATO as an instrument for the security of the capitalist world order, and did not explicitly call for its dissolution. The proposal was for 'civil disobedience', without specific mention of 'blockades and encirclements'. Notwithstanding, most of the radical originators of the campaign signed this diminished call, in order to maintain and demonstrate the breadth of the anti-NATO alliance (Schmidt n.d.).

The first meeting of the ICC was held on 1 December 2008 in Brussels. The majority of the twenty-five participants were of the traditional European peace movement, plus ATTAC. War Resisters' International and Vredesactie, with their strong interest in nonviolent direct action, sent representatives. There were a number from the radical left of both 'dogmatic' and 'undogmatic' varieties, including the Interventionist Left (ibid.). Issues that preoccupied the ICC at this and subsequent meetings in the four months' run-up to the Summit weekend were the location of the mass demonstration and counter-conference; the policing policy of the French state; and the nature of the civil disobedience and its bearing on the other activities.[21] The peace and anti-war networks continually stressed the importance of mounting a very inclusive, maximally large and strictly nonviolent demonstration in the form of a rally and march. The organizers very much wished the demonstration to take place in the city and near to the venue of the Summit. The French authorities emphatically refused this, and insisted on a location that was well out of the public eye, seven kilometres from the city centre. Time and again the ICC urged the local French group *Collectif Strasbourg anti-OTAN* (COSTAU) to return to its negotiations with the Strasbourg municipal authority and insist on citizens' right to demonstrate in the city centre. But the authorities would not budge. As the weekend approached it became very clear that the security forces intended a massive presence in Strasbourg, and the No-to-NATO organizers were increasingly alarmed at the prospect of heavy confrontations between demonstrators and police.

Acute concern was also expressed, by the *Mouvement de la Paix* among others, about the handling of the civil disobedience. They were anxious that the ICC should not be seen as 'organizing' blockades. They worried, further, that the blockades, which must logically happen during the morning of the Saturday if they were to have a hope of impeding delegates' access to the Summit meeting, might aggravate the security forces who would then turn aggressively against the 'authorized' mass demonstration in the afternoon. There was little to be done about this, however, since civil disobedience was precisely what some – pacifist exponents of nonviolent direct action, and the radical left and *autonomen* partners – were in No-to-NATO for, and they were not going to relinquish it. Besides, in truth, though some of the big movements' representatives said 'cancel it' (by means unspecified, and difficult to imagine), many of the mainstream organizations themselves saw an element of civil disobedience as being within the logic of the whole mobilization.

The question was, however, just what civil disobedience might mean. The expression can be taken to mean nonviolent direct action. But it is an envelope that contains the possibility also of a violent strategy, and is sometimes knowingly used as a euphemism for this. The French and German mainstream were more alert to this sub-text than the British participants, accustomed to using the term to describe a practice of peacefully blockading, entering bases and so on. A particular ambiguity arose from the presence of the Interventionist Left in the ICC. IL does not take a position *for* violence, but as a network it is known to contain some groups that do delight in 'tactical diversity', a.k.a. 'broken glass', and, in the interests of holding together a broad alliance, it refuses to make a public *rejection* of violent methods.

Though the anxiety of the mainstream movements persisted, confrontation diminished as those who were into civil disobedience formed a sub-group that met separately as the Summit weekend approached, while maintaining a dialogue with the ICC. Their first meeting was in Offenburg in late November 2008. It was organized by *Résistance des Deux Rives – Widerstand der Zwei Ufer* (Resistance of the Two Shores, a local French/German anti-NATO group spanning the Rhine), the group that subsequently took on the organization of the peace camp. As to civil disobedience, there was agreement on blockading some major roads in Strasbourg to impede world leaders arriving at the Summit, but there was a divergence on methodology. Among those present at the meeting, the pacifist War Resisters' International, Vredesactie and others proposed making a clear and public commitment to nonviolence. Others, including the Interventionist Left, *Dissent!* (France and Germany), *Luttes Désobéissantes* (Disobedience Struggles), and *La Fédération Anarchiste* (the Anarchist Federation), whatever their actual intentions for the Summit weekend, preferred not to make a categorical statement of this kind. While the former group took the name NATO-ZU (Shut Down NATO), a more inclusive, and more ambiguous, group formed around them, taking the name Block NATO. NATO-ZU and Block NATO put out separate 'calls', the former stressing 'means appropriate to ends' and 'respect for the person', the latter using words like 'disruption', 'mass' and 'different forms of action'. The former announced their intentions publicly, the latter kept theirs secret.[22] However even Block NATO excluded the use of material blockades (such as vehicles or trees) and attacks on the police.[23] On the day of the Summit, NATO-ZU and Block NATO took responsibility for separate blockades.

Reasons for opposing NATO

The Summit weekend, 3–5 April 2009, a date so long marked on our calendars, rapidly approached. This would be one of the first overseas appearances of Barack Obama, newly elected US President. The NATO commanders and the Heads of State were looking forward to the perfect photo opportunity on the Bridge of Europe, spanning the Rhine between France and Germany. They anticipated modernizing NATO's Strategic Concept to secure its stake in the unfolding millennium.[24] The No-to-NATO activists for their part were looking forward to showing the world, by feet on the street, photos and video-clips on the Internet and articles in the media, that a lot of citizens consider NATO a threat to peace. A few – who knows how many – were looking forward to a ruckus. The police were not about to disappoint them. As the weekend approached an estimated 30,000 police gathered in and near Strasbourg. It was a clamp of steel, monitoring and impeding road and rail ingress to the city, and penetrating and patrolling all the public spaces of the centre, requiring residents to take down all political signs and slogans. Even rainbow peace flags were removed from balconies. So empty of ordinary life were the streets of Strasbourg when we arrived, it seemed that any resident with the means to get out of town for the weekend had fled.

Around forty women responded to our call, assembling in Strasbourg on the Thursday evening from eight different countries. Many reported difficulty getting through security checks as they approached the city. The next day, Friday, was devoted to the No-to-NATO counter-conference, held in a suburban sports complex. It was attended by more than eight hundred participants from twenty-five countries, although some, including several well-known individuals due to speak in the plenary, were barred from entering the city. Nonetheless, there was a pleasingly wide age-range at the conference, and a good mix of women and men.

So what was the case being made here against NATO? The No-to-NATO 'Strasbourg statement', and other papers circulated before the event and at the conference itself, showed the most fundamental question to be whether NATO should exist at all.[25] The North Atlantic Treaty was signed in 1949, to counter the threat of post-war expansion on the part of the Soviet Union. Its general objective was stated as being to safeguard the 'common heritage and civilisation' of its members (that is, the capitalist system) by promoting 'stability and well-being in the North Atlantic area'. In 1955 a Soviet bloc alliance, the Warsaw Pact, was established. When, 36 years later in 1991 the Soviet Union disintegrated and the Warsaw Pact dissolved, NATO persisted. In fact it started a new phase of growth, and its seemingly unstoppable expansion was a second issue addressed in the No-to-NATO analysis. In 1997 a NATO-Russian Permanent Joint Council was established to enable dialogue on security matters, but the relationship was continually strained by NATO's clear intention to scoop into its membership all the countries on Russia's western and southern flanks. Secretary General Jaap de Hoop Scheffer underlined that even the risk of deteriorating relations with Russia must not be allowed to 'derail NATO enlargement', which 'is not negotiable'.[26] There is pressure now on Sweden and Finland to sign up to NATO – because, with the melting of the Arctic ice cap, the far north is becoming an economically strategic zone (Oberg 2010). Particularly worrying is talk of Israel joining the alliance, and of NATO eventually taking over security missions in the West Bank and Gaza (Korski 2008).

In 1994 NATO established what it calls its Partnership for Peace, a device for holding close a group of more than twenty countries, stretching from the North Atlantic into the Caucasus and Central Asia. Add to this the Mediterranean Dialogue process, which draws Algeria, Egypt, Israel, Jordan, Mauritania, Morocco and Tunisia into the NATO net, and the Istanbul Initiative which assures a military link-up with Bahrain, Qatar, Kuwait and the United Arab Emirates. Beyond that, NATO has a list of even more far-flung states it calls 'contact countries' – including Australia, Japan and South Korea.[27] 'NATO is at the heart of a vast and expanding network of partnerships with countries from across the globe', proclaimed the Secretary General.[28] It is beginning to make more sense if, instead of asking 'who's in it?', we ask 'who isn't?'. NATO is clearly a project to line up as much of the world as possible behind the USA, while defining and isolating certain perceived enemies, among which Iran is currently significant.

A third worry about NATO stressed in the No-to-NATO analyses is its increasingly 'expeditionary' posture. Already in 1995, by sending the Implementation Force (IFOR) to Bosnia, NATO began engaging in military activities outside the geographical area of its formal remit. They had a UN mandate, but that was not the case in 1999 when NATO bombed Yugoslavia to drive Serb forces from Kosovo.[29] When US targets were attacked in 2001, supposedly by Al-Qaeda, NATO's Secretary General invoked Article 5 of the North Atlantic Treaty, which states that an attack on one signatory state will be considered an attack on all. NATO did not at first join the US and its allies in the bombardment of Afghanistan, but two years later it took strategic command of the UN-mandated peacekeeping force, ISAF, in and around the Afghan capital Kabul, whence it would radiate out to fight a hot war far from Europe.[30] This tendency to 'mission creep' by NATO is signalled by talk of a deepening engagement in Pakistan[31] and the potential for more activity in Africa (Korski 2008).

It is sometimes argued that NATO's very existence as a military alliance of Western states is in contradiction to the notion of global solidarity and internationally agreed structures for peace and security. In September 2008, notwithstanding the very different composition and the contrasted purpose of their institutions, NATO Secretary General Jaap de Hoop Scheffer and UN Secretary General Ban Ki Moon signed a UN-NATO Joint Declaration of Co-operation. It was not widely publicized and there was little media comment.[32] The Declaration spoke not only of 'consultation and dialogue and co-operation' but also of 'effective and efficient co-ordination between our Organizations' in dealing with the 'threats and challenges to which the international community is called upon to respond'. Many found this initiative by the UN Secretary General inappropriate. Article 1 of the UN Charter states that peace shall be brought about by peaceful means. NATO is a war-fighting alliance. While the UN Security Council's membership arrangement is designed to ensure inclusion of countries of the global South as a brake on the powerful states of the global North, NATO is clearly an alliance of relatively rich northern states, and is heavily dominated by the USA (Weyl 1999). Article 52 of the UN Charter does permit of the creation of 'regional alliances' in the furtherance of peace. But, given NATO's expansion, can it still be considered 'regional'? Given that NATO's member countries account for three-quarters of world military expenditure today,[33] it appears increasingly oppressive and overbearing. In view of the special status the accord with the UN now gives NATO, how will the Security Council be able to uphold the necessary distinctions between NATO actions and UN actions? Will it be able to challenge breaches of international law by NATO?[34]

Furthermore, the anti-militarist movements of the member states deplore NATO's role in militarization of the European Union, the development of a military capability over and above that of its separate member states. The EU, they point out, was devised as an economic union to prevent, not pursue, the historic militarism of the European nations. Yet the Maastricht Treaty of 1992 already envisaged an inter-governmental Common Foreign and Security Policy, and two years later NATO endorsed the concept of Combined Joint Task Forces. In 1996 foreign ministers agreed to build up what was termed a 'European Security and Defence Identity' within NATO, seen as a means of rebalancing roles and responsibilities between Europe and North America. Institutionalized relations between NATO and the EU began in 2000. The collaboration involves both 'strategic dialogue at the political headquarters level in Brussels' and permanent military liaison to ensure 'co-operation at the operational level'. In 2004 France, Germany and the UK launched the idea of establishing EU rapid reaction units composed of joint battle groups.[35]

NATO also excites the strenuous opposition of the peace movements of European countries on account of its nuclear arsenal. The Alliance disposes of the nuclear capability of France (348 warheads) and the UK (160 warheads) as well as hundreds of US warheads, some located in states that, having signed the Non-Proliferation Treaty, should be nuclear-free. Further, the USA depends on the co-operation of European countries for the deployment of its highly controversial 'missile defence' system, a militarization of outer space. Influential military thinkers close to NATO, in a radical 150-page manifesto for a new NATO published in January 2008, openly endorsed a 'first strike' policy in situations of severe international tension and to pre-empt threats from nuclear-armed enemy states (Traynor 2008).[36]

A feminist case against NATO

Our own workshop at the No-to-NATO counter-conference endorsed this general critique, and added to it a consideration of how NATO and all its works are gendered, and how they impact on women in particular. The participants were mainly from our three networks, but included also women from *La Marche Mondiale des Femmes*, the *Collectif Feministe 'Ruptures'*, El-Fem, *Die Linke* and other organizations. We had received twelve short written submissions in advance of the workshop and now presented a summary of their content under four themes, in order to prompt a discussion on strategies: what could we do in our localities, and together, as feminist women, to oppose the expansion of NATO and the militarization of the European Union?[37] Having no formal interpretation, we took great care to put the participants' own language skills to best use, dividing into five language groups in which those with good English interpreted for the others. Although it was certainly a strain to understand each other, evaluations of this process were positive.

NATO, nations and patriarchy

The first case the women were making against NATO concerned its role as an actor on the world stage – in diplomacy, international relations and military policy. Margherita Granero and Anna Valente of *Donne in Nero* (Women in Black), Torino, Italy, pointed to the way NATO perpetuates the 'bloc logic' of the Cold War era. Women, they wrote, don't recognize themselves in this discourse of 'Atlantic alliance', 'European fortress', and 'Western civilization'. Other participants too felt NATO by definition marks some nations out as Others, threatening gross *in*security to those outside the compliant coalition.

Furthermore, NATO reinforces the idea that nation-states are the only units that count in world affairs. Along with the concept of nation as 'fatherland' or 'motherland' goes the racist idea of blood and belonging. Feminism absolutely rejects this, as dividing women on ethnic grounds and setting up women as the reproducers of race and culture, the ones who pass on the nation's bloodline to their children (Yuval-Davis 1997). Secondly, it reinforces the sense that these nations are in a natural hierarchy of strong and weak. In NATO, the USA represents itself as a protector of its weaker junior partners. Women do not welcome this 'husband and wife' model of human relations. So NATO's logic is condemned as a *patriarchal logic*. All of us have learned in these years of feminist anti-militarist theorizing and practice that nationalism, capitalism and patriarchy are deeply intersected and reinforce each other. Together they foster militarism and war. Nelly Martin, of *La Marche Mondiale des Femmes*, Paris, added, 'patriarchy and capitalism use war to maintain their dominion'.

Strategies of action at the international level are not easy to identify. But if, as *Mujeres de Negro*, Sevilla, wrote, we can 'crack the code of patriarchy', if we can see through it, we can understand that it is pure myth that international relations is something that takes place in the stratosphere, out of our reach, as diplomats and military policy-makers would like us to think. In reality they affect our daily lives, they are our natural concern, and it cannot be beyond our imagination to intervene as women and as feminist anti-militarists. Monique Dental gave an example. Her organization, the *Collectif Feministe 'Ruptures'*, with other organizations, had petitioned the French President during the Gulf War with a 'Women Citizens' Letter' calling for an international peace conference.

NATO's overbearing presence in member states

NATO has a very tangible presence in our countries – with bases, installations and production facilities surrounded by razor wire and security checkpoints. The paper by Simona Ricciardelli of *Donne in Nero*, Napoli, was outspoken against the impact of these on peoples' well-being. Italy is effectively 'a US aircraft carrier in the Mediterranean Sea'. Naples and its region is massively militarized, Simona says, because it is NATO's 'frontline for preventive wars against the Middle East and the African continent'. 'Neapolitans are at war,' she concluded, 'and they don't even know it.' Not only does the NATO weaponry threaten a supposed 'enemy', it is a security risk to local communities that host it. UK women stressed potential radiation hazard around the Atomic Weapons Establishment at Aldermaston. One of the ways we can see 'security' to be a deceptive notion, we argued, is that 'the nuclear umbrella also poisons those it's supposed to shelter, bringing risk of accident, explosion and radiation, turning us into targets'. But there are other pollutants too. The military often relocate from one place to another, leaving local people to speculate on what toxins are buried in their neighbourhood, and how a trash-filled site can ever be restored to life.

Then there is the more intimate matter of the sexual exploitation of women by military personnel. Sian Jones, active in Women in Black London and the Aldermaston Women's Peace Camp, contributed a paper detailing how NATO military personnel in Bosnia and Herzegovina, and in Kosovo, as well as in 'rest and relaxation' zones in Macedonia, have exploited women trafficked for forced prostitution. While NATO has a formal policy against trafficking it does not explicitly or effectively prohibit NATO forces from involvement in it. As it is, along with NATO contractors and UN police, NATO military personnel have been 'actively involved in the trafficking process, receiving trafficked women and girls at borders, smuggling them into military bases and acting as pimps'. With very few exceptions NATO military personnel who commit such crimes escape punishment due to the functional immunity from prosecution furnished by the terms under which the missions operate. During the trafficking process, Sian Jones' paper continued, 'women are coerced, threatened, beaten and raped by their traffickers to keep them compliant. Their documents are taken away, their movement is controlled, they are often imprisoned. The promised wages often don't materialize'. And even when women have not, as in this case, been forcibly trafficked, wrote Nelly Martin, of *La Marche Mondiale des Femmes*, France, their prostitution is often the result of having lost all other options for supporting themselves and their children because they are in flight from war, or have been rejected by their communities after being the victims of rape.

The militarization of daily life

Several of the papers submitted to the feminist workshop deplored the way NATO's strategies increase the militarization of everyday life and culture in our countries and regions. 'Militarism has widened in scope and intensity to become, like war itself, intrinsic to civil life and democracy,' wrote Margherita Granero and Anna Valente of *Donne in Nero*, Torino. 'It has become the Western way of life.' First, military budgets drain funding from education, health and housing services. Ana Azaria, of *Femmes Egalité*, Paris, added, 'When you are laid off, when your fixed-term contract is not renewed, when you struggle to pay always more for less and when at the beginning of the month your wallet is already empty ... you have nothing to gain from an increase of military spending'.

We saw in Chapter 3 how in the 1980s the anti-militarist movement campaigned fiercely but unsuccessfully against Spain's membership of NATO. Women of *Mujeres de Negro* (Women in Black), Sevilla, wrote now that this new phase of their national militarization, sold to them as something distant that would barely affect them, had 'actually poisoned our lives and installed itself ineluctably into our interpersonal relationships ... relationships of hierarchy, fear, oppression and arrogance'. Living up to NATO's expectations, Spain had started recruiting women to the military. In this way and many others women have felt how 'the long tentacles of patriarchal power, through the military system, reach into and contaminate every inch of our lives'. The military institution, wrote Nelly Martin, 'contributes in various ways to training young men to occupy their dominant place in the social relations of gender'. It is 'unfortunately a reference for growing young people'. The paper from Women in Black London added that the 'hyped-up violence in popular cultures, especially youth cultures, and specific forms of criminality including gun ownership' are examples of the militarization of everyday life. And Simona Ricciardelli wrote of how the military model shrinks women's citizenship rights and regulates interpersonal relations.

Security is represented by the military as defence against enemies abroad. However the surveillance is readily turned inward. NATO's retiring Secretary General wrote in the run-up to the Summit of NATO's need to forge closer links with political authorities, NGOs and other civilian institutions.[38] This threatens more spying on citizens, often selectively according to racist criteria, and leads to an erosion of civil liberties, wrote London WiB. NATO is recognizing that the 'risks' its security apparatus faces are actually not posed by foreign 'enemies' but by circumstances 'at home', such as depletion of the ozone layer by CO_2 emissions, fuel shortages and inward migration. Christiane Reymann, of EL-Fem, Berlin, wrote that even if migrants to Europe survive the watery grave of the Mediterranean they sink into miserable poverty and lack of rights in their countries of destination. Many feminist groups in Europe are concerned with the plight of women asylum-seekers in their countries. Just what can NATO, for all its huge budgets, contribute to averting such domestic hazards as these?

NATO as a perpetrator of wars

Finally, NATO is a war-making machinery and women have a great deal to say about wars. 'War always buries humankind's hopes for freedom and democracy,' wrote Monique Dental, *Collectif Feministe 'Ruptures'*, Paris. Irmgard Heilberger of WILPF, Munich, contributed a schematic map of NATO's effects, among which are wars inflicting trauma on body and soul. Civilians, predominantly women, suffer an increasing proportion (90 per cent in recent conflicts) of war casualties. They are the great majority of refugees, trying to keep dependents safe, fed and sheltered. 'Violence against women and girls in situations of conflict and post-conflict is extreme, systematic and general,' wrote Monique. Reduced to the rank of objects, the property of men, women are regarded as the 'spoils of war', 'bargaining chips', and the 'rest and recreation of warriors'. Rape is used to humiliate, shame and demoralize the enemy, as a means of propaganda, or as a means of ethnic cleansing, added Nelly Martin. 'War is easier for men, they just die, sometimes even as heroes. We women must cope with the burden of survival for years and years,' a Bosnian woman had told Marlène Tuininga of *Femmes en Noir Paris* and WILPF. Sometimes, though, as Marlène observed, 'staying behind or fleeing with their children, they develop unknown qualities and a new solidarity'. Women's anti-militarist movements often arise out of the empathy and common sense born among women because of their direct experience of conflict.

Annelise Ebbe, from Denmark, WILPF's International President, devoted her paper to addressing the war being waged in Afghanistan by twenty-six NATO member states, and the claim, among others, that it is improving Afghan women's wellbeing. A study by Womankind Worldwide had found, to the contrary, that 87 per cent of Afghan women report violent abuse, the illiteracy rate among women is 88 per cent, and one in nine women in Afghanistan dies in childbirth.[39] As Ana Azarias of *Femmes Egalité*, France, observed, 'After having reduced women to a state of destitution and poverty where the only right they have won is to live in conditions of total insecurity, after all this, still daring to affirm that this war is aimed at liberating women amounts to huge hypocrisy'.

The rally goes up in flames

So our workshop was deemed useful by many of those who took part. 'We brought to the conference a good dose of alternative thinking, very much our own and rather different from that of the other participating groups,' Sofía Segura Herrera wrote later. With our workshop, stalls and a couple of photographic wall displays we had made ourselves and our analysis visible at a conference in which women speakers were few and feminist speakers fewer, where the high-profile protagonists were men and the style was often militant. The weather was benign and the sports centre provided for an outside grassy space where people gathered to chat over food and drink. There was 'a climate of tranquility and co-operation', as Sofía put it.

The next day, the day of street actions, the weather held – the tranquillity did not. Many of us had hoped we might make ourselves visible in the city centre, in the busy Place Kléber, the normal vigil site of *Femmes en Noir* (Women in Black) Strasbourg, standing for an hour or two to put over our 'Women say No to NATO' message, in French, to passers-by. The local women, however, pointed out that there was no public to see us. The city this weekend was more dead than alive. Secondly, they were sure that if the ubiquitous police so much as glimpsed a placard or banner we would be apprehended. So a decision was made that we would all go directly to the site of the mass rally, far from the city centre but at least officially approved.

The ground designated for the rally was an open space of gravel known as the *champ de foire*, the fair ground, in the docklands between the canals and the river Rhine, seven kilometres by road from the city centre. Already by the Saturday morning, 4 April, bus and tram services were reduced to a minimum in Strasbourg and by the afternoon all public transport, including taxis, had been closed down. And so we walked the long road out of town, across the canals and into the docks. At the *champ de foire*, the women of *Femmes en Noir* led us through the gathering crowd to the front of the podium where we formed a long line, holding many colourful banners of WiB, WILPF and other women's organizations, and placards in several languages. We maintained our silent stand there for well over an hour, our feminist message clearly visible. But to whom? Only to fellow demonstrators. As the authorities intended, we were not seen by a single member of the public. We ourselves, however, had a vantage point from which we could see in the distance, gathering at the canal bridges, closing our return route to the city, large numbers of security vehicles and massed ranks of police in black-padded riot gear and helmets. The authorities, it became clear, had already penned us into the desolate area of the Rhine Port (*Port du Rhin*). We could see, to our right, the other side of a high brick wall, a district of working-class housing, with some flats, two hotels and a couple of churches. In front and to the left was a wilderness of railway sidings and goods yards. Behind us the police controlled the highway to the Bridge of Europe.

Demonstrators assembled gradually at the rally, but fewer than expected. Speakers from the stage told us that many coach-loads had been halted on the road to Strasbourg and several thousand German demonstrators were immobilized in Kehl, at the approach to the Bridge of Europe. They would not be allowed to cross the Rhine to join us. As we waited, listening to the speakers, a plume of black smoke rose from the residential area beyond the wall. Then another, and another. As smoke drifted low over the crowd, it caused coughing, gasping and fear. It precipitated a decision by the organizers to set off. But where? Should we process futilely round and round this industrial wasteland for the amusement of the watching police? A spokesman of the ICC, speaking over the loud hailer, instead called on the demonstrators to set off at speed towards the distant canal bridges. Some of us may still have hoped to form an orderly women's bloc in an orderly march. No way. What followed was not a march but a stampede.

It is ironic that the *champ de foire* is marked on the map of Strasbourg as the '*Square des Fusillés de 15 Juillet 1943*', commemorating a Second World War execution on this ground. The crowd headed for the only exits from from this bloody historic site – two tunnels beneath the railway embankment. But it now became clear that while we had been gathering at the rally, numbers of individuals in 'black bloc' style, their faces masked by hoods and scarves, had been running through the residential area, breaking the glass of petrol stations, bus shelters and phone booths, and ripping out street signs. The smoke had been caused by the torching of a hotel, a local pharmacy and an abandoned border post building. Now the black-clad figures mingled with the crowd. The police closed in, using tear gas, pepper spray, sound-shock grenades and water cannon. Some canisters were dropped from a helicopter low overhead.

Our group of women was split and scattered in the rush. Some tried to pass under the railway bridges, squeezing past police vans. But black bloc characters on the tracks above were raining down stones and lumps of concrete. So some chose the only alternative, clambering up the high embankment and across the railway line, crawling under rolling stock, slipping and sliding down the other side. One who took this route was Martine Toulotte of WILPF, Grenoble. She has a disability that means she must walk with crutches. She wrote later that she had at first searched fruitlessly for banners of recognizable organizations to follow as the crowd rushed by:

> There was nothing but people in black … I took my friend's arm and stayed on the edge so as not to be trampled in the rush. We could no longer move forward. We tried to go left, then right. Impossible. We were cornered. All around were people trying to find a way. We were in a crumbling mass of huge blocks of concrete. The railway embankment stretched ten metres above us. We climbed up it, slid, climbed again. We got out of the debris to find ourselves nose to nose with police lorries with officers inside them. Suddenly a lorry set off at speed. We jumped onto the pavement so as not to be hit.

Once out of the *champ de foire* some women headed for the canal bridges and tried in vain to pass the police barricades in order to get back to town. Some walked for kilometres round a military airfield looking for an alternative route. Some sat it out until, as evening approached, the police begin to allow people through, a few at a time. For a lucky few the day was redeemed by the kindliness of local people they met on their wanderings. Ursula Gelis wrote, 'A French couple invited us into their home, where we were introduced to their three daughters. We had a nice chat, people became interested in WILPF. They looked us up on the Web. The father told his children that the girls should follow our footsteps.' But it was ten in the evening before the last of our women made it back to our meeting place in town.

Picking through the ashes

We invited evaluations of the day from the women who had answered our call to come to Strasbourg. Not only our own, but many other accounts of the day pronounced this one of the worst-handled demonstrations anyone could remember.[40] The authorities were blamed for impeding access to the demonstration and denying our right to a meaningful, safe and central site in which to gather. The security sector was blamed for its overbearing and over-armed police presence, and for having attacked demonstrators in military style while neglecting to extinguish fires and treating with contempt the well-being of local people. The organizers of the demonstration were blamed for their capitulation to the authorities' imposition of an untenable site, for irresponsibility in launching the crowd against the police barricades and for negligence in having failed to foresee and forestall the violence among the demonstrators. They had neglected to provide sufficient trained and identifiable stewards, first aid units and legal advisers. The violent demonstrators, mainly but not exclusively young and male, were bitterly condemned for putting demonstrators' safety at risk and destroying the public image of the peace movement. They had trashed public amenities in a poor working-class area, regardless of the cost to its inhabitants. They were also blamed for exposing the movement to *agents provocateurs*, for some had observed balaclava-wearing figures chatting with uniformed police, even being ferried in police vehicles. And who gained most from the fact that in the following days all the public saw of No-to-NATO on TV, in the press and on the Internet, was smoke and flames?

We of the women's mobilization, however. also blamed ourselves for our misjudgment. We had been naïve in believing the organizers' claim that the demonstration would be nonviolent. We should have prepared as if for a civil disobedience action, in the way many of us are well familiar with. We should have taken steps the day before to form affinity groups of three or four women who would stay together, no matter what. We should have discussed together the potential dangers, equipped ourselves against tear gas with masks and scarves, and organized a training with role play to prepare us for dealing with the police and violent demonstrators. We should have studied the terrain, made sure everyone had maps, mobile phones and a list of numbers, first aid materials, water and food. Above all, during the rally, we should not have complied with the blustering call of that male voice over the loud-hailer urging us to march into chaos.

All of us put some effort in the following weeks into learning lessons from that day. It had been the biggest ever mobilization against NATO, with an estimated 40,000 demonstrators, notwithstanding the official obstruction that kept thousands more sitting at the French frontier. But the police and the black bloc had dictated the course of events and we felt we had lacked choice or influence. It led us to reaffirm the value of small, local actions that can be creative and educational, and operate beneath the radar of the security services. Anna Gyorgy and I represented our group at some of the evaluative meetings organized by the ICC in the weeks that followed the Strasbourg Summit. The issue of violence was central to the agenda. The divergences that had been apparent in the planning for the Summit weekend re-emerged in the aftermath. On the one hand there were the peace and anti-war movements, together with the main political parties, whose cherished project had been a nonviolent mass demonstration. They were bitterly disappointed in the outcome, mortified by the authorities' success in preventing many thousands of people reaching Strasbourg and the *Port du Rhin*, and effectively immobilizing those who did. They were shocked and angered by the intrusion of the masked individuals, set on attacking the police and destroying property. Who were they? Some were certainly from among the French anarchist and German *autonomen* groups, their actions deliberate and strategic. Some were thought to be disaffected French working-class youth, spontaneously hitting out at the state. But had the French security services had been involved as *agents provocateurs*? If so, it was clearly not the whole story, since some activists were openly if anonymously describing and acknowledging their actions, including the arson, on the Internet. While some openly celebrated the destruction,[41] others were self-questioning.[42]

There were some on the ICC, from the French left and IL, who undoubtedly knew who had been involved in the demonstrator violence. They had not themselves welcomed it, but were unwilling to have the ICC make a public statement condemning it. No such statement was issued, although some individuals were outspoken in media interviews. Kate Hudson, chair of CND, wrote an emphatic blog: 'These people are no part of our movement. They are an obstacle to effective resistance and must be isolated and recognized for what they are: wreckers whose actions turned the mass of people against our campaigns.'[43] She felt the ICC had been wrong from the outset to include among its members representatives of groups that refused to condemn violence.[44]

Strong determination was expressed to press on with No-to-NATO campaigns at future Summits, but there were differences of opinion on how to avoid a recurrence of violence. Some of the organizing group wanted to take a proactive approach, to identify and exclude the violent element. Others felt, well, you can't stop them. Boys will be boys. So long as they go and play somewhere else. A different view was expressed to me in interview later by John Rees, who had been involved with the ICC meetings as a representative of the UK's Stop the War Coalition. If you have a position of responsibility in the movement, he felt, you should not minimize and marginalize these groups in such a way. 'They shouldn't just be seen as expendable. That has too often been the attitude to us, to the revolutionary left.' Just as it is important to be wide enough on the one hand to draw in liberals, Rees feels, so you should be inclusive in the other direction, towards the *autonomes*. As to confrontation, that is inevitable, he says:

> You are up against imperialism and the state. You have to be strong enough to stand up to them. Police tactics have changed – they are bringing violence to us, not we to them. There is a problem with the left. It doesn't look radical enough to draw young people behind it. Instead of chopping off the radical bits of the movement, you have to create a pole of attraction to draw young people around you, then you can have a sensible discussion about the difference between mass resistance and autonomist tactics.

The point we contributed to this *post-mortem* was that, as feminists, we were concerned with the whole force-spectrum of violence, from nuclear weapons at one end to the daily and ubiquitous violence against women at the other. Violent activism in the peace movement lay somewhere in the middle of that spectrum, and we felt we should address it. Fine. But how? No more than the others did we have a practical answer to this question. Fortunately, the NVDA groups had already modelled a response, spending the week of the Summit engaging intensively with the perpetrators of violence. The activists' peace camp out in the fields at La Ganzau had been beset from the start by people wrecking cars, burning hay bales and spoiling for a fight, and this had drawn several tear gas attacks on the camp by the police. Reports by Angie Zelter of Trident Ploughshares[45] and Andreas Speck of War Resisters' International,[46] two groups centrally involved in the camp, show the continual efforts made by NATO-ZU activists during the week, and with some success, to de-escalate the violence in the camp.

However, most of the experienced practitioners of nonviolence, whose skills might have had a calming effect at the demo, were otherwise engaged. It is ironic that while the demonstration so desired by the peace movements and the parties had fallen into shambles, the civil disobedience they so feared turned out to be the most effective anti-NATO activity of the weekend, and of exemplary nonviolence. Three separate blockades by NATO-ZU and Block NATO, involving an estimated thousand people in total, succeeded in closing roads to the Summit conference centre from 7am, significantly disrupting traffic throughout the morning. These blockades were the positive result of several days of painstaking organization in the camp, during which affinity groups formed and came together in spokes-councils to coordinate decisions. Trainings were mounted and NATO-ZU met with the police, telling them in advance, without specifying precise locations, of their intention to blockade roads. When the moment came, the blockades were achieved with good humour and without violence. The police responded in two out of the three cases with tear gas, but did not persist in their harassment, and when the blockaders disbanded they did so voluntarily.

The counter-Summit conference had continued on the Sunday of the Summit weekend. A lesson had been learned on the first day, and this time efforts were made by the No-to-NATO facilitators to ensure women's voices were heard, both from the platform and the floor. There was less patience now with the hectoring male voices when they persisted as before, fists metaphorically raised, blaming the USA, NATO, the state – anybody but our movement, and anybody but men – for violence. One such speaker provoked Lisa Rigby to leap to her feet and shout, in desperation, 'Young women want peace!' She and Penny Stone, from Edinburgh CND, then invited anyone who might wish to join them in going to the Bridge of Europe, now opened as usual to transport and pedestrians moving between France and Germany. We could have a different kind of demonstration, they suggested, an act of peace. In this way fourteen or fifteen women and men walked up onto the bridge and formed a line along the pavement. One carried a baby in a sling. The green river coiled below us. On the French bank, smoke still rose from the embers of the customs post. Traffic streamed slowly in both directions across this border between France and Germany. There were a lot of Sunday trippers, come to stare in amazement at the wreckage. We held our rainbow banners, *PACE*. We sang some gentle songs, and spoke quietly to the passing pedestrians and families in their slowly moving cars, windows open on this sunny afternoon. We said 'nous refusons la violence', 'non à toute violence'. Some frowned and looked away. But more smiled and nodded. We only stayed a little while. Then we went home by bus and tram through a city that had returned to perfect normality.

Notes

1. Announced in March 2009.
2. Online at: www.no-to-nato.org/en/appeal (accessed 31 March 2009).
3. Website: www.mvtpaix.org.
4. Website: www.cnduk.org.
5. Website: www.stopwar.org.uk.
6. Website: www.swp.org.uk.
7. See the English flyer at their website: www.koop-frieden.de/./kooperation/Flyer_engl_2.pdf.
8. They appear to have no website, but see www.ag-friedensforschung.de/rat/.
9. Website: www.friedenskooperative.de.
10. The website of French ATTAC is www.attac.org; that of German ATTAC is www.attac.de.
11. Website: www.european-left.org.
12. Website: www.die-linke.de.
13. Website: www.pcf.fr.
14. Website: www.npa2009.org.
15. Website: www.lepartidegauche.fr.
16. Website: http://interventionistische-linke.org.
17. 'Call to Action by the Interventionist Left: Make Capitalism History', at: www.autistici.org/g8/eng/news/interventionist-left (accessed 1 June 2009).
18. Reference here is to an English translation, 'NATO is having its birthday party – we are celebrating with them!', source unknown. In addition to Schmidt (n.d.) see: www.dazwischengehen.org/de/story/2008/09/eckpunkte-des-buendnisses-bye-bye-nato (accessed 12 December 2010).
19. *Deutsche Friendensgesellschaft – Vereinigte Kriegsdienstverweigerer* (German Peace Society and United Conscientious Objectors, the contemporary form of DVG-IDK, see Chapter 2, p. 50).
20. 'No to war, No to NATO' Appeal. Online at: www.no-to-nato.org/en/appeal (accessed 31 March 2009).
21. Susy Snyder, representing WILPF, attended the international meeting at Stuttgart in October 2008. I attended an ICC meeting in Paris on 12 January 2009. Irmgard Heilberger (WILPF), Anna Gyorgy (WLOE), Marlène Tuininga (WiB and WILPF Paris) and I (WiB and WILPF London) attended the preparatory Activists' Conference in Strasbourg on 14–15 February 2009.
22. Online at: www.natozu.de/index.php?id=44 and http://block-nato.org/index_en.htm (accessed 9 May 2011).
23. Report of a Block-NATO meeting in Strasbourg on 7–9 March 2009, online at: http://wri-irg.org/node/7031 (accessed 9 May 2011).
24. 'The Alliance's Strategic Concept: approved by the Heads of State and Government participating in the meeting of the North Atlantic Council in Washington DC', 24 April 1999. From NATO's website: http://nato.int/cps/en/natolive/official_texts_27433.htm (accessed 12 May 2009).
25. Online at: www.no-to-nato.org/en/strasbourg2009 (accessed 9 May 2011).
26. 'NATO at 60: the Way Forward'. Remarks by Jaap de Hoop Scheffer, NATO retiring Secretary General prior to the Strasbourg/Kehl Summit, 9 February, 2009, at: www.nato.int/docu/review/2009/0902/090205/EN/index.htm (accessed 12 May 2009).

27. 'Profile: NATO'. BBC News online at: http://news.bbc.co.uk/1/hi/world/europe/country_profiles/1549072.stm (accessed 13 August 2010).
28. As footnote 26.
29. As footnote 27.
30. As footnote 27.
31. As footnote 26.
32. 'Joint Declaration on UN/NATO Secretariat Co-operation'. Originally from www.nato.int/docu/update/2007/01-january/e0124a.html, cited in commentary by the Transnational Foundation for Peace and Future Research (TFF), 3 December 2008, online at: www.transnational.org (accessed 12 May 2009).
33. As footnote 27.
34. As footnote 32.
35. 'NATO's Relations with the European Union', at: www.nato.int/issues/nato-eu/index.html (accessed 29 May 2009).
36. Roundly condemned by the Campaign for Nuclear Disarmament, who called it 'insane and illegal'. At: www.cnduk.org/index.php/20080122475/press-releases/global-abolition/threat-of-pre-emptive-nuclear-strikes-by-nato-drives-insecurity.html (accessed 8 June 2009).
37. The papers can be seen online at: www.wloe.org/Workshop-papers.551.0.html (accessed 30 May 2011).
38. As footnote 26.
39. 'Taking Stock: Afghanistan Women and Girls Seven Years On', a paper by Womankind Worldwide online at: www.womankind.org.uk/news-and-events.html (accessed March 2009).
40. See, for instance, Elsa Rassbach, 'NATO Demo in Strasbourg Ends in Disarray Following Attacks by "Hooligans" and Police', online at: www.gipfelsoli.org/Home/Strasbourg_Baden-Baden_2009/NATO_2009_english/6706.html; and Diana Johnstone, 'Ingredients for a Disaster: NATO, Strasbourg and the Black Bloc' at: www.counterpunch.org/johnstone04072009.html.
41. See, for instance, the statement by Autonome Antifa online at: www.autonome-antifa.org/spip.php?page=antifa&id_article=148&design=2 (accessed 9 May 2011).
42. Notably, an anonymous article 'Apres avoir tout brulé?' and ensuing discussion, online at Indymedia, July 2009: www.indymedia.org/fr/. For further discussion see Chapter 9, pp. 249–50.
43. Online at www.cnduk.org/index.php/kate-hudson-s-blog/the-battle-of-strasbourg.html (accessed 30 May 2011).
44. In interview with the author.
45. Online at www.wri-irg.org/note/7468 (accessed 1 June 2009).
46. Online at: www.wri-irg.org/note/7275 (accessed 1 June 2009).

6
Seeing the Whole Picture: Anti-militarism in Okinawa and Japan*

Cynthia Cockburn and Naoko Ikeda†

At the southern extreme of Japan's archipelago, deep in the East China Sea, is a string of one hundred and sixty islands and islets: Okinawa. Together they add up to only 0.6 per cent of the land area of Japan, and their 1.4 million inhabitants are little more than one in a hundred of the Japanese population. Yet this remote southernmost prefecture bears fully three-quarters of the concrete and asphalt, razor wire

---

*In the research on which this chapter draws we were afforded interviews by the following people to whom we would like to express our warmest gratitude for the generosity with which they shared their insights into the anti-war, anti-militarist, peace and feminist movements of Okinawa and Japan: Atsushi Tougoku of the Article 9 Association; Hiroji Yamashiro of the Okinawa Peace Movement Center and Prefectural Peoples' Conference; Hiromi Minamoto, radio journalist, and member of Okinawa Women Act against Military Violence (OWAAMV); Hiroshi Ashitomi of the Conference Opposing Heliport Construction (Nago City); Hisako Motoyama of the Asia-Japan Women's Resource Centre (AJWRC); Ichiyo Muto of People's Plan Study Group; Katsuaki Ando of Iraq Peace TV; Kaz Tamaki and Kim Maria of Peace Depot; Professor Kim Pu Ja of the Violence against Women in War Network Japan; Professor Kozue Akibayashi and her students at Kyoto University who constitute the Kyoto branch of the Women's International League for Peace and Freedom; Maki Okada, journalist and member of the Article 9 Association; Mariko Yokota of Okinawa Peace Network; Masaru Shiroma of Okinawa Citizens Peace Network; Mina Watanabe of the Women's Active Museum; Mitsuo Sato of the Japan Peace Committee; Muneyoshi Kanou and other members of the Life Protection Association in Henoko; Professor Michiko Nakahara of the Violence against Women in War Network Japan; Shinsaku Nohira of Peace Boat; Shikou Sakiyama of the Okinawa Peace Movement Center and Prefectural Peoples' Conference; Shimizu Akira of the Takae Residents Group against Helipads; Shinichi Kawamitsu of Okinawa Peace Network; Shinichiro Tsukada of Peace Depot; Suzuyo Takazato of Okinawa Women Act against Military Violence (OWAAMV); and Youichi Komori of the Article 9 Association.

and weaponry with which the United States of America burdens the Japanese people under the terms of the US-Japan Security Treaty. This chapter looks at the Okinawan movement of opposition to the US bases, and in particular the part of women's activism, in the context of the wider Japanese anti-war, anti-militarist and peace movements.

The islands now known as Okinawa were once the kingdom of Ryukyu, an independent political entity that had a trading and tributary relationship with China. In the seventeenth century the Japanese Shogunate began to see Ryukyu as a valuable foothold from which to secure its own economic relationship with China. It despatched the army of its most influential noble family, the Satsuma clan, to occupy the islands (Morris-Suzuki 1998). In the eighteenth century, as Japan came under growing pressure from the colonial powers to open up to European commercial and cultural penetration, the feudal regime gave way to a modernized Imperial State of Japan (*Dainippon Teikoku*), which now extended its administration into previously neglected peripheral regions, including Ryukyu. In 1879 the islands, renamed, were fully incorporated into Japan. In the following decades, while waging imperialist wars against China (1894–95) and Russia (1904–05), and colonizing

We would also like to express our thanks to the following who in various ways guided us in our work: Aya Takeuchi of *Femin* Journal; Eiko Asato, Okinawan historian; Fumika Sato of the Graduate School of Social Sciences, Hitotsubashi University; Professor Harumi Miyagi, historian, of Okinawa Women Act Against Military Violence; Professor Kimiko Kimoto of the Centre for Gender Research and Social Science (CGRASS), Hitotsubashi University; Kosuzu Abe, of the Project Disagree, International Relations, Okinawa Kokusai University; Makiko Matsumoto of Feminist Active Video; Michiko Taba, a protester at the Shinjuku vigil; and Yoshiko Ashiwa of the Centre for the Study of Peace and Reconciliation (CSPR), Hitotsubashi University.

We benefited from group discussions with many others in the course of various encounters. We particularly valued meetings with members of The Women's International League for Peace and Freedom in Kyoto, seminars organized by Okinawa Women Act against Military Violence in Naha City, and by CGRASS and CSPR at Hitotsubashi University, and a workshop organized for us by AJWRC. We very much appreciate the sustained advice and guidance of Ichiyo Muto of People's Plan Study Group. Finally, our very special thanks to Suzuyo Takazato of OWAAMV, who unstintingly shared with us her time, her friends and her thoughts. Without her this study would not have been possible. This chapter owes much to the experience and wisdom of those named above. It is important to stress however that any errors or misjudgments that may regrettably remain in this chapter are entirely our own responsibility.

† Naoko Ikeda is a Doctoral Candidate, York University, Toronto.

Korea (1910), Japan assimilated Okinawans to create the modern state. Educational, cultural and economic institutions were reformed so as to impose Japanese (*yamato*) identity, inferiorizing and marginalizing Ryukyuan languages and cultures. Notwithstanding, Okinawans today continue to feel significantly 'different': the *yamato* are 'not us'.[1]

The colonization and absorption of Okinawa is part of a wider and deeper history of racist domination in Japan. The state is continually represented in authoritative discourse as an 'ethnically homogeneous nation', in systematic delegitimation not only of Ryukyuan but of any other self-proclaimed minority identity. The *Ainu* of Northern Japan, and other less numerous 'first nation' peoples, are invisibilized. The claim of rights by the *burakumin*, people of a lower economic caste associated from feudal times with 'unclean' occupations, is denied. The many Korean residents of Japan are stigmatized as *zainichi*, and economic migrants from other neighbouring countries, even when they have acquired resident's rights, continue to be viewed as alien. The state perceives these differences, including that of the Ryukyuan people, not as enriching the nation but as 'frontiers' to be overcome in establishing the transhistoric Japanese subject (Morris-Suzuki 1998). Though minorities, sometimes with the support of the UN and other international agencies, have protested against their treatment, the Japanese state has consistently refused to concede their rights (Human Rights Now 2009).

War, occupation and war again

The closing moments of the Second World War were traumatic in the extreme for Okinawans. The five-year conflict in the Pacific had begun with the Japanese assault on the US fleet at Pearl Harbour in the Hawai'ian islands. Its final stage began when the US landed a large force on these other islands, Okinawa, which were defended fiercely by the Japanese military, intent on preventing a land invasion of the mainland. It is believed that a quarter of the Ryukyuan population may have died in the Battle of Okinawa and its aftermath. Many Okinawans were killed by US forces, but the Japanese Imperial army also treated the despised Okinawan people with great brutality. Rather than protecting the civilian population, they used them as human shields, and, when surrender looked inevitable, instructed them to commit suicide rather than fall into American hands. They also reportedly shot thousands of Okinawans without trial, accusing them of spying for the Americans (Cooley and Marten 2006).

On 6 August 1945 the USA detonated an atomic bomb over the city of Hiroshima, and three days later a similar weapon over Nagasaki. On 15 August, Japan surrendered and submitted to military occupation under the authority of US General Douglas MacArthur, the Supreme Commander of Allied Powers in the Pacific (SCAP). The following year the victorious Allies convened the International Military Tribunal for the Far East which condemned seven wartime leaders to execution and more to prison terms. The Emperor, however, was not brought to trial. The US administration pushed through a new Constitution providing for parliamentary democracy but saw uses for the Emperor, albeit reduced to a ceremonial role, in facilitating their occupation. The highly conservative, hierarchical, patriarchal and nationalist social system Hirohito embodied survived with him, in tension with a rapidly modernizing postwar culture.

Article 9 of the 1947 Constitution, often called the Peace Constitution (*Heiwa-Kenpo*), states that 'the Japanese people forever renounce war as a sovereign right of the nation and the threat or use of force as means of settling international disputes'. A further clause adds that no armed forces or 'war potential' shall be maintained. Article 9 was imposed by the victors in their own self-interest, to prevent the remilitarization of Japan, and it was resented by the Japanese élite. But it was popular with the majority of ordinary Japanese people, exhausted by the war, weary of imperial despotism and repelled by the revelations of their leaders' war crimes. Later, in the 1960s, in response to popular pressure, the Japanese government would supplement the peace clause with a resolution known as 'the three non-nuclear principles' (*hikaku san gensoku*): Japan shall neither possess nor manufacture nuclear weapons, nor shall it permit their introduction into Japanese territory.

The occupation of a defeated Japan continued for seven years, ending with the San Francisco Peace Treaty in 1952. A massive US military presence continued however, under the terms of a US-Japan Security Treaty signed the same year. What is more, Okinawa was specifically excluded from the Peace Treaty and remained under the resented rule of *Amerika-yu* for another twenty years. Excluded from civilian normality and deprived of citizens' rights, Okinawans felt they had been sold out by Japan. The islands also received a relatively small share of the investment and development that would soon make Japan one of the most powerful economies in the world. Its traditional land-owning class was diminished by appropriations of land for military use. The Okinawan labour force became heavily dependent on three categories of employment (the 'three k's'): *kokyo jigyo* (public works), *kankou* (tourism) and *kichi* (the US military bases) (Maedomari 2008: 193). The result is a per capita income only three-quarters of the Japanese average, making Okinawa the poorest prefecture in Japan (Cooley and Marten 2006: 572). It experiences persistent unemployment, a wide wealth gap, high indebtedness, relatively low average incomes and relatively costly housing. Okinawan women fill lower-status jobs, have little capital and lack land rights (IMADR-JC 2002).

The ending of the Second World War was, of course, simultaneously the beginning of the Cold War. Those atom bombs had been dropped not so much to bring about the surrender of Japan, already imminent, as to deter the Soviet Union from trespassing on US interests in the Pacific. Thus, US postwar policy in relation to Japan was soon confounded by a major contradiction. Its stated intention was to democratize and demilitarize Japan. But the rights conferred on the people by the US-inspired Constitution inevitably opened the door to an energetic left. The Japanese Communist Party (JCP, *Nihon Kyosan-tô*), which had paid a heavy price for its brave refusal to support the Japanese Imperial war, now recovered strength, identifying with the Moscow-led world communist movement. Its huge labour union, the Congress of Industrial Unions (*Zenrou-Ren*) was challenging to capitalist interests. The US soon felt obliged to inspire a 'crackdown' on 'red' militants. But the popular alternative to the communists, the Japanese Socialist Party (JSP, *Nihon Shakai-tô*) and its labour federation *Sohyo* were scarcely more desirable to a McCarthy-ite USA.

If 'democracy' was a boomerang, launched by the USA, that flew back as a threat, so too was 'peace'. In 1950 the Cold War turned hot as the United States and allies, under the political cover of the United Nations, embarked on a brutal three-year campaign on the Korean peninsula against the North Korean Communist regime supported by the new Peoples' Republic of China. From now onwards the USA would need Japan as a military ally and the Peace Constitution would be a growing embarrassment. Embarrassing, too, was the fact the Japanese politicians most inclined to support remilitarization and crush labour unions were those of the extreme right, including war criminals who had escaped the Tokyo Tribunal. Enraged by wartime defeat, they were hungry to recover influence and revert to pre-war Imperial culture.

Anti-Bomb and anti-Treaty: the emergence of a peace movement

On 1 March 1954 the US detonated a nuclear weapon on Bikini Atoll in the Marshall Islands, and the fall-out from the test irradiated the crew of a Japanese tuna-fishing boat, the 'Lucky Dragon'. The incident caused a surge in anti-nuclear activism in Japan. For political reasons, postwar governments had downplayed the Hiroshima and Nagasaki atrocity. Now *hibakusha*, the survivors of the atomic blasts, began to speak out. A petition for a ban on nuclear weapons quickly raised almost 30 million signatures. A World Conference was held in Hiroshima in 1955 and the organizing committee became the Japan Council against Atomic and Hydrogen Bombs, popularly known as *Gensuikyo*. From this time on, many ordinary people, particularly women, housewives, in thousands of localities were drawn into a peace movement that, as Mari Yamamoto sees it, became a 'popular lever, which helped to eliminate to a significant extent feudal remnants of the past'. It 'involved a struggle to establish anew a personal identity for the peace activists themselves and a national identity for their country' (Yamamoto 2004: 12).

Meanwhile, a second strand in the Japanese peace movement was emerging in response to the 1960 renewal of the US-Japan Security Treaty (known as the '*ampo*'). The reactionary Prime Minister of the time, Nobusuke Kishi, 'went all out ... to entrench postwar Japan in the Cold War structure as a subordinate ally of the United States' (Ota 2007–8: 34). He rushed the Treaty through the Diet, in defiance of massive demonstrations. United in opposition were the JCP, the JSP, the labour unions and the student movement (Fuhrt 2008). The *ampo-tôsô* (anti-Treaty struggle) was fuelled by the experience of the communities living close to US bases, whose land and livelihoods were most damaged by the military activity (Muto 2009). That the US war in Vietnam (1955–75) was largely waged from these bases increased opposition to their presence, for the war was seen by many Japanese as a criminal assault on a poor rural people by an over-armed superpower. Their forced complicity in the war brought home to them that the bases meant more than the theft of their land. They signified militarization of their society on another's terms.

The anti-militarist activists throughout Japan placed advertisements in US newspapers, monitored troop movements, demonstrated and picketed against arrival or departure of US ships on combat missions, campaigned for election of anti-base politicians to municipal and prefectural authorities, and used what few powers they had to restrict free use of facilities by the US military. A 'citizens' appeal' and protest march to the US embassy in Tokyo led to the formation of *Beheiren*, a 'citizens' coalition' for peace in Vietnam. Its spontaneity, structurelessness and horizontalism appealed to many who were alienated by both the dogmatism of the Japan Communist Party and the vanguardism of the

Trotskyist and other anti-Stalinist tendencies. However, from the late sixties *Beheiren* began to be outflanked by elements more inclined to violent methods. Student radicals clad in black helmets and armed with staves fought each other and the police (Fuhrt 2008).

When we came as researchers to Japan and Okinawa in 2009 to learn about contemporary anti-militarism, we found it a movement largely aligned with, but at the same time divided by, the left. The anti-Bomb movement has two major wings. *Gensuikyo*, identified with the Japan Communist Party, continues to exist, but so does a rival wing. In 1959 many Liberal Democratic Party affiliates left *Gensuikyo* in disagreement with the JCP's negativity towards the military alliance with the USA, and some years later the Japan Socialist Party (JSP) affiliates likewise defected, due to the JCP's refusal to condemn the Soviet Union's participation in the nuclear arms race. The socialists formed *Gensuikin*, the Japan Congress against Atomic and Hydrogen Bombs (Carter 1992). *Gensuikyo* and *Gensuikin* both hold an annual conference against nuclear weapons.

In the anti-*ampo* movement too we found distinctive political streams. In mainland Japan the demand 'scrap the Treaty' has less popular support than the other two nationwide campaigns, defending the Peace Constitution and banning nuclear weapons. The Japanese Communist Party (JCP) is the only parliamentary party that outspokenly and consistently opposes the Security Treaty. Its campaigning arm is the Japan Peace Committee (*Nihon Heiwa Iinkai*). Dating back to 1949, this is the oldest peace organization in the country, with branches in all 47 prefectures, and holds an annual mass gathering in one of the cities hosting US bases. Although many of its individual members are not party-affiliated, there is an overlap of key actors between the Committee, the Communist Party, and *Zenrou-Ren*, the Communist-allied labour federation. Since the demise of the Japan Socialist Party (*Nihon Shakai-tō*, JSP) in the mid-1990s, socialists are now mainly represented in parliament by the Social Democratic Party (*Shamin-tō*, SDP).[2] They seek to hold the middle ground, and do not call, like the JCP, for abandonment of the Treaty but for strategic and phased changes to it. For all that, the SDP is associated with an Action Committee of the Network against the Japan-US Security Pact (*Atarashii Han-Ampo wo Tsukuru Jikkou Iinkai*). A nation-wide network of 'peace movement centres', headed by the Tokyo Peace Movement Center founded in 1990, is also generally seen as part of the SDP stream.

The third major thematic focus of the movement in Japan is the defence of the peace clause of the Constitution. Here again, there is a

JCP-allied Constitution Conference (*Kenpo Kaigi*), and National Network against Reform of the Constitution (*Kenpo Kaiaku Hantai Kyodo Sentaa*), an umbrella of citizens' organizations in the prefectures, with a grounding in the Communist-allied National Confederation of Trade Unions (*Zenrou-Ren*). The socialist stream on this issue is represented by the Peace Constitution Pilgrimage (*Kenpo Angya No Kai*), established in 2004, and the Network for Protection of the Constitution (*Goken-Net*), which has a long history associating it with *Rengo*, the socialist labour union federation. The Peace Constitution League (*Kyu Jo Ren*) also has many individual SDP-oriented members. Peace Forum, an organization concerned more broadly with peace, the environment and human rights, is also linked to the SDP.

The Communist Party, the former Japan Socialist Party and latterly the Social Democratic Party, have undeniably furnished a mass base to the peace movement, and their trade union organizations have contributed energy and organizing skills. The extra-parliamentary tendencies of the vanguardist and internationalist left, to which the parliamentary parties are highly antagonistic, are also conceded to have added a certain dynamism, particularly in the context of the worldwide movement against the US 'war on terror'. Thus *Chūkaku-ha*[3] organizes Stop War! World Action!, *Kakumaru-ha*[4] has its No Retaliation War! and the Movement for Democratic Socialism (*Minshushugi-teki Shakaishugi Undo*, MDS) publishes the journal *Peace News* and partners the 'worker-communist' Iraqi Freedom Council in an anti-US (but also anti-insurgency) TV programme in Iraq. Nonetheless, many of the activists we interviewed told us they felt the movement to have been weakened by communist/socialist factionalism. Disunity prevails even on an issue of clear concern to both tendencies – the presence of nuclear-weapon-bearing ships in coastal waters in defiance of the anti-nuclear principles. In July 2008, when a US nuclear-powered vessel visited Yokosuka port, a report in *Japonesia Review* noted that 'there were large rallies over two successive weekends. The first was organized by the Japan Peace Committee and other groups close to the Japanese Communist Party, the other by the Peace Forum, a peace movement center working with the Japan Social Democratic Party and the Democratic Party of Japan' (Yamaguchi 2008).

Women activists, in particular, already critical of the left's tendency to instrumentalize women's organizations, deplore this divisiveness. Mina Watanabe of the Women's Active Museum (see pp. 173–4 below) was unsurprised when we told her we had difficulty delineating a 'general peace movement' in Japan. It was, she said, because 'in any organization in Japan there is a good chance that a party or a Marxist faction will be involved in it, even if they don't proclaim themselves'. And journalist Maki Okada told us, 'the male rival leaders allow themselves to be divided on inessential details. They exaggerate small differences. I want to plead with them: "see the main purpose". If only they united, we could win!' However, Ichiyo Muto, active in the People's Plan Study Group, urged a more positive point of view.[5] He told us: 'While it's valid to recognize the communist/socialist separation, it's also important not to overlook that there are quite a few grassroots locality-based multi-issue groups, many of them descending from the *Beheiren* tradition and other new left origins.' These are in many cases the cores of local coalition building, networking nationally when major political incidents occur, he said, and are a valuable feature of the Japanese peace movement.

Thus alerted, we gradually began to identify elements of the movement that maintain a detachment from the parties and draw activists from a wider community of people opposed to militarism and war. The Article 9 Association, once connected to the Japan Communist Party, has changed and become a diverse and inclusive network that emphasises the autonomy of its seven thousand branches. Likewise unaffiliated is the Peace Depot, a peace research, education and information institution, a 'citizen's think-tank'. So too is the remarkable Peace Boat, which carries activists on educational work across the oceans. Some of the non-party organizations address a particular issue such as banning landmines or supporting conscientious objectors. Some seek to mobilize particular sections of the community, such as musicians, port workers or members of a particular religious denomination. And many, like the Network for Non-defended Localities (*Hibuso Chiiki Jorei Net*), which mobilizes local citizens to make their municipalities 'weapons-free zones', have sprung up in cities or prefectures where people are fired by local circumstances. Many of these perpetuate the non-dogmatic, inclusive spirit of *Beheiren*.

Two elements of the contemporary Japanese anti-war, anti-militarist and peace movement however stand out from the national movement as described above. Both stem from a positionality of disadvantage in relation to power in Japanese state and society. First, the Okinawan movement expresses not only a strong anti-base perspective but also a standpoint formed in Okinawans' long history of struggle against colonization. Second, feminist anti-militarist organizations (both in the mainland and Okinawa) share a standpoint derived from the struggle against male domination in a patriarchal system. Each has a distinctive understanding of the causes and effects of militarization and the nature of the peace they seek through demilitarization. To start with Okinawa ...

The Okinawan anti-base movement

When survivors of the 1945 Battle of Okinawa, uprooted by the fighting, tried to return home, many found their property had been taken over by US forces. The US Civil Administration of the Ryukyuan Islands (USCAR) endowed themselves with the legal authority to lease any land they required. The village of Isahama was just one of many sites of struggle, where residents, in bitter disbelief, saw soldiers converting their farms to military use by filling carefully tended rice paddies with salt sand from the shore. Protests spread widely across the islands. Wherever the US started to enclose land, the land owners and local people placed themselves in passive resistance in front of the trucks and bulldozers (Yamazaki 2003: 38–9). At many moments it became what they called an 'island-enveloping struggle' (*shimagurumi-tôsô*) when the Ryukyuan people united in spontaneous riots and general strikes, and tens of thousands of people surrounded and confronted the bases (Shimada 2004).

It was particularly demeaning to Okinawans that, while they were bound to fight for release from occupation, the price of full citizenship under the Constitution could only be a renewal of Japanese hegemony. Contradictions continued after Reversion in 1972, for the state tried to buy off local politicians, the landowners' resistance movement and the labour unions with the inducement of public works, grants and subsidies. Badly needed though these were, they in no way matched the cost of the bases in damage to everyday life. Militarization brings environmental degradation and life-endangering pollution by unexploded ordinance, depleted uranium, heavy metals and hazardous chemicals. In the 1970s, in addition to fatal plane crashes, road traffic accidents caused by US soldiers were running at more than three thousand a year. The bases are a source of crime: an estimated one thousand offences a year, mainly homicides, rapes and burglaries, were recorded in that decade (Taira 2006: 148). And in 1969, at the height of the Vietnam war, more than seven thousand women were working in the sex industry around the bases, among whom several each year died at the hands of their clients (Takazato 1996). Even when suspects were identified, they were protected from prosecution under Japanese law by the Status of Forces Agreement (SOFA) between the Japanese and US governments. Of the few cases against US personnel that went to trial most resulted in acquittal or very light sentences.

Some hoped that the end of the Cold War would mean the withdrawal of US armed forces from the East Asia Pacific region. Far from it. A 1995 strategy document affirmed a long future for the array of US bases in Japan and Okinawa.[6] However, the undeniable injustice of 'Okinawa's burden' prompted the appointment of a Special Action Committee on Facilities and Areas Okinawa (SACO) comprising US and Japanese diplomats and officials, to re-articulate their basing strategy. SACO's report, issued in December 1996, conceded that eleven US facilities involving 52,000 hectares would be returned to Japanese control over a ten-year period and, to Okinawan people's special delight, the much-hated US Marine Corps Air Station at Futenma would be closed. Futenma was sited in a residential area near Ginowan City, inflicting on the inhabitants intolerable noise from helicopters flying day and night. However, when their cheers had subsided, Okinawans discovered that the US intended not to disband the Futenma facility but transfer its functions elsewhere. Various sites, in Japan, in Okinawa and elsewhere in the Pacific were hotly debated.

Even at the time of our 2009 visit to Okinawa, thirteen years after SACO, the relocation of Futenma's various facilities remained in question. The first plan considered by the US and Japanese governments involved building an offshore heliport on a coral reef near Henoko. A referendum showed the local residents to be vehemently opposed. An alliance of twenty-one protest groups, *Suishin Kai*, opened an office in Nago, the nearest city. Environmental issues were pivotal: the coral reef must be preserved. In addition, there had been fortuitous sightings in the coastal waters of the dugong, a rare sea mammal whose survival would be endangered by the development. A Dugong Campaign was formed, which filed a lawsuit against the US Defense Secretary, *Dugong v. Rumsfeld*, in the US Federal Court. Environmental experts were employed by the groups to help them make their case more widely in the 'court' of world opinion, invoking the Convention on Biological Diversity and other instruments (Spencer 2003). Locally, the Henoko resistance was coordinated by a Conference Opposing Heliport Construction (*Kaijo Heli Kichi Kensetsu Hantai*). They established a tented 'sit-in' from where, with binoculars, volunteers could keep watch over the reef area. When the workmen of the Defense Facilities Administration Agency (DFAA) arrived to mount scaffolding on the coral reef, nonviolent direct action was launched, with people swimming, diving and paddling canoes in the waters of the reef, while some occupied the scaffolding. In September 2005, after ten months of confrontation, the DFAA quietly dismantled its structure and withdrew.

However, in Okinawa the successful conclusion of one struggle usually means the start of another. The following month the government disclosed that Futenma's landing facilities were now destined for a nearby headland, which would be extended by landfill into the neighbouring shallow waters. Within an existing US military base, the site would be less accessible to protesters, they believed. But the movement only grew stronger as local fishery guilds mobilized against the threat to their fishing grounds in neighbouring Oura Bay (Yui 2006, 2007–8). We visited the seaside tent at Henoko in August 2009 and heard from Hiroshi Ashitomi, co-chair of the Conference, and Muneyoshi Kano of the Life Protection Association (*Inochi wo Mamoru Kai*), the story of their long resistance.

That afternoon we travelled fifty miles north of Henoko to visit another tented vigil, this time on the side of a road that traverses the dense forests of the Yanbaru region. A couple of years previously, the Americans had announced a plan to build a Jungle Warfare Training Centre here for the Marines. The construction of six helipads, multiple access roads and an influx of men, buildings, vehicles and Osprey helicopters would devastate an unspoiled stretch of tropical forest that is home to several rare species as well as a small human community. For two years some residents of the village of Takae, calling themselves The Association to Protect the Broccoli Forest (*Broccoli no Mori wo Mamoru Kai*), had been staging a continuous sit-in in front of the four access gates of the proposed US base, blockading the road when construction vehicles approached.

Back in the capital city too we found campaigners collecting signatures on petitions, writing articles and making speeches, as well as organizing rallies and other events in support of the local protests at Henoko and Takae. The anti-militarist movement of Okinawa is a partnership of citizens' organizations, party-based organizations and some progressive prefectural politicians and administrators. The umbrella organization of the civil society movement is the Okinawan Citizens Peace Network (OCPN). With thirty-three affiliated organizations and individual members, its concerns span anti-militarist, anti-base, human rights and environmental struggles in Okinawa, but extend also to world peace. It co-ordinates practical support for the sit-ins at Henoko and Takae, lobbies municipal, prefectural and governmental authorities on behalf of affiliated groups, and campaigns in support of anti-*ampo* candidates at election time.

As we made our journey among the anti-militarist activists of Okinawa we often heard them use the term *kakushin kyotou*, which means 'co-struggle among progressive forces'. The expression was coined in the late 1960s when the Okinawan branches of the progressive parties and their labour unions formed a *Kakushin Kyotou Kaigi* (the Conference for Co-struggle of Progressives) in the movement to end the American occupation. At the moment of Reversion, when Okinawa rejoined the Japanese political structure, although the mainland political parties (as one of our informants put it) 'piled in', the tradition of cross-party co-operation in Okinawa did not die. The Communist Party (*Okinawa Jinmin-tō*, formerly the Okinawa People's Party) and the Social Democratic Party (*Shamin-tō*) work closely not only with each other but also with a local independent party formed back in 1950, the Okinawa Social Mass Party (*Shadai-tō* or *Shakai Taishu-tō*). At times they put forward unity candidates in elections to win seats from the conservative Liberal Democratic Party.

The three parties co-operate in the anti-*ampo* movement by way of two organizations. The Okinawa Peace Movement Center (*Okinawa Heiwa Undo Center, OHUC*) is an alliance between the Social Democratic Party and the Okinawa Social Mass Party and related labour unions, bodies which together assemble thirty thousand members on the islands. The Prefectural People's Conference (*Kemin Kai Gi, KKG*) is an alliance of the Social Democratic Party and the Okinawa People's Party (a.k.a. the Communist Party). What is more, OHUC and KKG, federations that in the Japanese mainland would be respectively in the socialist stream and the communist stream of the movement, here in Okinawa share an office and have some officers in common. Citizens' organizations can also affiliate to KKG and benefit from the fact that its leaders, who are senior local representatives of the parties, have the ear of the Governor and prefectural authorities.

Though it is important not to romanticize Okinawan cross-party unity, it is nonetheless a fact that the kind of partnership exemplified by OHUC and KKG is rare in Japan. 'It surprises the mainland comrades sometimes!', Shikou Sakiyama, who is an officer in both organizations, told us in interview. 'In Tokyo, the organizations share the same aims but they get divided and don't respect each other's demands.' Furthermore, the Okinawan prefectural and city authorities sometimes show themselves more loyal to the islands than to the Japanese government, as when in 1995 Governor Masahide Ota refused to concur with the government's demand that he sign, as proxy for rebellious anti-war landowners, leases for land sought by the USA for their bases (Akibayashi and Takazato 2009). The relationship between ordinary citizens and political parties too is a little closer in Okinawa than on the mainland. 'The parties belong to the citizens more here', we were told. Even the conservative politicians of the ruling Liberal Democratic Party are accessible to Okinawan sentiment. 'They are visible to us,' Shinichi

Kawamitsu, director of the Okinawa Peace Network, said in interview. 'On the mainland they can cheat and conceal, but here in Okinawa the Governor is surrounded by many war survivors and he can be challenged by them.'

Hiroshi Ashitomi told us, as we sat on the sea shore awaiting the next attempt at base development, 'Okinawa is different. We are still colonized as well as occupied. The Japanese government is part of this, attacking the Okinawan people'. He felt 'as if there is a breakwater preventing us reaching the Japanese government'. However, it is not only the government of Japan from which Okinawans feel distant. Their movement also coheres, it must be said, around their disillusionment with the mainland peace movement. While there have sometimes been common actions against the Security Treaty and the bases, and some *yamato* activists make trips down to the islands to support the sit-ins for a day or two, the Okinawans perceive an absence in the mainland of any sustained campaign supporting their struggle, whether it is against the bases or against Japan's inferiorization of Ryukyuans. There is a feeling that 'they will cry for Iraq, but not for us'. Later, in Tokyo we were able to interview Ichiyo Muto, of People's Plan Study Group and the *Japonesia Review*, which are notable for maintaining a focus on Okinawa. He felt Okinawans had reason to be disappointed in the mainland anti-*ampo* movement. 'We in the mainland need to have our own anti-*ampo* struggle in solidarity with Okinawa. But the US and Japanese governments have deliberately and by stages shifted the major burden of the US bases to Okinawa in order to make it a non-issue in national politics, and in public consciousness. This manoeuvre has succeeded, and our anti-*ampo* struggle has almost disappeared.' Meanwhile the current of history is flowing the other way.[7] The USA has been engaged in a far-reaching 'realignment' of its relationship with Japan. 'In an 18-month working process begun in February 2005 and completed in June 2006,' Muto has written, 'Japan willingly surrendered command over its military forces to the United States, committing itself unconditionally to the American empire's global strategic imperatives' (Muto 2006: 19).[8]

Okinawa Women Act against Military Violence

For twenty-five years there has been a strong feminist movement in Okinawa, well connected with the women's movement in mainland Japan but independently linked to global feminism. The Okinawan delegation that attended the NGO Forum of the 3rd United Nations World Conference on Women in Nairobi in 1985 flew back inspired by their encounter with thirteen thousand women from all over the planet. One of the participants was Suzuyo Takazato, a social worker who had experience of working with prostitutes, and she was particularly encouraged by the common ground they had been able to establish with women from other countries who attended their workshop on prostitution and women's labour. The energy that flowed from Nairobi was an inspiration to Hiromi Minamoto, a feminist radio reporter back in Naha City. Working with Suzuyo and other women, she persuaded the local radio station to devote a 12-hour programme to women, to be produced by a woman-only team. The programme became an annual event, an enduring feature of Okinawan feminism to the present day (Takazato 1996; Tanji 2006). The *Unai* festival, it is called. 'Why *Unai*?' we asked Suzuyo. She explained that in Okinawa, as in mainland Japan, the traditional family system is profoundly patriarchal. In the Okinawan tradition, however, known as *tôtôme*, a sister, *unai*, is endowed with a modicum of value. She is believed to be a protective spirit, a kind of 'guardian angel', for her brother. Suzuyo went on:

> *Tôtôme* has been our basic source of indignity and deep sadness for women. Women who fall outside the family framework, who remain single, who can't conceive a son, or are disabled, are treated with just the same disrespect as elsewhere in Japan. So, we thought, in Okinawa women are supposed to have this spirit power – let's turn the tradition round. We can value each and every woman for herself, rather than for her role in the family. We can act on our own initiative.

So the Okinawan feminists reinvented 'sisterhood' as women for women. The *Unai* radio women's festival gained a following throughout the islands. Radio is a democratic medium, rooted in daily life and making no demands on literacy. People tune in when driving, listen while they work, take a transistor to the fields. The production group developed a unique process they came to call 'the *unai* approach', the *'unai houshiki'*. The programmes, year by year, drew into co-operation the women's sections of the communist and socialist parties and their labour unions, but also a wide range of women's organizations, some non-feminist, others on the feminist spectrum from liberal to radical. *Unai* was the feminists' version of 'co-struggle'. Hiromi Minamoto told us in interview:

> The organizations involved are not represented by their leaders, in the normal way. With us, any woman has an equal right and space.

It's enabled us to break down the boundaries between political ideologies. In mixed organizations when disagreements arise it's hard to get women's various points of view heard. But in *Unai* women can raise these differences among themselves. So many women's standpoints – yet we can act together.

The Nairobi conference marked the end of the United Nations Decade for Women (1976–85). The Japanese government was under pressure from UN agencies and a lively feminist movement throughout Japan to pay attention to the status of women. The indicators did not look good. While the UN Human Development Report of 1993 showed Japan to be the most 'developed' country in the world, it slipped down to seventeenth position when the index was adjusted for gender (Inoue 1996). This prompted the government to set up a Department for the Promotion of Gender Equality, with a unit in the Prime Minister's office (Shigematsu 2005). This unit in turn assured a substantial official presence of Japanese women at the 4th UN World Conference on Women in Beijing in 1995. However the NGO Forum at the Conference also received a big delegation of Japanese feminist activist women, including no fewer than seventy-one arriving on a chartered plane from Okinawa.

The Beijing *Platform for Action* had a section titled 'Women in Conflict'. But, the Okinawan women wondered, what about women like us, experiencing not conflict exactly but *occupation* – oppression by the military forces of an alien power? They met up with women from other countries hosting US bases and together they deepened their enquiry into the impact on women of *militarization*, a condition similar to, but different from, war. It is a condition that precedes war and continues when conflict ends, a condition that can make everyday life feel like a battlefield. It so happened that the delegation returned from Beijing to bitter news that illustrated their point: while they were away a 12-year old Okinawan girl had been abducted and raped by three US marines from Camp Hansen. The US authorities were refusing to surrender the suspects into the custody of the Japanese authorities. In partnership with other Okinawan women's organizations, the returning women called a press conference and mobilized a citizen's rally that drew an estimated eighty-five thousand to Ginowan Park. Half a million people signed a petition for justice and for closure of US bases. Then the women staged a 12-day sit-in, under a tent in Naha City's Peace Square. Twenty-five women went to Tokyo to lobby the Prime Minister and Foreign Minister.

Early in November 1995 the activists formally established an NGO, Okinawa Women Act against Military Violence (*Okinawa, Kichi Guntai wo yurusanai kodo suru Onna tachi no Kai*). Suzuyo Takazato was one of its co-chairs. What did OWAAMV want? In the short term they wanted an end to military violence against women, and a revision of the Status of Forces Agreement together with the Japanese laws that protected US perpetrators from punishment. They began compiling a case by case chronology from all available sources of US crimes against Okinawans since the end of the Second World War, revealing hundreds of incidents. In the long term, like the rest of the anti-*ampo* movement, they called for a concrete plan for dismantling the US bases.

OWAAMV have strong links with feminist anti-militarist groups in Japan, in the USA and elsewhere (see p. 173 below). But in Okinawa too they work in co-operation with other women's initiatives that have sprung up during the *Unai* years. Some have colourful names, like The Dugongs, up on the north-west coast, the Cooking Pots Gathering in Ginowan, and the Life is Treasure Spirited Women's Group. They differ in focus. These three have chosen to protest the environmental impact of base development. But such Okinawan women's protest groups share a certain style and spirit – a minimal organizational structure, an absence of hierarchy. Participation and sharing are valued more than status. They avoid the aggressive and repetitive chanting and sloganizing popular with the left. There is, besides, no question of discipline, of dogma or a 'party line'. Each individual decides for herself. Miyume Tanji describes Okinawan women's activism as challenging the 'old ways of protest', including 'the typically dictatorial and male-dominated *modus operandi* of the citizens' movements and anti-base organizations that tended to obliterate individuality and difference'. With their everyday language and more inclusive way of doing things they have brought 'change in the dynamics in the Okinawa community of protest' (Tanji 2006: para 54; see also Spencer 2003).

The political clamour over US military sexual violence tends to obscure the commonplace reality of rape and domestic assault by Okinawan males. Some of the women in and close to OWAAMV decided to act against civilian rape by establishing a sister organization, the Rape Emergency Intervention and Counselling Centre (REICO). REICO does advocacy and information work to educate the community about sexual violence. It tries to dispel the widespread 'myths' about rape: that women 'ask for it', that rapists are usually unknown to their victims. As a support organization for survivors, however, it must operate differently from OWAAMV, keeping its address secret to protect women from further violence, and maintaining a working relationship with hospitals, social services and police to ensure appropriate and sensitive responses to raped women.

Making connections between sources, forms and scales of violence

The partnership between REICO and OWAAMV is conceptually and politically significant for the link it makes between institutional and personal, military and civilian, US and Okinawan, violence against women. The two organizations persistently connect the presence of the bases with the violation of women's human rights. But they also bring to view the reality of sexual violence in Okinawan and Japanese society, which have their own oppressive gender power structures. 'Whether the perpetrator is a US serviceman or a Japanese, our shared anger is against sexual violence itself' (REICO Newsletter No. 3).

The left and the mainstream anti-*ampo* movement embrace OWAAMV warmly for their campaign against the violence emanating from the US bases, but are less enthusiastic about this finger pointed at local men. The women are sometimes looked on askance for collaborating with the police – aren't the state security services 'the enemy'? The women for their part sometimes find the response of the anti-base movement to US military violence unhelpful. The masculinized discourse of the mainstream movement can have the effect of further exploiting the rape victim, making her body an object of the public gaze. Sometimes a case of rape is used to legitimate a resentful polemic against 'those' men trampling on 'our women' and 'our Okinawan land'. Some of the media are prone to blame the victim instead of the perpetrator. Men will be men, soldiers will be soldiers: girls should know better than to walk into danger. OWAAMV responds, 'We don't need dangerous neighbours' (Motoyama 2008).

The media and public opinion often allow prostitution to cloud the issue of rape. As in other Asian countries, there is a great deal of prostitution in the camp towns near the US bases in Okinawa. It is questionable to what extent the sex workers involved are working under their own free will. Many come from the Philippines and other Asian countries. All are poor, driven to work overseas to maintain themselves and dependents. Many are 'trafficked', brought into the country on visas that describe them as 'entertainers', and subsequently tricked into prostitution and debt bondage by those who operate the bars and brothels. Nonetheless popular and media opinion often represents sex workers as delinquent women, selling themselves for US dollars. Yet there is a double standard at work here. Until the Prostitution Prevention Law of 1956, prostitution in Japan was organized in legal brothels. When, later, this law was presented in the Okinawan legislature, local politicians rejected it several times, because the dollars earned through the sex trade were a valued addition to the Okinawan economy. More publicly it was argued that without organized and legal prostitution the supposed libidinous 'needs' of US soldiers would be unsatisfied, resulting in yet more rape. Indeed women of certain categories (Okinawan working class and Asian migrants) were pushed towards serving as sex workers for the US military. It is certain, as Suzuyo Takazato reminded us, that 'raped women and prostitutes are not separate phenomena. It's the "structural violence" of militarization that produces both effects'.

Militarization is a source not of security but of insecurity, OWAAMV say. It is specially perilous for women. 'The bases don't protect us, they torture us,' Suzuyo Takazato told us. 'The "Security" Treaty violates *our* security.' Because they are so aware of the uses to which women are put, not only by nationalists and militarists but also, sometimes, regrettably, by anti-*ampo* activists, they are always at pains to couple campaigning with 'taking care'. When OWAAMV or REICO hear of a rape, whether by US or local men, their first reaction is the same: to check that the victim is receiving a proper response from the police, hospitals and social services. Suzuyo told us in interview, 'OWAAMV isn't just against the military presence. We are equally concerned *about the women themselves,* who are victimized by the US personnel'.

For all its distinctive concerns, OWAAMV do not stand apart from the Okinawan anti-*ampo* movement. On the contrary, they join wholeheartedly in the campaigns, the marches, the rallies. They visit and bring support to the sit-ins at Henoko and Takae. They are respected and active affiliates of the Okinawa Citizens' Peace Network, the Okinawa Peace Movement Center and the Prefectural People's Conference. Where they differ from the mainstream movement is in what they identify as causes and effects of militarization. Looking to causes, they see the militarization visited on Okinawa as deriving not only from the violence of the capitalist market, imperialist domination and the nation-state system, but also from the implicit/explicit/complicit violence of patriarchy, understood as an interlocking feature of all these systems. Suzuyo Takazato says, 'Behind the military are *societies* that value militarism – US and Japanese society – and both are *patriarchal.*' She has written that patriarchal societies, oriented towards militarism, 'place women in a subordinate position and legitimate their objectification as sexual machinery in order to achieve the goals of the nation' (Takazato 1996: 126).

As to the impacts of militarization, OWAAMV again differ from the mainstream in their perception of what it does to men, and what men do to women. They pay attention to the individual perpetrator and the victim of his violence. In this way their glance takes in on the one hand weaponry on a massive scale (the unwelcome US nuclear patrols in the skies and oceans of the Pacific region) and on the other forces of coercion on a comparatively puny, yet still murderous, scale – the fist, the boot, the penis, of a violent individual. Sometimes Suzuyo is told by those in the mainstream movement, 'You are very good at presenting the violence-against-women issue. But don't forget the whole structure!' Her reply is, 'I know the whole structure. If you are going to understand the picture as a whole, you have to take account of *this*. It's like a jigsaw, and this is a key piece, so that if it is missing the whole doesn't make sense. And since the rest of you don't touch the core issue, I do it.'

'Comfort women' and the rightwing agenda

The rape of an Okinawan schoolgirl by US soldiers was not the first time military sexual violence had appeared in Japanese news headlines. Towards the end of the 1980s an issue had arisen that shook mainstream Japanese politics to the core, in a way that women's issues rarely do. It was the matter of Japan's practice before and during the Second World War of enslaving women from neighbouring countries for the sexual servicing of their military personnel. Among the estimated 200,000 so-called 'comfort women' from all over Asia abducted and held in military brothels in the service of Japan's campaigns were a large number of Korean women, and it was Korean feminists who began researching and publicizing the history of the 'comfort stations'. In 1990 they filed a lawsuit against Japan but failed to get the compensation they demanded. Japanese feminists felt challenged now to re-examine their own history and admit some shared responsibility for the imperialist aggressions of the 1930s and the Second World War carried out in their name (Suzuki 2002: 7, 8). Meanwhile, Yayori Matsui, Michiko Nakahara and other Japanese feminists, in touch with women of nearby countries through the medium of the Asian Women's Association, had been exposing the contemporary problem of Japanese men's 'sex tourism' in the region. Now the Korean revelations prompted them to acknowledge an uncomfortable resonance between today's masculinist economic imperialism in the region and that earlier masculinist military imperialism. In the one way and the other, Asian women's bodies have been continuously exploited to meet Japanese men's sexual demands.

At first, the Japanese government's response to the women's disclosure of the wartime sexual slavery was to state that the 'comfort stations' had been run by private contractors. However in 1991 the historian Yoshiaki Yoshimi unearthed documents in the archives of Japan's Defense Agency that showed beyond doubt that the state military had abducted women. On 11 January 1992 *Asahi Shimbun* published his findings. The Chief Cabinet Secretary, Koichi Kato, responded immediately by acknowledging some of the facts and the following week, on a trip to South Korea, Prime Minister Miyazawa formally apologized for the suffering of Korean victims of the comfort women system. In 1993, Yohei Kono, the Chief Cabinet Secretary, issued a statement that acknowledged the involvement of the Japanese military in the prostitution and apologized to all who suffered the 'immeasurable pain and incurable psychological wounds' inflicted (Ota 2007–8).

Although these statements did not admit legal responsibility for military sexual slavery, they were sufficiently apologetic to enrage rightwing opinion. Japanese nationalist extremism was already on a surge inspired by the Gulf War. When Saddam Hussein invaded Kuwait in 1991, the US called on the Japanese Self-Defence Force to join its 'coalition of the willing' to throw him out. Parties and politicians disputed fiercely how far Article 9, the peace clause of the Constitution, could or should be ignored or 'bent' in order to comply. In the end Japanese funds, not armed forces, were contributed to Operation Desert Storm. The right writhed at the shame of Japanese manhood, its bloodshed evaded by a donation of cash. Now what they felt to be official grovelling over the matter of the comfort women fuelled new initiatives. One was the Japanese Society for History Textbook Reform (*Atarashii Rekishi kyokasho wo Tsukuru-kai*), set up to correct the 'masochistic' version of Japanese war history, to refuse guilt and restore the nation's military pride.

The year 1995, the fortieth anniversary of the capitulation of Japan, was a high point of all this dissension. It coincided with a severe economic setback that shook the confidence of the Japanese élite. In Okinawa, the scandal of the Camp Hansen rape had precipitated the creation of OWAAMV. In Tokyo, Yayori Matsui and others had just set up the Asia-Japan Women's Resource Centre, 'to end gender-based violence and discrimination, including sexual violence under armed conflict and around military bases, trafficking and sexual exploitation, domestic violence, and sexual harassment' and in so doing to 'challenge the conventional concept of peace and security'.[9] A couple of years later the Violence against Women in War Network (VAWW-Net) was formed. Comprising women of all the countries affected by the comfort women system, it had a branch in Tokyo. The aim now was redress – to end the impunity of the state and the Emperor.

The vehicle was a Women's International Tribunal on Japan's Military Sexual Slavery. Mounted in Tokyo in December 2000, it was a civil society rather than an official initiative, but it was conducted so far as possible in accordance with accepted juridical procedure, employed qualified lawyers and judges, and observed correct use of witnesses and evidence. Sixty-four surviving comfort women from eight countries attended and many gave evidence during the three-day hearing, which was attended by a thousand observers. The judges found guilt in the case of the Emperor Hirohito and several high-ranking war time officials, and called for official acknowledgment of responsibility and the payment by the state of reparations to the surviving comfort women. The subsequent final judgment in The Hague, in December 2001, found Japan's practice of military sexual slavery to have been a 'crime against humanity'. But the Japanese government, despite ongoing pursuit by VAWW-NET, has neither admitted guilt nor paid compensation.

We learned this history in long conversations with two of today's VAWW-Net Japan activists, Kim Pu Ja and Michiko Nakahara, with Hisako Motoyama of the Asia-Japan Women's Resource Centre (AJWRC) and with Mina Watanabe of the Women's Active Museum (WAM), a resource established with a bequest from estate of the now deceased Yayori Matsui. Although they are significantly less involved in struggle against the Security Treaty than Okinawa Women Act against Military Violence, these feminist organizations are close allies of OWAAMV, sharing with them a feminist and anti-nationalist agenda. Although the racism that affects them most directly in the mainland is xenophobic treatment of immigrant minorities, the mainland feminists are also alert to the negation of Ryukyuan identity and are aware that the rightwing project of 'recovering history' involves the denial of wartime atrocities against Okinawans as well as of crimes against women. At Kyoto University we met a professor of literature, Kozue Akibayashi, whose students have joined her in forming a local branch of the Women's International League for Peace and Freedom. They make it their task to increase awareness of the Okinawan struggle in the mainland peace movement.

We were in Japan during August 2009, when there are customarily many activities commemorating the end of the Second World War. Rola-Net, a support group for Filipina women migrants in Japan, had prevailed upon the Mitaka City municipal authority to make available a hall for a three-day showing of a mobile exhibition, *Let's See, Hear and Talk about the Comfort Women*, furnished by the Women's Active Museum. During this period they would also screen some of VAWW-Net's videos. The hall was picketed throughout the three days of Rola-Net's show by a large and noisy group from *Zaitoku-Kai*, the Association against the Privilege of non-Japanese Residents in Japan. Characteristic of the nationalist right, *Zaitoku-Kai* found two reasons for trashing the event. First, the organizers were hated because they supported the rights of ethnic minorities and migrants who, it should be added, far from being 'privileged', are in fact widely subject to discrimination. Second, the exhibition was promoting the 'masochistic view' of Japanese history. At moments the angry crowd numbered a hundred or more. They brought a campaign vehicle and loud-hailers, challenged and harassed visitors to the exhibition and impeded their arrivals and departures. They used cameras and camcorders to record the identities of those attending the event. They called the women 'whores' and 'traitors', grabbing and hitting anyone foolhardy enough to remonstrate with them.

The right, the peace movement and patriarchy

The extreme right in Japan is a force to be reckoned with (Matthews 2003; Tahara 2006). It is more than a handful of noisy populist groups like *Zaitoku-Kai*. It is the Japan Conference (*Nihon Kaigi*), with a caucus in the Diet. It is the Japan Policy Institute (*Nihon Seisaku Kenkyuu Sentaa*), feeding its reactionary analysis to the conservative Liberal Democratic Party. It is the Shinto Political League. It has compelling writers, ideologues and propagandists. With the weight of Imperial history behind it, feeding on every economic setback, every perceived slight to Japanese national pride, it stands at the shoulder of power, awaiting electoral advantage.[10] The right longs to remilitarize Japan, not as lieutenant to the USA but as commander of its own means and forces of coercion, including a nuclear arsenal. The left, of course, across the spectrum from the Trotskyist fringe to the social democratic centre, are its natural enemy. But the peace movement too, in its several forms – defending Article 9, insisting on the non-nuclear principles or inveighing against the Security Treaty – is anathema to the right. To succeed in its struggle with the right for popular understanding and allegiance therefore, the anti-war, anti-militarist and peace movements need an analysis and a strategy that are fully adequate to counter the right's programme. At present, they are equipped for this contest for hearts and minds across most of that agenda. They make a case against capitalism as a cause of war, against nationalism for its hatred and exclusions, and against militarism for its violence and profligacy. But there is one matter on which the peace movement is silent while the right is alarmingly vocal. That is the matter of gender relations. The gender project of the extreme right is explicitly patriarchal: the recovery of the traditional 'Emperor system' and its '*ie*' family structure, marked by male supremacy, primogeniture, patrilocality, profound gender dichotomy, the strict subordination of women and a tightly confining definition of femininity. They polemicize against a declining birthrate and call for women to play their 'customary role' for the nation. They resent feminists' challenge to the authority structure of the patriarchal family, and the metaphors used in their tracts often suggest a castrated and angry masculinity.[11]

The women of the AJWRC, VAWW-Net, WAM and OWAAMV and other feminist groups, along with individual feminists who have chosen to work in mainstream peace movement organizations of both women and men, bring to the movement a clear message, that is articulated not only in meetings, discussions and actions, but also in articles and other media output.[12] They are saying that militarization and nationalism are profoundly gendered phenomena. We cannot act effectively against them without a gender strategy. The struggle to transform gender relations, refuse family norms and 'disarm' hegemonic masculinity is a necessary part of the struggle against the Security Treaty, for the Constitution and for enduring peace. How well is the mainstream movement hearing them?

Not well, it seems, if at all. This much we had already learned from some of the men we had interviewed in the mainstream organizations. People's Plan Study Group is unusual, perhaps unique, among mixed-gender organizations in the Japanese and Okinawan peace movements in having adopted a feminist gender analysis, expressed clearly in its publications. Ichiyo Muto has had much to do with this. He told us: 'A consciousness and critique of patriarchy is not integrated at all into the activities of *general* peace movement organizations.' Of the left as a whole, he added:

> The right has a clear anti-feminist position and acts aggressively. It is an important component of their overall chauvinist agenda. The left do resist the right's offensive on this. Also the idea is current among the left that they ought to operate in a non-sexist way. But *gender analysis of war and peace issues* is not commonly shared by the

peace movement. Feminists are powerfully advancing their views, but the gender analysis is still sorely lacking in the peace movement in general.

We asked Youichi Komori, the Secretary General of the Article 9 Association, whether this was so. He answered, 'That is correct. Yes. This lack you are describing is a serious problem in our movements'. He added: 'In the 1970s and 1980s the Japanese social movements did not go through the agonizing experience of self-transformation under the feminist impact. Why this is so is a tormenting question I struggle to understand and answer.'

What was the view of women activists? The Asia-Japan Women's Resource Centre organized a workshop for us in Tokyo to try and gather some opinion. Well advertised, it drew around sixty women, with a good age span, activists from a wide range of groups and projects, and the discussion it generated was energetic and, it turned out, sharply critical of the mainstream movement. Many women spoke of an inhibition they felt, preventing them raising gender issues in mixed organizations. They have learned they will get a negative response from men – and not a few women – if they do so. Far from being heard and understood, therefore, it was difficult even to speak about these things outside woman-only spaces. 'When men hear the word gender they take a step backwards', we were told. 'The term gender irritates men here,' Hisako Motoyama said. 'Feminists are seen as radical, as too political.' They are labelled 'difficult' women.

Even progressive men, besides, lack political consciousness of their role and responsibility in the gender system, women said. 'Men don't want to *see* masculinity.' Even the ones who might theoretically recognize a link between patriarchy and militarism would not understand patriarchy as 'their *own* issue', Maki Okada said. Whereas women like OWAAMV see military sexual violence as a matter of both gender abuse and militarist abuse, mixed organizations tend to see it as only the latter. And this was indeed borne out by what we were learning in our interviews in the mainstream movement. Mitsuo Sato, for instance, co-chair of the Japan Peace Committee (*Nihon Heiwa Iinkai*) had been actively seeking justice for a particular victim of military rape. Rather than combining a critique of male violence and the base system, as the feminists do, he pinned the blame only on latter, telling us:

> This kind of incident would never occur if the bases are eliminated. The bases exist because we have the Security Treaty. So to problematize

the rape case, we problematize the US troops. We say let's get rid of the bases, and send the troops back to the USA ... We cannot separate the women's issue from the *ampo*.

In this environment, raising a critique of Japanese gender relations feels counter-productive to women. For one thing, it threatens harmony in the movement. Kaori Suzuki described a weekly street-side peace vigil she attends in central Tokyo: 'These are people from the committed movement. They are of various ages and sexes. They bring their own messages to the vigil. The only issue that is *never* addressed is gender.' Another woman who stands with this vigil added, 'It is only by people avoiding gender issues that they can keep doing anti-war actions. But such activism is incapable of making people change themselves – and that is what you have to do if you want to end war'. People in the peace movement live, like everyone else in Japan, in a society that still marks a clear distinction between *uchi* and *soto*, indoors and outdoors, the private world of family and home, the public world of business, politics and action. It is not in good taste to politicize *uchi*, as feminists do when they say 'the personal is political'. Decorum requires one's utterances to be appropriate for 'time, place and occasion' – the popular expression is 'TPO'. There are few spaces where gender politics can be introduced without it feeling like a gaffe.

To win over public opinion against militarism in Japan, therefore, it is often felt necessary to keep gender issues out of sight. For instance, we asked Maki Okada whether, in her local Article 9 Association, it would be thinkable to link defence of Article 24 to their defence of the peace clause of the Constitution. We had heard that the LDP's commission on the Constitution were considering a revision of this vital clause that gives women equal rights in marriage, divorce and family affairs (Tahara 2006). She replied thoughtfully:

There are members who *would* take Article 24 seriously. But not everyone would see its relevance. We don't take a collective position on it. With the Social Democratic Party and trade unions so down, with the right rising, and the threat of remilitarization of Japan, our aim has been to make the slogan 'Let's protect Article 9' famous. People know exactly what it means. If you were to add Article 24 it would become blurred, less clear.

The threat to the two clauses is meaningfully linked, however. Women at the AJWRC workshop spoke of the Japanese patriarchal family as 'a politico-military institution', a place where good little patriots and soldiers are nurtured. The nation's military in turn gives back to the family proper manly men (that is, when they are not returned in a coffin). 'The value system of the family is a value system that leads to war,' someone said. 'I want diverse forms of family.' Women are well capable of organizing love and care, relationships and bonds, without the deforming framework of official family structures. How could it be that men of the anti-war, anti-militarist and peace movements are, as one woman put it, 'all for smashing oppressive structures – except those of the family, which they preserve . . . Such a contradiction, opposing war but still internalizing family values!' Someone spoke of 'the family fantasy' of the peace movement.

Above all, women at the workshop were expressing exasperation – and not a little anger. They were exhausted by the burden of double militancy, resentful at having to take responsibility for changing men as well as demilitarizing the nation. They were all the more despairing because *Zaitoku-Kai*'s attack on the comfort women exhibition had occurred only days before. It was clear to everyone in the room that the extreme right have no shadow of doubt that the patriarchal principle holds the rest of Japan's conservative social order in place. The demagogues invoke *ryôsai kenbo* (good wife/wise mother) and inveigh against *yamato* marrying foreigners, against lesbian mothers, mixed-race children, children identified as Ryukyuan, children born out of wedlock. Out there on the street stands masculine authority – national majority-ethnic masculine authority – defining and outlawing multiple forms of bastardy. And progressives of the anti-militarist movement are perpetuating *family values*?

Notes

1. For example, Richard Siddle notes that in the 1997 survey into prefectural differences, 72 per cent of Okinawans considered their 'way of thinking' to be different from that of other prefectures, the highest figure among the prefectures (*Ryukyu Shimpo*, 10 Jan 1997, cited by Siddle 2003: 133).
2. After a brief interruption in 1993 to its decades of rule, the Liberal Democratic Party returned to power within a year, re-establishing its electoral majority by means of an alliance with the Japanese Socialist Party. The latter made itself acceptable to its conservative partners by performing a U-turn, modifying its opposition to the Security Treaty and Article 9. This was effectively the end of a significant left alternative in Japan. The most progressive parliamentary party since that time has been the Social Democratic Party.
3. Japan Revolutionary Communist League, National Committee – Middle Core Faction (*Kakumeiteki Kyōsanshugisha Dōmei, Zenkoku Iinkai*).

4. Japan Revolutionary Communist League – Revolutionary Marxist Faction (*Kakumeiteki Kyosanshugisha Domei, Kakumeiteki Marukusu Shugiha*).
5. In interview. The People's Plan Study Group was established in 1998 as a network of a few hundred committed intellectuals and social movement activists and is conducting action-oriented research while committing itself to social movements for peace and social justice. It engages in international networks in Asia and beyond, including the World Social Forum and the Asian Peace Alliance. It publishes the journal *Japonesia Review*, the subtitle of which is 'Critical Analyses for an Alternative World'.
6. *United States Security Strategy for the East-Asia Pacific Region* (1998) Washington, DC: The US Secretary of Defense. Online at: www.dod.gov/pubs/easr98/ easr98.pdf (accessed 9 May 2011).
7. When in opposition, the Democratic Party of Japan had backed removal of the base burden from Okinawa. Since entering government in 2008 it has backtracked, under pressure from the US government and the Liberal Democratic Party opposition.
8. The Security Treaty has effectively been rendered obsolete in the last decade by what is termed a 'realignment' of US policy regarding Japan and the Pacific. The realignment began with the adoption in September 1997, without discussion in the Japanese parliament, of new 'guidelines' that provide for Japan Self-Defence Force participation in wars of America's choosing anywhere in the world if considered relevant to Japan's security. Japan agreed to mobilize its economy to provide logistic support for such war-fighting. The policy 'realignment' continued after 9/11 in two reports commissioned by President Bush senior from his Deputy Secretary of State, Richard Armitage. *The United States and Japan: Advancing toward a Mature Partnership* was published in October 2000, and *The US-Japan Alliance: Getting Asia Right through 2020* in February 2007. They commit Japan's Self-Defence Forces to complete interoperability with US forces and to full participation in ballistic missile defence, counter-terrorism, search and destroy operations, intelligence, surveillance and reconnaissance operations in an 'arc of instability' stretching from Korea to the Middle East. The former document is available online at: http://homepage2.nifty.com/moru/lib/nichibei-anpo/pdf/ INSS%20Special%20Report.pdf; and the latter at http://csis.org/files/media/ csis/pubs/070216_asia2020.pdf (accessed 9 May 2011).
9. From their website: www.ajwrc.org.
10. In elections in 2007 and 2009 the Liberal Democratic Party lost its ruling position in both houses of the legislature to the more centrist Democratic Party.
11. See, for instance, a collection of essays 'correcting' Japanese history, awarded prizes in a competition organized by the Apa Corporation and published in English as Toshio Motoya (ed.) (2008) *The Shocking Truth About Modern History*.
12. In English language, see, for instance, *Women's Asia*, privately published by the Asia-Japan Women's Resource Centre.

7
A State of Peace: Movements to Reunify and Demilitarize Korea*†

Korea, like its near neighbour Japan, experienced occupation by the USA at the end of the Second World War and continues even now to play a crucial role in US military strategy for the Pacific region. The peace movements of the two countries therefore have several themes in common – ending US military hegemony, demilitarizing and democratizing society

---

*My colleague and co-researcher Elli Kim, formerly co-representative and director of research in Women Making Peace, to whom I express my warmest thanks, played a significant role in the research reported here and contributed greatly to this chapter. However, any errors of fact and opinion that remain in it are my own responsibility.

† In the research on which this chapter draws we were afforded interviews by the following people to whom we would like to express our warmest gratitude for the generosity with which they shared their insights into the reunification, anti-war, anti-militarist, peace and feminist movements of South Korea: Cho Young-Hee, representative of Women Making Peace; Chung Hyun-Back, Professor of History at Sung Kyun Kwan University, and active in the Korean Women's Association United; Chung Kyung-Nok (Kyle), of All Together (Dahamke); Kim Duk-Yeop of All Together (Dahamke); Kim Kyung-Mee of the Peace Network, and Center for Peace and Public Integrity, Hanshin University; Kim Sook-Im, former standing representative of Women Making Peace; Lee Daehoon Francis, representative of People's Solidarity for Participatory Democracy; Lee Kang-Sil, co-representative of the Korean Women's Alliance and Korean Alliance of Progressive Movements; Lee Tae-Ho, director of the Center for Peace and Disarmament, People's Solidarity for Participatory Democracy; Nam-Youn In-Soon, standing representative of the Korean Women's Association United; Oh Hye-Ran and Pyon Yeon-Shik of SPARK (Solidarity for Peace and Reunification of Korea); and Son Mee-Hee of the Movement for One Korea, co-representative of the Korean Women's Alliance.

We benefited from a group discussion with Choi Jung-Min of Korea Solidarity for Conscientious Objectors; Jie-Un of the Center for Peace and Disarmament, People's Solidarity for Participatory Democracy; Kang In-Wha of the Women's

and reducing violence in everyday cultures. However, the partition of the Korean peninsula since 1945 has given Koreans an additional and distinctive cause: reunification as one nation. Tensions between these diverse motivations in the South Korean peace movement, and people's creativeness in transcending them, are the topic of this chapter.

On 8 August 1945, just a week before the surrender of Japan, the Soviet Union entered the Pacific theatre of war by launching an attack on Japanese forces in Korea. Their aim was political: to obtain for the USSR a share of the victors' carve-up of the Japanese sphere of influence in North East Asia. The USA, however, determined to prevent the USSR gaining a postwar presence in the Pacific region, swiftly issued an order excluding its allies entirely from the occupation of Japan and its colony on the Korean peninsula, and dividing the latter at the 38th line of latitude. The USSR complied by withdrawing its forces north of the parallel and there supported guerrilla leader Kim Il-Sung, with a band of comrades who had long been fighting the Japanese in Manchuria, in establishing the Democratic Peoples' Republic of Korea (DPRK). In the southern zone of the peninsula the USA installed a puppet president, Syngman Rhee, flown in from the USA to head what would become the Republic of Korea (RoK). The arrangement was inherently unstable. For four millennia Koreans had thought of themselves as one nation and one people.[1] Within five years of the end of the Second World War, these two new factitious states and their sponsors would be engulfed in the first hot conflict of the Cold War.

The Korean War of 1950–53 began with provocative incursions across the demarcation line by the forces of Syngman Rhee, followed by an attack

Peace Research Centre (and member of the former Solidarity for Iraq Peace & Iraqi People); Na Tari Youngjung of the New Progressive Party (and former Women against War); and Yeo-Ok of World Without War and Korea Solidarity for Conscientious Objectors.

We had retrospective help with aspects of this research report concerning Women Make Peace from Jung Kyong-Ian, now director of its policy-making committee. We gained much from a visit to *Durebang* (My Sister's Place) and a conversation with its director Yu Young-Nim. We had an interesting talk with Han Kuk-Yom, Minister of the Presbyterian Church and director of the Women Migrants' Human Rights Center of Korea. Ms Han is also a co-chair of the Women's Committee of the Association of Religious Groups that participates in the Joint Committee for the Realization of the Declaration of 15 June 2000. Thanks to Chen Eun-Bok for a day of conversation and visits in Seoul. Finally, we had invaluable help from two talented interpreters: Lee Se-Hyon and Jeon So-Hee. In addition, Ok Hyun-Joo, in London, helped with translation work. Our very sincere and warm thanks to all the above for your generous co-operation in our research.

by the North Korean People's Army on RoK forces in the Ongjin peninsula at the western end of the demarcation line. The USA entered the war a few days later, landing 80,000 marines at the west coast port of Inchon, and during the summer months of 1950 quickly rolled back the Korean People's Army to the Manchurian border. Mao Zedong, honouring his obligation to the North Korean fighters who had contributed to his recent victory over Chiang Kai-Shek, ordered the People's Liberation Army across the Yalu River, doubling the forces available to Kim Il-Sung. For three years an appallingly destructive war was fought on land, while from the air, unresisted, the USA systematically reduced the North to rubble. The armistice of 27 July 1953 affirmed the 38th parallel as the border between North and South Korea. Not an inch of territory had been gained by either side, but the loss of life, especially in the north, was beyond calculation. In the absence of a subsequent peace agreement, the countries continued, and remain to this day, technically in a state of war.

Building two Koreas

The Korean people on both sides of the partition line applied themselves to rebuilding what remained to them – half a country, physically and economically shattered. But the twin regimes continued to evolve in markedly different ways.[2] In the north Kim Il-Sung's strategy had been from the start to build a local administration on the popular left-inclined 'people's committees' that had been a feature of Korea before and during the World War in the struggle against the hated Japanese colonizers. He made radical reforms of the land system and labour conditions, while women were granted rights and integrated into the workforce on terms of formal equality. However, the social movements that in other countries have struggled from below for such statutory gains did not exist in the Democratic Peoples' Republic of Korea (DPRK). The country was characterized, as it still is, by a one-party political system controlling an extensive bureaucratic structure, and by the almost complete lack of an autonomous civil society. It is effectively ruled by a unique leader. Kim Il-Sung retained this position till his death in 1994, when Kim Jong-Il, the son he nominated to succeed him, took up the reins of power.

Although Kim Il-Sung's political and economic strategy had an affinity with Marxism and Maoism, there were clear divergences. Dispensing with a capitalist phase of development and the historic role of an industrial proletariat, his project was to carry North Korea directly from a peasant society, by means of collectivization and modern farming techniques, to people's power. The centrally planned economy, modelled on Soviet lines, for a while kept pace with the South in heavy industrial development. Excluded from world markets, however, North Korea missed out on the technological revolution of the late sixties and seventies. It is vulnerable to food shortages and has been unable or unwilling to provide its populace with reasonably priced consumer goods such as the cars, televisions and appliances that are taken for granted by the employed working and middle class in the South. Due to the unresolved conflict, the government has felt obliged to spend massively on defence with the effect of militarizing society and empowering a military élite.

What most characterizes the austere culture of North Korea is *Juche*, a philosophy invented and inculcated by Kim Il-Sung. *'Juche'* valorizes 'Korean-ness' and self-reliance. The word actually means 'the subject', and suggests that the human being, not a social class, is the subject of history. In place of class struggle it invokes the striving of a small nation for its rightful independent place in a world of equal nation-states. Perpetuating the Confucian ideals of respect for authority, leadership and hierarchy, and a belief in the organic connection of family, party and state, *Juche* seriously inhibits the growth of diversity and autonomy, resistance or rebellion.

South of the partition line, in the Republic of Korea (RoK), the reactionary Syngman Rhee survived for seven years after the armistice, supported by the USA and, internally, by the old landowning and business classes. While in North Korea those who had collaborated with the Japanese were purged, in the South they continued to have influence. Indeed, security was placed in the hands of the hated ex-colonial Korean National Police which suppressed popular resistance by peasants, organized labour, ex-people's committees and former anti-Japanese guerrillas, students and academics. Rhee was eventually ousted in 1960 in a popular revolt against his police state. Within months however this 'April revolution' was scotched by a military coup. Major General Park Chung-Hee's first step on taking power was to close the National Assembly and ban political activity. South Korea would not return to civilian government until 1993. In the intervening three decades the country suffered periods of state terror in which political dissidents and suspected communist sympathizers were imprisoned, tortured or liquidated. The USA, though embarrassed by these excesses, continued to support the military government of the RoK for, whatever its shortcomings, it was assuredly anti-communist and could be relied on neither to seek alliance with China and the USSR nor tolerate internal leftwing revolt.

While democratic political life was in deep freeze, the South Korean economy flourished. In 1964, encouraged by the USA which favoured the renewal of Japanese influence in Korea as a buffer against communist Asia, the Republic of Korea signed a treaty that normalized the relationship between the ex-imperial power and its former colony. It brought an input of technology and capital investment to South Korea and hastened industrialization. Though there were extremes of wealth and poverty, a middle class grew and prospered. And despite the political repression, a radical political opposition, founded way back in the struggle against Japanese colonial rule, survived in South Korea during the 1970s and 1980s. It included a labour movement of organized workers and peasants. Students were sporadically active. Feminism was emerging, both within and independently of the left. Some of these malcontents were ready to resist the renewal of military rule by Park's successor, General Chun Doo-Hwan. In May 1980, as Chun consolidated power, a demonstration in the town of Kwangju was brutally smashed by the RoK armed forces, leaving many dead. Chun identified 37,000 'dissidents' to send to 'purification camps'. To this outrage the USA turned a blind eye (Cumings 2005).

In the course of our interviews for this research, we learned that 'Kwangju' had been a formative moment in the lives of those present-day activists of an age to have been students at that time. Lee Kang-Sil had been in her fourth year at university when the Kwangju massacre happened. She told us:

> I saw these same people living in the same country, killing each other. Why? The reason was partition! I realized that partition was the crucial issue. Reunification became the goal for me. And I began to see how the USA was controlling things from behind, how the USA was a barrier to democracy. If the USA hadn't given the green light to the South Korean government, the Kwangju massacre would not have happened. So that's when my anti-US perspective was born. We have to take account of both the South and North, together. That's where there is hope. (Lee Kang-Sil in interview)

Francis Lee Daehoon too had been deeply shocked by the Kwangju massacre, and the silence in the country about it. He and the young people around him had learned two lessons from that moment:

> First, the myth that the USA was 'protecting' us was blown. We saw that South Korea was actually under US control. Second, we learned

that students alone are weak. Who could be our ally? It had to be the workers. We rushed to the working class. Trade unions had been organized since the late seventies. Many of them had been concerned with liberal issues and workers' rights, but now they were radicalizing. ... From 1980 to 1987 we had the first class-based worker/student/farmer/urban poor alliance. Some women of that inclination were also involved, a left feminism, different from the largely Christian and liberal feminism of the previous decade. (Francis Lee Daehoon in interview)

Lee Kang-Sil and Francis Lee Daehoon were just two of a generation in whom the repression of the seventies and eighties forged a spirit of resistance and struggle against the South Korean state, and no less vehemently against its US sponsors. We can see however, from their reactions to Kwangju, that the shared experience was going to lead them into differing kinds of activism.

The movement for reunification

The movement to which Lee Kang-Sil would commit her skill and energy was the struggle to make meaningful contact with North Koreans and work with them for the end of partition. During the long decades of military rule, the North Korean and South Korean governments had occasionally expressed a cautiously worded wish for *rapprochement*, but ordinary citizens seeking contact across the line were persecuted as traitors. In South Korea, more began to take the risk during the late 1980s, encouraged by a joint governmental 'Declaration' in 1988. That year the national student movement umbrella organization, *Jeondaehyup*, had the nerve to propose a North–South student summit. The following year, a couple of rebellious South Koreans simply travelled to the North without permission as acts of individual defiance: one was the Reverend Moon Ik-Hwan, the other a female university student, Im Su-Kyung. On return, they were punished under the National Security Law. But to many South Koreans they were an inspiration (Lee Tae-Ho 2003).

In 1989 the people of Germany rebelled against their own partition by pulling down the Berlin Wall. Soon afterwards the Soviet Union, Kim Il-Sung's Cold War ally, went into meltdown. In a uni-polar world Kim understood the United States of America to hold the key to North Korea's future prosperity and international acceptance. He embarked on a course, to which the North Korean regime hold even now, of alternate compliance and provocation. It began development of a nuclear weapon, its principal bargaining chip. The USA responded by alternating carrot and stick (Grzelczyk 2008). Positive moments were marked by inter-governmental 'basic agreements' in 1991 and 1994, but between those dates the DPRK provoked a crisis by announcing its withdrawal from the international nuclear Non-Proliferation Treaty.

In the Republic of Korea the election of 1993 brought the return to civilian rule for which South Koreans had waited so long. Although the National Security Law was not annulled, and pro-democracy, left and labour activists were not yet free from persecution, what the Koreans call *simin undong*, or citizen-based social action, now became possible. A moderate sphere of reformist, intellectual and student organization and activism, involving many middle-class people, began to expand (Cho Hee-Yeon 2000; Jones 2006). Reports of crop failures and famine in the mid-1990s revealed North Korea as a country in desperate, if unadmitted, need. 'Pity' for the North looked less subversive in the South Korean government's eyes than 'admiration' for the North. In 1997 the progressive Kim Dae-Jung was elected President and launched what he called a 'Sunshine Policy' towards North Korea (Moon Chung-In 2001). The practice of manipulating North–South relations for electoral advantage in South Korea would end, to be replaced by transparency and a search for domestic consensus. In response, the North opened access to Mount Geumgang, a tourist spot near the Partition Line, and in November 1998 an estimated 200,000 southern visitors made the day trip. That year and next, thousands of South Koreans would visit the north for family reunions and business trips (ibid.).

The ten years that followed, under Kim Dae-Jung and his like-minded successor Roh Moo-Hyun, would be a remarkable period for the reunification movement, and it is this 'Sunshine decade' to which our account below refers. It was by no means all smooth-running. George Bush was elected US President in 2000 and in his State of the Union address in 2002 stigmatized North Korea as a 'rogue state', part of the 'axis of evil'. Kim Jong-il hit back by flaunting enriched uranium, kicking out UN inspectors and testing missiles. China, Russia and Japan held the USA and the Koreas into five rocky rounds of Six-Party Talks between 2003 and 2007 (Han Yong-Sup 2005). But by 2008, the year before our interviews in Seoul were carried out, a conservative President, Lim Myung-Bak, and the reactionary Grand National Party, had come to power in the RoK, reversing progress towards a peace agreement, returning the country to high military spending and unquestioning allegiance to the USA. Opening to the North ceased to be official policy and the reunification movement was curbed.

Kim Dae-Jung's Sunshine policy had three principles. Military threats from the North would not be tolerated. However, the South would officially abandon its aim of absorbing North Korea and would desist from undermining the Northern regime and its *Juche* system. Third, while the South retained a strong security posture and the RoK-US alliance was affirmed, 'unrestrained interaction' with the North was encouraged. In June 2000, a ground-breaking summit meeting between President Kim Dae-Jung and Chairman Kim Jong-Il took place in Pyongyang. They issued a 'Joint Declaration of 15 June 2000' proclaiming that North and South would solve the question of reunification by their own concerted efforts, on the basis of their different, though not incompatible, aspirations for some kind of federal system. They would do so 'independently', that is to say without the intervention of other powers.[3] In the meantime there was a promise of economic co-operation between enterprises and more people-to-people contact. Civil society could become, for the first time, a genuine actor in the process.

It took a number of years for an organizational structure to solidify through which the South Korean reunification movement could operate. On 4 March 2005 the founding statement was issued of a body calling itself 'The North-South-Overseas Joint Committee for Realization of the 15 June North-South Joint Declaration' (henceforth the '15 June JC'). It had a South Branch based in Seoul, a North Branch in Pyongyang and an Overseas Branch made up of Koreans living elsewhere in the world, with an office in Tokyo. The South and North branches were symmetrical in featuring an internal structure representing the interests of students, peasants, women and other sectors, but beneath this level the two sides inevitably became very lop-sided. The divergent political, social and philosophical movements that constitute civil society in the South are forbidden and penalized in the DPRK where the state and the Korean Workers Party control all public organized life. While the sectoral organizations of the South Branch of the 15 June JC are a device for linking a heterogenous, growing and adaptive mass of civil society organizations, those of the North Branch, including the Women's Headquarters, are official bodies, and any associations downstream from them are state-sponsored, not autonomous.

In South Korea, within and beneath the South Branch of the 15 June JC structure, are three major 'blocs' of civil society organizations. One is the Korean Association of Religious Groups (KARG). A second is the Korean Council for Reconciliation and Co-operation (KCRC) whose many affiliated civic groups[4] include two women's umbrella organizations, the rather conservative Korean National Council of Women (KNCW) and the more feminist-inclined Korean Women's Association United (KWAU). The third bloc is the Korean Alliance of Progressive Movements (KAPM), an umbrella organization for 'the progressive forces'. Whereas the KCRC is a 'consultative' structure, KAPM describes itself as a 'solidarity' structure. Made up of coalitions and organizations of various regions and sectors, including the Korean University Students Union, the Democratic Labour Party, the Korean Peasant Association and the Korean Poor Union, KAPM is 'not only a struggle force but also a people's political frontline'.[5] It too has a women's organization, the Korean Women's Alliance (KWA), of which more below.

In South Korean terminology the term 'progressive forces' is often used to designate what in other countries and cultures might be termed vaguely 'the left'. Importantly, however, here the progressive forces include two rather distinct elements. One is the 'national liberation' (NL) tendency, which comprises unions, parties and NGOs that are, broadly speaking, pro-North, pro-unification, and fiercely opposed to neoliberal global capitalism and US foreign and military policy. The other is the 'people's democracy' (PD) or *minjung* tendency, an array of unions, parties and NGOs that are clearly class-based, workerist, anti-capitalist and 'struggle-oriented'. Although reunification activity is an important focus for the progressive block, the KAPM, unlike the 'civic' block, the KCRC, it is not a 'dedicated' reunification structure, but additionally represents its affiliates on a range of other issues. Conversely, not all of the organizations affiliated to KAPM participate in reunification activity. Those that do so most energetically are of the national liberation (NL) tendency. Some people's democracy (PD) or *minjung* groups choose not to participate.

Crossing the Line

At first, as the humanitarian organizations developed contact with the DPRK, they faced a great deal of mistrust. North Korea was in many respects simply unknown to the visiting teams. None of the normal social statistics were available. When foreigners sought such data it seemed to Northern officials suspiciously like espionage. Hazel Smith carried out research on the humanitarian programme in the North. She wrote later:

> The implications of implementing standard operating procedures for humanitarian organizations were revolutionary. Collecting and disseminating information – a routine operation anywhere else in

the world – had potentially enormous consequences for the wider politics of the Korean peninsula. The immense distrust between the DPRK and major donors was such that every action or omission on either side could inadvertently become a potential trigger for serious political conflict. (Smith 2005: 11)

Eventually the very scale of the activity forced a degree of adaptation to Southern civil society's troubling ways. Shortly into the Sunshine period, thousands of people each year were travelling to the North, including technical experts such as the energy specialists from the Korean Energy Development Organization, and many business people seeking joint ventures.

For the Southerners too the process of engagement with the North required patience, tact and tolerance – a new kind of know-how. All visits and visitors had to be screened and cleared by the governments of North and South, and often an individual might be turned down as 'undesirable' due to some past history, real or imagined. There was no Internet link. Every contact had to be processed by fax through the Tokyo office of the 15 June JC Overseas Branch. Even when a meeting was achieved, it was clear that individual Northern participants could not freely speak their minds. Often they had to refer their decisions back to some authority before things could move forward. Particularly frustrating to many of the Southerners was that, after all these decades of separation, even now it was seldom possible to achieve any real intimacy with Northerners, to chat, exchange candid views, get to know each others' families, visit each others' homes. Even though one might gradually over a succession of meetings build up a practised relationship with a particular partner in the dialogue, the Northern rules rarely allowed it to flower into real friendship.

Experiences differed, however, for just as South Korean organizations varied in their approach to North Korean partners, Northerners also approached relationships with South Korean organizations selectively, distinguishing between their various political positions. Some projects were more sustained and productive than others. One that seems to have satisfied both sides in equal measure was the Bread Factory, a project of the Movement for One Korea (MfOK), an affiliate of the progressives' bloc, the KAPM. We heard the story from Son Mee-Hee, assistant general manager of the Bread Factory project, who, through this work had become a well-known woman in North Korea. The creative idea of the Bread Factory was to produce wheaten loaves to nourish the children in public nurseries and kindergartens around

Pyongyang. The Northern government provided a factory building, and undertook to pay the on-going labour costs of the bakery. MfOK supplied the machinery and regular consignments of wheat flour and other materials, paid for by small monthly donations on the part of many thousands of individual subscribers. The MfOK conceived of this not as charity but as co-operation. Parents of the South would share with those in the North some of the burden of child-rearing. Son Mee-Hee said:

> We thought it would be good to enable South Koreans to actually spend money on the North. In the capitalist South you try to maximize the money you put in your pocket. It would be significant somehow to voluntarily send our own money to people thought of as 'our enemies'. Sending donations of materials and equipment to the North, bought with our personal money, is like saying, 'We want you to prosper along with us'. At the same time it would raise public awareness in the South. It would be a corrective to the customary view of the North.

On one occasion, in a spirit of reciprocity, the North donated a day's production, ten thousand loaves of bread, to the South. MfOK distributed it to the volunteers and activists in their ten centres around the South, giving them a taste of the bread their contributions were baking.

A different left: anti-militarist, anti-war and peace movements

It was not only the movement for reunification with the North that gained momentum during the liberalization of the 1990s. A movement addressing the situation in South Korea also emerged, involving many of the progressive organizations of the people's democracy (PD) or *minjung* tendency, but also many non-aligned individuals and groups. This was the activism into which the Kwangju massacre impelled the then young Francis Lee Daehoon. There were workers' strikes in South Korea, democracy issues were acute. So PD groups, oriented as they were towards class struggle, felt it urgent to address the problems at home, leaving reunification to diplomatic processes. Another Lee, Lee Tae-Ho, told us how, as a student, he had aspired to be active in both movements, but it had seemed to be a matter of either/or. 'One of the hottest issues was how to choose in campaigning between two priorities, summed up in the slogans "reunification" and "anti-war, anti-nuclear".

How to balance these? It was a huge topic for us. And that was the start of long-lasting tensions between the two approaches.' Rightly speaking, the second approach had several aspects: some initiatives were anti-militarist, others were opposed to specific wars, while a third group were more positively defined as concerned with peace and nonviolence in everyday cultures.

The anti-militarist initiatives within the new movement took off slowly during the 1990s, and intensified in the new millennium. As in Japan, the activists were in part responding to damage caused by bases and crimes committed by US personnel. Here too there was a movement to re-examine history, calling for investigation into massacres by US troops during the Korean War (Lee Tae-Ho 2003). Anti-militarist activists also mobilized against the importation to South Korea by the US forces of particular weapons such as Patriot Missiles and F-15K combat aircraft. There was continual suspicion that US vessels docking in Korean harbours might be carrying nuclear weapons. The USA's Missile Defence Initiative, which involves locating technology in South Korea to defend against a putative missile attack by China or Russia, was and still is unpopular. A defining moment occurred in June 2002, when a US military vehicle accidentally killed two school-age girls, and the authorities failed to bring the perpetrators to book. The unprecedented anguish and rage the incident provoked was expressed in a huge national candlelight vigil (ibid.).

Anti-militarism has also involved a critique of the RoK's own military. This is still in theory under UN supervision, but that body devolves the task onto the US military, which exercises joint command with the RoK government. As early as 1991 activists protested against the Ministry of Defence's sponsorship of an international 'arms trade fair'. In 1992 a Joint Committee for Reduction of the Defence Budget was set up to campaign against the high level of military expenditure. Women were active in this, as they still are, calling for a transfer of public funds from military to social and welfare budgets (Kim, Elli 2005). When, in 2005, President Roh Moo-Hyun published a comprehensive plan for 'defence reform', it was welcomed for seeming to consolidate civilian control of the military, but fiercely opposed for proposing an annual increase of 11 per cent in the military budget (Lee Tae-Ho 2005).

There is considerable overlap in membership and actions between this anti-militarist movement and mobilizations against specific wars. There was a strong reaction against the proposal to contribute RoK troops to the Gulf War of 1991. A decade later, the Afghan and Iraq wars sparked huge demonstrations in South Korea, indicating that many activists were beginning to look beyond peninsula politics and identify with the growing international anti-war movement. The South Korean government concurred with US requests to contribute forces to the UN/NATO intervention in Afghanistan, and, to the astonishment of many of those who voted him to power in 2002, the new President Roh subsequently committed RoK troops to Iraq. Both moves evoked large protests. Francis Lee Daehoon told us in interview:

> When the US can simply call in South Korean forces, it raises questions among us about the legitimacy of the US presence in South Korea, and that is fundamentally linked to the legitimacy of South Korea as a state. Roh was supposed to be a liberal. And he sends South Korean troops at the bidding of the US. We thought, 'Who *are* you?'.

The anti-war movement came together as a coalition calling itself Joint Action against War (*Ban-Jeon Gong Dong Haeng Dong*), with a particularly broad following among the young, including students and many women. It organized mass demonstrations and civil disobedience through nonviolent direct action. One such action was the despatch, by an organization calling itself the Iraqi Peace Team, of a group of women and men into the Iraqi war zone as 'human shields'.

Women made a strong input to the 1990s surge in activism. Some women's initiatives were directed against aspects of militarization. For example, in 1992 a women's Joint Committee for the Reduction of the Defence Budget was set up, calling for the transfer of public funds from the military to the social budget, and 1994 saw the formation of a group called Women against Patriot Missiles. Some were specifically anti-war, such as the group that came together in 1991 as 'Mothers Unite to Oppose the Gulf War and Deployment of RoK Troops to the Gulf' (Kim, Elli 2005; Shim and Kim 2005; Hahn Jeong-Sook 2009). Some prefigured the coming reunification activity. Between 1991 and 1993, while still under military government, women organized conferences with North Korean women under the rubric 'Peace in Asia and Women's Role' and later in the decade women initiated a project of cross-border work called 'Sharing Food, Sharing Love' (Kim Sook-Im 2002). But one thing was characteristic of much of women's activism in this field – it was not just against something, it was *for* something. In 1997, a number of women who had been active in these various ways came together to form a substantial organization that would endure till the present day. They gave it the positive name Women Making Peace (WMP). Whenever they engaged in the wider movements WMP always did so from a perspective and with a programme of 'peace' – this positive word was their signature (ibid.).

In the course of our case study in South Korea we interviewed several activists currently involved in these anti-militarist, anti-war and peace movements of South Korea. We visited People's Solidarity for Participatory Democracy and its Center for Peace and Disarmament where we spoke with Francis Lee Daehoon, Lee Tae-Ho and other members. It is on the office and staff of the Center that the responsibility for organizing work for mass demonstrations often falls. We spoke with members of Peace Network, which carries out research and policy analysis; Peace Ground (formed by returners from the Iraq intervention); Solidarity for Peace and Human Rights (set up in 1998) and the more recent World without War. The latter two organizations are both closely related to Korea Solidarity for Conscientious Objectors, campaigning against obligatory military service and supporting the several hundred young males who are at any one time serving prison sentences for refusing militarization.

We also met Oh Hye-Ran and Pyon Yeon-Shik (Regina) at the office of SPARK (Solidarity for Peace and Reunification of Korea). This activist NGO, formed in 1994, has nine district offices and 900 members throughout Korea. The organization participates in some reunification events, but is not primarily located in the reunification movement. Rather, it campaigns for reduction of the RoK military budget. To this end they organize petitions, hold meetings with ministers in the Ministry of Budget Planning (the Treasury), lobby parliamentarians and policy advisers to the President, and hold arms-reduction workshops. They have engaged in sit-down protests out on the street. SPARK's second goal is the replacement of the current unequal Korea-US relationship with one based on equality, revision of the military treaties between the two countries, and gradual withdrawal of all US Forces in Korea. For this they coordinate a rally on alternate Tuesdays in front of the US Embassy and the Ministry of Defence. One evening we joined a small peaceful assembly against the war in Afghanistan, organized by SPARK to coincide with a visit of President Barack Obama to Seoul. It was first surrounded then violently dispersed by police in riot gear.

A second organization in the forefront of the movement against both South Korean military expenditure and the international wars in Afghanistan and Iraq is 'All Together' (*Dahamkke*). We had a chance to interview two of its leading activists, Kim Duk-Yeop and Chun Kyung-Nok (Kyle). They told us how this group started out as part of the International Socialist (IS) tendency in 1991, took shape as an organization in 1999 and adopted the name All Together in 2001. With some 1500 individual members and a newspaper, *Left 21*, they are in the revolutionary and vanguardist Trotskyist tradition, though without subscribing to the over-arching notion of the Fourth International. Kim and Kyle told us that All Together prioritize grassroots activity in a working class conceived as much broader and more diverse than the organized industrial proletariat. They strongly oppose the inequities of race and gender, which they define as effects of the capitalist mode of production and the hierarchical society it generates.

Two women's initiatives

In the context of the Sunshine policy introduced in 1998 and the struc-ture for its realization that followed, women's organizations interested in participating in reunification activities positioned themselves under one of those three blocs of the 15 June JC South structure mentioned above.[6] Women Making Peace was located within an umbrella organi-zation, the Korean Women's Association United (KWAU), beneath the overarching wing of the 'civic' bloc, the Korean Council of Reconciliation and Co-operation (KCRC). From this place in the Sunshine structure WMP participated in many cross-border activities during the decade.

It is informative to compare and contrast Women Making Peace, located under the KCRC, with the Korean Women's Alliance (KWA), located under that other bloc, the Korean Alliance of Progressive Movements (KAPM). While in many ways the two organizations are partners with shared interests, there are also significant divergences between them, deriving from their different political analyses.

Our main sources of information on the Korean Women's Alliance (KWA) and the KAPM, the progressive bloc, were Lee Kang-Sil and Son Mee-Hee, both co-representatives of the former body. While Women Making Peace from the start had interests in both the reunification move-ment and the anti-militarist, anti-war and peace movements, the Korean Women's Alliance was set up in 2007 with a single focus: reunification. Among all South Korea's women's organizations, it is the one that dedi-cates the greatest proportion of its energies to reunification. It is, in a sense, the women's wing of the Korean Alliance of Progressive Movements, and strongly informed by national liberation (NL) thinking. The KWA aims to educate other groups and organizations in the progressive spectrum on gender issues and gender equality. Lee Kang-Sil explained to us that they may be distinguished from women's organizations outside the 'progressive' bloc by their focus on 'grassroots' women, that is to say 'labourers, peasants and the poor'. In countries where a language of class is more readily used than in South Korea, these would be termed women of the working class. KWA's objective is 'to take action for reunification from a women's perspective'. In so far as it addresses matters beyond and other than reunification, it has a strong concern with women's employment and economic circumstances.

As to Women Making Peace, my main source of information was my co-researcher, Elli Kim, one of its founding members and a former co-representative. But we also had a chance to interview other members and former activists in WMP, including Cho Young-Hee, its current representative (equivalent to a chairperson), and Kim Sook-Im, a former standing representative. We also interviewed Chung Hyun-Back, at one time a co-representative of WMP. WMP co-operates with the Korean Women's Alliance in women's work for reunification, and has been active alongside them in all the major North–South encounters of the Sunshine period. What marks a difference is that in addition to reunification activity WMP is, as we have seen, also active in the anti-militarist, anti-war and peace movements.

WMP has individual membership and its main income derives from subscriptions. It has an office, with three full-time and five part-time staff, located with eleven other feminist organizations in the Women's Center for Equality and Peace. WMP positions itself distinctively within the autonomous feminist tradition, stressing inclusion and refusing dogma. As Cho Young-Hee told us in interview, 'We believe there's always more than one answer'. They feel it is impossible for individuals who are not peaceful in their own lives to engage effectively in struggles for peace. Violence is present in the language we habitually use, in the home, and even in movements against militarism and war. They recognize the gendering of this violence. Elli Kim wrote that 'the violence of war occurs not only in times of war, but [is] intricately related to patriarchal gender discrimination in daily lives and sexual violence committed by men' (Kim, Elli 2002). WMP therefore addresses this continuum of violence through cultural work including meditation, discussion groups and peace education from a feminist perspective.

* * *

The organizations and individuals mentioned in the above account cannot be said, in methodological terms, to be a representative sample of the contemporary movement in South Korea. They do however add up to a substantial component of the movement, and together constitute an informative 'panel of discussants', covering between them a wide span of concerns in the field of activism for a peaceful, demilitarized and reunified future for both Koreas. It will already be apparent that this is a complex and shifting field. Groups and initiatives are for ever emerging and being eclipsed, changing name, grouping under this and that umbrella organization which in turn also now and then change name. The evolving elements are also diversified, not only by focus but by political analysis and strategy. Views polarize around certain contested issues. The divergences of opinion, however, do not only or always separate organizations and networks from each other. They are sometimes internal to them. Either way, they strain relationships and require painstaking negotiation if the disparate elements are to cohere as a social movement.

Below we distinguish three persistent issues, and try to illustrate the way the organizations and individuals introduced in the foregoing section relate to them, the analyses they deploy. They are, first, the question of Korean nationhood and nationalism; second, attitudes towards North Korea; and, third, contrasted strategies for bringing the peninsula from its state of war to a state of peace.

The once and future 'nation' of Korea

Given more than half a century of partition preceded by thirty-six years under the imperial rule of Japan, it is not surprising that ordinary Koreans are highly susceptible to national sentiment (Chung and Ro 1979). It affects even the young, and is expressed for instance in massive enthusiasm for Korean teams in international sporting events (Lee Sook-Jong 2006). The peculiarities of Korea's history mean that some tendencies among the progressive forces in South Korea invoke national identity with an enthusiasm not found on the left elsewhere. During the colonial period, as Bruce Cumings remarks, 'Socialists and communists were always Korean nationalists as well ...' (Cumings 2005: 158. Shin Il-Chul 1979 also makes this point). The reunification movement taps into this deep reservoir of feeling for the nation.

Lee Kang-Sil and Son Mee-Hee of the Korean Women's Alliance were helpful in explaining to us the national liberation tendency's positive invocation of 'nation'. For their organizations, so long the partition persists, the ideal of Korean nationhood, combined with emphatic opposition to neoliberal global capitalism, is an irreducible necessity. Of course they are aware of the deep mistrust of ethno-nationalist movements felt by progressives in Europe, due to the struggle with Nazism in the 1930s and 1940s, and more recently the nationalist wars that destroyed Yugoslavia in the 1990s. They are therefore careful in their use of terms, distinguishing 'national*ism*', the passion of the right, from the concepts of 'nation', 'nationhood' or 'national identity', which the NL tendency consider necessary and positive organizing concepts. They believe a destructive, extremist interpretation of nation is averted so long as the aims of the national movement are to end imperialism and bring peace. This, they point out, is the nationalism espoused by many of the twentieth-century independence movements of Asia, Africa and Latin America, in which the word nation signals not exclusion and supremacy but self-reliance and resistance.

Some South Korean activists, however, feel that the national liberation tendency's appeal to national identity, though popular and, in the context, understandable, is nonetheless dangerous. In particular, feminists such as those of Women Making Peace, who subscribe to a theory that the structures and ideologies of nationalism, patriarchy and militarism are irreducibly intersected and together a source of violence and war, are bound to be uncomfortable with the assertions of national identity and nationhood.[7] Kim Sook-Im for instance said:

> The concept of nation is outdated, old fashioned. Today we talk about multi-culturalism, across the world. You see signs, banners in the street in North Korea, invoking our 'nation-first' ideology. [. . .] The 15 June Joint Committee structures are deeply imbued with nationalism. [. . .] We would prefer to approach reunification as something that's necessary for us as human beings, rather than as Koreans. We want to be able to simultaneously raise issues of peace, demilitarization – things that get overshadowed by the concept of 'Korean nation'.

Elli Kim similarly believes we should 'oppose the logic of power' and give no credence to the idea of 'national territories'. 'Distancing from the national interest,' she wrote, 'going beyond the boundaries ... are the characteristics of women's peace movements that stand out since 9/11' (Kim, Elli 2007: 288).

To the feminist case against nationalism, Lee Kang-Sil responds, 'Women who live in imperialist countries haven't experienced colonization and national liberation struggles'. An excess of nation-mindedness leading to national*ism*, she admits, leads both to patriarchy and subjugation by the state. However that is no reason for abandoning a nation-*orientation*. 'If women are included in the national discourse, then it won't develop along patriarchal lines'. Lee Kang-Sil is thus critical of the kind of structuralist feminist theory that represents patriarchy and nationalism as enduring and mutually shaping power systems. At the same time she is critical of postmodernist feminist deconstructions that posit a multiplicity of national identities, but in her view do so 'thoughtlessly', abandoning the 'big story' of nation and capitalism.

The discomfort with 'nation' articulated by feminist anti-militarists is shared by some of the mainstream anti-militarist and anti-war movement organizations, including People's Solidarity for Participatory Democracy (PSPD) and its Center for Peace and Disarmament (CPD). Francis Lee Daehoon said, in interview:

> The pro-North nationalists will argue that South Korea is a US colony, subject to US imperialism, and that democratic human rights are not possible in these circumstances. They believe the anti-US struggle must come first, and that too is represented as being 'for our national good'. Nationalism encompasses all their political agenda.

What WMP and PSPD/CPD, and those who share their perspective, most mistrust in the popular invocation of nation is its essentialism, its representation of the Korean nation as primordial, eternal, fixed and given. Even in the apparently innocent 'football nationalism' of contemporary Korean youth, the word *minjok* is current, which invokes bloodline and ancestry, as well as cultural factors such as common language (Lee Sook-Jong 2006). But, the sceptics ask, does a Korean nation objectively exist? Is it the same today as a century ago? Will it be the same a hundred years from now? The idea of countries with shifting populations in an everchanging and more interactive world is what inspires the anti-nationalism of the people's democracy (PD) tendency among the progressive forces. Anti-nationalism in their repertoire is expressed most fiercely in campaigns against racism in South Korea. Likewise, All Together, with its emphatic class analysis, sees racism as a dangerous source of division in the working class. Kim Duk-Yeop said of the NL tendency's stress on nation: 'It's one of their greatest weaknesses. Often we worry that it might lead them to scapegoat minorities in South Korea. Sometimes they say insensitive things, for which we criticize them.'

Negotiating a coherent position on the Korean 'nation', whether for oneself, for an organization or for a movement, necessarily consumes a deal of thought and energy. Kim Kyung-Mee is a young woman active in the Peace Network. In interview she described to us how, coming new to the peace movement, 'a normal person, like anyone else', she had been confused. 'To reunify we need nationalism, we need the idea of Korea. It's in the logic of the movement. But among peace activists, nationalism is a negative value.' When she first dipped her toe into all this, she told us, she didn't know how to resolve this contradiction. Her thinking went in circles. 'Why unite anyway – when there is no particular inconvenience living as we are? Because we are one people! BUT ... that is being nationalist!' She was trying to learn, searching around for an answer and finding none. Her fear was that the nationalism invoked in reunification work could turn out to be a 'bad nationalism' such as she had witnessed elsewhere. 'It could be a will to make us strong *against* other countries.' She didn't want to be part of such a movement.

However, we found people on all sides producing formulae for a shared understanding, or at least a mutual tolerance, of different positions on nation and nationalism. In the end, a certain pragmatism comes into play. Chung Hyun-Back said:

> The position of Korean feminists is bound to be different from that of feminists in the West on the matter of nationalism because we have to start from Korean realities. [...] For me, nationalism *cannot* be a primary ideology. *But* the movement will always have to consider the national question.

One way of dealing constructively with the divergence is to clarify that in the Korean context, and particularly in reunification thinking, nationalism is not incompatible with internationalism. As Cho Young-Hee put it, 'Nation in the context of Korea is not chauvinistic. Internationalism is not its opposite'. It is closer to meaning simply 'a respect for Korean self-identity'. Oh Hye-Ran, active in SPARK, also insists that Korean nationalism should be seen not as contradicting, but as complementing, the left's aspiration to internationalism. This perspective imagines a Korean nation equal with and respecting of other nations in an internationalist world.

Attitudes towards North Korea

People of South Korea, as would be expected, vary widely in their opinions of and attitudes towards the North Korean regime. Some on the right see it as a long-lived tyranny that must be swept away, the North absorbed into the South. A few South Koreans, on the contrary, are so critical of their own society that they view the Northern regime as preferable. Most hold a view between these extremes. Even among those who seek to sustain a programme of contact and exchange with the North, many harbour serious reservations about the economic rigidity, lack of democracy and disregard for human rights they perceive in the DPRK. Conflicting attitudes to North Korea are sometimes termed the 'South–South ideological conflict' and seen as a major impediment to a peace process (Kwak and Joo 2003).

The most solidary position in relation to North Korea is that invoked by the national liberation (NL) tendency, so deeply involved in the reunification movement. Unlike the conservative forces, on the one hand, and the people's democracy (PD) or *minjung* tendency on the other, both of which perceive the Northern regime as little other than a dogmatic and repressive dictatorship, NL thinking understands North Korea's economic and political deficits always in the context of the attitude of the USA to North Korea. The poor economy and heavy militarization of North Korea are both explained, in this view, by the long-standing blockade and, indeed, pseudo-war, that exists between that wealthy giant and its impoverished 'enemy'. Lee Kang-Sil told us, 'The North Koreans would like to focus on economic development, but it simply can't afford to. They are obliged to spend their resources on military defence'. The NL tendency urges a positive reading of the DPRK. They stress its huge growth potential, with masses of undeveloped natural resources and a highly educated labour force. The only thing preventing the DPRK becoming an economically thriving and politically 'open' society is US enmity. Lee Kang-Sil stresses, 'The North Korean side and our group in the reunification movement are in agreement about these thoughts'.

As to the democracy deficit, again NL makes a case for the North. There are, after all, other forms of democracy than the liberal democracy of 'the West', which in any case has many shortcomings. The North Korean People's Congress permits of genuine representation of the population, they argue, albeit with the exception of certain disfavoured ex-capitalist and feudal classes. In the framework of the state, though decisions are strongly shaped by the Party, there does exist a grassroots, deliberative, policy-shaping system to which local communities and agricultural co-operatives have an input. There may be no access to international media, but, after all, the 'free' media of South Korea and Western countries often purvey misinformation and bias.

The attitude to the DPRK of the PD tendency in South Korea is less unified than that of the NL tendency. Some Marxists and communists justify the Northern regime, despite its divergence from Third International orthodoxy. The original leaders of the North won admiration and legitimacy among many Koreans by their heroic and costly liberation struggle against Japan. Their successors have inherited this positive reputation. Such a view is considered deeply subversive in the South, and for this reason alone is attractive to some on the left. On the other hand, those South Koreans of Trotskyist, anti-Comintern and international socialist inclination categorize the DPRK as a degenerate authoritarian state-capitalist regime.

The sympathetic-yet-critical activists of the reunification and anti-militarist, anti-war and peace movements face a dilemma. Should we speak out honestly in criticism of the North Korean state and society, show ourselves for who we are and what we really think, at the risk of forfeiting our Northern partners' confidence in us? Or on the contrary should we, even if it compromises us, tactfully hide our doubts and disagreements in order to keep the conversation going (and avoid giving fuel to the North's enemies)? For the national liberation tendency there is no dilemma. They are clear that a critique of North Korea for its denial of human rights is inappropriate in the circumstances. Lee Kang-Sil explained to us that North Korea is too often singled out for judgment by Western observers, using Western criteria, and ignoring the workings of global political power. In a world context, in which North Korea is struggling for its very survival, the USA exploits the theme of 'North Korea's human rights deficit' for its own political interests. Civil society groups should take care not to get drawn into the US discourse. The North's democracy should and eventually will be addressed by North Koreans themselves. Lee Kang-Sil added: 'Every country has a human rights issue and we cannot say that one is better than another in this respect. Direct comparisons are inappropriate.'

Even the women of Women Making Peace, who harbour serious reservations about the nature of the Northern regime, understand the need for caution. Cho Young-Hee said:

We shouldn't criticize North Korea from a Western point of view. We need to be sensitive. And we should take care not to criticize North Korea too publicly. Any democratic or human rights shortcomings in the North are immediately jumped on and exploited in the US media.

She added, however:

At the same time we shouldn't simply become pro-North and adopt everything they represent. We need to meet them in person, face to face. It's important to be able to acknowledge and understand the differences between us, and engage with them. That is a basic step in all conflict reconciliation.

South Korean women's organizations that have dealings with the North encounter the regime's authoritarianism in one particularly acute form: gender relations. Patriarchalism persists in both societies, but the greater prosperity in the South, combined with an active civil society in which a feminist movement has flourished, make for marked differences. In the North women have had formal equality in employment since 1948 and a representational quota gives them an assured presence in the political and administrative system. The traditional patriarchal 'family head' system has been abolished, as it has in the South. Literacy is almost 100 per cent, and North Korean women have the highest rate in the world of participation in paid employment. Maternity leave is generous. Health care is universal and free. Nonetheless, women's institutionalized benefits do not translate into status and influence for women in the power system. Women continue to fill the lowliest jobs in the economy. During the years of crop failure in the 1990s they bore the brunt of the famine, benefited least from state food allocations, and experienced a drastic maternal mortality rate of forty-one per thousand (Smith 2005: 48, 89). Recent economic crises have also adversely affected women's status. Besides, the society is even more militarized than that of the South, with a consequent devaluation of women and the feminine. The machismo penetrates not only the military but the North Korean political and economic system. A catchword often heard is 'powerhouse' (*gang seong dae guk*). It signifies powerful army, powerful economy, powerful country and, at the top, a supremely powerful man.

What divides women in the South Korean movements is how to respond to the apparent acceptance of patriarchalism by Northern women. Some feminists in the Southern branch of the reunification movement find the Northerners painfully deferential to men and to masculine authority, and strangely uncritical of militarism. They suffer from the lack of feminist partners in North Korea, which has no autonomous women's movement with the freedom to explore, express and fight for women's needs and rights. Kim Sook-Im, of Women Making Peace, told us:

> When we have women's exchange events I try to make a critique of the militarist and nationalist aspects of North Korean society and the reunification process. But North Korean women always argue that

those matters must be considered subordinate to the huge task of reunification. The differences between us were always very visible on issues like arms reduction, denuclearization, building international solidarity for reunification, and securing women's participation in all reunification processes. Those issues arose when drafting joint statements at exchange meetings. We would say, 'We are an NGO for women's rights and for peace, and we must be capable sometimes of co-operating with, but sometimes criticizing, our respective governments'. But the North Korean women didn't accept this point of view.

There is, however, an issue dividing the different tendencies in the reunification and anti-militarist, anti-war and peace movements of South Korea that is, quite literally, more explosive than gender relations. It is the matter of North Korean nuclear capability. The nuclear tests of 2006 and 2009 had a deeply divisive effect on the movements. Anti-militarists were outraged and unforgiving. But the NL tendency continued to defend the North's nuclear policy. Lee Kang-Sil insists:

We must take account of the national issue, the national context in which North Korea makes this choice. The US wants regime change in the North. It's just too costly for North Korea to compete with the USA by conventional means. The only way they can defend themselves is by means of nuclear weapons. So they have become a nuclear state. It has been a successful strategy, which should be seen as having prevented war here, and brought peace nearer.

Son Mee-Hee of the Movement for One Korea concurred. 'We feel,' she says, 'that it's unfair to forbid North Korea to have a nuclear weapon when the USA has a whole arsenal of them. The US should dismantle theirs first.'

In the middle ground of opinion, in the movements and in society at large, some prefer simply to keep silent on the issue of North Korea's weapon. Some national liberationists hush their support for North Korea's strategy for fear of appearing too radical, while some moderates hush their criticism of it for fear of seeming to align with the right. But many organizations and individuals are more creative in seeking out a position of compromise on which to work together towards what everyone in these movements, in the end, wants to achieve: regional and global nuclear disarmament. One organization that works constructively on the issue of nuclear weapons is Peace Network. They carry out research and policy work and publish papers, addressing nuclear weapons in the context of achieving a peace treaty involving a non-nuclear zone in North East Asia, together with an all-round reduction in conventional arms. They hold a monthly forum drawing activist organizations together around this difficult and divisive issue. Kim Kyung-Mee told us the Network believe the first priority is to make North Korea feel more secure. The bomb, they say, is a systemic problem, not a manifestation of North Korean evil. South Korea should respond to the nuclear tests by acting as a peacemaker, bringing the US and North Korea to the negotiating table.

Roads to peace

One way of understanding the divergences between the various elements of the South Korean movements is to see them as proposing different routes along which the people of the peninsula imagine they might travel to reach a unified and demilitarized society. For instance, can Korea achieve this 'by ourselves', as the North Korean mantra proclaims, and their NL partners in the Korean Alliance of Progressive Movements also believe? Or is the mediation of friendly neighbours needed to defuse the animosity between North Korea and the USA? The latter view motivated the intergovernmental Six Party Talks of 2003 to 2007, drawing into conference the two Koreas, the USA, Russia, China and Japan. Women Making Peace and other likeminded women's organizations, noting the absence of women from these official talks, set up a 'Track 2' process to parallel the government's 'Track 1' diplomacy. In their North East Asia Women's Peace Conferences of 2008 and 2009 they brought together women of these same countries (except for North Korea itself which at that time was withholding its participation from such international moves) (Hahn Jeong-Sook 2009). Women of the Korean Women's Alliance did not support the idea of these women's talks on the 'six party' model, Lee Kang-Sil explained: reunification should be pursued 'between and within our nation first'. The Six Party process at the governmental level was, in the NL view, merely a ploy by the USA to put pressure on the North. Why would women wish to replicate this approach?

Another divergence of routes concerns demilitarization. The passionate desire of the anti-militarist movement is to divest North Korea of its massive military machinery, to cut South Korea's defence budget and rid it of US bases. But is all militarization reprehensible? Here a divergence occurs between the Korean Women's Alliance and Women Making Peace that parallels closely the divergence we have already noted on nationalism. The autonomous feminist movement, not only in South Korea but worldwide, tends to a view of militarism and militarization as profoundly gendered and inevitably oppressive (Cockburn 2007, Korean edition). Kim Sook-Im, of Women Making Peace, concurs with this. She says: 'Our analysis is that militarism and patriarchy are related, and that relationship is something we have to take account of in our activism'.[8] However, this intersectional understanding of militarism and militarization as having a necessary and malign association with patriarchy does not win universal agreement among South Korean women activists. Women of the Korean Women's Alliance do not see militarization as necessarily enhancing male domination, militarizing masculinity and exacerbating the oppression of women. Lee Kang-Sil believes this concept leads to an erroneous opposition to militarism *per se*. She told us, yes, of course, the long-term aim must be a demilitarized world free of war. In the meantime, however, militarization in 'third world' countries should not be judged by the same criteria as that of imperialist countries, with which they are in a power relation. 'We have to put militarism in the context of nation. We have to ask, what is the militarism for? Who is it for? It is making a serious error to put imperialist militarism and defensive militarism in the same bag.'

A third point at which the imagined route to a solution bifurcates is where it appears necessary to choose between 'reunification' and 'peace'. There are those who say 'if you want peace you have no choice but to work first for reunification' and those who reverse the causality and say 'reunification will not be achieved without prior work for peace'. The NL tendency naturally prioritizes reunification, which for them is about the survival of Korea as a nation. It cannot and should not be reduced to one among many different activities needed to make the world a more peaceful place. The ultimate goal, yes, is peace. But as long as imperialism remains, the struggle must continue. Peace will only be possible when the USA and other imperialist countries have given up their military bullying of weak nations such as North Korea.

For Women Making Peace, SPARK and the PSPD's Center for Peace and Disarmament, on the contrary, an important aim in being involved in reunification activity is to contribute a 'peace perspective'. They believe (as our informants in SPARK put it) that the 'problems' in and of the North are caused by 'the whole structure of North East Asia, the arms race, the legacy of the war'. They therefore prioritize a civil society quest for peace and disarmament – for the whole peninsula. Listening carefully to the women and men we interviewed, we came to understand that this 'peace first' idea, though subtle, is passionately held. Jie-Un of the Centre for Peace and Disarmament said that, for her, 'Reunification isn't, and it shouldn't be seen as, the ultimate goal of our movement. What we need to do is put an end to the Cold War on the Korean peninsula and reframe the relationship between North and South'. And Kim Kyung-Mee of the Peace Network sees the process towards a peace settlement in North East Asia as a step-by-step affair. 'That's why we shouldn't focus on reunification as such and subordinate all else to that.'

All Together, from their sharply anti-capitalist perspective, also disagree with prioritizing reunification, but for a different reason. It is not that work for 'peace' must come first. It is that reunification activity stakes too much on the ruling classes of North and South Korea. The only road to an ultimate peace, for All Together and similar left tendencies, is a revolutionary transformation of society in both halves of Korea. The workers of both countries must unite and overthrow their governments to create a single workers' state.

Some, however, refuse to choose between 'reunification' and 'peace', finding it a false dichotomy. Reunification should be seen as just one of several valid routes to peace. Kim Sook-Im, for instance, said:

> It's about where you place reunification in your vision, whether you see it as an ultimate goal or a means to an end. That creates differences in the approach to reunification and in the process – whether you make sure it contains the perspective of peace, of ending militarization.

In this sense she believes Women Making Peace 'are interested in the reunification movement *as a form of peace movement*, as part of the process of establishing peace in the Korean peninsula'. Elli Kim has a slightly different position from others in Women Making Peace. She inserted here:

> I don't take 'reunification', that word, as my own agenda. I would rather say 'overcoming the partition' or 'de-partitioning'. The partition is such a huge barrier to peace. We need to overcome the difficult conditions that the partition has established in the peninsula. It is not the case that a single state and one system is the only way to reunification.

Park Sun-Song, in his preface to an edition of *Korea Peace Report* dedicated to this theme, wrote of the need to resolve the tensions and close the gap between the Korean reunification and peace movements, in the interests of building a greater solidarity without which no progress would be possible (Park 2005: 17). People's Solidarity for Participatory Democracy and its Center for Peace and Disarmament, publishers of this journal, have been key actors in developing and framing such a shift. The new principle at work is the idea that reunification can be achieved only through the simultaneous reform of *both* North and South Korean political and administrative systems and cultures. As Lee Tae-Ho puts it, 'the issue of overcoming national division and the reform of the North and South Korean civil society are becoming increasingly linked with each other' (Lee Tae-Ho 2003: 112). Whereas the conventional reunification movement thinking is 'North and South must unite to fight the USA', their fresh thinking, which potentially transcends the main contradiction in the movement, is to 'concede the existence of problems in both North and South, and unite to deal with them simultaneously'. Both sides have reproduced injustice in this distorted system; both have taken advantage of the hostility. Now both should redress the injustices and deal with them together.

PSPD call their initiative the 'peace state'. They mean a state in which the security paradigm is replaced by a peace paradigm. They are proposing that security affairs, 'exclusively monopolized by the state agencies' should be 'social-ized' and 'civil-ized', brought under the surveillance of civil society (Lee Daehoon 2008). It is a bold move, inciting civil society organizations to trespass on the terrain of security, a 'prohibited arena' in Korea (Center for Peace and Disarmament 2005: 199). It means, what is more, putting ethics into an ethics-free arena, introducing norms such as tolerance, co-operation, co-existence and respect for diversity that are currently far from the minds of conventional security specialists. Francis Lee Daehoon, of PSPD, believes the security state constructs fictitious external threats for purposes of internal control, a process 'guaranteed through the combination of patriarchy, authoritarianism, male-supremacy and other non-democratic belief-systems' (Lee Daehoon 2005: 150). South Korea, these analysts propose, should declare itself a 'peace state', cutting military expenditure on both sides and producing 'a gain in "real security" for both North and South Koreans'. Such a move would involve increased participation and control of governance by civil society. And it would involve mechanisms by which to internationalize the process, so that the civil societies of countries in the region would together monitor their militaries and create an 'East Asian Common House'.[9] In interview Francis Lee Daehoon described the consensus in PSPD on treating 'security' as a social construct, inviting reinterpretation:

> Violence is generated by the state and the social structures within it. The new government [of 2008] is confrontational and 'national-security-nostalgic'. It is not enough to limit ourselves to criticizing defence and foreign policy. We need to address the social dimension of state violence. Show how new policies on police behaviour, migrant workers, the urban poor and so on, have changed, with the effect of heightening the general level of violence in Korea. Let's introduce this social dimension into our discussion of security.

This initiative for a 'peace state' at the national level has resonance with the work of Women Making Peace towards 'peace in everyday life'. As we have seen, the women of WMP feel it is important to change people's way of thinking, to 'mobilize peace as a value for people' rather than to simply denounce war policies. Thus by 'peace' they mean no violence of any kind, of thought, word or action. Kim Sook-Im told us in interview:

> A lot of politicians and activists use 'peace' instrumentally, just as a form of rhetoric. Peace is a condition free of violence, a value that opposes all forms of violence, including 'structural violence'. But, due to our shortcomings, often people don't think of peace this way.

Cho Young-Hee explained graphically. She drew a diagram representing violence as a chain, which showed the USA (symbolized by the stars and stripes) at one end, leaning heavily on the South Korean riot police who are delivering violence to ordinary citizens, who then (next step in the chain) go back home and transmit violence there. That is to say, the man beats the woman, victim becomes offender. And finally, 'the woman beats the dog'. She said:

> For activists this chain of violence presents challenges and problems. Because there is sometimes violence, for instance, in the way we communicate with one another. It is sometimes not mutually respectful, but authoritative and based on force. Whether in the larger social structure or everyday life, the rule of force dominates our lives, affects the way we communicate, and renders every part of our lives un-peaceful. We see the task of Women Making Peace as

both resisting the structure and changing the way we live and relate to each other.

In other words, instead of ascribing insecurity only to external threats, these South Korean peace thinkers are including in their frame of reference the human insecurity generated within and by the state, and violence lived in and through the cultures of everyday life. They are, in a word, redefining the meaning of peace and the scope of a peace movement.

Notes

1. Contemporary Koreans locate the origin of 'Korea' as a 'nation' in the foundation of the dynasty known as Old Choson in 2333 BCE (Uichol Kim 2001).
2. Histories of the Koreas vary widely in their evaluation of the respective political regimes of the Democratic People's Republic of Korea and the Republic of Korea. In compiling this very summary account I have referred to Paul French's *North Korea: The Paranoid Peninsula* (2007), sharply critical of the DPRK, and Bruce Cumings' *Korea's Place in the Sun: a Modern History* (2005) which is more even-handed about the Northern regime but unforgiving regarding US tolerance of misrule in South Korea.
3. Text available online at: http://en.wikipedia.org/wiki/June_15th_North-South_Joint_Declaration (accessed 8 January 2010).
4. Note that the term 'civic group' (*si-min jib-dan*) is used in Korea to designate a citizen-based initiative, in contrast for instance to a class- or labour-based initiative. All these are encompassed within the broader term 'civil society' (*si-min sa-hoe*) defined as non-economic organization outside the confines of the state and political system.
5. A useful online source of information on the Korean Alliance of Progressive Movements (KAPM) is: http://jinbocorea.org/main_eng.php. See also: www.iacenter.org/korea/afghan_kapm121609 (accessed November 2009).
6. As with the mainstream movement of men and women, so with women's organizations – while some entered the reunification structures after the millennium others continued to focus their activism against the US military presence in South Korea and against the deployment of RoK troops in the international wars in Iraq and Afghanistan. Some women's organizations that made the latter choice were SAFE Korea (Korean Women's Network against Militarism) which formed in 2000 and became the part of the East Asia-US-Puerto Rico Women's Network against Militarism; Women against War which met for the first time the following year; and Women against the USA which came together in 2002 – and would later be renamed the Women's National Alliance.
7. The complex relationship of nationalism and feminism in the South Korean context has been argued extensively in a collected work edited by Elaine H. Kim and Chungmoo Choi (1998).

8. This intersectional theory, which is characteristic of the feminist anti-militarist movement worldwide (see my Introduction, but also many instances in Cockburn 2007), has been developed and promoted in South Korea by the feminist academic Kwon In-Sook, whose work is well known to the women cited above (for instance Kwon In-Sook 2006). A debate occurred between Professor Kwon and Lee Kang-Sil of the Korean Women's Alliance at a conference titled 'Dialogue between the Reunification Movement and Feminist Movement' organized by the Women's Committee of Korean Council of Reconciliation and Co-operation in 2007.

9. PSPD's concept of a 'peace state' is in tune with the approach of a South Korean scholar, Paik Nak-Chung. A significant leader in South Korean civil society, until recently he was a 'representative' of the South Korean Branch of the 15 June Joint Committee. In his book, *The Division System in Crisis* (2001) he develops a concept he terms 'regime of partition'. He suggests that the capitalism of the South and the socialism of the North are not simply unconnected, contrasted and hostile systems, but are mutually dependent and mutually shaped. The analysis leads to building a wider solidarity by embracing the differences between North and South, instead of focusing on and criticizing the shortcomings of one or the other. In similar vein, PSPD are developing the concept of the 'system of division' in which the two Koreas have been locked for more than half a century. It is characterized by two overlapping sets of power inequalities; that between foreign and peninsula forces, and that between élites and peoples on both sides of the line. Like Paik, they see the twin polities as distorted by their shared history and visualize them together as the single object of transformation (Park Sun-Song 2005).

8
Guns and Bodies: Armed Conflict and Domestic Violence*

There is a class of weapons known to arms manufacturers, arms traders and arms control activists as 'SALW': Small Arms and Light Weapons. They do not excite as much public concern as nuclear devices and chemical weapons, but arguably, given their numbers, their spread and death toll, they too are 'weapons of mass destruction'. The Small Arms Survey estimates there are currently around 900 million in circulation worldwide. They are produced by more than a thousand manufacturing companies located in nearly a hundred countries, and assembled from components whose origins are still more widespread. Only a quarter of these weapons are thought to be in the armouries of state security sectors, the remainder are in the hands of 'non-state' military elements, or of ordinary civilians. Guns are a material element in the time-and-space continuum of violence. They span pre-war, war, postwar and peace. Of the estimated

*My co-researcher in his case study was Sarah Masters, co-ordinator of the Women's Network of the International Action Network on Small Arms. Her partnership was invaluable, and I thank her warmly. The chapter benefits greatly from her first hand experience and insights, but any shortcomings it may have are my responsibility. For the information and opinion gathered in the course of the case study I am indebted to the following, who generously gave time for an interview and commented on draft reports: Marren Akatsa-Bukachi, executive director of the Eastern Africa Sub-regional Support Initiative for Women's Advancement (EASSI); Rose Othieno, executive director, and Grace Tukaheebwa, staff member, of the Center for Conflict Resolution (CECORE); Canon Joyce Nima, executive director of the Uganda Joint Christian Council (UJCC); Joe Burua, UNDP staff member of the Uganda National Focal Point on Small Arms; Richard Mugisha, executive director of the Uganda Action Network on Small Arms (UANSA); and, in London, Rebecca Peters, director, International Action Network on Small Arms (IANSA). My warmest thanks to you all.

three-quarters of a million deaths in armed violence annually worldwide, around two-fifths are believed to occur in actual armed conflict while three-fifths occur far from the battlefield – or rather they happen in the battlefield of everyday life, in murders, suicides and accidents.[1]

The 'small arms' category in SALW refers to revolvers, self-loading pistols, rifles and carbines, assault rifles, sub-machine guns and light machine guns. This is the kind of weapon usually owned or carried personally by an individual, a soldier, police officer, security guard, insurgent or civilian. The 'light weapon' category refers to heavy machine guns, hand-held grenade launchers, portable rocket launchers and the like. These are designed for use by a crew of two or three people, and are characteristically the equipment of state forces or insurgent units rather than individuals (UNDP 2008a: 2). In this chapter we shall be concerned mainly with the former category, though the campaigns we refer to, especially at international level, are often concerned with the control of both small arms and light weapons.

Like earlier successful international movements to ban land mines and chemical weapons, and the current movement to rid the world of nuclear arsenals, concerted action to curb the proliferation of SALW may be seen as one element of the world's anti-war, anti-militarist and peace movements. In this chapter we trace the political and gender dynamics in three components of the movement: in and around the United Nations in New York; within a civil society organization, the International Action Network on Small Arms (IANSA); and in the East African state of Uganda.

A movement to stop the proliferation of small arms

Research and policy discussions reflecting a concern about the proliferation of SALW began in the early 1990s, as the collapse of the Soviet Union released huge numbers of second-hand weapons into shady markets. The international and inter-governmental authorities concerned with the issue tended to focus particularly on the movement of weapons, their import and export. Internationally agreed standards and processes do not yet exist. Some countries have a voluntary licensing process in place to prevent export to countries deemed potential enemies. The problem however is that much of the movement of SALW is illegal, slipping beneath the bar of such prohibitions as exist. Often the movement is effected by unscrupulous brokers who are difficult to detect and prosecute because they disguise their identities behind 'front companies', work through intricate networks of sub-contractors, use devious transportation routes and make fraudulent financial transfers through offshore banking and shell companies (Stohl et al. 2007). Furthermore, detecting brokerage is complicated by the fact that international crime networks do not necessarily specialize in gun-running, but trade also in drugs and other prohibited goods, and traffic people. Besides, much of the proliferation of SALW in the hands of non-state actors and civilians occurs internally within borders, through what is known as 'diversion'. A country may have gun laws in place, yet licit weapons still drift by theft, loss and casual sale into illicit ownership.

Mobilizing an effective international social movement for the control of SALW is impeded by lack of unanimity. There are differences between states, between government institutions within states, between authorities and civil society, and sometimes within civil society. State governments oppose the uncontrolled proliferation of small arms because their presence in the hands of non-state actors threatens the state's monopoly of force. Most governments will tolerate no questioning of their rights or powers in this respect. The United States for instance, by far the most heavily armed power in the world and also by far the biggest arms exporter, has been unwilling to tolerate any curb on its right to buy weapons in the quantity it wishes from whomever it wishes, to sell them without constraint and to manage internal gun ownership as it sees fit. But some US citizens, notably those in the anti-militarist movement who would like to see a reduction in military budgets and greater responsibility in manufacture and export of arms, disagree with their government's position. Likewise, many people living under undemocratic regimes on various continents consider their over-armed state militaries and police less a source of security than a threat to their rights and safety. So, very often, do countries with whom they share borders. Besides there is the question of what is a reasonable level of armament for a state's armed forces – how many guns are enough guns? Are weapons ever deemed surplus to requirement and safely destroyed (GIIDS 2008)?

While many civil society organizations agitate about the misuse of security sector weapons by state personnel, and their widespread diversion into illegal uses, others are emphatic about a citizen's right to bear arms. Again the USA is a case in point, where the National Rifle Association (NRA) asserts this right under the Second Amendment of the US Bill of Rights. Though the Obama administration has been less supportive of the NRA than those that preceded it, the US government is aware of the gun lobby at its shoulder when considering international measures for control of SALW. The claim of a citizen's right to a gun is not unique to the NRA, which has links to similar movements in Canada, Brazil and elsewhere. Many of those who remember how the Nazi regime of the 1930s denied weapons permits to German Jews and Communists argue for the right to protect oneself from genocidal attacks or political repression (GIIDS 2009).

Despite these divergences, by the millennium there had been sufficient investigation, documentation and agitation by concerned governments and international NGOs to stir an official response. The action began in Africa, where the widespread availability of guns was wrecking the social fabric of many countries. In June 2000, the twelve states of the Great Lakes Region and Horn of Africa agreed the politically binding 'Nairobi Declaration' on curbing SALW proliferation.[2] Shortly afterwards, an Eminent Persons Group on the small arms problem in Africa prompted a Ministerial Conference in Mali of the Organization of African Unity (later to become the African Union). It issued the 'Bamako Declaration' of November 2000, elaborating an 'African Common Position' on the gun problem.[3] The following July the United Nations joined the act, with a Conference on the Illicit Trade of Small Arms and Light Weapons in All Its Aspects. Although it was a high-level intergovernmental affair, non-governmental organizations had a prominent role in this New York conference. Key among them was the International Action Network on Small Arms (IANSA), the global alliance of eight hundred civil society organisations in one hundred and twenty countries working to stop the proliferation and misuse of small arms and light weapons.

IANSA and other anti-SALW non-governmental organizations scored a notable success in this New York conference of 2001. The outcome was a concrete measure – a UN Programme of Action on the Illicit Trade in SALW in All its Aspects (PoA).[4] Though not legally binding it remains the primary international agreement on the control of small arms and light weapons. It sets out a range of measures for UN member states to consider in managing the SALW problem, including the control of small arms transfers, regulating small arms brokering, managing stockpiles, and marking and tracing small arms. Among other things, states committing to the PoA would make illicit gun production or possession a criminal offence; ensure complete disarmament of combatants after conflicts; and identify and destroy stocks of surplus or illegal weapons. In most countries full implementation would necessitate new national legislation. A UNDP 'How To' manual published in 2008 for the guidance of governments and civil society suggested new laws should cover among other things: regulating arms in civilian hands; controlling international transfers; regulating manufacturers, dealers and gunsmiths; marking weapons and keeping records of their location; and improving state security sectors' practices concerning their own SALW (UNDP 2008a). Most importantly, governments should establish an agency, some kind of 'national focal point', to have oversight of the efforts of the several government ministries and agencies that would be concerned in implementing the Programme. It should have at least two full-time staff and a broad and inclusive membership, including civil society organizations. It should carry out research, engage in awareness raising, information management and communication, and mobilize and allocate resources for action on SALW (UNDP 2008b).

Implementation of the UN Programme of Action on the Illicit Trade in SALW was fostered by a series of five biennial conferences in New York between 2003 and 2010, including a Review Conference in 2006. A report to the 2008 Biennial Meeting of States (BMS) showed that by that year one hundred and forty-eight states (and the Pope's Holy See, no less) had supplied contact details of their National Focal Point (UNIDIR 2008). Other international initiatives followed the Programme of Action. A UN Firearms Protocol – the Protocol against the Illegal Movement of and Trafficking in Firearms, their Parts, Components and Ammunition – entered into force in 2004, supplementing the only existing relevant binding treaty, the Convention against Transnational Organized Crime.[5] In 2006, a hundred and fifty-three of the world's governments voted to start work on a binding international Arms Trade Treaty (ATT) to control the trade in conventional weapons, including SALW (Amnesty International 2008). Things were on the move.

The International Action Network on Small Arms that mobilized the civil society input to the UN Conference and Programme of Action on SALW provides our point of departure in this chapter. Established in 1998, it comprises a wide range of types of organization as well as individuals concerned with small arms, including policy development organizations, national gun control groups, research institutes, aid agencies, women's groups, faith groups, survivors, human rights and community action organizations. Rebecca Peters, IANSA's director at the time of our research, explained in interview that rather few member organizations are actually specialized in gun reduction:

> The proliferation of guns isn't a problem in and of itself. It's significant because it undermines larger goals. So our member organizations are often concerned primarily with one of those larger issues – peace and reconciliation, development, public health, justice or governance.

The Network has a board, a secretariat with eight staff in London, and additional full-time paid staffers in Johannesburg and New York. Global meetings of members take place every two years to discuss progress and strategy, and regional meetings occur more frequently. IANSA's objectives are to reduce small arms violence by raising awareness among policy-makers, the public and the media about the global threat to human rights and human security caused by small arms; promote civil society efforts to prevent arms proliferation and armed violence through policy development, public education and research; and provide a forum for NGOs to share experiences and build skills. At one end of the spectrum of action it aims to facilitate civil society participation in high-level global and regional processes, while at the other it promotes the voices of individual survivors, in solidarity with them and their families. Funding support for IANSA comes from several governments, including that of Norway, as well as international NGOs. Its affiliated organizations in more than thirty nations are grouped in regional networks. The West African network is preparing a strategic plan for its region, while in the Latin American network (CLAVE), member organizations are pushing for the harmonization of national firearm laws, and co-ordinating transnational public education and advocacy campaigns. In addition, regional networks are emerging in South Asia, South East Asia, the South Pacific, East Africa and Eastern Europe. In 2003, together with Oxfam GB and Amnesty International, IANSA set up the international Control Arms Campaign, its main aim being the achievement of a global, legally binding agreement, an international Arms Trade Treaty.[6]

Gender and guns

Women had been active in IANSA from the start, both in the Network's secretariat in London and in the affiliated organizations working for gun control worldwide. Their entry point into the debate on SALW was the clearly, even dramatically, gendered nature of the gun phenomenon. Men are overwhelmingly the sex that, whether legally or illegally, manufactures, markets and transports, buys and sells guns, and in the last resort pulls the trigger. The women found, however, that this was simply taken for granted. No-one believed any differently, yet the fact was seldom elaborated. Indeed, gender awareness was almost entirely absent from the official discourse on SALW. The Nairobi Declaration mentioned women once, to allude to them as passive victims of guns. The Bamako Declaration made a passing reference to women as a vulnerable group. The UN Programme of Action on Small Arms and Light Weapons was just as gender-blind as these forerunners. It merely mentioned, in Clause 6 of the Preamble, a concern about the 'devastating consequences' of small arms and light weapons 'on children ... as well as the negative impact on women and the elderly'.[7]

There was really no excuse for this neglect, given the consciousness-raising on women and gender in relation to violence and armed conflict achieved in the international fora during the previous decade. 'Gender mainstreaming' had been United Nations policy since 1997. All UN departments and agencies were supposed to be 'ensuring that gender perspectives and attention to the goal of gender equality are central to all activities – policy development, research, advocacy/dialogue, legislation, resource allocation, and planning, implementation and monitoring of programmes and projects'.[8] Indeed, an Assistant Secretary-General and Special Adviser to the Secretary-General on Gender Issues and the Advancement of Women had been charged with overseeing the mandate's implementation. Besides, by the time the UN launched its own SALW process in 2001 the Security Council had already adopted its ground-breaking Resolution 1325 on *Women, Peace and Security* of October 2000, which could not have been more emphatic about the urgency of including women as stakeholders and actors in security policy-making. The UN's Office for Disarmament Affairs had quickly responded with a briefing note on 'Gender Perspectives in Disarmament'.[9] It was painfully clear, however, that the international stepping-stones so carefully laid by women activists in civil society and reformers in the UN system had not led to the intended gender awareness. A study of how gender language was used in UN meetings and documents concerned with small arms and light weapons, carried out by Emily Schroeder and Lauren Newhouse for the Institute of Security Studies, concluded that 'UN debates on SALW do not yet address gender in the SALW context in a way that encompasses the differing social, economic and political effects of these weapons on men and women'. The report urged efforts to bridge the gap between SALW policy-makers and those with gender expertise (Schroeder and Newhouse 2004).

So women set about producing evidence and argument. Vanessa Farr, a graduate of the Women's Studies Programme at York University, Toronto, was one of several researcher-writers who began to create a new sub-genre of gender-and-militarism literature: gender and guns. In 2002, while working at the Bonn International Centre for Conversion, with others she produced a substantial briefing paper, *Gender Perspectives on Small Arms and Light Weapons*, with material from several African countries

(Farr and Gebre-Wold 2002). A year later the Control Arms Campaign produced a report on *The Impact of Guns on Women's Lives* (Control Arms Campaign 2005). By 2009 there would be enough material to assemble a substantial volume, *Sexed Pistols: The Gendered Impact of Small Arms and Light Weapons*, with evidence from thirteen countries stretching from Northern Ireland to Papua New Guinea (Farr et al. 2009a).

In the meantime, many local and regional studies began to appear. Some focused on the relationship between men and guns. An exceptionally well-grounded research report came from South Africa, a country with high gun-related mortality. It was carried out by the Ekupholeni Centre in the township of Alrode with the co-operation of IANSA member Gun Free South Africa. The Centre set up an action-research project with a group of fifteen boys who had been referred to them for behavioural problems. The lads were encouraged to become researchers, gathering information about their area and those who live in it, and reflecting on their own lives. The boys' report had a lot to say about gun ownership, all of it related to their masculine self-identity. First and foremost, they saw a gun as a source of livelihood, 'a way of getting money' in their conditions of extreme poverty. In a context where you otherwise feel routinely unvalued, a gun could be a source of self-respect. To have a gun 'makes you feel like a human being'. In a very dangerous environment in which boys and men are often afraid of each other, a gun confers confidence. 'You aren't scared anymore, you feel like you are the king who can control everybody.' Owning a gun makes you one of the 'clevers' or 'bully brothers', the ones who exact fear. Fatalistically, the boys said 'crime is all there is' and 'I think I will be killed young' (Clacherty and Kistner 2001).

The Caribbean and Latin America have one of the highest rates in the world of SALW-related violence. With less than 10 per cent of the global population the region accounts for approximately 42 per cent of the global total of gun-related homicides. These statistics come from a report on the Caribbean by Jasmin Blessing and co-authors, who lay particular stress on 'gun culture'. They argue that enactments of violent masculinity are deeply embedded in local popular culture, expressed in music, videos and movies 'in which gun ownership and hyper-masculinity are equated with economic and social power, sexual prowess and respect'. Guns, they say, are cast as 'tools for gaining these benefits as well as being fetishised symbols in and of themselves' (Blessing et al. 2010: 7). They stress that gun ownership and use are a class phenomenon as well as a gendered one. It is to marginalized males, darker-skinned and thus underprivileged, that the 'gangsta' culture most appeals. For them, 'the gun can become "the great equaliser" in obtaining what they feel has been denied them in a postcolonial, and continuing exclusionary, society' (ibid.: 15).

Some women activists now began to feel that, ironically, while the belated focus on masculine gun cultures was very welcome, it had the effect of relegating women to the sidelines. While women are not wedded to guns in the same way as men, they are not entirely lacking agency, for both good and bad, when it comes to firearms. In many countries women are in the forefront of action against guns. Yet women and girls are evidently also implicated in storing, smuggling and hiding weapons. In some countries they are increasingly being enlisted to the state armed forces and police forces that were once the exclusive pre-serve of men. They are also recruited to insurgent militias, very often as forced conscripts or by abduction, but sometimes as motivated volun-teers. The numbers of women involved can be very great. For instance, in Liberia the disarmament programme of 2004 involved, among 96,000 combatants, 17,000 women and 9250 children of both sexes. However, women bearing and using guns are frequently also victims of the men who command them. They are 'simultaneously the perpetrators and victims of violence' (Control Arms Campaign 2003: 30).

The relationship of women and girls to guns in peace-time is equally ambiguous. Brazil is a country where the cost to men of masculinity has begun to be recognized. Men account for more than 91 per cent of the thirty to forty thousand gun-related deaths recorded annually.[10] Taking homicide and dangerous driving as linked phenomena, it is estimated that in a span of 50 years' there will be six million men miss-ing from the Brazilian population (Centre for Human Dialogue 2006). Such figures, argued Tatiana Moura, of the Observatory on Gender and Armed Violence at the University of Coimbra, Portugal, give men 'hypervisibility'. In a qualitative research study she set out to 'look at the silences' about women. She found that women and girls become involved with armed criminality, but because they do not readily fit the categories used to describe male crimes they go unnoticed, unless to be sexualized and sensationalized in the media. She learned from girls themselves that many of them are seduced by the glamour of gun-toting men. 'Girls go out with guys who use guns because they want a good life, easy money, brand-name clothes, feeling superior to others ... If [a girl] goes out with a regular working guy her life won't be like that' (Moura 2007: 38). On the other hand women undeniably suffer, both indirectly and directly, from gun crime. When men are killed women are likely to become the main breadwinners for their dependents. When men are wounded they must nurse and care for them. Besides, women are disproportionately affected by the strain imposed on already inadequate health, education and other social services caused by armed violence. And women suffer directly from the bullets. They are that ten per cent of victims invisibilized by the ten times greater number of male fatalities.

The implication of these studies published in the decade following the millennium is that if there is one thing that has to change before the world will be rid of guns it is the gender relation, as a relation of differentiation, hierarchy and power. In particular there has to be a change in men – or more precisely in the hegemonic masculinity that mandates, even requires, a man to be disposed to the use of force to assert his power over women and other men. Vanessa Farr and her co-authors concluded that we must 'encourage positive, peaceful expressions of male identity: this is a corner-stone of controlling and managing small arms' (Farr et al. 2009b: 432). However, it had long been apparent to the women activists that it is not only the manufacture, sale and use of guns that are masculine worlds. Men likewise are the overwhelming majority of the policy-makers, civil servants, military personnel, security specialists, technical experts and NGO representatives that people the corridors of the United Nations at SALW conferences. How were the women going to lodge, in these processes presided over by men at national, regional and international levels, the heretical message that 'hegemonic masculinity is a problem'?

Women's anti-gun activism

From that first UN Conference in 2001 a handful of women had been present, IANSA members from various countries. They began to talk to each other, generating an informal women's caucus. In 2005 the IANSA Secretariat obtained funding from Norway's Ministry of Foreign Affairs to develop this into a Women's Network. Before long the Network had a couple of hundred individual and group members. When Sarah Masters was appointed its co-ordinator in 2007, she set about energizing interaction between them, creating a space of mutual support. She established an e-mail list and continued to produce a quarterly Bulletin in which women could share news of their activities. She gave the 'women's portal' on the IANSA website a facelift and filled out its content. With a new logo – a woman's sign containing a handgun, cancelled by a diagonal line – the Women's Network gained a sense of identity and a recognizable brand image. Their short message was, said their leaflet, 'applying a gender perspective to the small arms issue – understanding the different ways that men, women, boys and girls engage in, are affected by, and respond to gun violence – is key to developing effective solutions to the problem'.

As we started the research partnership that would result in this chapter, Sarah and I sat down and talked. She reviewed her three years in post, and the process in which she had been involved at the United Nations. Here the Network, as she saw it, faced two distinct tasks. They had to bring the small arms issue into the annual conference of the Commission on the Status of Women (CSW), and they had to bring women and gender into the proceedings of the principal small arms forum, the UN small arms process relating to the UN Programme of Action. At the 2008 CSW they made a good start on the first task. In a productive partnership with the head of the Conventional Arms Branch of the United Nations Office for Disarmament Affairs (UNDODA) they organized a panel of women from different countries on gender and small arms. The following year the same partnership brought to the Conference on the Status of Women a number of women activists working for an Arms Trade Treaty. The fact that the CSW and an ATT meeting were taking place in parallel provided a valuable opportunity to bring these two sets of interests together. It was acknowledged as an important moment of advocacy with regard to the ATT. The women pressed for the ATT's criteria for legitimate export of small arms to include certainty that in the context of the importing country the weapons will not be likely to perpetuate or facilitate high levels of gender-based violence, in particular rape and other forms of sexual violence.[11] In 2010, again with UNDODA, the IANSA Women's Network held a side event on 'Girls in Settings of Armed Violence'.

The second task was more of a challenge. The Biennial Meeting of States on SALW is held in New York on alternate years in June. Before the 2008 meeting Sarah prepared and circulated a policy paper on 'women, guns and domestic violence'. She had had to think hard about how to insert this theme into the recognized SALW framework, so that it would be seen as legitimate by the delegates. She decided to use the concept of 'diversion', a term in common use in SALW discourse, referring to the shift of a weapon from legal to illegal hands. The women's paper argued that domestic violence is one of the criminal acts to which otherwise legal guns often get 'diverted' – for example when an off-duty member of the security services takes his gun home with him and there threatens his spouse or partner. The women were saying that the UN Programme of Action should be obliged to take cognizance of statistical evidence of the growing use of guns in deaths from domestic violence.

Despite this conceptual circuitry, it was not going to be easy to introduce the theme of 'armed domestic violence' convincingly into the BMS environment. The discussion there focuses relentlessly on technicalities, on hardware. Human beings, the social issues surrounding SALW, are understated, undervalued and mostly ignored. The themes prioritized at the 2008 BMS were typical: 1) stockpile management; 2) marking weapons; and 3) tracing weapons. There was only one space on the agenda where the women might conceivably lodge their paper: under 4) 'other'. 'So we put it right there,' Sarah said. But how to grab some attention? They decided to organize their session as a simulated TV talk show. To the 'Oprah Winfrey' role, they were lucky to be able to recruit a black woman radio journalist working in New York. She questioned a lively panel of women drawn from different countries. As the participants arrived at the event they were faced with items of women's clothing pegged to a twenty foot clothesline. Pinned to each garment was a card with the name and details of one woman killed somewhere in the world in an act of armed domestic violence. The women activists followed up this performance at the subsequent Biennial Meeting of States in 2010 with a paper developed with UNDODA that took the main points of the Programme of Action one by one and highlighted the gender implications. These efforts produced scarcely a ripple however in the mainstream proceedings. In the report of the 2010 BMS, paragraph 49 listed twenty-four contested items on which no agreement had been reached, due to the expression of contrary points of view. Fifteenth in the list was 'gender perspective'. In the context, Sarah was advised, this ambiguous mention should be considered 'a success'.

The inertia Sarah encountered was not limited to the UN system. Even in dealings with the major civil society campaigns such as the Control Arms Campaign she had to struggle to get women seen and heard. The people and organizations whom feminists might reasonably assume to be their natural allies, people with whom they clearly shared a commitment to the SALW theme, turned out to be uncomprehending, or misapprehending, of the gender issue. She says: 'Those who do not have a specific gender brief simply do not get, or do not like, the women's message. They water down women's statements, and place obstacles in the way that require time-consuming navigation.' She found she had to be continually vigilant, continually pushing the agenda forward. The moment she let up, the ball stopped rolling. Even in the IANSA Secretariat in London it was an uphill task to get director and staff to 'routinely think about gender'. Out there in the Women's Network women reported a similar response.

Uganda: awash with weaponry

In the spring of 2010 the two of us decided to visit Uganda for IANSA's annual 'Global Week of Action against Gun Violence' to see what challenges women's organizations in that country were facing. Resource-rich and with a benign climate, Uganda is nonetheless desperately poor, down at No. 157 in the UN's Human Development Index of 182 countries. Life expectancy is 52 years, adult literacy only 26 per cent.[12] The World Bank puts per capita GDP at a mere $420.[13] In the colonial era Britain exploited the country for its primary products, turning it into an exporter of its natural wealth and an importer of manufactured goods. Development of an industrial sector was neglected. A more recent cause of Uganda's failure to thrive is the unstoppable sequence of internal wars since independence in 1962. They have been fought almost entirely with small arms and light weapons, which have continually drifted from the state's armed forces to insurgent militias, from the hands of rebels to those of non-combatants, from the police officer to the petty thief. In the jargon, massive 'diversion'. The uncountable, and ever-growing, number of firearms in the country ensures that gun-use in fighting, crime and casual violence is everyone's daily reality.

In 1962, Milton Obote became Uganda's first president. The colonialists had left a country deeply divided on lines of tribe, language, region and religion. Obote's party and power-base, the Uganda People's Congress, was dominated by Protestants and had its main source of support in the north. The opposition party was dominated by Catholics and was stronger in the south, whose Bantu-speaking people perceived Obote's rise as a take-over by the Nilotic north. Obote's ruthless treatment of his opponents was surpassed only when his army general, Idi Amin, seized power and instituted a reign of scarcely imaginable brutality, in the course of which possibly 300,000 Ugandan citizens were killed. The nightmare was brought to an end by an invasion from Tanzania. After a short interregnum, Obote and the UPC returned to power, instituting a regime even more destructive than their earlier rule. The oppression was particularly inflicted on the Luwero Triangle, the West Nile region, the Banyarwanda people of southwest Uganda and on Karamoja, to the east. It is estimated that between 150,000 and 500,000 people were driven from their homes in this period, to become internally displaced people of whom about 80,000 were held in concentration camps in dire conditions. 'Imprisonment without trial, bad prison conditions, and extreme violation of human rights became an accepted way of life in Uganda ...' (Kasozi 1994: 4).[14]

In 1981, as Obote was consolidating this second term in power, Yoweri Museveni, a militant from Western Uganda, mobilized an armed force to oppose him, claiming that the 1980 elections had been rigged. His National Resistance Movement (NRM) and Army (the NRA) appealed to many in the oppressed south, eager to overthrow a 'government of northerners', doubly resented because the British had recruited their colonial army from among the Acholi and other northern tribes. In 1985 the NRA seized Kampala, and Museveni was installed as president. He is still head of state at the time of writing. Though credited with some progressive legislation, his regime is deficient in human rights and clings to power only by elections of disputed integrity.

The advent of Museveni did not mean the end of armed conflict in Uganda. On the contrary, the national army (the NRA, now renamed the Uganda People's Defence Force, UPDF), was above the law and a major source of insecurity to ordinary Ugandans (Amnesty International 1992). Blaming the Acholi for the atrocities of the Obote regime, Museveni visited on them atrocities of his own, 'including rape, abductions, confiscation of livestock, killing of unarmed civilians and the destruction of granaries, schools, hospitals and bore holes ...' (Conciliation Resources 2002: 13). Some former Obote supporters formed a militia, the Uganda People's Democratic Army (UPDA) to fight the government. In the early 1990s, in a curious development from this struggle, a bizarre character, Joseph Kony, claiming to be possessed by spirits and directed by God, formed the Lord's Resistance Army (LRA), comprised in the main of Acholi fighters, and began a campaign of terror in Northern Uganda, which, spreading to southern Sudan and more recently to the Democratic Republic of Congo, has continued ever since. Kony's sadistic treatment of his own and 'enemy' people, including abduction and abuse of thousands of girl and boy children, are well known to human rights organizations and his arrest for war crimes is sought by the International Criminal Court (Human Rights Watch 2003, 2005; Allen and Vlassenroot 2010; Borzello 2009).

The government has responded to the LRA by alternating armed force with peace moves, yet there is no sign of the northern war ending. In the meantime, during these years of conflict, at least three other insurgencies have been brutally put down by the government: a rebellion by the Teso in Eastern Uganda from around 1987 to 1992; two offensives by the Uganda National Rescue Front in the West Nile Region; and most recently an uprising by the Allied Democratic Forces in the Rwenzori region of Western Uganda, which did not end until 2004. Each of these wars has added to the total of small arms and light weapons circulating in the country.

Ugandan government measures to control arms

To this history of Uganda's internal conflict must be added the fact that this landlocked country is part of a regional gun belt. Its eastward neighbours in the Great Lakes and the Horn of Africa, and Sudan, Rwanda and Congo to north and west, are all conflict zones, generating an unregulated flow of arms across borders. Inter-governmental consultation and co-ordinated action is therefore vital if the SALW problem is to be reduced. We saw above that East Africa was ahead of the United Nations with its intergovernmental Nairobi Declaration on SALW. Now Nairobi is the site of a Regional Center on Small Arms (RECSA), while Uganda and a number of other countries in the region have, in line with UN expectations, 'domesticated' the Programme of Action, established their National Focal Point (NFP) and set about reviewing legislation and practices concerning firearms.

We interviewed Joe Burua, a staff member of the Ugandan National Focal Point, who described the system they had devised. The Ministry of Internal Affairs, responsible among other things for peace and security, had been designated lead agency, with fourteen other ministries and departments, including the armed forces and police, represented on the NFP. Private security firms, significant weapons users, were also involved. Each of these partner organizations was expected to have a small arms 'desk' to ensure that the gun issue would be addressed in every institutional work plan. Practical measures were delegated to Uganda's regional and district 'Task Forces for Arms Management'. Meanwhile the NFP had already produced a five-year Plan.[15] Uganda's existing Firearms Act of 1970 being far from adequate to present circumstances, new legislation was being drawn up to facilitate the marking and tracing of weapons and ammunition, provide for tougher controls over the security sector's armouries and enable the introduction of a licensing system with tough criteria for civilian gun ownership and a higher minimum age – possibly 25 years.[16]

Civil society organizations were also represented on the National Focal Point, Joe told us. IANSA has a branch in Uganda, the Uganda Action Network on Small Arms (UANSA). However it did not form until after the NFP was constituted and is thus represented thereon through some of its member organizations. The NGOs are selected from four constituencies: 'faith groups'; groups representing victims and survivors of gun violence; development organizations; and groups working for peace and reconciliation. We asked Joe, 'Why were "women's organizations" not designated a constituency?' We had noted, besides, that there were no women on the Management Committee of the NFP, and only one among its seven staff. There was no mention in the National Action Plan of men and masculinity in relation to gun ownership and use, the impact on women of guns, or the gendered statistics of gun crime. Was gender as neglected in SALW thinking here 'on the ground' as it was in New York? Joe Burua confirmed this lack. But, he assured us, in response to the strong advocacy of women's organizations and the engagement of the Ministry of Gender, Labour and Social Development in small arms issues, things were now beginning to change. Several women's organizations were working directly with the National Focal Point. The NFP was seeking 'gender balance', and gender would have its own chapter in the forthcoming revision of the National Action Plan.

These questions we asked of the state sector we also put to the key civil society actor, the Uganda Action Network on Small Arms. UANSA has a number of active women's member organizations, but when the possibility of bringing them together in a Uganda section of the IANSA Women's Network has been raised, a move which could empower them and help them raise the profile of gender concerns, it has been dismissed. In the view of Robert Mugisha, UANSA's executive director, 'Unity is strength'. If they were to recognize women as having a distinctive interest, other self-identified groups 'might come up with a similar idea, and UANSA will be in pieces'. As we shall see, however, this discouragement has not stopped women and women's organizations committing a lot of time and energy to the gun-control campaign.

Women's projects of disarmament

In the field we found it was often women who were most active for peace, disarmament and gun control. The women's movement has been called 'one of the strongest mobilized societal forces in Uganda' (Tripp 2000: 23). Women have developed a strong sense of their entitlement to equality of opportunity and rights, and the government has had to respond to their pressure with positive measures that include a 30 per cent quota in political representative bodies. Women's organizations are numerous, and in the main the movement here has retained a degree of feminist autonomy, avoiding the lure of governmental co-optation (ibid.).

We spent time with three Uganda member organizations of the IANSA Women's Network: EASSI, UJCC and CECORE. One of the women we interviewed was Marren Akatsa-Bukachi, executive director of EASSI, the East African Sub-regional Support Initiative for Women's Advancement.[17]

A Kenyan herself, she is proud of the African women's movement, which is 'very strong, very feminist':

> Feminists have a different way of looking at things. We have a Charter of Principles of African Feminism. A group of feminists from different African countries drafted it. We are the only region in the world to have such a charter. And every three years we have an African Feminist Forum. We have met in Accra, in Kampala and the next meeting will be in Senegal. We are supposed to manage our lives according to that feminist charter. We speak out a lot.

Marren feels the Ugandan government has responded reasonably well to women's demands. Responsibility at national level for furthering the status of women lies with the Ministry of Gender, Labour and Social Development, which has proved a reliable advocate of women's rights. 'They are good partners to work with.' The overall Minister of Labour is a man, but the person specifically responsible for gender is a woman. 'All of them,' Marren said, 'are gender-sensitive women and men, so they will help us to push issues, and they involve us in everything.' The response is weakest in the matter of women and gender in relation to conflict, violence and disarmament. The implementation of UNSC Resolution 1325 on *Women, Peace and Security* had become 'ghetto-ized' in this Ministry, she said, rather than being mainstreamed across the defence and security sector, including the National Focal Point on small arms.

Marren believed EASSI could make a useful intervention on the gun problem. 'Women were dying,' she said. 'The issue of guns was being treated [by the government] only as a military matter. How could we penetrate the patriarchal system?' They began to build their own expertise in small arms issues and passed it on to others in training events. They edged their way into RECSA, the Regional Centre on Small Arms, in order to put across at this transnational level the message that the proliferation of guns can be neither understood nor halted without an understanding of gender-specific roles and gender-specific impacts. RECSA's executive secretary appeared to be listening. But Marren found, just as Sarah Masters had found in London and New York, that if for the slightest moment women relaxed the pressure, gender awareness slipped away. For instance, quite early on they pressed on the RECSA executive secretary the need to appoint a gender officer. This appeared to be accepted. But then RECSA called in specialists to make an organizational development assessment. Why do you need a *gender* officer?, these 'experts' wondered. The executive secretary did not persist, so no gender post was included in the consultants' recommendations. Eventually RECSA created a job titled 'Research and Gender Officer'. But the man who was appointed to the post admitted to Marren, 'Usually I tell people I'm the Research Officer. Only when I go specifically to a gender meeting I say "I do gender"'. Marren comments, in exasperation, 'These SALW people are just men. And they don't get it. They just don't get it. Up to now'.

A second civil society organization involved in the small arms issue is the Uganda Joint Christian Council (UJCC).[18] We learned about its work from Canon Joyce Nima. The Council has historic significance as an ecumenical alliance between Catholic, Anglican and Orthodox churches, which from colonial times to the present have been rivals, with their own denominational churches, hospitals and schools. The UJCC formed an Inter-faith Peace and Small Arms Network and made it their job to link this faith-based constituency into the activities of the National Focal Point. With the help of the international NGO Saferworld they developed training materials and carried out trainings among civil society organizations in each of the twelve regions of Uganda. Further afield, they got active within a regional peace-building network called the Fellowship of Councils and Churches in the Great Lakes and Horn of Africa (FECCLAHA), initiating trainings for religious leaders in the member states on how to collect data on SALW and how to develop early-warning indicators. With the funding support of Christian Aid, they established cross-border small arms committees in four border areas, through which the counterpart organizations either side could communicate about stolen animals and the movement of arms. This was grassroots stuff. Joyce said:

> We wanted to build the capacity of the communities to deal with the problem themselves, rather than wait for the army to come from Kampala and deal with it. We wanted to own the peace process. I kept asking, 'Where are the people?'. For us, security has to belong to the people. They must be able to contribute to their own feelings of safety, rather than wait for external forces. They can negotiate and dialogue, as neighbours, as communities.

Canon Joyce has been among those insisting on gendering all the UJCC's programmes. As former headmistress of a girls' school, she was disposed to notice that commonly 99 per cent of those attending the meetings of the various religious organizations were men: 'You have to have affirmative action,' she said. In their 'peace village' camps and in all their trainings they try to ensure that women make up 50 per cent of the participants, and all their cross-border projects have had a specific women's component.

A third NGO active on the gun issue is the Center for Conflict Resolution (CECORE), 'an initiative of Ugandan people working to seek alternative and creative means of preventing, managing and resolving conflicts'.[19] By 'alternative and creative' they mean to contrast their own method to that of the government, which is often violently repressive in dealing with breaches of the peace. We met and interviewed both Rose Othieno, CECORE's executive director, and staff member Grace Tukaheebwa. CECORE is highly unusual among mixed organizations in having a strong, even dominant, presence of women. They comprise five out of the nine Board members and six of the ten paid staff. In fact, in contrast to Joyce's experience in the UJCC, in CECORE Rose had found it was men they lacked. They needed men because some groups would not accept women as conciliators. Grace Tukaheebwa told us she hears no complaints from the men about the strong presence of women in the organization. On the contrary, 'the men always say "women are our mothers, we must be guided by them"'. Other organizations sometimes wonder at CECORE, she says. They comment to the men, 'You are in a woman-dominated organization'. But the men, Grace says, tell their critics, 'You're missing out a lot by not working with women'.

One of CECORE's programmes is working to rid communities of small arms and light weapons. The Karamoja region presents a particular challenge. It is a dry region in north-eastern Uganda, where cattle herding is the only viable livelihood. Largely neglected by governments, the Karamojong are extremely poor, and educational and literacy levels very low. There is a lack of fuel, and roads are few and badly maintained (Närman 2003). The people are divided by religion, some being Muslim, others Catholic or Anglican Christians. The patriarchalism of all three faith structures buttresses a traditional male-dominated tribal and family structure. Many men have more than one wife. Women own no property or land. It is the man of the family who owns the cattle, though he may lend a cow to his wives for purposes of feeding the family. Apart from supplying all daily needs, cattle ownership has symbolic value as a measure of men's relative status. Marriage involves payment of 'bride price' in the form of a defined number of cattle (Jabs 2007; Mkutu 2008; Yeung 2009).

There is a long tradition of cattle raiding between Karamoja's tribes, and between them and other neighbouring cattle-herding people. In the past the practice was, up to a point, functional and adaptive – a rough and ready way of sharing of resources in scarcity. It was not considered crime, nor was it termed theft, but rather had its own term translated as 'taking by force'. Women did not take part in the raids, but encouraged them and would goad men to prove themselves. Young men leaving for a raid have traditionally crawled through the arched legs of a standing woman, wife or mother, who in that way blessed the raid and guaranteed safe return. When the husband returned, the wife would ritually carry his shoes and spears into the house and be responsible for the weapons' safe-keeping.

Then things changed. Karamojong men stumbled on an armoury of 60,000 assault rifles left behind by Idi Amin's forces. To these have been added many other firearms filtering across the nearby national border. As a result, inter-tribal cattle raiding now resembles modern warfare. The rise in cattle prices and depletion of cattle stocks has undermined the customary provision for marriage. The patriarchal system is therefore under stress. A young man cannot gain respected adult status because he cannot afford to marry. A woman often has to submit to 'temporary' marriage that gives her no security. Widowed women are passed from brother to brother, losing respect and status along the way. On the other hand women's contribution to the economy through gardening, beer-brewing and trading (often exchanging beer for bullets) has become a matter of survival for the family, and men resent this. Domestic violence, as well as other kinds of criminality, often alcohol-related and exacerbated by guns, is increasing (Jabs 2007; Mkutu 2008; Yeung 2009). The state attempts to deal with the disorder in Karamoja, now by offering incentives to give up weapons, now by sending in the army to seize them. There are many reports of atrocities by the government troops in the region (Human Rights Watch 2007).

Failing to recognize the role of women in the gun drama, the government's incentives to the Karamojong have been addressed to men. So CECORE, first and foremost, encourage women's participation:

> After all, in the refugee camps women are heading families – they are competent. When their sons come in from the bush, they can send them to us for disarmament and training. We encourage women to step forward for leadership positions, to stand for elections to local councils.

However, a gender analysis of the patriarchalism of Karamoja society also leads CECORE to work with the warrior men to encourage them to see the advantages of a gun-free life. Many men are reluctant to walk into a government centre to hand over their guns, so CECORE provides for them to deposit their weapons in local churches, where 'no questions are asked'. They include men in projects for generating alternative sources of income. Grace told us:

> I used to ask myself, 'Where are the men?' All the man does is get up in the morning, be given his breakfast by his wife, and sit under a tree and drink. The woman is good at everything. The man doesn't need to do anything. If you give women gardens, chickens, goats, this just doubles their workload, since they continue to look after house and home.

So they are trying to interest the men in bee-keeping for honey production. They call their approach mental disarmament. 'Minds have to be changed, attitudes: is it possible to imagine another way of life other than cows and guns?'

The gun, or the hand that holds it?

We found that IANSA's Disarm Domestic Violence campaign, now involving thirty countries, had been taken up energetically by Ugandan women. Women were saying that men's behaviour towards women has been changing in recent years. Rape is more common, both in armed conflict and out of it. Domestic violence has escalated. Increasingly, guns are involved, so injuries are more serious. More assaults become murder. The presence of a firearm greatly reduces the victim's ability to escape, evade or resist attack. It deters intervention and assistance by others. During the Week of Action, the Ugandan network organized a workshop on the gender significance of SALW and disarming domestic violence. Participants from EASSI, UJCC, CECORE and other groups were pressing the Ministry of Internal Affairs, currently drafting gun-control legislation, to take women's experience of gun violence into account. Some changes are not disputed. The new law must introduce a system of licensing. Any civilian seeking to acquire a firearm should have to apply for a licence in order to buy it, while anyone currently in possession of a gun must be required to bring it in to the authorities, have it marked, registered and licensed. However, it is not only 'illegal' guns that are causing women's deaths but also those of the so-called 'security sector' which are taken home by off-duty personnel, or are lost, stolen or otherwise permitted to 'leak' into illegal, civilian use. So the law must require accountability of movement in the case of 'official' and 'company' guns and ammunition. Weapons must be specifically issued for use and returned after use, with severe penalties for negligence.

However, we heard a great deal of confusion and disagreement at the workshop over how intrusive into people's lives and relationships the new measures could or should be. Traditionally, domestic violence has been considered a private 'family' matter in Uganda, but recently women have been 'outing' the issue and a Domestic Violence law has been passed. Despite the divergences of opinion that became apparent at the workshop, among women, between women and men, and between the representatives of the state, the male-led anti-gun movement and women activists, it was clear that the occasion of drafting new legislation had to be used to harmonize gun law with domestic violence law. There were men present at the workshop from the security sector, the National Focal Point and even UANSA who clung to the idea that a person – read 'man' – has an inalienable right to a gun. It was therefore not a question of the new law bestowing a right but rather of defining behaviours that could nullify an existing one. Some participants, of both sexes, felt that to give a spouse a right of veto if her partner applied for a licence would destabilize the patriarchal family, community and society. It could have the effect of putting the woman at even more risk. Besides, we should remember that a woman's resistance to her partner getting a gun licence might be an expression of 'simple malice'. On the one hand it was felt women should be more assertive, know their right to a life free from violence, and stand up for it. 'It's a power game, it's about who controls whom and what.' But, then again, were women perhaps themselves to blame for the violence they were experiencing? Women gaining more economic independence, getting 'above themselves', refusing subordination, departing from tradition – this was a provocation to men.

In Uganda, as in the wider world, feminists are now fully alert to the policy significance of the affinity between men and guns. Gun possession and use is a respected way, among men, of 'doing manhood'. Some women see a parallel affinity between states and their arms. States, they point out, especially their security sectors, are replete with men both in senior positions and in the ranks who likewise demonstrate an addiction to weaponry. Fostering an arms industry, building impressive arsenals, basing policy on a readiness to resort to force – these are respected ways, among states and statesmen, of 'doing statehood'. Uganda is no exception. Marren Akatsa-Bukachi told us:

> Small arms are in the hands of small boys and big men. We can ask: does any woman own a gun-manufacturing company? No, it is men

who own and fund the industry. They influence the senior people in government. And who are they? Men again.

One of the features of the Global Week of Action against Gun Violence was a ceremonial destruction of seized ammunition. It proved Marren right. The gathering, stacking and setting fire to the ammunition was carried out by male labourers in blue overalls. Those who were there to witness and relish the explosions, who presided and spoke at the meeting were men. The military officers and other uniformed personnel present were almost all males. The masculine affinity with guns, whether expressed at the individual human level, or at the level of the army, the police and their political masters in government, is what makes 'DDR' – disarmament, demobilization and reintegration – into a process that is, at best, focused on guns rather than people, and, at worst, a military action to disarm by force. In Uganda many people are killed or injured by state personnel every year. It is likely, although there are no statistics to prove it, that more people die at the hands of police and soldiers than from shooting by civilians. The Week of Action included a visit to the Kampala hospital to meet survivors of gun violence. The visitors found the majority of patients they talked to had been wounded by 'legal' rather than 'illegal' gun users.

Joyce Nima, in interview, made an impassioned critique of the militarization of Ugandan society and state. Successive leaders, she said, have been war makers. 'Fighting, fighting, fighting. None of them have clean hands. The thinking has been so militaristic. We have resorted to military action, time and again. People are impatient. They see it as the quick fix.' The Ugandan government, like other governments, is caught in a contradiction. One of its roles is collecting and destroying small arms and light weapons, while another role is to import them, buy them, and commission their local manufacture. The various ministries and their portfolios might therefore be seen as pulling in contrary directions. The contradiction is resolved, officially, by discriminating between problematic guns and unproblematic guns, problematic people and unproblematic people. The exercise of DDR is one of reinforcing the state's monopoly of the means of coercion. There is no discussion of reducing the number of weapons in the state armoury, only those 'in the community'. What we need, Joyce feels, is 'a paradigm shift', a shift of government policy away from the present emphasis on state security and towards a concern with human beings. We need to reduce expenditure on the military, little by little, and increase the funding for social services. But such a call for reducing the military budget is rarely heard in Uganda. An event such as the terrorist attack by Somali Islamic extremists that killed 74 Ugandans, and injured many more, at two sites in Kampala a few weeks after our visit of course leads to calls for a more heavily armed, rather than a disarmed, state.

The major actors on SALW, whether at international level, or in a state such as Uganda, tend to privilege a technicist, 'expert' approach, founded primarily in the experience and know-how of the security sector. Thus 'masculine expertise and opinions are absolutely privileged' (Farr 2002: 22). The primary aim is to control the weapons, rather than reduce the violence. Civil society, and particularly women's organizations within it, are bringing a different approach to the problem of SALW. They combine the necessary technical knowledge with an emphasis on root causes, on the social and cultural reasons people value guns. Some take a community-based approach, tapping into local knowledge, resources and effective traditions, bearing in mind, nonetheless, that these may reflect highly gendered structures of power. Others start from the idea of 'public health'. How much harm is caused to wellbeing in this country by guns? The starting point is the idea that violence is a social phenomenon, and can be prevented (GIIDS 2008). Neither of these approaches receives much respect or support in official circles (Farr et al. 2009b). Joyce Nima urges this 'human security' approach to post-conflict:

> The men who deal with these issues don't see the human perspective. If they are bureaucrats they look at improving the infrastructure. If they're dealing with disarmament they look at weapons, tracing, marking and destroying arms. None of them look at the impact on people. We, the civil society organizations, are the only ones doing that. It's we who keep saying, 'Small arms are a human security issue, not just a military issue'. Let's look for ways of detaching society, and especially men, from the very idea of guns, their value, their supremacy, their normality. We need to offer people practical ways of living without a gun.

Notes

1. Geneva Declaration, *Global Burden of Armed Violence* (September 2008) cited in IANSA, *How an Arms Trade Treaty Can Help Prevent Armed Violence*, available online at: www.iansa.org/system/files/ArmsTradeTreaty-Web.pdf (accessed 4 April 2011).
2. Online at: www.recsasec.org/pdf/Nairobi%20Protocol.pdf (accessed 4 March 2011).

3. Online at: www.africa-union.org/root.au.AUC/Departments/PSC/Small_ Arms.htm (accessed 1 July 2010).
4. 'Programme of Action to Prevent, Combat and Eradicate the Illicit Trade in Small Arms and Light Weapons in All Its Aspects' (UN Document A/CONF.192/15). Online at: http://disarmament2.un.org/ddasite.htm (accessed July 2010).
5. Online at http://multimedia.unodc.org/unodc/en/treaties/CTOC (accessed 4 March 2011).
6. Online at: www.controlarms.org (accessed 4 March 2011).
7. As footnote 5.
8. Online at: www.un.org/womenwatch/osagi/gendermainstreaming.htm (accessed 4 March 2011).
9. Online at: www.un.org/disarmament/HomePage/gender/gender.shtml (accessed 4 March 2011).
10. The figures are contested. See: www.comunidadesegura.org/en/STORY_ Controversy-surrounds-gun-death-numbers-in-Brazil; and: http://en. wikipedia.org/wiki/Gun_politics_in_Brazil (accessed 4 April 2011).
11. Online at: www.iansa-women.org/node/600 (accessed 4 April 2011).
12. Figures for 2009, online at: http://hdr.undp.org/en/statistics (accessed 18 June 2010).
13. Cited in: http://news.bbc.co.uk/1/hi/world/africa/country_profiles/1069166. stm (accessed 18 June 2010). On Uganda's poverty see also Borzello (2009).
14. This brief account of Uganda's recent history draws substantially on Kasozi (1994), Finnström (2008) and Rice (2010). On the effects of armed conflict and post-conflict transformation, see Buckley-Zistel (2008).
15. National Action Plan 2004–2009, *Uganda's Coordinated Efforts to Deal with Proliferation of Illicit Small Arms and Light Weapons*, and *Uganda National Action Plan on Small Arms and Light Weapons* (Kampala: Ministry of Internal Affairs). Currently being reviewed.
16. As required by the UN Programme of Action. The Regional Center on Small Arms has developed 'best practice' guidelines to ensure harmonization of such new gun laws across the region.
17. Website: www.eassi.org (accessed 4 March 2011). Eastern Africa Sub-regional Support Initiative for Women's Advancement (EASSI), with its headquarters in Kampala, serves eight countries: Burundi, Eritrea, Ethiopia, Kenya, Rwanda, Somalia, Tanzania and Uganda. Its membership includes both civil society organizations and individuals. EASSI publishes a twice-yearly newsletter.
18. Website: www.insightonconflict.org/conflicts/uganda/peacebuilding-organisations/ujcc (accessed 4 March 2011). The Ugandan Joint Christian Council (UJCC) is an ecumenical organisation established in 1963 to provide a platform for its members to work towards greater mutual understanding and unity of purpose. It provides a forum to articulate and address issues of common concern including peace building, health, education, and social and economic justice.
19. Website: www.cecore.net (accessed 4 March 2011). The Center for Conflict Resolution (CECORE) is a non-profit and non-governmental organization, formed in 1995. At the start it was a representative in Uganda of

the International Fellowship of Reconciliation, a worldwide organization founded in 1919, after the First World War, with a vision of human community founded in peace through active nonviolence. CECORE's objective is 'to empower individuals, organisations, institutions and the community to transform conflict effectively by applying alternative and creative means in order to promote a culture of active tolerance and peace'.

9
Towards a Different Common Sense

The groups, organizations and networks I have described in the preceding chapters, as I warned in the Introduction, can hardly be taken to 'represent' peace movements, especially if we use this term in its most inclusive sense. What we have seen here is simply a number of informative cases, lively components of a putative movement of movements, in widely dispersed places at different moments in time. We've stepped back into the past to see the peace movement in Britain changing as war itself changed over a century and a half. We've visited Japan and South Korea to see aspects of their anti-war, anti-militarist and peace activism today. Two international networks have featured. The first, War Resisters' International, supporting conscientious objection world wide, appears in historical perspective, alongside a study of its associate, the Alternativa Anti-militarista – Movimiento de Objección de Conciencia, challenging the militarist policies of the Spanish state. The second, the International Action Network on Small Arms, is a more recent initiative, and we have seen both its transnational lobbying of the UN and, in Uganda, the grassroots anti-gun activism of typical member groups. We have also glimpsed a local alliance in a single British city, shocked into action in protest against an episode of aggression against Palestinians; and seen an early phase of what promises to be a sustained transnational campaign of protest against NATO.

Each of these organizations, or clusters of organizations, contributes in some way to an overall field of analysis, polemic and action in civil society that calls for peace (variously defined) in place of (broadly speaking) militarism, militarization and war. For the most part they are not the only one of their kind – cases from other times and places could have served as well. Instead of the campaign against guns we might have looked at the international movement to ban nuclear weapons.

237

Korea is not the only partitioned country: we could have examined the case of Cyprus, half a world away, similarly stuck in non-peace. In Okinawa we saw a group calling for the removal of US military bases from their land, but we know there are such movements wherever US bases are imposed and resented.

My aim has not been to define and describe a 'social movement' as such, but to examine and show what can and sometimes does go on inside a particular formation. In the ever-growing literature of social movements there are many encyclopaedic definitions, many attempts to trace the history of their emergence and development, and list their distinguishing features. Among the theorists to whom I've turned,[1] however, it is Alberto Melucci who comes closest to an understanding of social movements that would be recognizable to the peace activists I met. More than twenty years ago, in *Nomads of the Present*, he stepped beyond earlier accounts that had portrayed them as ignorant mobs in the grip of agitators, as masses reacting to systemic crisis, or classes marching towards their destined liberation (Melucci 1989). These things peace movements are certainly not. Instead he suggested a less categorical approach. Social movements are, as he saw it, forms of collective action always in the making ('socially constituted') by people who think about what they are doing ('conscient actors'). This reminds me very much of Rafael Ajangiz who wrote of AA-MOC (Chapter 3):

> [W]e live the uncertainty of a project that is always unfinished, always in process of being decided ... a project that is not built by necessary steps or to a pre-established design, but which makes continual reference to certain outlines that are as impossible to achieve as they are to renounce ... [T]he social and the personal are mixed up, they are mutually determining. The assembly was the triumph of the collective, and consensus was the triumph of the individual (MOC 2002: 271).[2]

As the women and men of AA-MOC clearly understood, social action is never a given fact. Melucci said, 'It is always socially produced within the boundaries of certain structures, people participate in cognitive, affective and interactive relationships and creatively transform their own social action and to a certain extent their social environment as well' (Melucci 1996: 197). In collective action people can be seen to 'produce meanings, communicate, negotiate and make decisions' (ibid.: 20). From such a starting point it makes sense to come with an open mind and ask empirical questions about a social movement. What's it against, what's it for? What aspect of the system's logic does it defy? What processes does it involve? What's the source of unity and how is cohesion produced and maintained? How, why and when do individuals join this collective action, or leave, or carry it in a new direction?

In a later work, Melucci wrote of a social movement's actions as 'a breach of the limits of compatibility of the political system', its interests as 'formed before and beyond the boundaries and the rules of the political game'. Responding to needs experienced in the social fabric of everyday life, a movement is a 'constant reminder of the limits of politics' (Melucci 1996: 287). And in the foregoing case studies we have indeed seen individuals of a range of political tendencies – socialist, communist, anarchist, pacifist, religious, secular and feminist – putting their hopes and energies into something other than conventional engagement in the political structures (voting at given intervals, participating in the legislature, controlling the executive powers), aiming instead to mobilize a street presence, a media response and a popular consciousness that will demand the attention of that formal political system (governments, the United Nations) from an outlying position of strength among 'the people'.

Just as this study does not aim to be definitive of 'social movement', neither does it aim to draw a line around a particular movement and mark its perimeter. Instead my approach has been to describe some illustrative cases: clusters of groups, organizations and networks that share the broad objective of dismantling the war system, diverting foreign policy from the military option, stopping organized aggression and achieving durable peace and real security. We know this putative movement of movements exists in many countries, regions and continents, and its component parts vary by spatial scale and temporal longevity. We can confidently say, besides, that it has at least three elements differentiated by focus. We see some groups whose members describe themselves as 'anti-war' organizations, focused on preventing, or ending, a given conflict such as the attack on Afghanistan by the USA and its allies in 2001. Second, we've come across others that term themselves 'anti-militarist', because their members feel themselves to be in a sustained struggle against militarism as a mindset, and the processes of militarization that deform their societies. Think of Okinawa. Third, we have met yet other entities that go straight for goal and call themselves 'peace' groups. Their focus is often a creative one, attempting to replace the violence paradigm in international relations, politics and everyday life with a peace culture. A good example is Women Making Peace in South Korea.

Often, however, the focus of a given group spans two or all three of these types. Women Making Peace had, in fact, campaigned against the Republic of Korea's purchase of F-15K combat fighter aircraft in the late 1990s and joined anti-war demonstrations in 2003. Besides, within each element are groups articulating the focus in a variety of ways. We've seen the Palestine Solidarity Campaign working in the UK to discredit Israel's unending war against Palestinians, while in Israel itself New Profile supports individuals who refuse to perpetuate that conflict by soldiering in the Israeli Defence Force. Some groups are doing anti-militarism by focusing on the fundamental issue of the defence budget (as in military tax resistance), while others are campaigning against particular installations (a jungle warfare training base), or particular weapons (small arms).

Divergences of thought and action

My purpose in setting out on the research was to learn about internal differences in our movement, and how well we handle them, because on that depends whether we can be an effective collective actor. What I hoped for, of course, was that I would find, despite differences, that we understand each other so well, convince each other so profoundly of our shared purpose and support each other's campaigns so generously and effectively that we represent a powerful alliance capable of changing the world. Do we? The answer of course is, 'Well, not *exactly*'. My perspective has shown up a number of tensions, even antagonisms.

It is not, I have learned, differences in the spatial scale of organizations and their longevity, or in objective and focus, as described above, that challenge our cohesion. On the whole such variety is appreciated: we can't all do everything, we can't be everywhere at once. Even our values, it seems to me, are broadly speaking shared and a source of unity. I found groups as widely different as the internationalist left and the Christian Church, anti-NATO activists and women opposing military sexual violence, sharing adherence to the values of peace, justice and democracy. War Resisters' International say their aim is a world 'based on relationships of equality, where basic human needs are fulfilled, where women and men have an equal voice, different cultures and ethnic groups are accepted by one another, borders do not divide, and the natural environment is respected'.[3] WRI is one of the most deeply pacifist of the organizations we have examined. Yet this world for which they strive would be accepted as an ideal by the most 'militant' left of anti-war and anti-militarist activists.

What my case studies have shown, rather than a conflict of values in the movements, is a divergence of analysis. Each of the various political tendencies that converge in the movement brings its unique understanding, its account of the roots of the 'war problem', and, flowing from that, its preferred oppositional strategy. That's the biggest challenge to coherence and cohesion. Let me draw out and discuss in more detail three major divergences. First, differences in and among the left, broadly defined, on the significance of capitalism and the state as causes of war. Second, the divergence between feminists and other political tendencies deriving from the former's intersectional understanding of power, and particularly the significance women ascribe to patriarchal gender relations as predisposing societies to war. Third, differences of strategy and the difficult issue of activist violence.

Capitalism and state as causes of war: a plural left

It has been a long-standing hope in peace movements that the left will be a trustworthy supporter of anti-militarism. It has often proved to be so, and we have seen many examples in the foregoing accounts. At times the hope is disappointed, however, as political parties such as the Labour Party in Britain, Izquierda Unida in Spain or the Socialist Party in Japan abandon the movement in order to seek or gain parliamentary power. Likewise leftwing trade unions (for example the Unión General de Trabajadores in Spain) have sometimes been experienced as unreliable anti-militarists because they fear job loss if weapons manufacture is closed down. The extra-parliamentary left groups for their part have been a significant mobilizing force within wider movements to end war. It is the capitalist mode of production these identify as the unique exploitative and aggressive system at the root of war, sometimes characterized as 'global capitalism', 'corporate capital', 'neoliberalism' or 'imperialism'. Thus, the Socialist Workers Party, a founder of the Stop the War Coalition in the United Kingdom, as we saw, writes of itself, 'we strive to be the anti-capitalist, anti-imperialist voice of the movements we build'.[4] The divisiveness of this analysis is not due to the parties' identification of capitalism as implicated in war – many if not most of the other groups, organizations and networks I spoke with share the view that corporate interests steer national policies. In fact, with their sharp critique of the 'military industrial complex', the anti-militarist movement adds something to the anti-capitalist analysis. Ultra-left positions only become divisive if and when a singleminded focus on capitalism precludes identifying other potential or actual sources of violent conflict, and when nonviolent methods are condemned as a 'reformism' that inhibits 'revolution'.

One of the most long-lived and heartfelt differences in the Marx-oriented anti-capitalist left is between communists (of varying specifications) and socialists (including 'international socialists' in the Trotskyist tradition). During the Cold War, 1945–89, contrasting attitudes towards the USSR led peace movement organizations, such as the *Mouvement de la Paix* in France (Chapter 5), to belong to the World Peace Council, while others kept a distance, seeing this as a tool of the Soviet Union. We saw in Chapter 2 how War Resisters' International had to negotiate differences between those of its member organizations that supported and those that condemned revolts against the USSR in Czechoslovakia and elsewhere. We know from the study of the South Korean reunification movement that the positioning of activist groups with regard to North Korea is determined in part by tolerance or intolerance of Kim Jong-Il's (albeit uniquely inflected) communism. We have seen (Chapter 6) the fault line running through the contemporary movement in Japan, with communists on one side, socialists on the other. Two organizations, *Gensuikyo* and *Gensuikin*, the former communist, the latter socialist in allegiance, share a belief that nuclear weapons are a serious menace to humankind. Yet their political analysis, rooted in the Cold War period, threw them into conflict with regard to the legitimacy of the Soviet Union's nuclear arsenal. Notwithstanding the uni-polar world in which they now co-habit, doctrinal differences continue in this way to sustain rival initiatives, and not only in Japan.

Linked with the identification of capitalism as the unique cause of militarism and war, we have seen that some movements virtually equate the USA with the capitalist system, to the point of neglecting other states' responsibility for war. This is characteristic of some anti-war groups opposing the US-led 'war on terror'. We have seen how some in the South Korean reunification movement hold the USA uniquely responsible for North Korea's political and military intransigence. One of the most vehement and visible rifts in and among the left is in the USA itself, where in the period since 9/11 two major groups have been observed negotiating their differences with great difficulty in an attempt to present a solid front against US war ventures such as the attacks on Iraq and Afghanistan. One is United for Peace and Justice, a very broad alliance of local, regional and national groups, including secular and religious, variously progressive and democratic, women-only and mixed organizations. The other is the more unitary ANSWER (Act Now to Stop War and End Racism) in which the key role is played by the Workers World Party (WWP). The latter founds itself in Marxist and Leninist thought, works for the replacement of 'the unjust world economic order' by socialism, and defines the present occupation of Iraq and Palestine as 'colonial'.[5] It diverged sharply from most of the peace movement in justifying the Chinese government's attack on protestors in Tiananmen Square in 1989, and supporting the defence of Slobodan Milošević against a charge of war crimes. In the present epoch such reactions are prompted less by support for any residual communism in the Chinese or Serbian regimes than by the simple fact that the USA defines them as enemies of democracy. Fury over the US claim to be a fount of democracy is understandable in a country like South Korea that suffered decades of military tyranny sponsored by the USA (Chapter 7). This does not mean however that everyone bombed by the USA is a democratic role model. The War Resisters League, the US affiliate of War Resisters' International (Chapter 2), is represented on the board of United for Peace and Justice. Like many critics of ANSWER, its members strongly condemn what they see as an undiscerning politics of 'the enemy of my enemy is my friend' (Weinberg 2008). As do many other activists I met in the course of these studies, WRL believe the only constructive politics for peace is one that is capable of saying 'neither/ nor'. They say, in effect, 'We do not tolerate US war policies. But neither do we condone the injustice or belligerence of other regimes. It is possible for both sides in a conflict to be wrong'.

Socialist and communist tendencies are usually highly identifiable, at pains to present themselves in clearly 'branded' form, and explicit to the point of dogma in their analyses. Anarchism, a second source of strength in peace movements, is of its very nature less easy to pin down to named groups with clearly articulated platforms. Those I spoke with who defined themselves as anarchist share with other left tendencies a critique of capitalism as system. What characterized them most clearly however was their refusal of state power. Anti-authoritarian elements of the First International in the 1860s and 1870s aimed to replace state authority with spontaneous working class organization. An anarchist current, defining the state as a source of violence, was evident in peace movements throughout the twentieth century. Alex Comfort, for example, whose writing linked a critique of state authority with a critique of war, was active in the early years of the UK's Campaign for Nuclear Disarmament (Comfort 1950). We have seen in the war resistance movement (Chapter 2) that same defiance of the authority structures of the nation-state expressed as nonviolent resistance to militarism and war, particularly in Spain (Chapter 3) where activism in the spirit of anarcho-syndicalism has been an influential pacifist current resisting Spain's membership of NATO and the modernization of its armed forces.

Sometimes the divisive dichotomy of 'capital or state' as alternative sources of war is transcended, or at least smoothed over, within movements by a focus on 'militarism' itself, represented as an ideology and set of structures that are themselves a war-generating force. We saw the nonviolent activists of Vredesactie in Belgium (Chapter 2) naming 'militarism' rather than 'capitalism' or 'the state' as a focus of action capable of drawing social democrats, socialists and anarchists side by side into actions, for example against nuclear weapons. Contemporary anarchist groups in peace movements can act as a pacifist, nonviolent counterweight to those groups of the socialist and communist left who, despite being 'anti-war', support specific armed struggles. However, anarchism itself has been a problematic partner due to its bifurcation into deeply nonviolent and extremely violent tendencies, a point to which I return in the discussion of strategy below.

War in 3-D: the feminist anti-militarist standpoint

In the Introduction I described the concepts of feminist standpoint and intersectionality that, drawn from my earlier research in the feminist anti-militarist movement, furnished the 'interpretive paradigm' with which I approached this study. We've seen in the foregoing case studies too, many women embracing an analysis of war that, while it features capitalism as a major cause, does not see that as the whole story. They suggest that power is more complex than socialism alone, derived from the proletarian standpoint, can reveal. It has more than one dimension. Yes, there is economic power. In the capitalist mode of production that structures our society, a class empowered by the ownership of wealth exploits and oppresses a class deprived of access to the means of production, a class that has only its labour power to sell – and that on disadvantaged terms. That class relation, however, is cross-cut by other kinds of power relation, of which two are specially significant. The first is the patriarchal gender order, in which men as a sex are, historically and currently, empowered by the appropriation of women's bodies, their reproductive labour, their offspring and their investment in love and care. The second is ethno-national domination, in which a people is empowered by a cultural self-definition that excludes and marginalizes others, is often associated with control of a territory and borders, and sometimes deploys religion as a differentiator. Capitalism, patriarchy and ethno-nationalism, all three predicated on violence (as women's experience leaves them in no doubt) are bound together in the pursuit of war – capitalism by the imperative to control markets, nationalism by its cultural and territorial ambitions, patriarchy by its dependence on a form of masculinity honed for combativeness, authority and ascendancy.

We've seen this feminist variant of war theory emerging in the nineteenth-century British peace movement and developing in the context of the the First World War (Chapter 1). We've seen its reinvention in the late 1970s in War Resisters' International (Chapter 2), and by women in Spain a little later (Chapter 3). In South Korea the issues of patriarchy and nationalism arise when women debate the politics of Korean reunification (Chapter 7). In Okinawa women apply an intersectional analysis of power to an understanding of both Okinawan subordination to Japan and men's violence against women. And in Japan women recognize the malign partnership of misogyny, xenophobia and militarism in the resurgent fascist right (Chapter 6).

Women have learned, too, from recent wars in other parts of the globe. Capitalism may have precipitated the collapse of the Soviet system, but nationalist impulses were clearly at work in the disintegration of the USSR into ethno-culturally defined territories (Muslim Chechnya, Christian Armenia and so on) separating from a resurgent Russia. When the Yugoslav Federation collapsed into war, it hardly took a feminist to see that reversion to a fully market economy was accompanied by reawakened nationalisms, reascendent Orthodox and Catholic Christian churches, a patriarchal and racist panic over a declining Serbian birthrate, and a retreat from gender equality to gender difference. The phenomenon of mass rape, the presence of large numbers of women among 'ethnically cleansed' populations and a growing proportion of women among recruits to military and paramilitary forces, highly visible features of the so-called 'new' wars of the 1990s, have made it harder to ignore a gender analysis of war.

All the same, we've seen that women are still finding it difficult to win acceptance for feminist anti-militarist theory in the mainstream movement. Perhaps the reluctance should not surprise us, because the theory tells activists something painful about themselves. It is a reminder that the 'we' that constitute peace movements, while we may identify ourselves as the ordinary people, the workers, the oppressed, are ourselves implicated in power, often as the oppressors of others – by the way we live our national identity, by the way we live our gender. Feminists are suggesting that, if our movements are not to be vitiated by mutual oppression, and so disempowered in the struggle against militarism and war, we have to change ourselves and our relations with each other as we change the world. It is a highly demanding agenda, and one from which many mainstream activists turn away.

Choice of strategy: the significance of nonviolence

Analytical divergences within the left and between the several left, anarchist, feminist and other actors in anti-war, anti-militarist and peace movements are sometimes expressed in differences within the repertoire of activist strategy. We've seen, by my reckoning, the use of five forms of action: mass mobilization; using locality; campaigning; cultural activity; and nonviolent direct action.

First, there is the method favoured particularly by the socialist and communist tendencies, especially the vanguardist groups, of inspiring a huge presence on the street at a given time and place, usually a major city. Demonstrations of hundreds of thousands of people, shoulder to shoulder for a day, give participants an encouraging sense of solidarity. They are sometimes capable of winning the attention of the media and the politicians, although even the largest marches and rallies (such as those against the threatened attack on Iraq on 15 February 2003) are not guaranteed to cause governments to change their policies. Some activists deplore the privileging of the capital city, the waste of funds on transport. Others say that too much importance ascribed to discipline and mass turn-outs can stem from, and lend legitimacy to, domineering, centralizing and hierarchical leadership that alienates partners who prioritize inclusivity and structurelessness. But still others set store by vanguardist organizations for their efficiency, if nothing else. They ask themselves: who else will hire fleets of buses and produce tens of thousands of placards reiterating 'no war' or 'troops out'?

The second strategy, by contrast, emphasizes place and community. Many groups, while they will turn out to the occasional mass demonstration organized by somebody else, choose to concentrate their efforts on their own patch. The women from across Europe who experienced the No-to-NATO mobilization in Strasbourg (Chapter 5) as counter-productive went away to set up an e-mail network and share information about actions they would generate locally.[6] At the time of the following NATO Summit, in 2010, they took to the street in several cities in Italy and Britain with the message 'women say No to NATO'. In some cases these responded to women's liking for the still and silent vigil. But others feel that the advantage of a local approach is that, trading on familiarity with your home patch, it is possible to reach out and engage with local people. In London we distributed a thousand leaflets in a few hours as we moved through the city centre performing in our printed T-shirts. We had many useful conversations with passers-by who till then, to our surprise, had no idea what the initials N – A – T – O stood for, or the bearing this military alliance has on them. Such local actions are sidelined within the No-to-NATO movement however, which, as with Strasbourg in 2009, at the time of the Lisbon Summit of 2010 again focused uniquely on achieving an international mass presence in sight of the world's leaders and media.[7]

Some activists eschew banners, placards and feet on the street, regardless of whether the street is in their home town or in the capital city, in favour of sustained campaigning in an altogether different register – with less rhetoric, more engagement. This third method involves generating and distributing information, writing in the local press or blogging, organizing public meetings and petitions, keeping a good relationship with local parliamentarians, lobbying municipal councils and government departments, and campaigning at the United Nations. In Britain many branches of the Campaign for Nuclear Disarmament and the Women's International League for Peace and Freedom are skilled in this style of work.

Fourth, some organizations, especially those that invoke 'peace', choose to work directly with individuals and communities to achieve change in behaviours. I remember Elli Kim describing the desire of Women Making Peace (Chapter 7) as 'taking personal responsibility, making the changes in ourselves, rather than telling the government what to do'. The highly developed field of conciliation is not included in my study, but cultural campaigns for disarmament have been mentioned. For instance, anti-gun activists in Uganda (Chapter 8) work with women and men in a gender-sensitive way to help them imagine a viable weapon-free household and community. They use both material incentives and consciousness-raising to achieve 'mental disarmament'. Perhaps here, too, we should recall the Bahá'í community in Leicester (Chapter 4), who might well be joined by adherents of other faiths represented in the peace movement when they say that, for them, prayer is a powerful form of action.

The patience, tolerance and optimism called for by educational and cultural work for peace is not everyone's *forte*. Some want to express more vehemently their distress and anger about militarism and war, and this is the attraction of the fifth strategy, nonviolent direct action. We've seen examples from Spain (Chapter 3), for instance, where AA-MOC deliver their message by trespassing in military installations, and France, where anti-NATO activists sat down to block the route of Heads of State to their meeting (Chapter 5). NVDA has its own principles, processes and techniques. Care is taken to use as little force as possible, even against property, and to use passivity rather than provocation in face of the police. Where possible, activists are open about their intentions, for instance telling the authorities in advance about a planned action, concealing only the time and location. Such civil disobedience has the effect of making visible the militarization in our own neighbourhood, the local base, barracks or engineering firm, showing that 'war starts here'. Women sometimes inflect the action in a particular way, to avoid reproducing either masculine heroics (taking risks) or feminine passivity (lying prone and immobile). But often, as at the Greenham Common Peace Camp (Chapter 1), or in MOC Sevilla (Chapter 3), women find ways of putting their bodies into play on their own terms, with dramatic and transgressive effect. Like other strategies, civil disobedience has its critics. Some see it as childish and self-indulgent, as no more likely to achieve its goal than prayer in the evaluation of an atheist. But for many who engage in it, the 'directness' of NVDA is empowering. More than in any other strategy, 'prefigurative struggle' is in play, the belief that it is important to use means that exemplify ends. In particular, if you want a nonviolent world, in which people's wellbeing is prioritized, you devise direct actions which, though challenging, use nonviolent, circumspect and caring methods.

Direct action and mass mobilizations, however, are sometimes joined by groups that see merit in using violence to provoke the state into revealing its own violent nature. Those who choose violent methods, no less than nonviolent direct activists, often name themselves, or are named by others, as anarchists. In the nineteenth century many anarchists practised anti-authoritarian violence, 'the propaganda of the deed' (Graham 2005). It is this tradition that lives on in the contemporary phenomenon of the black bloc. We saw an example in Chapter 5. The black bloc, comprising mainly but not exclusively young males, is not an organization but rather a practice, with a particular style of dress and group behaviour. These activists do not seek realistically to defeat the state by force of arms, but deem violent acts against the state's security personnel (stone throwing, 'molotov cocktails') and against property (breaking glass, setting fires) a cogent symbol of resistance to authority.

Should we call this the sixth method in the movement's repertoire? It is questionable. First, the dislike of this tactic among non-practitioners is of an altogether different magnitude than any lack of enthusiasm felt for the other five kinds of strategy. The great majority of activists condemn violence and feel undermined by it. The black bloc have been highly visible in protest movements against global capital and the international trade and monetary institutions. Although it is difficult to be sure, it may be that individuals and small groups of activists move readily between movements, so that those that join mobilizations of anti-war, anti-militarist and peace movements do not have a particular loyalty or commitment to them. Certainly they do not share, as other organizations do, in the collective life of the movements, identifying themselves, stating their intentions and arguing for them. They are secretive not only in relation to the security services but also in dealings with other activists.

The arguments of those who reject violent methods are, first and foremost, pragmatic. If you are challenging the state to put down its weapons it is counterproductive to pick up weapons of your own. You have no chance of defeating the forces of 'law and order', and your actions are likely to lead them to step up their baton or tear gas attacks on unarmed demonstrators. Besides, the sight of stone throwing and arson alienates public opinion and diminishes the number of people willing to participate in demonstrations. But violent methods are condemned for moral reasons, too. For some peace movement activists, including some religious groups as well as nonviolent anarchists and libertarians, nonviolence is an ethical principle.

If, as I shall suggest below, one of the rather few things we hold in common in our very mixed movements is a desire for all-round violence reduction, to use violence as a method of protest is illogical and divisive. For all that, there is a grey area in respect to violence in the movements. In the first place activists who claim nonviolence vary in what they categorize as 'violent' behaviour. Those at the absolutist extreme of pacifism would say that any use of force, even against inert objects, is a violent (therefore undesirable) method. Probably the majority of activists on the other hand consider quite reasonable the limited and precise application of force to property that symbolizes military or state power, such as using bolt cutters to open a way through a fence, or painting peace symbols on a military aircraft. Besides, we saw in Chapter 5 that the representative of at least one group participating in the anti-NATO weekend of action in Strasbourg in 2009 did not wish to cast out from the movement those liable to use violence, his priority being to mobilize people from the broadest possible social and political spectrum.

In the second place, among those who do engage in violence during demonstrations there is disagreement on what is an acceptable and productive use of force. After the Strasbourg demonstration there was an exchange of views on the Web by anonymous black bloc participants.[8]

One article, described as being compiled from several accounts, adopted the authorial persona of an older than average, and female, black bloc activist. 'She' expressed relish for 'the sound of breaking glass, the swinging of batons, the powerful smell of adrenaline, of petrol, of testosterone and of tear gas', pleasure at the burning of the frontier post and hotel, and delight in 'being "sexy", all in black, offering new poses to the riot-porn cameras'. Nonetheless the authors acknowledged feelings of malaise and confusion. In particular they felt troubled by

> the lack of respect or interest on the part of those in the black bloc towards other participants of anti-NATO actions, not least for the fact that without us, they could have easily carried out their actions. But that is not true for us: without them, we wouldn't be able to carry out ours.

We took our actions, these correspondents acknowledged, into spaces where they adversely affected other demonstrators who had not had the chance to debate and decide on these tactics.[9]

Co-existence or cohesion?

These divergencies of analysis and strategy in the anti-war, anti-militarist and peace movements are sometimes relatively easy to ignore. When faced with an acute issue (a crisis such as the launching of the war on Iraq, which brought together disparate groups worldwide), or when an alliance is understood to be temporary, occasional or narrowly focused, we are able to suspend disbelief and act 'as if' we all agreed. Often, however, differences of analysis and strategy are an ongoing impediment to united action locally, nationally and internationally. A further question arises, then: are we addressing or evading differences? Are we developing and using purposeful methods for negotiating them? As Alberto Melucci puts it, 'constructing a collective identity entails continuous investment and unfolds as a process – a process that must be constantly activated'. It calls for 'a network of active relationships between actors who interact, communicate, influence each other, negotiate, and make decisions' (Melucci 1996: 67, 71). My perception is that the mechanisms for addressing and resolving tensions in the anti-war, anti-militarist and peace movements we have seen here are in most cases poorly developed. The organizations and networks I spent time with, when they mapped for me their relationship with significant 'others' in their immediate environment, were able to say clearly, of some of them, 'these are our partners' and of others 'we avoid them', 'we each do our own thing'. But I didn't often hear people say, 'well, we have difficulties with them, but we're working on it'. To meet, listen, acknowledge, understand and perhaps eventually agree takes not only time and goodwill, but courage, skill and technique. If those are lacking, it may seem safer to skate over the thin ice of differences.

In theory, new electronic communication technologies should assist cohesion and coherence. Mobile phones and e-mail are a huge advance on the phone-tree and the photocopier. Information about and from organizations can be made permanently accessible and be continually updated on the Web. It does not seem, however, that the new technologies' full potential is yet being used. A recent research project in the UK found that, 'by and large, the anti-war movement uses the manifest rather than latent functionalities of new media. It tended to adopt ICTs in orthodox and predictable ways ...'. More imaginative uses of technology exploiting interactivity to allow discussion and collaborative, wiki-style writing were 'scarce' (Gillan et al. 2008). Given this finding, although it was not a focus of my questions, it seems likely that the Internet is being used more to put out calls to action than to facilitate the careful negotiation of differences in analysis.

For the most part, people evade disagreement by joining a group, organization or network in which they can be sure to find like-minded people. Indeed, that fact may account for the huge proliferation of initiatives, and for the very small size of some of them. In many cases overlapping memberships help to bond various groups into a movement. Those half dozen people in a microscopic grouplet may well be simultaneously members of several other and perhaps bigger organizations and networks, which, having less precisely defined analyses and strategies, are tolerable – if less dear to their hearts. Sometimes, though, we do witness a sustained effort to hold together a movement with strongly divergent tendencies. We saw that in Japan (Chapter 6) a third, non-aligned, stream of anti-war, anti-militarist and peace activism furnishes some organizations that can transcend the socialist/communist dichotomy and strive to give a wider public a sense of contributing to a nation-wide peace movement. In Okinawa, the widespread feeling of being a 'colonized' people furnished such common ground. We observed activists in South Korea (Chapter 7) applying care and caution to the divisive concepts of nation, nationhood and nationalisms, some of them transcending the profound contradictions resulting from Korea's disastrous twentieth century with the notion of a 'peace state'.

One instance of a creative move towards mutual understanding remains in my mind. When I was in Leicester, where (as we saw in Chapter 4) the movement that came together for Gaza involved highly disparate groups, two people had just begun an initiative they called Dialogues. One of them, Richard Johnson, you may remember, was active in the Campaign for Nuclear Disarmament; the other, Zina Zelter, had started a Women in Black vigil in Leicester and was also part of an affinity group doing NVDA against local firms involved in the arms industry. They were very conscious of the contingency and fragility, yet at the same time the value and potential, of the relationships embodied in the demonstrations for Gaza at the Clock Tower. Relationships among the various left and pacifist groups in the city were comparatively well-worn and non-contentious, and a practised mutual tolerance prevailed among the organized secularists and the organized Christians. However, when the large and influential Muslim organizations were added to the peace terrain, together with the leftwing (mainly Hindu) Indian Workers' Association, many activists from all sides found themselves on untested ground. Richard and Zina believed there was need for a secure, unthreatening environment in which people from the various currents could meet, talk about themselves, learn about others and explore differences. In Dialogues, their plan was to hold a sequence of informal evening gatherings in people's homes, inviting a particular mix of individuals from the movement. Each person would bring along a dish to the shared meal. Richard and Zina planned to experiment with semi-structured ways of prompting conversations across differences – conceived both as differences of political analysis, and of positionality in terms of personal history, ethnicity, class and gender. In all my travels round the movements, this was the nearest thing I encountered to a thought-through transversal politics. There is potential, and a great need, for so much more.

In particular there seems to be an impasse when it comes to the adoption of feminist insights. There is not a chapter in this book in which women have not been heard saying, of their experience in anti-war, anti-militarist and peace movements, words to the effect that 'gender is never seen as the real business', and 'the men just don't get it'. Women report that it is hardly ever possible to raise gender issues in mixed organizations without feeling 'the time isn't right', you're 'making a gaffe'. And when it does come about that a man accepts that male dominance and sexism are verifiable problems, rather than the fictions of self-interested women, he seldom recognizes (Japanese women told us) that the phenomenon refers not just to men in general, but to *him* – that it calls for a response by him.

It's as if there is an inhibition in the case of gender that is less evident in the cases of race and class. 'White' Western activists do not on the whole permit their own positionality in relation to white supremacy, in the world or in the nation, to inhibit them from antiracist activism – indeed many take it as a point of honour to engage in solidarity with racialized 'others'. Similarly, the many activists born into the property-owning class do not allow their advantaged positionality in relation to economic power to inhibit them from blaming capitalist class interests for war, or participating in working class struggles. How is it then, women wonder, that so many men allow their positionality as males in relation to patriarchal power to prevent them acknowledging the part played by phallocracy in militarism, to impede them from joining the struggle to subvert the system of male supremacy?

The inability of so many male comrades to hear, understand and adapt leaves women activists with a difficult choice. Should they stay in a mixed organization, persisting in an exhausting and often fruitless double militancy, or opt for the women-only alternative? Though it's costly to abandon a project in which you have invested a lot of yourself, often for years, we have seen many cases in the foregoing case studies where feminists have walked away from the mixed movement to join or create a women-only organization, attracted by the possibility of creating an environment in which it is easier to speak and be heard, a space in which to highlight war's gender-specific impacts (on men as well as women), to develop and deploy a holistic, gendered analysis of militarism, and to choose campaigning strategies with which they feel comfortable.

On the other hand many feminist women remain in the mixed organizations. What holds them there is often a belief in the irreducible necessity, if militarism is to be effectively opposed and war ended, of men themselves being made aware of the way manhood, masculine strengths and values, are exploited and deformed by war-makers, of perceiving that gender-transformative work is necessary work for peace. If men are part of the war problem, such women feel, they must be part of the anti-war solution. If it is only women who can awaken this consciousness among men in the mixed movement, they must hold on and persist in the work.

Making connections: a 'continuum' of violence

In conclusion I turn to some perceptions I bring, from my exposure to these many organizations and networks, concerning their current thinking on violence. My feeling is that since the end of the Cold War there has been a shift from seeing war as a matter of policy decisions by governments towards seeing it as one manifestation, if the most extreme, of a society-wide, socially constituted, propensity to violence. Many of the women and men I've talked with, and some of the many books and articles I've read, have expressed two ideas that are symptomatic of such a shift. The first is that instances and kinds of violence are not discrete and unconnected – they can be characterized as a *continuum*. Second, that violence is, for the most part, not inevitable. It is a *choice*. The continuum can be interrupted.

The term 'the continuum of violence' was initially coined to convey the idea that when violence is our concern, episodes of armed conflict and periods called peace cannot and should not be considered entirely separate and different. All our countries are, more than we are disposed to notice, in a permanent state of militarization. Don't think, Cynthia Enloe warned us, that militarization is limited to where you see that tell-tale khaki. It's 'not just the executives and factory floor workers who make fighter planes, land mines, and intercontinental missiles but also the employees of food companies, toy companies, clothing companies, film studios, stock brokerages, and advertising agencies' (Enloe 2000: 2). Daily life in countries where the homicide rate is very high, such as Mexico and South Africa, is war without the name. Police states where torture and extrajudicial killings are routine could be classed as conflict zones.

Women in particular have been alerted to a continuum of violence by perceiving a thread of gender running through the different moments of violence. Rape is common at the best of times, increases with the level of criminality in society, is a favoured form of torture in police states, and is often epidemic in armed conflicts. Women observe that the inferiorization of women in 'peaceful' societies disposes armed forces to sexually abuse women in war. Conversely, the experience of war shapes men's behaviour towards women in peace time. Thus, there is evidence that domestic violence is particularly prevalent in families in which a man has served in the military (Mercier and Mercier 2000). A significant increase in domestic violence during the Yugoslav wars was noted by Serbian and Croatian women's help-lines, that also found the abuse occurring disproportionately after violent war reports were screened on TV news (Korac 1998). Besides, as Joanna Bourke showed in her book *A History of Intimate Killing*, a study of veteran soldiers' recollections of the battlefield, performing violent acts of an apparently non-sexual nature is sometimes experienced as erotic (Bourke 1999). Lisa Price describes this effect as 'an eroticization of dominance and submission such that violence is experienced as sex, and, too often, sex is experienced as violence' (Price 2005: 110).

In the early days of second wave feminism in Britain, militarization and war were not on the feminist agenda. As Jill Liddington describes the late 1960s and early 1970s, they were 'the nadir of a popular women's peace movement in Britain. Feminism and anti-militarism seemed a million miles apart' (Liddington 1989: 203). All the more remarkable then was the insight of those women activists who got together in 1979 to study 'feminism and nonviolence' (Chapter 2) who came up with the idea that 'individual men attacking individual women is one end of the *continuum of violence* which leads inexorably to the international military abuse of power' (Feminism and Nonviolence Study Group 1983: 39, my italics). A quarter century later, as we have seen, the perception of a continuum of violence linking war and peace has become commonplace among feminist anti-militarists. A Ugandan woman told us how the prevalence of guns in her community sustains it. 'When you have a war you look for a weapon. When you have a weapon you look for a war,' she said.

The term 'continuum of violence' has emerged from, and in turn inspired, fresh thinking about violence. But it tends to be used casually rather than analytically. A number of different dimensions of continuity are suggested, sometimes explicitly but often only implicitly. The first and most common is a time continuum – the notion of an uninterrupted flow or current of violent events spanning periods of war and peace. This was my main intention in an article with the title 'The Continuum of Violence' written in 1999 where I traced the gender thread through times of pre-war, war-fighting, disarmament and peace (Cockburn 2004b).[10] However, in a later edition of the article I felt the need to be more explicit about other dimensions of continuity of which I had become aware: a spatial continuity of violence stretching from home and street to battlefield and stratosphere; a continuum linking types or kinds of violence; and a scalar continuum, as in the scale of force (from fist to bomb), or social unit (two people in a punch-up, wars between nations) (Cockburn 2012).

One important dimension along which a continuum of violence runs is between harm by oppression and harm by physical force. Forty years ago Johan Galtung pointed out that social structures, particularly the system by which life chances (wealth, resources, services) are distributed in a population, can result in injury, sickness and death for those they disadvantage. As I mentioned in the Introduction, he termed this 'structural violence' (Galtung 1969: 171). A similar extension of the scope of the term violence was suggested around the same time by Newton Garver, who wrote of 'a kind of quiet violence' which 'operates when people are deprived of choices in a systematic way by the very manner in which transactions normally take place' (republished as Garver 2009: 180). We are now less likely to forget that government policies or official neglect, no less than baton charges and airstrikes, can kill and maim.

The existence of continua of violence, whether of time, space, scale or type can be persuasively suggested. The imagination can easily fill in the detail. However, the word continuum itself means no more than a continuous series of instances. Its interest to peace movements lies in supposing the existence of a link between instances, a chain of causality. If one violent act gives rise to another, we can believe that reducing violence at one point along the continuum will have the effect of reducing violence of another kind or in another place or moment. The continuum of violence is a thematic trope in the anthology *Violence in War and Peace*, edited by Nancy Scheper-Hughes and Philippe Bourgois. In their introduction they stress cause and effect. Violence they say is reproductive, mimetic, it 'gives birth to itself' (Scheper-Hughes and Bourgois 2004: 1). They cite, for instance, the frequency with which abusers within families turn out to have been themselves abused as children, and observe that militant revolutionaries often substitute their own forms of violence for the repressive regimes they overthrow. In a similar vein, in an article on 'The Continuum of Violence in Post-war Guatemala', Beatrix Manz showed the violence of insurgency and counter-insurgency that racked that country for thirty years arising out of prior repression and leaving behind devastating levels of criminal violence (Manz 2008: 1).

Although there are more assertions than proofs concerning the 'infectiousness' of violence, it is a logic that many activists clearly feel offers them a strategy. If by weakening a link, breaking a sequence, violence can be averted, it makes sense to seek an accessible point of intervention. For instance, if the normalization, even valorization, of violence in popular culture leads individuals to enact violence in real life, it will be productive to work at the cultural level to discredit gratuitous representations of violence. A great deal of the activism described in this book, the interventions we have seen activists choose, implies a belief in such a theory.

The movements' problematic: where to draw the line?

Reviewing the thinking we have heard expressed within contemporary anti-war, anti-militarist and peace movements in the foregoing chapters we can see arguments being mounted and choices being made as to where along the various continua of violence a boundary marker is to be put down, separating the issues we shall address with our activism and those we shall leave to others.

I see one line as being drawn, for the most part and without acrimony, between structural and overt violence. I perceive the principal focus of these organizations and networks as being characteristically on *direct, overt, physical violence*, and the organizational machinery – command systems, weapons and personnel – that deliver it. Their emphasis on the physical does not imply they fail to recognize the continuum that links physical violence to indirect harm. Rather, they have made a practical, tactical, choice: 'You can't do everything.' Thus, while I've heard many organizations state their objective to be 'peace *with justice*', most appear to mean by this that they recognize 'justice' as a necessary condition for the emergence of durable peace, not that it's a theme on which they themselves actively and presently work. There are exceptions of course – in the case of Palestinians under occupation and blockade by Israel, for instance, it is scarcely possible to separate the military repression from the harm done by economic means. And the Women's International League for Peace and Freedom in the aftermath of both World Wars put a great deal of its effort into campaigns for greater economic and social justice in the international peace settlements (Bussey and Tims 1980). For the most part, however, the oppression generated by the mode of production and governmental policy 'arrangements' is understood by anti-war, anti-militarist and peace activists as the theme of a parallel, though not unrelated, movement, the *altermondialisme* that strives for global economic and social justice. This is not to say that individuals aren't involved in both movements. Many surely are – as well as being active in others such as the environmental and women's movements.

Considering direct, overt, physical violence alone, we can see the anti-war, anti-militarist and peace movements now currently challenged, and disunited, concerning whether to pursue the wrongs they address along the time continuum of violence, from 'war time' to 'peace time', with the effect of redefining peace. Those who wish to take this route argue that the violence of war is but an extreme case, an epidemic, if you like, of endemic violence. And if violence is 'mimetic', if instances of violence are causally linked, then interventions against the use of physical violence in everyday life can be thought of as part and parcel of anti-war activism and *vice versa*. Why draw a line between campaigning against rape in peace-time and rape in war? This time-extended view, though argued most cogently by feminist anti-militarists, does not relate to gender-based violence alone. If power systems predicated on violence – most significantly those of economic class, the territorial ethno-national state, and the male-dominated gender order – are causal of war, there is an argument for addressing the violence to which all those same intersected systems give rise in 'peace time'. Peace then comes to mean a condition defined by an absence of the threat of physical violence against the person. Yes, it means a condition in which women's bodies are no longer considered territories for group conquest, property men can lay claim to, or toys for them to use and break at will. But it also means a condition in which corporate thugs do not attack striking workers, vagrant children on the streets are not seen as refuse to be eliminated in the name of 'social cleansing', in which 'foreigners' are not threatened by racist attacks, and in which homosexuals, disabled people and others are not the targets of hate crime. It also implies the cessation of the banal violence men and boys inflict on each other, with guns, knives or fists, and a transformation of the everyday cultural practices that normalize violence, particularly those that foster violent forms of masculinity. One way of seeing the broadening of horizons to bring societal violence into the scope of analysis and activism against war is to think of it as an overlapping of membership and objectives between several movements. In the nineteenth century, after all, the peace movement shared many members with movements to end slavery, outlaw duelling, ban flogging in the military and abolish capital punishment.

Violence and nonviolence as choices

Peace activists are often seen as naïve for pitting themselves against violence. After all, the world itself heaps harm on us – volcanoes erupt, *tsunamis* drown us, storms batter us. But the peace activist responds, with good reason, that we do better to exclude such events from our definition of violence. We may speak figuratively of the 'violence' of a hurricane, but the forcefulness of the forces of nature do not evoke violence in response. Then again, the sceptics invoke primate biology: 'violence is human nature'. To which the peace activist replies: be that as it may, human beings have modified, in the course of our social evolution, many instinctual behaviours. Besides, historically the growth of organized violence in human society is more closely associated with the onset of civilization than with the simpler cultures of hunter-gatherers that preceded it (Eckhardt 1992). And in the contemporary world some societies are less violent than others.

Among those who decry the pacifist ideal are (as we've seen) some of the supposed allies on the political left, those who view revolutionary violence as not merely inevitable but in some circumstances desirable, cathartic and heroic. In *The Wretched of the Earth*, Frantz Fanon wrote of the colonial subject: 'At the level of the individual, violence is a cleansing force. It frees the native from his inferiority complex and from his despair and inaction; it makes him fearless and restores his self-respect' (Fanon 1967: 74). And Jean-Paul Sartre endorsed this view. In his Preface to Fanon's book, both of them devastating indictments of colonial repression, he wrote 'no gentleness can efface the marks of violence; only violence itself can destroy them' (Sartre 1967: 18).

Given popular belief in the inevitability, even the desirability, of violence, it is not difficult for the 'realist' school of politics and diplomacy, stressing the tough realities of power and self-interest in a world of rival nation-states, to make a persuasive case for the enduring necessity of military might as an instrument of international relations. It is a school of thought that, developed in the 1930s both in the USA and European countries, has proved resistant to the revisions of two or three generations of critical IR theorists (Halliday 1994). The latter cite plentiful evidence that the effects of military coercion are highly unpredictable (Sidman 2001) and that physical violence proves no more reliable a strategy than nonviolent political methods, even in the case of direct confrontations with other violent actors (Howes 2009). Yet the dubious outcomes of military adventures do not seem to dull the militarist reflex of politicians. Even when the security of their own state is not directly threatened, they sell the idea that 'humanitarian intervention', that is, bombing, is an appropriate response to the internal conflicts of other states.

It may be useful to think of the inevitability of violence as a hegemonic idea, one that holds sway over the minds of the majority in our societies at the present time. The use of the term hegemonic in this sense owes much to Antonio Gramsci. Observing the way that the rulers of most European states avoided the same fate as those of Russia in the October Revolution of 1917, he observed that rule is not always reliant on force. The bourgeoisie may indeed dominate its class rivals by the threat or use of armed might, police repression, imposing imprisonment and other forms of punishment. But alternatively, as occurred in 1920s Germany, Britain and France, it may win consent by 'the exercise of moral and intellectual leadership' – hegemony, as Gramsci termed it (Gramsci 1971: 57).[11] In such cases the state's role is cultural and educational, disseminating a world view which, though it may serve the interests of the ruling class, is nonetheless convincing to the majority of civil society. Those who refute this 'common sense' appear marginal and unreasonable.

The inevitability of violence is one of these pervasive and persuasive ideas that forestall progressive social change. It serves ruling interests by legitimating a state with a strong security sector, capable of imposing internal order as well as defending investments, markets and other national interests abroad. It fosters a lucrative industry manufacturing warships and planes, weapons and ammunition, for domestic use and export. It favours racist suspicion of foreign 'others' and 'the enemy within'. Calling for tough leadership, it fosters the patriarchal gender order, bolstered by a 'hegemonic masculinity' (the term is R. W. Connell's, 1987) that is combative and authoritarian. It makes it seem reasonable to train a proportion of the citizenry in military values and fighting technique, and prepares the remainder to sacrifice them to the interests of the nation, should the need arise.

There is a constant 'battle for hegemony', a struggle in society at the level of ideas. Subaltern, subordinated, excluded or exploited classes have a different and subversive story to tell of how things are, how things work. A critical awareness may emerge. Spreading among more and more people and areas of society, presenting a serious challenge to the dominant rationality, the new idea may become 'counter-hegemonic'. It may prevail and bring about deep change in society. The work of the peace movement, then, could be seen as the substitution of a different 'common sense', as Gramsci termed it, about violence and war. The peace movement is not a class subject, in the Marxist sense of class relations arising in the capitalist mode of production. Its anti-war, anti-militarist and peace components span classes, drawing membership from a very wide cross-section of society, including state and service employees, professionals, intellectuals and students, as indeed do other contemporary global social movements. These have joined the manual working class as agents of change. Benedetto Fontana, in an essay on Gramsci's concept of hegemony, writes of the possible emergence of 'a reflexive and conscious movement, from passive acceptance of the given reality to active engagement with it ... a movement from fragmentation to integration'. The question debated by today's peace activists is whether our movements can achieve the coherence and cohesion to be more than a fluctuating array of contingent alliances, to become what Fontana calls 'a social and political subject capable of acting in history' (Fontana 2006: 41).

An objective shared by anti-war, anti-militarist and peace organizations, perhaps we might call it their common denominator, is not the utopian vision of a world free of all violence. Even the most pacifist among peace activists find it hard to imagine, and persuade others to imagine, that all violence between human beings can be eliminated. Life teaches us that stress and insanity, as well as intractable antagonisms, will always disturb the peace. Rather, what I have heard them express is a more pragmatic, more achievable, goal: *violence reduction*. We can (and sometimes already do) work backwards, scale down, seek alternatives: foreign policy that favours negotiation over troop deployment, trade policy that does not promote arms exports, play schemes without toy guns. A step at a time, we can illegalize landmines, next cluster bombs, eventually nuclear weapons.

Violence reduction for many of these organizations is a means as well as an end. Peace groups in the libertarian tradition lead the way in this by electing in their own relationships with each other to use words, gestures and strategies that are studiedly less violent, that prefigure the less violent world they want to bring into being. (It is this impulse that makes black bloc violence as a strategy so questionable and divisive.) Feminists contribute by insisting on a process that rejects machismo. At the moment of choice between a more or less violent practice, whether in a stand-off between rival states or a road rage incident, gender can play a decisive role. Which value in our gender-dichotomous value system is going to predominate? Care or combat, compromise or honour, co-operation or control? A gendered reflex here may be the iota on the scale that tips the balance.

The counter-hegemonic idea, as I see it expressed in the movements, is that *violence is a choice*. It is a conviction that there is, much more often than commonly supposed, a more violent and a less violent course of action – policy, programme, stance, gesture, turn of phrase – and that we can prefer one over the other. The woman can choose not to slap the child. The man can choose to put down the gun. The cabinet can choose to cancel the contract for the aircraft carrier. Violence is *discretionary*. Here I am echoing Lisa Price who wrote, neatly, that even wartime rape is in most cases 'a discretionary power' (Price 2005: 82).

As I write the closing pages of this book, one extremely violent event has dominated the news headlines and caused a spate of e-mails, blogs and tweets. Before dawn on 2 May 2011, a US hit squad helicoptered into Pakistan and assassinated Osama bin Laden, leader of Al-Qaeda and presumed architect of the terror attacks on US targets on 11 September 2001. Two shots to the head, the bloody corpse bundled away by air and hastily buried at sea. According to the popular media, America erupted in joy: 'justice has been done'. But there was a minority that saw no cause for celebration. This comment was circulated by Veterans for Peace, in the USA:[12]

> Killing will lead only to more killing. There will be no review of bin Laden's alleged crimes, as a trial would have provided. There will be no review of earlier US support for bin Laden ... Instead there will be bitterness, hatred, and more violence, with the message being communicated to all sides that might makes right and murder is the way in which someone is, in President Obama's words, brought to justice ... When their revenge comes, we will know exactly what we are supposed to do: exact more revenge in turn to keep the cycle going.

In the days following 2 May, communicating with each other transnationally through their many electronic networks, peace activists remarked above all on the fact that bin Laden had been unarmed, that the US military had had the option of arresting him and delivering him to stand trial under international law. It is above all the unusual clarity of this *choice* to kill rather than capture that has shocked people. One thing the anti-war, anti-militarist and peace movements, for all their diversity, unite in saying is: there is almost always a choice.

Notes

1. I have looked to Zirakzadeh (1997), Waterman (1998), Castells (1996–99), McIntyre-Mills (2000) and Tilly and Wood (2009) among others, for insights into social movements.
2. '[V]iviamos la incertidumbre de un proyecto siempre inacabado, siempre decidiéndose ... Un proyecto que no se construia sobre pasos necesarios o un deseño preestablecido, sino en referencia constante a unas líneas maestras tan imposibles como irrenunciables ... [L]o social y lo personal se confundían, se determinaban recíprocamente. La asamblea era el triunfo de lo colectivo y el consenso era el triunfo del individuo.' My translation.
3. Extract from War Resisters' International *Statement of Principles*, accessed on: www.wri-irg.org (22 January 2009).
4. Online at: www.swp.org.uk (accessed 1 June 2009).
5. Online at: www.workersworld.net/wwp (accessed 20 April 2011).
6. See reports and photos on the website: www.wloe.org.
7. The report of the International Co-ordinating Committee on No-to-NATO's work presented to the annual conference held in Dublin in April 2011 made no mention of local actions.
8. 'Après avoir tout brûlé ...: Suite au sommet de l'OTAN à Strasbourg en avril 2009 – Correspondance à propos de stratégies et émotions révolutionnaires', was published in July 2009 on Indymedia, seen online at: www.infokiosques. net/spip.php?article733 (accessed 16 May 2011).

9. '... du son des vitres cassés et des moulinets de bâtons, des odeurs tenaces de l'adrénaline, de l'essence, de la testostérone et des gaz lacrymogènes'; '... nous sommes "sexy", tous en noir, offrant une nouvelle pose de riot porn aux caméras'; '... le manque de respect ou d'intérêt montré par les participants aux black blocs pour les autres participants aux actions anti-OTAN, tout particulièrement parce que si un certain nombre d'entre eux auraient pu mener leur actions à bien sans nous, nous ne pouvions entreprendre nos actions sans eux'. My translation.

10. For a World Bank conference on Gender, Armed Conflict and Political Violence, Washington, DC, 10–11 June 1999.

11. Antonio Gramsci, Marxist thinker and leading figure in the Italian Communist Party, was imprisoned from 1926 to 1934 by Benito Mussolini. The notebooks he compiled in prison contain his insights into the functioning of class-divided societies and amplified Marx's theory of politics and the state. He evolved the concept of cultural hegemony to explain how, while a Bolshevik revolution had overthrown the ruling class in Russia, in the Western European states bourgeois rule survived the working class challenge (Gramsci 1971).

12. Authored by David Swanson, it was online at: http://warisacrime.org/node/57708 (accessed 3 May 2011).

References

Ajangiz, Rafael (2002) 'Es posible una sociedad insumisa?', in MOC: Movimiento de Objección de Conciencia, *En Legítima Desobediencia: Tres Décadas de Objeción, Insumisión y Antimilitarismo* (Madrid: MOC, with El Proyecto Editorial Traficantes de Sueños), 269–74.

Akibayashi, Kozue and Suzuyo Takazato (2009) 'Okinawa: Women's Struggle for Demilitarization', in Catherine Lutz (ed.), *The Bases of Empire: The Global Struggle against US Military Posts* (London: Pluto Press), 243–69.

Allen, Tim and Koen Vlassenroot (eds) (2010) *The Lord's Resistance Army: Myth and Reality* (London and New York: Zed Books).

Amnesty International (1992) *Uganda: Time for Action to Safeguard Human Rights*, AI Index: AFR 59/06/92 (London: Amnesty International).

Amnesty International (2008) *Blood at the Crossroads: Making the Case for a Global Arms Trade Treaty*, AI Index: ACT 30/011/2008 (London: Amnesty International).

Amnesty International (2009) 'Israel/Gaza: Operation "Cast Lead": 22 Days of Death and Destruction', AI Index No.15/015/2009. Online at www.amnesty. org/en/library/info/MDE15/015/2009/en (accessed 2 April 2011).

Arunburu, Xabier Agirre (2002) 'Están ustedes hablando con un delincuente', in MOC: Movimiento de Objección de Conciencia, *En Legítima Desobediencia: Tres Décadas de Objección, Insumisión y Antimilitarismo* (Madrid: MOC, with El Proyecto Editorial Traficantes de Sueños), 275–80.

Berkman, Joyce (1990) 'Feminism, War and Peace Politics: The Case of World War 1', in Jean Bethke Elshtain and Sheila Tobias (eds), *Women, Militarism and War: Essays in History, Politics and Social Theory* (Savage: Rowman and Littlefield), 141–60.

Beyer, Wolfram (1980) *War Is a Crime against Humanity*. A thesis in Political Science at the Free University of Berlin. Unpublished typescript. Translated into English by Hilda Morris.

Blackwood, Caroline (1984) *On the Perimeter* (London: Fontana Paperbacks).

Blessing, Jasmin, Henri Myrttinen, Nicola Popović and Nicole Stolze (2010) '"Como te haces entender?" Gender and Gun Cultures in the Caribbean Context'. Working Paper of the Gender, Peace and Security Programme (Santo Domingo, Dominican Republic: United Nations International Research and Training Institute for the Advancement of Women).

Borzello, Anna (2009) 'The Challenge of DDR in Northern Uganda: The Lords Resistance Army', in Mats Berdal and David H. Ucko (eds), *Reintegrating Armed Groups after Conflict: Politics, Violence and Transition* (Abingdon, New York: Routledge), 144–71.

Bourke, Joanna (1999) *An Intimate History of Killing: Face-to-face Killing in Twentieth Century Warfare* (London: Granta Books).

Braudy, Leo (2003) *From Chivalry to Terrorism: War and the Changing Nature of Masculinity* (New York: Vintage Books).

Braunw, Esther et al. (1984) *Mujer, Paz y Militarismo* (Madrid: Fundación de Investigaciones Marxistas).

Buckley-Zistel, Susanne (2008) *Conflict Transformation and Social Change in Uganda: Remembering after Violence* (Basingstoke, New York: Palgrave Macmillan).

Bussey, Gertrude and Margaret Tims (1980) *Pioneers for Peace: Women's International League for Peace and Freedom 1915–1965* (Oxford: Alden Press).

Butler, Sandra E. and Claire Wintram (1991) *Feminist Groupwork: Self, Identity and Change* (London, Thousand Oaks, New Delhi: Sage Publications).

Carter, April (1992) *Peace Movements: International Protest and World Politics since 1945* (London, New York: Longman).

Castells, Manuel (1996–99) *The Information Age: Economy, Society and Culture*, Vols. 1–3 (Oxford: Blackwell Publishers).

Ceadel, Martin (1996) *The Origins of War Prevention: The British Peace Movement and International Relations 1730–1854* (Oxford: Clarendon Press).

Ceadel, Martin (2000) *Semi-detached Idealists: The British Peace Movement and International Relations, 1854–1945* (Oxford: Oxford University Press).

Center for Peace and Disarmament (2005) 'From Security Paradigm to Peace Paradigm: Proposed Agenda and Points for Northeast Asian Consultation on GPPAC', *Korea Peace Report 2005* (Seoul: People's Solidarity for Participatory Democracy), 197–200.

Centre for Human Dialogue (2006) *Hitting the Target: Men and Guns*. Revcon Policy Brief presented at the First Review Conference on the UN Programme of Action to Prevent, Combat and Eradicate the Illicit Trade in Small Arms and Light Weapons in all its Aspects. New York, June-July (Geneva: Centre for Human Dialogue; Rio de Janeiro: Instituto Promundo).

Cho Hee-Yeon (2000) 'Democratic Transition and Changes in Korean NGOs', in Korean National Commission for UNESCO, *Korea Journal*, Vol. 40, No. 2, Summer, 275–304.

Chung Chong-shik and Ro Jae-Bong (eds) (1979) *Nationalism in Korea* (Seoul: Research Center for Peace and Unification).

Clacherty, Glynis and Johanna Kistner (2001) 'Guns, Power and Identity: A Research Project of the Zimiseleni Researchers'. Report of research by Clacherty and Associates Research and Ekupholeni Mental Health Centre. Alrode, South Africa, October.

Clark, Howard (1981) *Making Nonviolent Revolution*, Peace News Pamphlet No. 1, Nottingham. Second edition.

Clark, Howard (2007) 'WRI and Nonviolent Intervention', article at www.wri-irg.org/node/3252 (accessed 14 June 2009).

Cockburn, Cynthia (1998) *The Space between Us: Negotiating Gender and National Identities in Conflict* (London and New York: Zed Books).

Cockburn, Cynthia (2000) 'Women in Black: Being Able to Say Neither/Nor', *Canadian Women's Studies/Les Cahiers de la Femme*, Vol. 19, No. 4, Winter, 7–10.

Cockburn, Cynthia (2004a) *The Line: Women, Partition and the Gender Order in Cyprus* (London and New York: Zed Books).

Cockburn, Cynthia (2004b) 'The Continuum of Violence: A Gender Perspective on War and Peace', in Wenona Giles and Jennifer Hyndman (eds), *Sites of Violence: Gender and Conflict Zones* (Berkeley, Los Angeles, London: University of California Press), 30–44.

Cockburn, Cynthia (2007) *From Where We Stand: War, Women's Activism and Feminist Analysis* (London and New York: Zed Books). Korean edition, tr. Elli Kim (Seoul: Sam In Publishers).

Cockburn, Cynthia (2010) 'Gender Relations as Causal in Militarization and War: A Feminist Standpoint', *International Feminist Journal of Politics*, Vol. 12, No. 2, June, 139–57.

Cockburn, Cynthia (2012) 'A Continuum of Violence: Gender, War and Peace', in Ruth Jamieson (ed.), *The Criminology of War* (Farnham: Ashgate Publishing Group).

Cockburn, Cynthia and Lynette Hunter (1999) 'Transversal Politics and Translating Practices', *Soundings: A Journal of Politics and Culture*, 12, Summer, 88–93.

Collins, Patricia (1986) 'Learning from the Outsider Within: The Sociological Significance of Black Feminist Thought', *Social Problems*, Vol. 33, No. 6, 14–32.

Collins, Patricia (1990) *Black Feminist Thought: Knowledge, Consciousness, and the Politics of Empowerment* (Boston: Unwin Hyman).

Comfort, Alex (1950) *Authority and Delinquency* (London: Routledge and Kegan Paul).

Conciliation Resources (2002) *Protracted Conflict, Elusive Peace: Initiatives to End the Violence in Northern Uganda*. Issue 11 of *Accord*, an International Review of Peace Initiatives (London: Conciliation Resources).

Connell, R. W. (1987) *Gender and Power* (Cambridge: Polity Press; Oxford: Basil Blackwell).

Control Arms Campaign (2005) *The Impact of Guns on Women's Lives* (London: Amnesty International, International Action Network on Small Arms and Oxfam International).

Cook, Alice and Gwyn Kirk (1983) *Greenham Women Everywhere: Dreams, Ideas and Actions from the Women's Peace Movement* (London: Pluto Press).

Cookson, J. E. (1982) *The Friends of Peace: Anti-war Liberalism in England, 1793–1815* (Cambridge: Cambridge University Press).

Cooley, Alexander and Kimberley Marten (2006). 'Base Motives: The Political Economy of Okinawan Anti-Militarism,' *Armed Forces & Society*, Vol. 32, No. 4, 566–83.

Crenshaw, Kimberlé (1991) 'Mapping the Margins: Intersectionality, Identity Politics and Violence against Women of Color', *Stanford Law Review*, Vol. 43, No. 6, 1241–99.

Cumings, Bruce (2005) *Korea's Place in the Sun: a Modern History* (New York, London: W. W. Norton and Company).

Davidoff, Leonore and Catherine Hall (1987) *Family Fortunes: Men and Women of the English Middle Class, 1780–1850* (London, Melbourne, Sydney, Auckland, Johannesburg: Hutchinson).

Denzin, Norman K. and Yvonna S. Lincoln (eds) (1998) *Strategies of Qualitative Inquiry* (Thousand Oaks, London, New Delhi: Sage Publications).

Dudink, Stefan and Karen Hagemann (2004) 'Masculinity in Politics and War in the Age of Democratic Revolutions, 1750–1850', in Stefan Dudink, Karen Hagemann and John Tosh (eds), *Masculinities in Politics and War: Gender in Modern History* (Manchester, New York: Manchester University Press), 3–22

Eckhardt, William (1992) *Civilizations, Empires and Wars: A Quantitative History of War* (Jefferson, NC, London: MacFarland & Company Inc).

Elster, Ellen and Majken Jul Sørensen (eds) (2010) *Women Conscientious Objectors: An Anthology* (London: War Resisters' International).

Enloe, Cynthia (2000) *Maneuvers: The International Politics of Militarizing Women's Lives* (Berkeley, Los Angeles, London: University of California Press).

Fairhall, David (2008) *Common Ground: The Story of Greenham* (London, New York: I. B. Tauris).

Fanon, Frantz (1967) *The Wretched of the Earth* (London: Penguin Books).

Farr, Vanessa A. and Kiflemariam Gebre-Wold (eds) (2002) *Gender Perspectives on Small Arms and Light Weapons: Regional and International Concerns*. Brief 24. July (Bonn: Bonn International Center for Conversion).

Farr, Vanessa, Henri Myrttinen and Albrecht Schnabel (eds) (2009a) *Sexed Pistols: The Gendered Impacts of Small Arms and Light Weapons* (Tokyo, New York, Paris: United Nations University Press).

Farr, Vanessa, Henri Myrttinen and Albrecht Schnabel (2009b) 'Conclusions: Recommendations for Further Research and Activism', in Vanessa Farr, Henri Myrttinen and Albrecht Schnabel (eds), *Sexed Pistols: The Gendered Impacts of Small Arms and Light Weapons* (Tokyo, New York Paris: United Nations University Press), 421–32.

Feminism and Nonviolence Study Group (1983) *Piecing It Together: Feminism and Nonviolence*. Published by the Study Group in co-operation with War Resisters' International, London.

Finnström, Sverker (2008) *Living with Bad Surroundings: War, History, and Everyday Moments in Northern Uganda* (Durham, NC, London: Duke University Press).

Flick, Uwe (2009) *An Introduction to Qualitative Research* (Thousand Oaks, London, New Delhi, Singapore: Sage Publications).

Fontana, Benedetto (2006) 'State and Society: The Concept of Hegemony in Gramsci', in Mark Haugaard and Howard H. Lentner (eds), *Hegemony and Power: Consensus and Coercion in Contemporary Politics* (Oxford: Lexington Books), 23–44.

French, Paul (2007) *North Korea: The Paranoid Peninsula* (London, New York: Zed Books).

Fuhrt, Volker (2008) 'Peace Movements as Emancipatory Experience – *anpo tôsô* and Beheiren in 1960s Japan', in Benjamin Ziemann (ed.), *Peace Movements in Western Europe, Japan and the USA during the Cold War* (Essen: Klartext Medienwerkstatt GmbH), 77–90.

Galtung, Johan (1969) 'Violence, Peace and Peace Research', *Journal of Peace Research*, Vol. 3, 167–91.

Garver, Newton (2009) 'What Violence Is', in Vittorio Bufacchi (ed.), *Violence: A Philosophical Anthology* (Basingstoke, New York: Palgrave Macmillan), 170–82. Originally published in *The Nation*, 1968, No. 209, 24 June, 822–34.

GIIDS: Graduate Institute of International and Development Studies (2008) *Risk and Resilience: Small Arms Survey 2008* (Cambridge: Cambridge University Press).

GIIDS: Graduate Institute of International and Development Studies (2009) *Shadows of War: Small Arms Survey 2009* (Cambridge: Cambridge University Press).

Gillan, Kevin, Jenny Pickerill and Frank Webster (2008) *Anti-War Activism: New Media and Protest in the Information Age* (Basingstoke, New York: Palgrave Macmillan).

Gordillo, José Luis (2002) 'Ni ejército profesional sustitutoria, 1989', in MOC 2002, 257–60.

Graham, Robert (2005) *Anarchism: A Documentary History of Libertarian Ideas* (Montreal, London: Black Rose Books).

Gramsci, Antonio (1971) *Selections from the Prison Notebooks* (London: Lawrence and Wishart).

Greenwood, Davydd and Morten Levin (1998) *Introduction to Action Research: Social Research for Social Change* (Thousand Oaks, London, New Delhi: Sage Publications).

Grzelczyk, Virginie (2008) 'Carrots and Sticks: The Construction of an American Foreign Policy toward North Korea', *Korean Observer*, Special Issue on *Security and Peace in the Korean Peninsula*, Vol. 39, No. 4, Winter, 539–70.

Hahn Jeong-Sook (2009) 'Issues of Peace on the Korean Peninsula and the Role of Women's Peace Movement: Peace in Northeast Asia from the Perspective of Korean Women', in *Negotiating Regional Peace, Reconciliation and Co-operation. Report of the Second Session of the North-East Asian Women's Peace Conference 2009* (Washington, DC: George Washington University).

Halliday, Fred (1994) *Rethinking International Relations* (Basingstoke: Macmillan).

Han Yong-Sup (2005) *Peace and Arms Control on the Korean Peninsula* (Seoul: Kyungnam University Press).

Haraway, Donna (1988) 'Situated Knowledge: The Science Question in Feminism and the Privilege of Partial Perspective', *Feminist Studies*, Vol. 14, No. 3, 575–99.

Harding, Sandra (1986) *The Science Question in Feminism* (Milton Keynes: Open University Press).

Harding, Sandra (ed.) (2004) *The Feminist Standpoint Theory Reader: Intellectual and Political Controversies* (New York, London: Routledge).

Harford, Barbara and Sarah Hopkins (eds) (1984) *Greenham Common: Women at the Wire* (London: The Women's Press).

Hartmann, Heidi (1979) 'Capitalism, Patriarchy and Job Segregation by Sex', in Zillah R. Eisenstein (ed), *Capitalist Patriarchy and the Case for Socialist Feminism* (New York: Monthly Review Press).

Hartsock, Nancy (1985) *Money, Sex and Power: Towards a Feminist Historical Materialism* (Boston: Northeastern University Press).

Hartsock, Nancy (1998) *The Feminist Standpoint Revisited and Other Essays* (Boulder and Oxford: The Westview Press).

Hinton, James (1989) *Protests and Visions: Peace Politics in Twentieth-century Britain* (London: Hutchinson Radius).

Horne, John (2004) 'Masculinity in Politics and War in the Age of Nation-states and World Wars, 1850–1950', in Stefan Dudink, Karen Hagemann and John Tosh (eds), *Masculinities in Politics and War: Gender in Modern History* (Manchester, New York: Manchester University Press), 22–40.

Howes, Dustin Ells (2009) *Toward a Credible Pacifism: Violence and the Possibilities of Politics* (Albany: SUNY Press).

Hudson, Kate (2000) *European Communism since 1989* (Basingstoke: Palgrave Macmillan).

Hudson, Kate (2005) *CND – Now More than Ever: The Story of a Peace Movement* (London: Vision Paperbacks).

Hudson, Kate (2009) 'Political Opportunities for the Left in the "Post-Communist/ Post-Neoliberal" World: The Case of *Die Linke*', Conference presentation. University of Padua, Italy. Typescript.

Human Rights Now (2009) 'Kokuren ga Zesei wo Motomeru Nihon no Jinken Jokyo- Kankoku no Ichiran', at http://hrn.or.jp/activity/kokuren-ga-zesei-wo-motomeru-nihon.pdf (accessed 30 May 2011).

Human Rights Watch (2003) *Stolen Children: Abduction and Recruitment in Northern Uganda.* Vol. 15, No. 7(A), March.

Human Rights Watch (2005) *Uprooted and Forgotten: Impunity and Human Rights Abuses in Northern Uganda.* Vol. 17, No. 12(A), September.

Human Rights Watch (2007) *'Get the Gun!' Human Rights Violations by Uganda's National Army in Law Enforcement Operations in Uganda's Eastern Region.* Vol. 19, No. 13(A), September.

IMADR-JC (2002) 'International Movement against All Forms of Discrimination and Racism, Japan Committee', *Newsletter* No. 119, at www.imadr.org/publica tions (accessed 9 May 2011).

Inoue, Reiko (1996) 'Introduction: Looking toward Beijing', in AMPO (ed.), *Voices from the Japanese Women's Movement.* An edited volume of articles from *AMPO: Japan Asia Quarterly Review* (New York, London: M. E. Sharpe), xvii–xxi.

Jabs, Lorelle (2007) 'Where Two Elephants Meet, the Grass Suffers: A Case Study of Intractable Conflict in Karamoja, Uganda', *American Behavioral Scientist*, No. 50, 1498–519.

Jones, Adam (2000) 'Gendercide and Genocide', *Journal of Genocide Research*, Vol. 2, No. 2, June, 185–211.

Jones, Nicola Anne (2006) *Gender and the Political Opportunities of Democratization in South Korea* (Basingstoke: Palgrave Macmillan).

Junor, Beth (1995) *Greenham Common Women's Peace Camp: A History of Nonviolent Resistance 1984–1995* (London: Working Press).

Kasozi, A. B. K. (1994) *The Social Origins of Violence in Uganda 1964–1985* (Montreal, Kingston, London, Buffalo: McGill-Queen's University Press).

Kim, Elaine H. and Chungmoo Choi (eds) (1998) *Dangerous Women: Gender and Korean Nationalism* (New York, London: Routledge).

Kim, Elli (2002) 'Militarism, Women and for Demilitarization.' Paper presented at the International Meeting of the East Asia-Puerto Rico-US Women's Network Against Militarism, Seoul. Typescript.

Kim, Elli (2005) 'Women's Disarmament and Anti-war Movements', in Shim Young-Hee and Elli Kim (eds), *Korean Women's Peace Movement: Its Unfolding and Issues* (in Korean language) (Seoul: Han-Woo Publishing), 139–201.

Kim, Elli (2007) 'Women who Redefine Security and Peace: With a Focus on Korean Women's Anti-war Movements since 9.11', in *World Women's Peace Forum, Gwangju, Korea Women's Rights and Culture.* Report. Seoul, 26–28 June, 283–88.

Kim Sook-Im (2002) 'Korea Women's Peace Movement: Concentrated on Peace Movements of Korea Women since 1990.' Paper presented at the International Meeting of the East Asia-Puerto Rico-US Women's Network against Militarism, Seoul. Typescript.

Korac, Maja (1998) 'Ethnic Nationalism, Wars and the Patterns of Social, Political and Sexual Violence against Women: The Case of Post-Yugoslav Countries', *Identities: Global Studies in Culture and Power*, Vol. 5, No. 2, 153–81.

Korski, Daniel (2008) 'The Summit of NATO's Ambitions?', *The Guardian*, 2 April, at: www.guardian.co.uk/commentisfree/2008/apr/02/thesummitofnatosambi tions (accessed 12 May 2009).

Kuhlman, Erika (2008) *Reconstructing Patriarchy after the Great War: Women, Gender and Postwar Reconciliation between Nations* (London: Palgrave Macmillan).

Kwak, Tae-Hwan and Seung-Ho Joo (2003) 'Introduction', in Tae-Hwan Kwak and Seung-Ho Joo (eds), *The Korean Peace Process and the Four Powers* (Aldershot: Ashgate), 1–10.

Kwon In-Sook (2006) 'Feminists Navigating the Shoals of Nationalism and Collaboration', *Frontiers: A Journal of Women Studies*, Vol. 27, No. 1, 39–66.

Laity, Paul (2001) *The British Peace Movement 1870–1914* (Oxford: Clarendon Press).

Lee Daehoon, Francis (2005) 'Democratic Reform of Security Sector-Civil Society Relations', *Korea Peace Report: Proposals for Peace, Disarmament and Co-operation* (Seoul: People's Solidarity for Participatory Democracy), 149–54.

Lee Daehoon, Francis (2008) 'How to Cope with the Military', in Kimijima Akihiko (ed.), *To People Who Learn Peace Studies* (Kyoto: Sekai Shiso Sha), Typescript.

Lee Sook-Jong (2006) 'The Assertive Nationalism of South Korean Youth: Cultural Dynamism and Political Activism', *SAIS Review*, Vol. XXVI, No. 2, Summer-Fall, 123–32.

Lee Tae-ho (2003) 'Overcoming National Division on the Korean Peninsula and the Peace Movements', *Korea Peace Report: Proposals for Peace, Disarmament and Co-operation*, December (Seoul: People's Solidarity for Participatory Democracy), 94–115.

Lee Tae-Ho (2005) 'A Civil Society Evaluation of the Defence Reform 2020', *Korea Peace Report 2005* (Seoul: People's Solidarity for Participatory Democracy), 111–32.

Liddington, Jill (1989) *The Road to Greenham Common: Feminism and Anti-Militarism in Britain Since 1820* (New York: Syracuse University Press; London: Virago Press).

Lukács, Georg (1968) *History and Class Consciousness* (London: The Merlin Press). First published 1923.

Maedomari, Hiromori (2008) 'Okinawa no Sangyo/Keizai: Jiristu heno Michi' (tr. 'Industry and Economy in Okinawa: Path towards Independence'), in Arasaki Moriteru, Maedomari Hiromori and Shizuo Ota et al. (eds), *Kankou Koosu de nai Okinawa* (tr. *Okinawa for non-tourists course*) (Tokyo: Koubunken), 191–230.

Manz, Beatrix (2008) 'The Continuum of Violence in Post-war Guatemala', *Social Analysis*, Vol. 52, No. 2, 151–64.

Marshall, Catherine and Gretchen B. Rossman (2011) *Designing Qualitative Research*, fifth edition (Thousand Oaks, London, New Delhi, Singapore: Sage Publications).

Mattausch, John (1989) *A Commitment to Campaign: A Sociological Study of CND* (Manchester, New York: Manchester University Press).

Matthews, Eugene (2003) 'Japan's New Nationalism', *Foreign Affairs*, Vol. 82, No. 6, 74–90.

McCall, Leslie (2005) 'The Complexity of Intersectionality', *Signs: Journal of Women in Culture and Society*, Vol. 30, No. 3, 1771–800.

McIntyre-Mills, Janet M. (2000) *Global Citizenship and Social Movements: Creating Transcultural Webs of Meaning for the New Millennium* (Amsterdam: Harwood Academic Publishers).

McNiff, Jean with Jack Whitehead (2002) *Action Research: Principles and Practice* (London, New York: Routledge Falmer).

Melucci, Alberto (1989) *Nomads of the Present: Social Movements and Individual Needs in Contemporary Society* (London: Hutchinson Radius).

Melucci, Alberto (1996) *Challenging Codes: Collective Action in the Information Age* (Cambridge: Cambridge University Press).

Mercier, Peter J. and Judith D. Mercier (eds) (2000) *Battle Cries on the Home Front: Domestic Violence in the Military Family* (Springfield: Charles C. Thomas Publishers Ltd).

Mies, Maria and Vandana Shiva (2004) 'The Subsistence Perspective', in Sandra Harding (ed.), *The Feminist Standpoint Theory Reader: Intellectual and Political Controversies* (New York, London: Routledge).

Mill, John Stuart (1991) *On Liberty and Other Essays*, edited and with an Introduction and Notes by John Gray (Oxford: Oxford University Press). First published 1869.

Miller, Pavla (1998) *Transformations of Patriarchy in the West, 1500–1900* (Bloomington: Indiana University Press).

Mkutu, Kennedy Agade (2008) 'Uganda: Pastoral Conflict and Gender Relations', *Review of African Political Economy*, No. 116, 237–54.

MOC: Movimiento de Objección de Conciencia (1998) *Antimilitarismo y Feminismo: la Campana Insumisión y 25 anos Desobedeciendo* (Madrid: Movimiento de Objección de Conciencia), A5 booklet, 22pp.

MOC: Movimiento de Objección de Conciencia (2002) *En Legítima Desobediencia: Tres Décadas de Objección, Insumisión y Antimilitarismo* (Madrid: MOC, with El Proyecto Editorial Traficantes de Sueños).

MOC: Movimiento de Objección de Conciencia, Grupo de Mujeres Antimilitaristas (1991) *Mujer y Antimilitarismo* (Madrid: Movimiento de Objección de Conciencia), A5 booklet, 70pp.

Moon Chung-In (2001) 'The Sunshine Policy, the Korean Summit and Aftermath: A Critical Assessment of Inter-Korean Relations', in Henriette Sinding Aasen, Uichol Kim and Geir Helgesen (eds), *Democracy, Human Rights and Peace in Korea: Psychological, Political and Cultural Perspectives* (Seoul: Kyoyook-Kwahak-Sa Publishing Company), 121–69.

Moraga, Cherrie and Gloria Anzaldúa (1981) *This Bridge Called My Back: Writings by Radical Women of Color* (Watertown: Persephone).

Morris-Suzuki, Tessa (1998) *Re-inventing Japan: Time, Space, Nation* (New York, London: M. E. Sharpe).

Motoya, Toshio (ed.) (2008) *The Shocking Truth about Modern History* (Tokyo: The APA Group), 4–6.

Motoyama, Hisako (2008) 'Not a "Yankees-Go-Home" Solution to the Sexual Violence of the US Military', *Off Our Backs*, Vol. 38, No. 1, 24–7.

Moura, Tatiana (2007) *Invisible Faces of Armed Violence: A Case Study on Rio de Janeiro* (Coimbra, Rio de Janeiro: Centre for Social Studies, University of Coimbra, and Viva Rio, Brazil).

Mujeres de Negro Sevilla (2007) '*Memoria*', a typescript paper by Mireya, María Angeles, Sofía, Carmen, Manuela and María of Mujeres de Negro Sevilla.

Mullen, John (2009) 'Almost Revolutionary', *Red Pepper*, February/March, 26–30.

Murray, Andrew and Lindsey German (2005) *Stop the War: The Story of Britain's Biggest Mass Movement* (London: Bookmarks Publications).

Muto, Ichiyo (2006) 'Japan's Willing Military Annexation by the United States: "Alliance for the Future" and Grassroots Resistance', *Japonesia Review*, No. 2, 19–31.

Muto, Ichiyo (2009) 'Japan, Pacifist movement, 1945-Present', in Immanuel Ness (ed.), *International Encyclopedia of Revolution and Protest* (Oxford: Blackwell Publishing), 1884–9.

Närman, Anders (2003) 'Karamoja: Is Peace Possible?', *Review of African Political Economy*, No. 95, 129–69.

Oberg, Jan (2010) 'Help Stop Sweden's Furtive Accession to NATO', 9 February, at: www.internationalpeaceandconflict.org/profiles/blogs/help-stop-swedens-furtive (accessed 13 August 2010).

Oldfield, Sybil (2000) *Women against the Iron Fist: Alternatives to Militarism 1900–1989* (Lampeter: Edwin Mellen Press).

Ota, Masakuni (2007–8) 'Abduction and "Comfort Women": Two Stumbling Blocks to Abe Shinzo's Dream Come True', *Japonesia Review*, No. 4, 34–8.

Paik Nak-Chung (2001) *The Division System in Crisis: Essays on Contemporary Korea* (Berkeley: University of California Press).

Park Sun-Song (2005) 'Preface: Let Us Broaden the Horizon of the Peace Movement', *Korea Peace Report 2005* (Seoul: People's Solidarity for Participatory Democracy, Center for Peace and Disarmament), 5–19.

Pateman, Carole (1988) *The Sexual Contract* (Cambridge: Polity Press).

Pettit, Ann (2006) *Walking to Greenham: How the Peace Camp Began and the Cold War Ended* (South Glamorgan: Honno Autobiography).

Phelps, Christina (1930) *The Anglo-American Peace Movement in the Mid-nineteenth Century* (New York: Columbia University Press).

Prasad, Devi (2005) *War Is a Crime against Humanity: The Story of War Resisters' International* (London: War Resisters' International).

Price, Lisa S. (2005) *Feminist Frameworks: Building Theory on Violence against Women* (Halifax: Fernwood Publishing).

Reason, Peter and Hilary Bradbury (eds) (2006) *Handbook of Action Research* (London, Thousand Oaks, New Delhi, Singapore: Sage Publications).

Richards, Janet Radcliffe (1990) 'Why the Pursuit of Peace is No Part of Feminism', in Jean Bethke Elshtain and Sheila Tobias (eds), *Women, Militarism and War: Essays in History, Politics and Social Theory* (Lanham: Rowman and Littlefield), 211–25.

Robbins, Keith (1976) *The Abolition of War: The 'Peace Movement' in Britain 1914–1919* (Cardiff: University of Wales Press).

Rose, Hilary (1994) *Love, Power and Knowledge: Towards a Feminist Transformation of the Sciences* (Cambridge: Polity Press).

Roseneil, Sasha (1995) *Disarming Patriarchy: Feminism and Political Action at Greenham* (Buckingham, Philadelphia: Open University Press).

Rousseau, Jean-Jacques (1998) *The Social Contract or Principles of Political Right* (Ware: Wordsworth Editions). First published 1762.

Ruddick, Sara (2004) 'Maternal Thinking as a Feminist Standpoint', in Sandra Harding (ed.), *The Feminist Standpoint Theory Reader: Intellectual and Political Controversies* (New York, London: Routledge).

Sartre, Jean-Paul (1967) 'Preface' to Frantz Fanon, *The Wretched of the Earth* (London: Penguin Books), 7–26.

Scheper-Hughes, Nancy and Philippe Bourgois (2004) 'Introduction', in Nancy Scheper-Hughes and Philippe Bourgois (eds), *Violence in War and Peace: An Anthology* (Malden, Oxford: Blackwell Publishers), 2–31.

Schmidt, Reiner (n.d.) 'Die NATO hat Geburtstag – wir feiern mit'. Article on the website of the journal *Analyse & Kritik*, at: www.linksnet.de/de/artikel/24010 (accessed 9 May 2011).

Schroeder, Emily and Lauren Newhouse (2004) *Gender and Small Arms* (Pretoria: Institute of Security Studies).

Shaw, Martin (1987) 'War, Peace and British Marxism, 1895–1945', in Richard Taylor and Nigel Young (eds), *Campaigns for Peace: British Peace Movements in the Twentieth Century* (Manchester: Manchester University Press), 49–72.

Shigematsu, Setsu (2005) 'Feminism and Media in the Late Twentieth Century: Reading the Limits of a Politics of Transgression', in Barbara Molony and Kathleen Uno (eds), *Gendering Modern Japanese History* (Cambridge, MA: Harvard University Asia Center and Harvard University Press), 555–83.

Shim Young-Hee and Elli Kim (eds) *Korean Women's Peace Movement: Its Unfolding and Issues* (in Korean language) (Seoul: Han-Woo Publishing).

Shimada, Masahiro (2003) 'US Bases in Okinawa', from *US Military Bases in Japan: An Overview*, Asia/World Social Forum: Support Project for Participants from Japan, at: www.jca.apc.org/wsf_support (accessed 1 October 2009).

Shin Il-Chul (1979) 'Nationalism in Resistance: Its Internal Character', in Chung Chong-shik and Jae-Bong Ro (eds), *Nationalism in Korea* (Seoul: Research Center for Peace and Unification), 125–46.

Siddle, Richard (2003) 'Return to Uchina: The Politics of Identity in Contemporary Okinawa', in Glen D. Hook and Richard Siddle (eds), *Japan and Okinawa: Structure and Subjectivity* (London, New York: Routledge).

Sidman, Murray (2001) *Coercion and Its Fallout* (Boston: Authors' Cooperative).

Silverman, David (1985) *Qualitative Methodology and Sociology* (Aldershot: Gower Publishing).

Sluga, Glenda (2004) `Masculinities, Nations, and the New World Order: Peacemaking and Nationality in Britain, France, and the United States after the First World War', in Stefan Dudink, Karen Hagemann and John Tosh (eds), *Masculinities in Politics and War: Gender in Modern History* (Manchester, New York: Manchester University Press), 238–54

Smith, Dorothy (2004) 'Women's Perspective as a Radical Critique of Sociology', in Sandra Harding (ed.), *The Feminist Standpoint Theory Reader: Intellectual and Political Controversies* (New York, London: Routledge).

Smith, Hazel (2005) *Hungry for Peace: International Security, Human Assistance, and Social Change in North Korea* (Washington, DC: United States Institute for Peace Press).

Somekh, Bridget (2006) *Action Research: A Methodology for Change and Development* (Milton Keynes: Open University Press).

Speck, Andreas (1998) 'Militarismus und Männlichkeit', *Schwarzer Faden – Vierteljahreschrift fur Anarchie und Luxus*, No. 64, 2nd quarter, 37–44, at: http://wri-irg.org/node/10562.

Speck, Andreas (2007) '"Being a Man": Willingness to Serve and Masculinity', paper presented to the War Resisters' International/New Profile seminar on 'Gender and Militarism', Neve Shalom, Israel, at http://wri-irg.org/node/6521.

Spencer, Caroline (2003) 'Meeting of the Dugongs and the Cooking Pots: Anti-military Base Citizens' Groups on Okinawa', *Japanese Studies*, Vol. 23, No. 2, September, 125–40.

Stohl, Rachel, Matt Schroeder and Dan Smith (2007) *The Small Arms Trade* (Oxford: One World).

Strauss, Anselm and Juliet Corbin (1990) *Basics of Qualitative Research: Grounded Theory Procedures and Techniques* (London, Newbury Park, New Delhi: Sage Publications).

Suzuki, Yuko (2002) *Tenno-sei, Ianfu, Feminizumu* (tr. *The Emperor System, 'Comfort Women' and Feminism*) (in Japanese language) (Tokyo: Impact Press).

Tahara, Maki (2006) 'Japanese Neo-cons Infest Gender Discourse', *Japonesia Review*, No. 2, 58–65.

Taira, Natsume (2006) 'Henoko kara' (tr. 'From Henoko'), *Gendai Shiso*, Vol. 34, No. 10, 147–51.

Takazato, Suzuyo (1996) 'The Past and Future of *Unai*, Sisters in Okinawa', in AMPO (ed.), *Voices from the Japanese Women's Movement*. An edited volume of articles from *AMPO: Japan Asia Quarterly Review* (New York, London: M. E. Sharpe), 133–43.

Tanji, Miyume (2006) 'The *Unai* Method: The Expansion of Women-only Groups in the Community of Protest against Violence and Militarism in Okinawa', *Intersections: Gender, History and Culture in the Asian Context*, No. 13. August.

Taylor, Richard (1987a) 'The Labour Party and CND: 1957 to 1984', in Richard Taylor and Nigel Young (eds), *Campaigns for Peace: British Peace Movements in the Twentieth Century* (Manchester: Manchester University Press), 100–30.

Taylor, Richard (1987b) 'The Marxist Left and the Peace Movement in Britain since 1945', in Richard Taylor and Nigel Young (eds), *Campaigns for Peace: British Peace Movements in the Twentieth Century* (Manchester: Manchester University Press), 162–88.

Taylor, Richard (1988) *Against the Bomb: The British Peace Movement 1958–1965* (Oxford: Clarendon Press).

Tilly, Charles and Lesley J. Wood (2009) *Social Movements, 1768–2008* (Boulder, London: Paradigm).

Tosh, John (2004) 'Hegemonic Masculinity and the History of Gender', in Stefan Dudink, Karen Hagemann and John Tosh (eds), *Masculinities in Politics and War: Gender in Modern History* (Manchester, New York: Manchester University Press), 41–58.

Traynor, Ian (2008) 'Pre-emptive Nuclear Strike a Key Option, NATO Told', *The Guardian*, 22 January. at: www.guardian.co.uk/world/2008/jan/22/nato.nuclear (accessed 8 June 2009).

Tripp, Aili Mari (2000) *Women and Politics in Uganda* (Oxford: James Currey; Kampala: Fountain Publishers; Madison: University of Wisconsin Press).

Trott, Ben (2007) 'Moving Against', *Red Pepper*, June, at: www.redpepper.org.uk/moving-against (accessed 9 May 2011).

Uichol Kim (2001) 'Ethnography of Korean People and Culture', in Henriette Sinding Aasen, Uichol Kim and Geir Helgesen (eds), *Democracy, Human Rights and Peace in Korea: Psychological, Political and Cultural Perspectives* (Seoul: Kyoyook-Kwahak-Sa Publishing Company), 245–78.

Ülker, Ferda (2010) 'Turkish Women Awaken to Conscientious Objection', in Ellen Elster and Majken Jul Sørensen (eds), *Women Conscientious Objectors: An Anthology* (London: War Resisters' International), 102–10.

UNDP: United Nations Development Programme (2008a) *Small Arms and Light Weapons Legislation*, 'How to Guide', July (Geneva: Bureau for Crisis Prevention and Recovery, United Nations Development Programme).

UNDP: United Nations Development Programme (2008b) *The Establishment and Functioning of National Small Arms and Light Weapons Commissions*, 'How To Guide', April (Geneva: Bureau for Crisis Prevention and Recovery, United Nations Development Programme).

UNIDIR: United Nations Institute for Disarmament Research (2008) *Implementing the United Nations Programme of Action on Small Arms and Light Weapons. Analysis of the National Reports Submitted by States from 2002 to 2008*, UNIDIR, Geneva, 2008/15 (New York, Geneva: United Nations).

Waterman, Peter (1998) *Globalization, Social Movements and the New Internationalism* (London, New York: Continuum).

Weeks, Kathi (1998) *Constituting Feminist Subjects* (Ithaca, London: Cornell University Press).

Weinberg, Bill (2008) 'The Politics of the Anti-war Movement: The Intractable Dilemma of International ANSWER', *The Nonviolent Activist*, magazine of the War Resisters League, December.

Weyl, Roland (1999) 'L'OTAN et la legalité internationale', *Droit-Solidarité*, publication series of the *Association Internationale des Juristes Democrates*, Paris, 19 November.

Yamaguchi, Hibiki (2008) 'People of Yokosuka Resist US Nuclear Carrier', *Japonesia Review*, No. 5, 67–9.

Yamamoto, Mari (2004) *Grassroots Pacifism in Post-war Japan: The Rebirth of a Nation*, Sheffield Centre for Japanese Studies (London, New York: Routledge Curzon).

Yamazaki, Takashi (2003) 'Politicizing Territory: The Transformation of Land Struggle in Okinawa, 1956', in *Jinbun kenkyu* (tr. *Studies in the Humanities*), No. 54, Vol. 3, 31–65.

Yeung, Christina M. (2009) 'Missing Men, Lost Boys and Widowed Women: Gender Perspectives on Small-arms Proliferation and Disarmament in Karamoja, Uganda', in Vanessa Farr, Henri Myrttinen and Albrecht Schnabel (eds), *Sexed Pistols: The Gendered Impacts of Small Arms and Light Weapons* (Tokyo, New York, Paris: United Nations University Press), 390–417.

Young, Daniel Dylan (2001) 'Autonomía and the Origin of the Black Bloc', A-Infos: Multilingual News Service by, for and about Anarchists, June, at: www.ainfos.ca/jun/ainfos00170.html (accessed 9 June 2009).

Young, Nigel (1987) 'War Resistance and the British Peace Movement since 1914', in Richard Taylor and Nigel Young (eds), *Campaigns for Peace: British Peace Movements in the Twentieth Century* (Manchester: Manchester University Press), 23–49.

Yui, Akiko (2006) 'Okinawa Disagrees: A Historic Turning Point in the Struggle for Peace and Dignity', *Japonesia Review*, No. 2, 6–18.

Yui, Akiko (2007–8) 'Okinawa's Resistance Reaches a New Height on Falsification of History and US Bases', *Japonesia Review*, No. 4, 9–17.

Yuval-Davis, Nira (1994) 'Women, Ethnicity and Empowerment', in Kum-Kum Bhavnani and Ann Phoenix (eds), *Shifting Identities, Shifting Racisms: A Feminism and Psychology Reader* (London, Thousand Oaks, New Delhi: Sage), 179–98.

Yuval-Davis, Nira (1997) *Gender and Nation* (London, Thousand Oaks, New Delhi: Sage Publications).

Zamarra, Cthuchi (2009) 'Conscientious Objection in Spain: Disobedience', in Özgür Heval Çinar and Coşkun Üstercí (eds), *Resisting Militarized Society: Conscientious Objection* (London, New York: Zed Books).

Zirakzadeh, Cyrus Ernesto (1997) *Social Movements in Politics: A Comparative Study* (London and New York: Longman).

Index

277